AN ILLINOIS READER

AN ILLINOIS

CLYDE C. WALTON
EDITOR

READER

NORTHERN ILLINOIS UNIVERSITY PRESS

DEKALB, ILLINOIS

Painting by Otto Krans adapted for use in cover design and title page, courtesy of State of Illinois, Department of Conservation, Division of Parks and Memorials.

First Printing 1970
Second Printing 1973

Copyright © 1970 by Northern Illinois University Press
International Standard Book Number 0–87580–014–9
Library of Congress Catalog Card Number 70–105676
Published by Northern Illinois University Press, DeKalb, Illinois

Manufactured in the United States of America
Designed by John B. Goetz

An
Illinois
Sesquicentennial
Book

In 1968, the State of Illinois observed its 150th anniversary. Three years earlier, Governor Otto Kerner appointed a commission authorized by the General Assembly to decide upon the most effective and suitable means of commemorating this milestone in the state's history. The commission decided that a series of historical publications was called for and a committee of prominent historians selected the subjects to be covered. High on the list was an anthology describing Illinois from the beginning of its recorded history to the present. This volume of selected articles published by the Illinois State Historical Society was compiled and edited by the former editor of the society's publications who was also the State Historian.

For their support of the sesquicentennial historical program I wish to thank former Governors Otto Kerner and Samuel H. Shapiro, the Illinois General Assembly, and the members of the Illinois Sesquicentennial Commission:

Hon. Hudson R. Sours, Hon. Thomas A. McGloon, Hon. Paul J. Randolph and J. W. "Bill" Scott, Vice Chairmen; Gene H. Graves, Secretary; William K. Alderfer; Hon. Thomas J. Awerkamp; Hon. Francis J. Berry; James W. Cook; Hon. Lawrence DiPrima; Hon. Joseph F. Fanta; Hon. Robert F. Hatch; Hon. G. William Horsley; Patrick H. Hoy; Goffrey Hughes; Hon. Henry J. Hyde; Hon. George P. Johns; Hon. J. David Jones; Hon. Richard R. Larson; Lenox R. Lohr; Hon. Edward Lehman; Daniel MacMaster; Virginia L. Marmaduke; Hon. Edward McBroom; Hon. Robert W. McCarthy; Hon. Elmo "Mac" McClain; Hon. Tom Merritt; Hon. Clarence E.

Neff; Hon. Richard H. Newhouse; Hon. James Philip; Hon. Paul Powell; Hon. William J. Schoeninger; Walter Schwimmer, John H. Sengstacke; Glenn H. Seymour; Hon. Paul Simon; Hon. Roy Curtis Small; Burnham P. Spann; Hon. Harold D. Stedelin; Milton D. Thompson; Clyde C. Walton. The director of historical publications was Paul M. Angle.

RALPH G. NEWMAN
Chairman

PREFACE

My participation in *An Illinois Reader* began in Springfield in 1967, when I had lunch with two old friends, Ralph G. Newman and Paul M. Angle. Mr. Newman, proprietor of the Abraham Lincoln Bookshop, newspaper columnist, authority on the Civil War, and chairman of the Board of Trustees of the Chicago Public Library, was also serving as chairman of the Illinois Sesquicentennial Commission. Mr. Angle, Lincoln scholar, keen student of the American scene, and until recently director of the Chicago Historical Society, had been the general editor for all the historical publications of the Illinois Sesquicentennial Commission. Our discussion centered on the high quality of the material published over a long period of time by the Illinois State Historical Society, material not ordinarily well known or readily available to the general reader. At the end of the luncheon it was suggested that such an anthology be compiled and issued under the auspices of the Sesquicentennial Commission.

What Messrs. Newman and Angle asked me to do was compile and edit a collection of articles taken exclusively from the periodical publications of the Illinois State Historical society, namely, the annual volumes of *Transactions of the Illinois State Historical Society* (and its successor, *Papers in Illinois History*) and the quarterly *Journal of the Illinois State Historical Society*. (Because the anthology was intended primarily for adults, articles would not be taken from *Illinois History*, the Society's magazine for teenagers.) *Transactions* was first published in 1900 and continued until 1942; the *Journal* was in its sixtieth volume in 1967. Clearly, there would be a large number of articles from which to choose.

Perhaps I should explain that I was then the executive director of the Illinois State Historical Society and Illinois State Historian (positions I had held for the preceding ten years), as well as the general editor of the *Journal*. Although I was therefore familiar with the contents of the *Journal* and *Transactions,* I carefully examined every page of these publications and initially selected material that would fill three volumes the size of this one. Slowly and reluctantly, I reduced the material to manageable size and finally chose the twenty-five articles that make up this volume.

The Society has published very little about the prehistory of Illinois because it has long held that other agencies have been better qualified to do so. Indeed, most of the Society's publications concern Illinois in the nineteenth century, and especially the years between statehood and about 1900. There are articles about the Revolutionary War and the decade that preceded it, and articles that deal with twentieth-century events, but by and large its publications have concentrated on the last eighty years of the nineteenth century. However, because it is hoped that this anthology will appeal to the layman who has some knowledge of Illinois history but would like to know still more about our state, the selections cover almost two hundred years of Illinois history and the topics discussed should be of general interest.

Writings that deal with subjects of limited interest or minor points in Illinois history as well as those that are highly speculative or theoretical in nature have been excluded. With but one exception, articles that are principally documentary in form also were omitted because it was thought that discursive, narrative, and interpretative articles were best suited to the purpose of the volume; diaries, letters, speeches, and state papers are therefore not included. In no case was an article selected solely because of the reputation of the man or the woman who wrote it. As editor-compiler, I believe the selections are either interesting or important —and occasionally both; but always, I liked the way in which the information was presented.

Regrettably, several of our most distinguished Illinois historians do not appear in this volume. Dr. Harry Pratt and Paul Angle, for example, both of whom have edited the *Journal,* for the most part published their work either in other learned journals or in book form. However, major American historians are represented in *An Illinois Reader*—in many cases Illinoisans who wrote about topics that intrigued them or events in which they participated. A few of the articles that appear here have been expanded to book length, such as the late Benjamin P. Thomas's article on New Salem, which became *Lincoln's New Salem* (Chicago: Americana House, 1961).

Unfortunately, some aspects of Illinois history are not represented, because pertinent material has not been published by the Society. In a few cases, I rejected an apparently valuable article because it was badly written or inaccurate. Finally, another editor, presuming to address the same audience, might have selected very different articles, or choosing from the same body of material but for a different audience, would have chosen differently. In other words, the selections that make up *An Illinois Reader* are my personal choice and I alone am responsible for selecting them.

The reader begins with Allan Nevin's brilliant, interpretative essay, "Not Without Thy Wondrous Story, Illinois," which also stands as an excellent introduction to the volume. The other twenty-four selections are grouped in rough chronological order and five rather arbitrary periods: (1) *Outpost of a New Nation*, (2) *The Frontier State*, (3) *The Age of Lincoln and Douglas*, (4) *The Maturing State*, and (5) *In Recent Times*.

In Part I, *Outpost of a New Nation*, James Alton James provides an overview of two difficult years in Illinois at the time of the Revolutionary War, and Theodore C. Pease concentrates on 1780, a critical year for military operations in the Illinois country. In contrast, John H. Hauberg points out the multiplicity of problems the settlers faced in 1780 and the hard times they endured. The section closes with Nelson Vance Russell's discussion of social customs and the ways in which the French and British occupied their leisure time in the Illinois country during the last forty years of the eighteenth century.

Part II, *The Frontier State*, opens with Ray A. Billington's survey of the effect of the frontier upon the people of the infant state of Illinois. Benjamin P. Thomas considers the central Illinois frontier settlement of New Salem and its influence upon young Abraham Lincoln, while John Allen examines Negro slavery and conditions of near slavery in Pope County in southern Illinois. Grant Foreman, in presenting the only documentary piece in the book, reveals the conditions of daily life in Illinois as the frontier period was coming to an end. This section closes with George R. Gayler's summary of the Mormons at Nauvoo and Paul W. Gates's review of the acquisition and use of Illinois prairie land by landlords and tenants.

Part III, *The Age of Lincoln and Douglas*, opens with reminiscences of two Springfield weddings by Mrs. John M. Palmer, the wife of one of the governors of Illinois. William H. Smith and Clinton L. Conkling also reminisce: Smith about an important Lincoln campaign meeting and Conkling, who knew Lincoln, about the ways in which the Great Emancipator learned of his nomination for the presidency in 1860. David Donald studies popular legends about Lincoln and discusses their significance. Allan Nevins closes the section with a penetrating and sympathetic analysis of Lincoln's great opponent, Stephen A. Douglas.

Part IV, *The Maturing State*, discusses various events and personalities at the turn of the century and some of the problems with which the full-fledged industrial state of Illinois now had to cope. Two articles deal with the Haymarket Riot. Francis X. Busch relates the events that preceded the riot and describes the trial of the anarchists; the late Harvey Wish then explains the factors involved in Governor Altgeld's courageous decision to pardon the convicted anarchists. Two great Illinois women, Jane Addams and Mary E. McDowell, detail their concern for the poor and underprivileged in their articles about social conditions and problems in the slums of Chicago. Concluding this section, Harvey Wish, in a second article, describes a major event in American labor history, the Pullman Strike of 1894.

Part V, *In Recent Times*, covers disparate subjects. David R. Wrone tells how Illinois "pulled itself out of the mud" by building a statewide network of paved highways. Grace Wilbur Trout writes her recollections of the struggle for women's sufferage; Richard L. Beyer tells of the catastrophic flood of 1937; and Walter Trohan, in a humorous but affectionate portrayal, "My Life with the Colonel," discusses the influential publisher of the *Chicago Tribune*, Robert R. McCormick.

To achieve something like uniformity of style (particularly for the early publications), certain changes have been made, but for the most part nothing more important than uniform renderings of dates, numbers, and titles. Also, because this book is intended for the general reader, it was decided to dispense with all footnotes that did not expand the author's narrative. The scholarly reader can find the citations in the publications from which the selections were taken, and detailed bibliographical information is given in the biographical sketches.

Whenever I have had to ask for help, it has been given cheerfully —by Miss Margaret A. Flint, Assistant State Historian; by Albert Von Beheren and Mrs. Norma Darovec of the Illinois State Histori-

cal Library in Springfield; and by Miss Esther Park, Mrs. Lorene
Linder, Mrs. Dorothy Jorstad, and Mrs. Maurine Cottew of the
Swen Franklin Parson Library, Northern Illinois University,
DeKalb. I am also indebted to Mrs. Edith Childs and Miss Carolyn
Leifheit of Northern Illinois University for typing the manuscript.
If I have not already acknowledged Paul M. Angle's help, I wish to
do so; and I am most grateful for the editorial assistance of Miss
Mary Lynn McCree and Don Russell of the Sesquicentennial Com-
mission's publications staff.

I believe that *An Illinois Reader* is an interesting and at times
impressive "record of her years," and if the casual student of Illinois
history gets but half the pleasure from reading it that I have had in
editing it, I shall count my time well spent.

CONTENTS

LIST OF MAPS

AN ILLINOIS READER

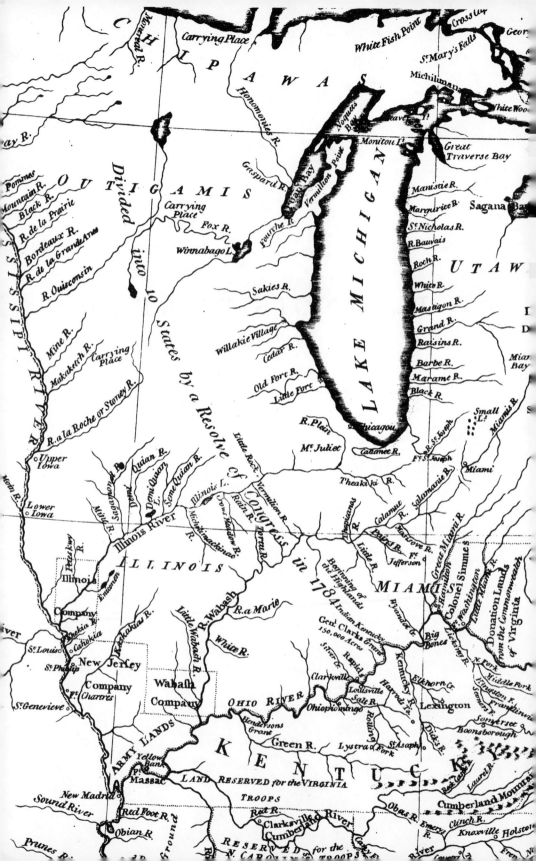

INTRODUCTION

Not Without Thy Wondrous Story, Illinois

ILLINOIS, they say, is flat. It has no mountain peaks, no fiords, no vales rivaling Kashmir or Tempe. In McLean, Cass and Adams counties, the prairie just rolls on and on. The history and social life of the state also are pronounced by some observers a bit flat. For the most part Illinois has enjoyed plump, uneventful years. The people of Aurora, Bloomington, Quincy, and Carmi appear in outward aspect much alike; to the Southerner they seem a little flat of speech, and to the Yankee rather flat of temperament. Flat, flat, flat, say the critics, repeating the revised version of Kipling:

> Oh, East is East, and West is West,
> But the Middle West is *terrible*.

In truth, however, this verdict is wide of the mark. The Illinois landscape is actually full of beauty; the history, temperament, and character of Illinoisans are in no sense flat. The state has qualities of its own which merit a more precise analysis.

When the Jesuit missionaries came to the Illinois country, they referred to the landscape as a sea of grass and flowers. When

Charles Dickens visited the young state, he was eager to view the
great Looking-Glass Prairie east of Lebanon, long a much publi-
cized wonder of nature. The prairies seemed at times to mirror the
calm blue sky. But when a breeze sprang up in the Ozarks and
crossed the Mississippi shore, or when a northwest wind whistled
down from Minnesota to the Rock River, the land ceased to seem
flat. The endless miles of grass—and later of grain—sprang into
life; they rippled in long undulating swells until they seemed, as
Francis Grierson writes in *The Valley of Shadows*, a rolling sea. As
the wind rose the sea became stormy; the grass lifted in heavier
billows, and in the distance the tossing branches of a copse along
some stream recalled a flight of sea gulls against the horizon. Or,
on a sultry day, Nature piled up in the west high ranges of cloud,
inky black below, dazzling white at the crest; and these vapory
Alps, to the music of their own artillery, swept conqueringly across
the land.

We have no fiords. But the watcher on Lake Michigan's shore
gazes out on an inland sea that joins Illinois to all the oceans of the
world. We have no bays. But to stand on the bluff at John Hay's
Warsaw, where the Mississippi drops from the north over the
Keokuk rapids, its never-ending flow linking the iron ranges of the
distant Mesabi with the cane fields of far-off Louisiana, binding
North and South with an indissoluble ribbon, is to gain a sense of
the pulse beat of the continent that is discernible nowhere else. An
airplane pilot hovering above Madison County can see the junction
of three great streams, the Missouri, Mississippi and Illinois; a
meeting-place of continental powers, "where philosophers might sit
and ponder on the mysteries of time and eternity." We have no
Vale of Ida. But the valleys of the Spoon, the Sangamon, the
Kaskaskia offer numberless shady nooks full of hickory and papaw,
of squirrels and doves, of buttercup and goldenrod.

Even falser than the suggestion of a mediocre landscape is the
concept of mediocrity in Illinois history. Many events that at the
time seemed tame take on, in perspective, a certain grandeur. Carl
Schurz in his autobiography relates that in the fall of 1858 he
boarded a train running from Galesburg to Quincy; some flat, dusty
cars, carrying men through flat, dusty cornfields to flat, dusty
errands. Suddenly he observed a commotion among his fellow
passengers, who sprang from their seats to cluster about a tall man
who had just entered. They hailed him with jovial shouts: "Hello,

Abe, how are you?" and he replied in kind. As the train rumbled along, Schurz measured the somewhat flat appearance of Abe Lincoln. He wore a battered stovepipe hat. His long, brown, corded neck emerged from a white collar turned down over a black string tie. "His lank, ungainly body was clad in a rusty black dress coat with sleeves that should have been longer. . . . His black trousers, too, permitted a very full view of his large feet. On his left arm he carried a gray woolen shawl, which evidently served him as an overcoat in chilly weather. His left hand held a cotton umbrella of the bulging kind, and also a black satchel that bore the marks of long and hard usage." In short, he was the most uncouth man Schurz had yet seen. Seating himself by Schurz, he presently began talking in simple, familiar, homely speech—political talk of the day in a flat Kentucky accent.

But mark the real drama of the scene, and its Olympian elevation. Here was an exiled German Patriot, whose escape from the besieged fortress of Rastatt had been one of the striking episodes of the revolutionary year 1848, and whose subsequent liberation of his fellow-patriot Gottfried Kinkel from the prison of Spandau had made Europe ring. Now an adopted American, he was observing a contest unique in our history. Lincoln and Douglas, like two knights of old selected to champion opposed armies in single combat, were fighting one of the great moral battles of the century. The state of Illinois was closely divided and intensely excited by a discussion as momentous as any since the adoption of the Constitution. On the morrow, at Quincy, the rival champions were to grapple like Ivanhoe and Front de Boeuf, but in a struggle incomparably grander than any of feudal days. Carl Schurz identified himself heart and soul with the free-soil cause; and his eager greeting of Lincoln was a token of world interest in the slavery convulsion.

Two years later a delegation of Republican leaders was in Springfield to give Lincoln a formal notification of his nomination for the Presidency. When the Pennsylvanian William D. Kelley was presented, Lincoln asked him: "How tall are you, Mr. Kelley?" "Six feet three, sir," replied Kelley; "and how tall are *you?*" "Six feet four," rejoined Lincoln. "Then Pennsylvania bows to Illinois," said Kelley. "My dear sir, for years my heart has been aching for a President I could look up to." Out of the Illinois prairies rose a statesman to whom, more than any other, the country is still looking *up.*

So far as history goes, Illinois has enjoyed an exceptional amount of it, and much of it has been extraordinarily picturesque. If we revert far enough, according to Clarence W. Alvord, we find Illinois "inhabited by huge reptiles eighty feet long, by gigantic kangaroo-like saurians, by dragons flying on twenty-foot wings, and by innumerable crocodiles." Perhaps in the social swamps of Chicago, Peoria, and East St. Louis a few crocodiles still survive!—but our written history provides color enough without going back to the saurians. That history begins with 1670, when the gallant La Salle, if we may believe his admirers, descended the Illinois River; or at least in 1673, when the wagonmaker's son, Louis Jolliet, followed the Mississippi southward, found a village of the Illini Indians, and on approaching the wigwam of the chief met him, stark naked, shielding his eyes with his hands. "Frenchman," said the chief, "how bright the sun shines when you come to visit us!" What state has a history that begins with a compliment more courtly—or a scene more emblematic of the impact of Europe and the wilderness on one another than this prairie state?

For one cardinal fact respecting the history of Illinois must never be forgotten: the fact that the Illinois country always lay squarely in the stream of world events. Our first chapters of history were written by the French and British; our earliest capitals were Paris and London. When in the 1670s French agents of Louis XIV planted themselves at the Sault Ste. Marie, and British agents for Charles II appeared in the passes of the Alleghenies, their eyes were on the Illinois valley. When the French created Louisiana, it was partly as a shield against English traders on the Tennessee and Ohio, whose goods were reaching the old southwest and the Illinois prairies. In the time of Frontenac, behind the rivalries of missionaries, fur traders, and soldiers stood two hostile empires, contending for the mastery of the continent. The weapons were often squalid enough. To win Indian support, French brandy was pitted against English rum; and the latter had the advantage, for it was cheaper—"The English liquor made an Indian drunk for a muskrat skin, while the French liquor cost a beaver pelt." When in this century-long struggle the British seized the final victory in Wolfe's capture of Quebec, the force of the stroke was felt all the way to the Mississippi. The treaties of Utrecht and Paris were no less world-shaking events, indeed, to the settlers of Kaskaskia and Cahokia, and the wild tribes along the Sangamon, than they were to the people of Europe.

In the years of British rule over the West, speculators in Philadelphia and London struggled over tracts of Illinois lands. One of the most potent elements in bringing on the American Revolution was the fact that in mismanaging Illinois and the West as in mismanaging the seaboard colonies, the English genius for government for once failed. During the Revolution, Illinois and the West were still a part of European politics, as no one realized better than George Rogers Clark. If exact justice were done, the state of Illinois would some day raise a statue to Lord Shelburne, the liberal British prime minister at the time of the peace of 1783, for he was one of our greatest benefactors. When many New Englanders were ready, nay, anxious, to let Great Britain keep the Illinois country in exchange for a secure title to fishing rights on the banks of Newfoundland, Lord Shelburne took a generous view. Seeing that the quarrels of fur traders and settlers could easily make a new Anglo-American war, and anxious to draw America toward Britain and away from France, he insisted on giving up the Illinois region; indeed, he offered it to Benjamin Franklin even before the other American negotiators, John Adams and John Jay, reached Paris. When Illinois entered the Union in 1818, of its 35,000 people the old French *habitants* still numbered one tenth; and the richest cultural element in the new state was the British community in Edwards County under Morris Birkbeck and George Flower.

Nor did Illinois ever lose its place in world events. When the Illinois Central was built, British capital, represented in part by Richard Cobden, figured largely in its construction. Idealistic Germans came, bringing the classics, music, and a world outlook on such issues as slavery. Muscular Irishmen arrived in armies, first to build canals and railways, and later to build political machines. Scandinavians formed settlements like that at Rockford and Moline, full of Lutheranism, literature, and laughter. Tell John P. Altgeld who was born in the duchy of Nassau, or Carl Sandburg whose parents came from Sweden, or James Keeley who migrated from London, that Illinois was not in the world stream, and they would smile derisively. In time, two world wars proved that it was. Reviewing the events of 1914, Arthur C. Cole wrote: "Illinois was, from the point of view of international relations, the most impor-

tant state in the Mississippi valley—in the opinion of many the
most important state in the Union." If there are still men who
perversely refuse to see the light, they know little of the real history
of the state.

Individualism has naturally marked Illinois history; the individualism of unfettered energy, which leveled the forest, broke the
soil, built the railways, and founded the cities. It was the individualism of which William Jennings Bryan, born and educated in
Illinois, spoke when he said: "Whenever a thing is necessary, it is
possible."

That individualism long had its violent and even lawless side—
and still has. An Illinois commander, rallying his troops in the
Mexican War, roared at them: "Come on, you Illinois blood-
hounds!" And bloodhounds Illinoisans could be at times. The pioneer Illinoisans were singularly brutal and savage in their onslaught upon Black Hawk and his band of Sauk and Foxes. They
were equally harsh in their excision of what they called the Mormon cancer from Nauvoo, to which they applied the knife of mob
violence. Like the crushing of the Sauk and Foxes, the dispersion of
the Mormons was effective; like that blow, its method was excusa-
ble only on the ground that the raw young state was as yet imper-
fectly civilized. The tradition of violence remains. But happily the
variegated history of Illinois shows individualism constantly at
work in more constructive ways—often with dramatic results, as in
the rebuilding of Chicago after her fire. And better still, it shows
individualism tempered by a sense of world responsibility.

That the quality of democracy in Illinois should be such as to
possess a significance for the whole world was a fact of which the
state's best leaders never lost sight. That truth was enunciated by
an early governor, Thomas Ford, in his rare *History of Illinois*. In
the Jacksonian era Ford agonized over the seamy aspects of a crude
frontier democracy, and his book, mercilessly exposing the mean-
ness of little men and little measures, called for purer, larger
attitudes. Edward Coles, the friend of Thomas Jefferson and secretary to James Madison, who emancipated his slaves and fought for
the antislavery cause in Illinois, believed, like Jefferson, that democracy was for world consumption. It was one of Lincoln's distinctions as a democratic leader that he always thought of Illinois,
and America, as object lessons for mankind. At Gettysburg he
exulted, not in victory over the South, but in the vindication of

democracy as a global force—in the fact that government of, by, and for the people should survive as an example to the whole earth. The governors of the First World War period, Edward F. Dunne and Frank O. Lowden, alike shared the Wilsonian idea that our democracy must be even more than an object lesson—that it must be a dynamic force, keeping the world safe for its spread. If the recent campaign of Adlai E. Stevenson had any paramount significance, it was that our democracy is a living world force. These are the true historic voices of Illinois.

When we turn from history to temperament and character, again we may claim for Illinois certain possessions—far indeed from flat—that are all her own. Of the various circumstances which have given the state a peculiar heritage, the chief is unquestionably its combination of remarkable diversities within a general unity. From the Wisconsin boundary to Cairo on the extreme south is a stretch of nearly five hundred miles; a distance greater than from New York to North Carolina. The elongated state was naturally first populated half by Southerners, half by Yankees. It grew up to combine, like New York, a great metropolis and a rich rural area. Its people before long were half native, half immigrant. The vagaries of glaciation gave it some of the richest soils of the globe, and some of the poorest, barrenest clays. It lies halfway between East and West, halfway between the Gulf of St. Lawrence and the Gulf of Mexico. Of necessity, Illinois was a state of compromises, concessions, and mergers. Because of its diversities, it always had a certain difficulty in getting along with itself. Pudd'nhead Wilson said he would like to own half of a troublesome dog, because if he did he would kill his half. But one half of Illinois was never able to kill the other half; it had to enlarge itself—to take on traits of universality.

The soul of early Illinois gained a stimulating discipline from the fact that the people were half Yankee, half Southerners. Oliver Wendell Holmes distinguished between two kinds of New Englanders, the fine-grained white pine sort, and the coarse-grained pitch pine type. As material for statebuilding, both were invaluable; but they are best when mingled with other timber. Parts of northern Illinois were once rather more Puritan than the Puritans themselves; the Galesburg of Jonathan Blanchard, for example, and the Jacksonville of the "Yale Band." When that consecrated Yankee, Elijah Lovejoy, settled in Alton, trouble blazed up like a flame in each footstep. The hair-triggered New England stock required a certain tempering, and the Virginians and Kentuckians, slow, easy-going, tolerant to a point and then implacable, supplied it. The Dick Oglesby who came from Kentucky to Illinois was a good Union man who led a brigade against Fort Donelson. But Oglesby had Southern charm and tact; when he fought a political battle against that chill, critical Yankee Lyman Trumbull, he won the votes; thrice elected governor and once senator, he was long the most popular man in Illinois. Well it was for Chicago that Yankees like Gustavus Swift, Marshall Field and William B. Ogden could furnish surpassing business acumen and enterprise; but it was also well that Southerners like John M. Palmer and the two Carter Harrisons could supply elements of geniality, grace and dignity. In the Lincolns, the best moral qualities of the North and the best social qualities of the South were admirably blended. As children intermarried, central Illinois—as brought out in Clark E. Carr's *The Illini*—became an area where Yankee and Southerner fused to finer effect.

It was still more salutary for the soul of Illinois that the state became half rural, half urban. No doubt it is uncomfortable for the great progressive city of Chicago to have to live with backward rustic areas. No doubt it is uncomfortable for our virtuous country-sides to have to live with the flaunted sins of Chicago. But discomfort is good for character.

The rural frontier was a land of natural idealism: the idealism of pioneers who endured hardship because they were sustained by a vision of the Promised Land yet to come. It was a practical, materialistic idealism, but intensely real. Its great defect was that it was not a social idealism. Although the frontiersman and his farmer sons, so well depicted in Edward Eggleston's *The Graysons*, saw a bright future civilization for which they were laying the foundation, it was a competitive, not a co-operative, civilization. The spirit was too much affected by the "git a plenty while you're a gittin'" temper which Eggleston presented as part of another novel. The Chicagoan for decades showed the same fiercely competitive temper.

But a crowded city, with its problems of crime, injustice, and poverty, necessarily generates in time a social idealism. We are able, even, to lay a fairly precise finger on the date when this transformation became fully visible in Chicago. Those who read the tenth chapter of Jane Addams' *Twenty Years at Hull House* will find set forth the evidence that Chicago entered the Pullman strike of 1894 a city of almost unregenerate individualists, and that it emerged from the rioting, the misery, the class conflict, of that grim labor war with a changing outlook. Social consciousness had spread; humanitarian grace had taken deeper root; the strike had illuminated the minds of innumerable Chicagoans previously blind —and the illumination widened.

The culture of rural Illinois might well have produced a radical leader like John P. Altgeld, as it did produce the Grangers and William Jennings Bryan. It remained for urban Illinois, however, to bring forth such apostles of social democracy as Jane Addams and Florence Kelley, Julius Rosenwald and Clarence Darrow. One fault of Chicago was simply that it grew too fast. The rise of a city of four millions in a single century is a phenomenon almost unexampled in history. Growing so rapidly, it was inevitably full of brutalities and greeds. "The larger toleration," wrote Charles E. Merriam, "emerges slowly in communities hastily built and without traditions upon which to rest." Such toleration began to emerge more rapidly when the four fine spirits just named, with Raymond Robbins, Brand Whitlock, Grace Abbott, Julia Lathrop, Frank J. Loesch, Jenkin Lloyd Jones, and Merriam himself entered the scene.

These leaders, and others like them, created the new social conscience of Illinois. Clarence Darrow had a passion for the underdog—the maltreated individual, the minority group. Whitlock, as a Chicago newspaperman and secretary to Governor Altgeld, cherished a passion for social justice. Florence Kelley, Julia Lathrop, and Grace Abbott felt a passionate interest in better working conditions, the stopping of child labor, and the rescue of neglected children. Jane Addams was a passionate battler against vice and the slum. Rosenwald, a gifted mercantile organizer who never sought office, by virtue of his weight of character, complete unselfishness, and tremendous earnestness in the struggle for better education, better housing, and better race relations, gave first Chicago and then the whole state a social leaven. Loesch had a passionate hatred of crime, and Merriam of corruption. The essential conditions of urban life have made for a bigger, deeper democracy. When Professor T. V. Smith of the University of Chicago ran for the Illinois Senate, he found inspiration in the diversity of his community. His constituency, he has recalled, was "half white and half Negro; one-third Jewish, one-third Catholic, one-third Protestant; it was one-half rich, one-half poor; it was half sophisticated, with the proud University of Chicago in its center, and one-half underprivileged educationally." These differences, as he says, "were the raw stuff of community richness."

Were we to name the two greatest exponents of democracy in Illinois, one would be the son of the soil, Abraham Lincoln; the other the daughter who turned to city slums, Jane Addams. Both, like St. Augustine, had their city of God; both would build it in Illinois—Lincoln amid farms and villages, Jane Addams amid city streets. Lincoln, who liked breadth, would have read appreciatively Santayana's statement: "Great empty spaces bring a sort of freedom to both soul and body. You can pitch your tent where you will; or, if ever you decide to build anything, it can be in a style of your own devising." Jane Addams would have liked that too; but she would have said that social co-operation, in areas too cramped and crowded for the old individualistic freedom, is also essential. Lincoln's democracy was primarily political and spiritual. He well expressed it when he explained why, in the fall of 1860, he had not gone to the railway station to see the Prince of Wales pass through Springfield. "I remained here at the State House," he said, "where I met so many sovereigns during the day that really the Prince had come and gone before I knew about it." Jane Addams' democracy was primarily economic and social. She, too, regarded the common man as a sovereign. But she knew that the unemployed workman, the sweated seamstress, the slum-housed immigrant, found it harder to hold a sovereign status than the yeoman of Lincoln's day. Well it is for the soul of Illinois, we repeat, that it has had to fuse the individualistic democracy of the prairies with the social democracy of Hull House.

Because of the rich history of Illinois—its place in world history; because of its diversity in unity, the commingling of North and South, of East and West, of immigrant and native, of rich and poor; because city masses and prairie farmers have had to dwell together in our state, Illinois has been able to put into art and poetry a more fluid, spacious, and searching democracy than that known in some states of greater homogeneity and less eventful growth. Lorado Taft, a son of the university created by the state, held an intense faith in the possibilities of a truly democratic art.

He taught thirty years at the Art Institute in Chicago and ten years at the University of Chicago; he gave more than two thousand lectures on art to general audiences; he was an apostle of the artistic enrichment of Illinois and the Middle West. In such imaginative sculptural groups as that of "The Great Lakes" and such impressive statues as the one popularly called "Black Hawk" towering over Rock River, he beautified his state with art the masses could understand. Hamlin Garland, in his Chicago days, gave the mute farmers of the West an eloquent voice; and he was anxious not only to help these farmers gain a square deal, but to see their lives touched with cultural grace. It was in Chicago in the period of the World's Columbian Exposition, itself one of the shining American achievements in bringing art to the people, that Daniel Burnham and others first made city planning a potent force. Vachel Lindsay, who called his second book *Adventures While Preaching the Gospel of Beauty*, and who taught that his own Springfield might be made another Florence, held a fervent belief in the necessity of giving democracy a set of living cultural and aesthetic values. Carl Sandburg, a western Walt Whitman with something added of the mass appeal of Robert Burns, believed in a union of democracy, humanitarianism, and art—a union blessed by unflinching honesty.

Like other communities from the time of ancient Athens, Illinois has lifted itself to its highest levels in time of crisis, and particularly when the crisis produced a devoted leader. In placid eras, Illinoisans too often allow the real to corrode the ideal. They fail to square the abstract with the concrete. They talk about enlightenment, but they pay their schoolteachers minimum salaries. They praise democracy, but think it is served merely by holding frequent elections, even if Hinky Dink and Bathhouse John are the men elected. They are eloquent about freedom, but let demagogues define it as telling King George and the United Nations to keep their snoots out of American affairs. They descant upon justice, but permit the successors of Al Capone to go right on with kidnapping and thuggery. The people respect nomenclature but are careless about substance. In relaxed moods they listen to voices appealing to their worst instincts, for Illinois like other states has such voices; it has one in particular, a journalistic voice of isolationism, cynicism, and social reaction, which comes into hundreds of thousands of homes every morning. In periods of relapse, Illinois becomes really flat. But when the crisis and the leader appear, then at times the spirit of the people is exalted. The brave romanticism which inspired Vachel Lindsay to place the courthouse square in Springfield on a level with the Agora in Athens then finds its response.

We are in the throes of a many-sided crisis today; but we shall still be enduring it tomorrow. One of its facets is a challenge to the willingness of Illinoisans to play their due role in world affairs. Actually, we have been in the midst of world affairs for two and a half centuries; we cannot escape playing a role on that great stage; but we can play it courageously and generously, or skulkingly and meanly. We can interpret the part of our democracy in the modern world as Lincoln interpreted it, or as the Copperheads interpreted it; we can accept it as Frank O. Lowden accepted it, or clown it as Big Bill Thompson clowned it. Another facet of the manysided crisis is the struggle between social advance and social reaction. We stagger under a terrible economic strain; debt, taxation, and living costs have reached unprecedented levels. Inevitably, voices are lifted demanding that we economize on education, that we stint our social services, and that we cut back the gains of labor and the farmer. They are the same voices that Florence Kelley and Grace Abbott heard in their day, and that excited their blazing moral indignation. Still another aspect of the crisis is a challenge to our civil liberties. The United States has lost its old security; we are living in what President Eisenhower calls "not an instant of danger but an age of danger." Placed in this situation of long-continuing peril, we face a severe test of our ability to preserve the great principles of moderation, compromise and scrupulous justice. Demagogues in two neighboring states have taken advantage of the tension to bring our elementary civil rights under attack; and we must stand on our guard.

We should remember that Illinois has its own pages of history pertinent to this last challenge. It is a tradition of valorous defense of the principles of the first ten amendments to the Constitution— not excluding the fifth; a tradition of the vindication of free inquiry, of the right of individuals to protection against browbeating and slander, and of the title of every citizen, when accused, to a calm and impartial trial. This is essentially a conservative tradition. It objects to any effort to use mob passion in time of excitement to ruin the weak, to suppress free discussion, and to force conformity to the dictates of a mob leader.

This is the tradition of Elijah Lovejoy, who lifted his voice at Alton when demagogues and mobs sought to suppress it, and accepted death rather than an infringement of his civil liberties. It is the tradition of Edward Coles, who left a slave state to fight the proslavery sentiment of southern Illinois and maintain the provisions of the Northwest Ordinance. It is the tradition of Lyman Trumbull, who from his early antislavery days until his final espousal of Populist doctrines, never hesitated to insist on the rights of the dissenter and of the minority, and to demand a broadening of social freedom. It is the tradition of John M. Palmer, ever a brave fighter for advanced views and policies. It is the tradition of Robert G. Ingersoll, who dared to think for himself in social and religious matters, and used his wit and eloquence to denounce a sterile conformity and expose the specious pretenses of demagogic bulldozers. It is the tradition of Clarence Darrow, who in one unpopular case after another threw his talents and his blunt honesty on the side of those who seemed in danger of obtaining less than a full hearing or a fair trial. It is the tradition of John P. Altgeld, who in the aftermath of the Haymarket affair braved a storm of misrepresentation and obloquy to pardon three unjustly condemned men, and in one of the best state papers ever written in America asserted the elementary rules of justice involved.

In any critical period—and we are certainly passing through one of the greatest crises of the modern era—the best lamp on our pathway is that of history. And what a glorious history, when we look at its better aspects, Illinois has had! The record is one, in the main, of moderation, compromise, and common sense, as befits a state inheriting the old Anglo-Saxon principles, holding a central position in the American continent, and uniting so many varied elements. The citizens of the state can surely be relied upon to reject with equal vigor the Communist and the demagogue, the enemies of our government and the enemies of our civil rights. Our record, with few deviations, is that of a people aware of their place in the stream of world events and their duty to what Lincoln called "man's vast future." Our history is that of a broadening social consciousness; a growing sense that the individual freedom of the pioneer must be blended with the communal privileges and protections of the great conglomerate—white and black, alien-born and native, laborer and white-collar man—which populates our ever-growing cities.

To the rising generation the state commits this heritage. To one part of that emerging generation in particular does it look for responsible action and imaginative leadership: its university-trained youth. What a privilege they have in preserving their heritage! What a challenge they should feel in the duty of enlarging and brightening it—in writing new pages more lustrous than the old! As they rise to that challenge, they will give more pregnant meaning to the lines:

> Not without thy wondrous story . . .
> Can be writ the nation's glory,
> Illinois.

This article by Allan Nevins was first published in the *Journal of the Illinois State Historical Society*, volume 46, number 3 (autumn, 1953), pages 231–246. It was the address he presented at the University of Illinois when he received the honorary Doctor of Law degree in June 1953. See page 260 for a biographical sketch. Ed.

PART I

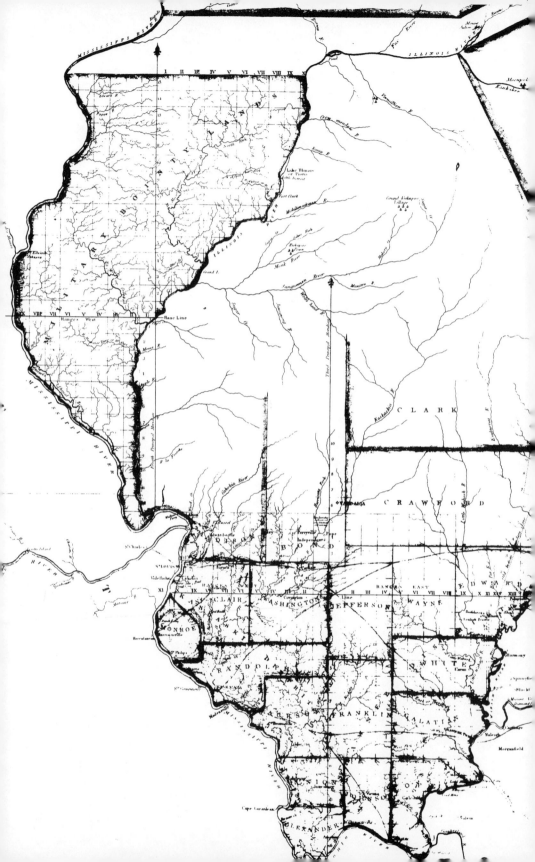

PART I

Outpost of a New Nation

1760–1796

THE RECORDED HISTORY OF ILLINOIS begins
with the voyage of Father Jacques Marquette and Louis Jolliet
along the west shore of Lake Michigan, through Green Bay and up
the Fox River to the Wisconsin River, and down the Wisconsin to
the Mississippi River. They reached the Mississippi on June 17,
1673, and followed it as far as the mouth of the Arkansas River.
Although they did not land on Illinois soil on the journey south,
they were the first Europeans to see our state. On their return
north, the small band of explorers turned up the Illinois River,
proceeded by portage to the Chicago River, and thence into Lake
Michigan. The first European settlement in Illinois dates from the
winter of 1674–75, which Father Marquette and two companions
spent with great difficulty near the mouth of the Chicago River. In
1675 Marquette founded a mission near Utica, and then, in ill
health, tried to return to Canada, but he died on the way, near
Ludington, Michigan.

Although French fur traders were active in Illinois, we know almost nothing about them, and the next European who we are sure came to Illinois was Father Claude Allouez, who succeeded Marquette at the Illinois mission in 1676. Robert Cavelier, Sieur de LaSalle, built Fort Crevecoeur near Peoria in 1680 and Fort St. Louis on Starved Rock in 1682; Henri de Tonti built the second Fort St. Louis at Peoria in 1691 and 1692. French Jesuits and seminarians established missions at Chicago in 1696 (and Kaskaskia in 1703) but, it was in March 1699, when Jolliet de Montigny and Jean Francois Buisson de St. Cosmé, priests of the Seminary of Foreign Missions, stopped at Cahokia and began to build the Holy Family mission, that the first permanent European settlement in Illinois was established.

The first French commander of Illinois, Pierre Duqué, Sieur de Boisbriant, arrived at Kaskaskia in December 1718, and Fort de Chartres, destined to be the major military installation in Illinois, was begun the next year. Rebuilt in 1727, it was so dilapidated by 1747 that the troops were withdrawn. The last and most secure Fort de Chartres was constructed between 1753 and 1756. Although Indians continued to menace the French for many years, Illinois was a securely held French possession by 1718, rich in furs and populated by Indians whom the missionaries would attempt to Christianize.

Almost as much in need of Christianity were the *coureurs de bois*, the voyageurs, crude, tough, hard-working and hard-drinking men whose lives were compounded of monotony, back-breaking labor, and the perils associated with taking items of trade into the wilderness and bringing valuable furs to the settlements. When they returned to civilization, perhaps after being away a year or more, their debauches were of epic proportions.

In contrast, other French settlers—some of the clergy, government administrators, wealthy traders, and members of the "old families"—lived pleasantly and comfortably in sturdy houses that were well kept and beautifully furnished. Many of these people were well educated, and their social lives centered on lavish, formal dinners that were characterized by excellent food, imported wines and liquors, and sprightly, sophisticated conversation. Some of these Frenchmen kept slaves, owned herds of cattle, and altogether lived quite well; the privations and terrors of the wilderness seldom touched them.

But most of the French seem to have led a free, day-to-day

existence, hunting and fishing as much for pleasure as from necessity. They often disappeared for long periods of time to roam
through the woods and across the prairies. In their aimless, improvident manner, they gambled beyond their means, danced to
exhaustion night after night, delighted in horse racing and wrestling, and smoked and drank to excess. Their lives were an unbroken, undisciplined frolic. They brought little to Illinois, and left
little behind when their era passed.

The destiny of Illinois, however, was controlled not by its French
inhabitants but by events in far-off Europe. The culmination of the
struggle between France and England to dominate America was
the French and Indian War, which began in 1754. By the Treaty of
Paris, which ended the fighting in 1763, France ceded all its territory east of the Mississippi to England, and Captain Thomas Stir-
ling arrived at Fort de Chartres in 1765 to take command for the
British.

Although Indians were again a serious problem, particularly
those led by the Ottawa chief, Pontiac, the English controlled
Illinois until the Revolutionary War brought new conflict to the
West. The British abandoned Fort de Chartres in 1772 and moved
their soldiers to Kaskaskia, and in 1776 Captain Hugh Lord moved
his troops from Kaskaskia to Detroit, having designated Philippe
François de Rastel, Chevalier de Rocheblave, as British agent in
Illinois. Without money, supplies, or troops, de Rocheblave gov-
erned as best he could while constantly begging British headquarters at Detroit for assistance. Meanwhile George Rogers Clark, who
had been charged by Virginia with the defense of Kentucky, decided this could best be accomplished by capturing Vincennes (Indiana) and the nearby Illinois towns, from which he would launch
an attack on Detroit. Accordingly, he transported a force of about
175 men down the Ohio River to Fort Massac, and then marched
overland to surprise Kaskaskia, which was not defended by the
British. After Clark captured the town, on July 4, 1778, he sent
agents to Vincennes and the citizens of that important town readily
swore allegiance to the colonies. By an act of the Virginia assembly,
Illinois became a county of Virginia on December 9, 1778, and
John Todd of Kentucky was appointed county lieutenant.

The British reaction to Clark's occupation of the Illinois country
was quick and positive; the lieutenant governor of Detroit, Henry
Hamilton (the "hair buyer"), immediately mounted a successful

expedition against Vincennes. Fearful that the British would use Vincennes as a base from which to attack the Illinois towns, Clark again decided that his best defense was to attack, even though winter still lingered. As they advanced towards Vincennes, Clark's men overcame incredible hardships, marching across flooded prairies and sometimes wading through neck-deep icy water. But their courage and persistence brought them success, for they reached the Wabash River and by means of half bluff and half military dash accomplished their mission: the capture of Vincennes and its military post, Fort Sackville, on February 24, 1779.

But Clark's position was still difficult; his only dependable source of supplies was New Orleans, where Oliver Pollock, one of the forgotten heroes of the Revolution, would bankrupt himself by accepting Clark's bills of credit. Despite the many problems created by depreciated currency, and other problems as well, Todd was able to establish civil government in the "county," and judges were elected at Kaskaskia, Cahokia, and Vincennes in May 1779. Clark wanted to pursue his plan to lead an expedition against Detroit in 1779, but men from Kentucky who were supposed to join his army were diverted in an unsuccessful attack on Indians and without these men Clark did not have sufficient strength for the expedition. However, the British, aware of Clark's intention, adopted a defensive posture, and the threat of Clark's proposed expedition temporarily relieved some of the pressure on the frontier.

The year 1780 was hard and uncertain for everyone who lived in the Illinois country. Food, clothing, and supplies were scarce; the French civilians in the occupied towns were hostile to Clark's soldiers and the handful of American settlers; the weather was unusually severe and wild game seemed to have disappeared. And never was Illinois more intimately involved with international policies. Wary of the intentions of a new partner in arms, Spain, which controlled the mouth of the Mississippi and most of its west bank, Clark also had to be concerned with the British at Detroit and to the east. Moreover, the Illinois country suffered from the inconsistent actions of her nominal ally, France, and from the lack of support or outright indifference of the government in Virginia.

It also was in 1780 that the British launched a three-prong attack on the Illinois country from Mackinac and Detroit. One column marched through Ohio toward the falls of the Ohio River; the second column moved across Lake Michigan and down the

Illinois River to the Mississippi; and the third column followed the Wisconsin River route to the Mississippi. In the West, the targets were Kaskaskia, Cahokia, and St. Louis; and in the East the objective was harassment of the frontier and isolation of the Illinois country from Kentucky. Clark fought off the attack on Cahokia and the Spanish defeated the British and Indians at St. Louis; the British expedition into Kentucky achieved no significant result. Clark sent troops up the Mississippi after the British and Indians who had attacked Cahokia and St. Louis, and his burning of the Indian villages at Rock Island was the westernmost action of the Revolutionary War. In August, Clark made a punitive raid against hostile Indians at Piqua in Ohio.

The curious armed advance upon Detroit by the mysterious Augustin Mottin de la Balme and the Franco-Spanish capture and one-day occupation of St. Joseph, Michigan, compound the confusion of military events in the West in 1780. They were, however, the last important episodes in the Illinois country during the Revolutionary War.

At the end of the Revolutionary War, the new nation theoretically gained control of all the territory (except East and West Florida) east of the Mississippi. In Illinois, however, federal control was tenuous for more than ten years. In 1784, Virginia gave up her claim to Illinois, and three years later, after Congress passed the Ordinance of 1787, Illinois became part of the Northwest Territory. Arthur St. Clair was appointed governor of the territory and a slow but steady trickle of settlers began to arrive in Illinois. By 1800, when the Indiana Territory (which included Illinois) was created, many of the French had left and Illinois had approximately 2,500 new European inhabitants.

JAMES ALTON JAMES

was professor of history at Northwestern University, 1897–1935, and dean of the Graduate School, 1913–1941. He was the first chairman of the Illinois State Parks Commission, 1909–1917, and president of the Illinois State Historical Society, 1935–1940. Among his better known works are *George Rogers Clark, Letters and Papers; The Life of George Rogers Clark,* and *The First Scientific Exploration of Russian America and the Purchase of Alaska.*

This article first appeared in *Transactions of the Illinois State Historical Society* for 1910, pages 63–71.

ILLINOIS AND THE REVOLUTION IN THE WEST, 1779–1780

JAMES ALTON JAMES

The position of George Rogers Clark was a desperate one when at the beginning of the year 1779 he determined to risk all he had gained by at once taking the offensive and attempting the reduction of Vincennes. "It was at this moment," he declared; "I would have bound myself seven years a slave to have had five hundred troops." The wish was vain, for not only had he received no reinforcements from Virginia but for nearly a year he had not received any communication whatever from Governor Henry.

His confidence in the success of the expedition seemed to inspire his men, and "in a day or two the country seemed to believe it, many anxious to retrieve their characters turned out, the ladies began also to be spirited and interest themselves in the expedition, which had a great effect on the young men." With this enthusiasm, provisions and stores were soon collected. On February 5, the *Willing,* an armed row-galley, the first armed boat on a Western river, mounting two four pounders and four swivels, with a crew of forty men commanded by Lieutenant John Rogers, set off under orders to take station a short distance below Vincennes and prevent any boat from descending the Wabash, for it was surmised that in case of defeat the British would attempt to escape by this route.

The following afternoon, Clark, with his one hundred and thirty men, nearly one-half of whom were French volunteers, Father

Gibault having granted them absolution, marched out of Kaskaskia. It is not the purpose of this paper to discuss the extreme trials encountered by this little band of men in their wintry march to Vincennes nor to relate the events connected with the capture of that post. On February 25, the garrison of seventy-nine men were made prisoners of war. Lieutenant Governor Hamilton and twenty-five of his men were sent under guard to Williamsburg.

Preparatory to his return to Kaskaskia, with the remaining prisoners, Clark carefully arranged for a satisfactory government at Vincennes by appointing the faithful Captain Helm to take control of all civil matters and act as superintendent of Indian affairs. Moses Henry was made Indian agent. The garrison of forty picked men was left in command of Lieutenant Richard Brashears, assisted by Lieutenants Bailey and Chaplin. Letters were sent John Bowman, then county lieutenant in Kentucky, urging him to begin collecting men and provisions for the proposed march on Detroit.

No victorious army ever returned with spirits more elated than the eighty men who, on March 20, accompanied Clark on his return back to Kaskaskia. Within a year the authority of Virginia over the region stretching from the Ohio to the Illinois and 140 miles up the Wabash had been established by conquest. The danger that the frontier settlements would be cut off by savages under the leadership of British agents was greatly lessened. These results had been accomplished against odds that would have competely overcome men not already inured to the harsh conditions incident to life on the frontier. No assistance had been rendered by the Virginia authorities, and for nearly a year Clark had not even received, as he expressed it, "a scrape of a pen" from Governor Henry. The six boats pushed off down the Wabash amidst the rejoicing of the people who had assembled to wish them a "good and safe passage." A few of those who lingered to watch the boats until they were lost to view fully comprehended the results which had been attained. Their thought was expressed by one of their number as follows:

> Although a handful in comparison to other armies, they have done themselves and the cause they were fighting for, credit and honor, and deserve a place in History for future ages; that their posterity may know the difficulty their forefathers had gone through for their liberty and freedom. Particularly the back settlers of Virginia may bless the day they sent

out such a Commander, and officers, men, etc., etc., I say, to
root out that nest of Vipers, that was every day ravaging on
their women and children; which I hope will soon be at an
end, as the leaders of these murderers are taken and sent to
Congress.

When the boats reached Kaskaskia, "Great Joy" was manifested
by the garrison, then commanded by Captain Robert George, who
had recently returned with sixty men from New Orleans. The
villagers, too, were not less gratified at the return of Clark, for he
was the one American who had gained and continued to hold their
love and confidence.

The problems and disappointments Clark was forced to meet
with during the succeeding three months were among the most
trying of his whole career. Upon arrival he found the people excited
over the recent conduct of a party of Delaware warriors. Learning
also of depredations committed at Vincennes by another party,
Clark, by way of warning to the other tribes, ordered a ruthless war
against the marauders. In the attacks on their villages which followed, no mercy was shown except to the women and children. The
Indians soon sued for peace.

Without money for the support of his army Clark had begun
after the capture of Kaskaskia to issue bills of credit on Virginia in
exchange for provisions. These were satisfactory to the merchants
and traders, for they were received and paid at their face value in
silver by Oliver Pollock, agent for the state at New Orleans. In a
letter of July 18, Clark said to Pollock: "I have succeeded agreeable
to my wishes, and am necessitated to draw bills on the state and
have reason to believe they will be accepted by you, the answering
of which will be acknowledged by his Excellency the Governor of
Virginia. . . ." Large batteaux rowed with twenty-four oars, loaded
with goods sent by Pollock, under the protection of the Spanish
flag, slipped past Natchez, then under the control of the British,
and in from eighty-five to ninety days arrived at St. Louis or the
Illinois posts. Full credit was given by Clark to Pollock for this
assistance, by which he was able to hold the Illinois country. "The
invoice Mr. Pollock rendered upon all occasions in paying those
bills," Clark declared, "I considered at the time and now to be one
of the happy circumstances that enabled me to Keep Possession of
that Country." During September, 1778, goods were sent by Pollock
to Clark, amounting to $7,200. The following January 500 pounds

of powder and some swivels were received by Clark from the same source. By February 5, 1779, bills were drawn on Pollock by Clark amounting to $48,000. Of this amount, $10,000 were paid by Pollock after he had disposed of his own remaining slaves at a great disadvantage.

By July, 1779, however, Pollock had so far exhausted his credit that in meeting an order from Governor Henry for goods amounting to $10,000, he was forced to mortgage a part of his lands. He had at that time paid bills drawn on the state amounting to $33,000. The flour and meal which had been promised him had not been forwarded. He wrote:

> Being already drained of every shilling I could raise for the use of yours and the rest of the United States, I went first to the Governor of this place, and then to every merchant in it, but could not prevail upon any of them to supply said goods, giving for their reason the few goods they had were imported, would in all probability become double the value of what they were just now, particularly at this juncture, as war between Spain and Great Britain was daily expected, and the little probability there was of getting paid for your quarter in any reasonable time, by depending only on the Letter of Credit and Mr. Lindsay's contract. In fine finding it impracticable to obtain any by that means, and at same time being fearful of the bad consequences that might attend your being disappointed in those goods, I have voluntarily by mortgaging part of my property for the payment at the latter end of this year, purchased the greater part of them from a Mr. Salomon; you have therefore invoice and bill of loading amounting to 10,029 dollars 1 Rial.

Twenty-five thousand dollars worth of the bills drawn by Clark were under protest at New Orleans.[1] They were issued in favor of a number of the inhabitants of Illinois. These drafts had been received by the French merchants and traders in preference to the Continental money, which had recently appeared in the west in small quantities.

While borrowing money on his own credit, Pollock, in order to encourage the shipment of arms, Indian goods, rum, sugar, etc., to the Illinois country, and in order to encourage down cargoes, in exchange, made up of deer-skins, beaver, otter, and flour while at

---

[1] Fully one-half of these represented the expense incident to the fitting out of the expedition against St. Vincents.

the same time keeping up the credit of the continental currency, continued until July, 1779, to pay "Bateauxmen and Traders silver dollars for Paper Currency Dollar for Dollar."

Continental currency had been used but little in the west previous to the expedition against Vincennes. The confidence of the people in the government, together with the efforts of Pollock, sustained this money at par when it had so far depreciated in the east as to be worth only twelve cents on the dollar. Traders from the east became aware of this situation, and rushed to this region, where goods might be procured with the "continentals" at their face value. They brought with them such large sums and distributed the money so liberally in trade that the inhabitants became alarmed and refused to receive it.

On returning to Kaskaskia, Clark was not surprised to learn that his credit at New Orleans was exhausted. He wrote Pollock:

> I am sorry to learn you have not been supplied with funds as expected your protesting my late bills has not surprised me. As I expected it being surrounded by enemies Mr. Hamilton and his savages being obligated for my own safety to lay in Considerable Stores I was obliged to take every step I possibly could to procure them unwilling to use force.

He was confronted also with the problems growing out of a depreciated money, of which he says in writing Governor Henry:

> There is one circumstance very distressing, that of our own moneys being discredited, to all intents and purposes, by the great numbers of traders who come here in my absence, each out-bidding the other, giving prices unknown in this country by five hundred per cent, by which the people conceived it to be of no value, and both French and Spaniards refused to take a farthing of it.

To the great joy of Clark he was informed that his friend, John Todd, had been appointed by Governor Henry to take charge of civil affairs in the Illinois country. His undivided attention might thus be given to "military reflections." December 9, 1778, a bill passed the Virginia legislature establishing the County of Illinois, which was to include the inhabitants of Virginia north of the Ohio River. This type of government had been brought into general usage by Virginia in her western expansion. The act providing for the County of Illinois was to remain in force for a year, and "thence to the end of the next session of the Assembly, and no longer." The establishment of some temporary form of government was thought to be expedient, for, as stated in the act, "from their remote situation, it may at this time be difficult if not impracticable to govern them by the present laws of this commonwealth, until proper information, by intercourse with their fellow citizens, on the east side of the Ohio, shall have familiarized them to the same." The chief executive officer was the county-lieutenant or commander-in-chief, who was appointed by the governor and council. He was to appoint at his discretion, deputy commandants, militia officers, and commissaries. The civil officers, with whom the inhabitants were familiar, and whose duties were to administer the laws already in force, were to be chosen by the citizens of the different districts. Officers with new duties were to be maintained by the state. Pardoning power was vested in the county-lieutenant in all criminal cases, murder and treason excepted. In these cases he was empowered to stay execution until such time as the will of the governor, or, in case of treason, of the assembly, should be ascertained. Provision was made for the protection of the inhabitants in all their religious, civil, and property rights.

The instructions issued by Governor Henry and the council, December 12, 1778, to Todd and to Clark, who was to retain the command of all Virginia troops in the County of Illinois, showed a grasp of the situation. They were to coöperate in using their best efforts to cultivate and conciliate the affections of the French and Indians. The rights of the inhabitants were to be secured against any infractions by the troops, and any person attempting to violate the property of the Indians, especially in their lands, was to be punished. All Indian raids on Kentucky were to be prevented. The friendship of the Spaniards was to be maintained. As head of the civil department, Todd was to have command of the militia, "who are not to be under the command of the military until ordered out by the civil authority and act in conjunction with them." He was directed on "all Accasions [sic] to inculcate on the people the value of liberty and the Difference between the State of free Citizens of the Commonwealth and that Slavery to which Illinois was destined. A free and equal representation may be expected by them in a little Time, together with all the improvements in Jurisprudence and police which the other parties of the State enjoy."

Todd reached Kaskaskia early in May, 1779. His coming was hailed with joy by the inhabitants who, having experienced some of the harshness incident to military control, were enthusiastic for a change, no matter what the new form of government might be. The county-lieutenant was well fitted to fill his office acceptably. Besides receiving a good general education, he had studied and practised law for a time. Unable to resist the call of the frontier, he enlisted for service in Dunmore's War, and in 1775, when but twenty-five years of age, Todd went to Kentucky, where he was selected as one of the representatives to form a constitutional government for the settlement of Transylvania. In 1777 he was elected delegate to the Virginia House of Burgesses from the County of Kentucky. The intimate friendship existing between Todd and Clark, and their known ability and bravery, promised a successful solution of the problems with which they were confronted.

May 12 was a notable day among the villagers of Kaskaskia, for on that day they assembled at the door of their church upon the call of Clark to hear the proclamation of the new government, and participate in the election of judges. The address prepared by Clark, who acted as presiding officer of the meeting, was well suited to the occasion.[2] He said:

> From your first declaration of attachment for the American cause until the glorious capture of post St. Vincent, I had doubted your sincerity, but in that critical time, I proved your faithfulness, I was so touched with the zeal that you have shown that my desire is to make you happy and to prove to you the sincere affection I have for the welfare and advancement of this colony in general, and of each individual in particular. The young men of this colony have returned from Post St. Vincent covered with laurels, which I hope they will continue to wear. Although there are a few who did not have anything to do with this glorious action, I do not esteem them less, hoping they will take revenge, if the occasion presents itself, who, during my absence, have with great care done their duty as guardians of this fort.

He promised, as soon as it was within his power, that they should become partakers in the liberty enjoyed by Americans, and that a regiment of regular troops was to be sent for their protection. They were assured that the new government was one of such "kindliness" that they would bless the day they had chosen to favor the American cause. Presenting Colonel Todd, he referred to him as his good friend and the only person in the state whom he desired to

---

[2] Translated and read by Jean Girault, who was Clark's interpreter.

have take charge of that post. He spoke of the great importance of their meeting for the purpose of selecting the most capable and enlightened persons, to judge their differences, and urged that only those most worthy of the offices should be chosen.

The brief response made by Todd was likewise full of promise for the success of the new government, which was to serve as guardian of their rights as citizens of a free and independent state. Elections of judges for the district courts at Cahokia and Vincennes took place shortly afterwards, and resulted, as at Kaskaskia, in the selection of Frenchmen.[3] On May 21, 1779, the commission for the court at Kaskaskia was issued by Todd. He had previously appointed a sheriff and state's attorney. The court named its own clerk.

One week earlier (May 14) military commissions were made out. A number of the men given officer's commissions had been elected judges, and were thus expected to assume the duties of both offices.[4]

Within a few days, Todd was called on to hear a recital of the grievances of the French inhabitants which had been formulated by the Kaskaskia justices. He was informed that a number of the oxen, cows, and other animals belonging to the petitioners had been taken and killed by the soldiers; that liquor was being sold to Indians, and trade carried on with slaves without the consent of their masters. Both kinds of traffic, they complained, were contrary to French custom.

Licenses for carrying on trade were issued by Todd. Fearful lest there would be a repetition of the abuses under the Virginia land law, as practised in Kentucky, and that adventurers and speculators would get possession of the rich bottom lands, he decreed that no new settlements should be made on the flat lands "unless in manner and form as heretofore made by the French inhabitants."

No problem proved more trying for Todd and Clark than the effects produced by depreciated currency. Complications were greater on account of counterfeit money. By the close of April, the price of provisions was three times what it had been two months previously, and Clark was enabled to support his soldiers only by

---

[3] The court of Kaskaskia consisted of nine members; Cahokia, seven; and Vincennes, nine.

[4] Five of the judges at Cahokia were also given military commissions.

the assistance of a number of the merchants. While in Kentucky, Todd learned that the issues of currency bearing the dates April 20, 1777, and April 11, 1778, had been ordered to be paid into the Continental loan offices by the first of June, 1779, otherwise they would then become worthless. He hoped that the time would be extended for the Illinois holders. Upon his arrival at Kaskaskia, Todd found that the paper money had depreciated, so that it was worth only one fifth of its face value in specie. On June 11 he addressed the court in the following letter, the evident purpose of which was his desire to sustain public credit:

> The only method that America has to support the present war is by her credit. That credit at present is her bills emitted from the different Treasuries by which she engages to pay the Bearer at a certain time gold and silver in Exchange. There is no friend to American Independence who has any judgment but soon expects to see it equal to Gold and Silver. Some disaffected persons and designing speculators discredit it through Enmity or Interest; the ignorant multitude have not sagacity enough to examine into this matter, and merely from its uncommon quantity and in proportion to it arises the complaint of its want of Credit.

To stay depreciation Todd proposed to retire a portion of the bills through exchanging them for land certificates. Twenty-one thousand acres of land in the vicinity of Cahokia were set aside on which it was planned to borrow $33,000 in Virginia and United States treasury notes. The lender might demand within two years his proportion of the land or a sum in gold or silver equal to the original loan, with 5 per cent annual interest. Land or money might be given at the option of the state. Large sums of money were exchanged for these certificates, but the project could not be carried further.

It was, however, the capture of Detroit which was uppermost in the minds of the two leaders, and preparations were rapidly made for the expedition, which promised complete success. In this they were following the orders explicitly given by Governor Henry. The instructions to Ford read:

> The inhabitants of Illinois must not expect safety and settled peace while their and our enemies have footing at Detroit and can interrupt and stop the Trade of the Mississippi. If the English have not the strength or courage to come to war against us themselves, their practice has been and will be to

hire the savages to commit murder and depredations. Illinois must expect to pay in these a large price for her freedom, unless the English can be expelled from Detroit. The means of effecting this will not perhaps be found in yours or Col. Clark's power. But the French inhabiting the neighborhood of that place, it is presumed, may be brought to see it done with indifference or, perhaps, join in the enterprise with pleasure. This is but conjecture. When you are on the spot you and Col. Clark may discover its fallacy or reality.

Captain Linctot, a trader of great influence with the Indians, who had recently joined the Americans, was sent up the Illinois with a company of forty men to secure the neutrality of the Indians, and at the same time cover the design of the main expedition against Detroit. He reported, on his return, having gone as far as Wea, that peace and quietness was general.

Great enthusiasm was manifested on the part of officers, troops, and the French militia. Not only were the villagers ready to enlist, even the old men volunteered their services. They gave further evidence of their zeal by proffering boat-loads of flour, cattle and horses.

The arrival of Colonel John Montgomery from Virginia with 150 men, about one-third the number expected, was a keen disappointment to Clark. But he did not lose confidence, for he had been promised 300 Kentuckians by Colonel John Bowman, their county lieutenant.

On July 1, 1779, Clark, with a party of horsemen, reached Vincennes, the place of rendezvous. Here he was joined by the remainder of the Illinois troops with the exception of a company of mounted men dispatched under Captain Linctot to reconnoiter and to obtain permission of the Wea and Miami for Clark to pass through their country on his way to Detroit.

Before leaving Kaskaskia, Clark learned that Colonel John Bowman had led the Kentucky forces against Chillicothe, a Shawnee town, and was fearful of the effect on his Detroit plans. This expedition consisted of 296. The Indians fortified themselves so strongly in a few log cabins that the whites were repulsed. The greater part of the town was burned and Bowman retreated with a large amount of plunder.

Clark had now to experience some of the adverse results of his earlier success. Influenced by his victories, immigrants in large numbers had entered Kentucky during the spring. Some returned to the older settlements for their families, and the others were scattered over such a large area that it seemed impossible to Bowman to secure the number of men he had promised Clark by the time appointed, and especially since the militia were so disheartened by the campaign against the Shawnees that only the most tried among them were ready to enter upon a new enterprise.

The arrival of only thirty Kentucky volunteers was a severe blow to Clark. The capture of Detroit, even though its fortifications were incomplete and its garrison numbered but a hundred men, was out of the question at the time, he thought, with his available force of about 350. Most of his men were barefoot, and Vincennes was able to supply scarcely enough provisions for its own inhabitants, and could not, therefore, furnish food for several hundred men on a campaign of uncertain length. All commerce with Detroit had ceased, and supplies could be gotten by the way of the Mississippi only with great difficulty, owing to the attachment of the southern Indians to the British.

Although abandoned, the influence of the preparations for the expedition proved of great significance. Threatenings from Vincennes led the British officials at Detroit to give up their plans for the recapture of that post. A summer campaign against Pittsburgh, with a force of regulars and Indians, was likewise abandoned. Instead of taking the field for an offensive campaign in 1779, the British at Detroit and Mackinac were engaged in considering defensive operations and in re-enforcing these posts with all possible dispatch. Even after large expenditures by the British for rum and presents for the warriors, and food for the old men, women and children, disaffection among the Indians became constantly more open. They and their French neighbors were frightened over the report that an alliance between the French, Spanish, Germans and Americans had been formed with the object of driving the English out of America.[5]

---

[5] "Fear acts stronger on them than all arguments can be made use of to convince them of enemy's ill designs against their lands." Brehm to Haldimand, May 28, 1779. *Mich. Pioneer and Hist. Collections*, IX., p. 411. In a letter of DePeyster, at Mackinaw, to Haldimand, June 1, 1779, he excused the increased expenditures as follows: "As the Indians are growing very importunate since they hear that the French are assisting the Rebels. The Canadians are a great disservice to the Government, but the Indians are perfect free masons when intrusted with a secret by a Canadian, most of them being much connected by marriage." *Mich. Pioneer and Hist. Collections*, IX., p. 382. Only the Menominee and Sioux remained true to the British.

Despite their apparent demoralization the British showed signs of activity. Lieutenant Bennett was sent from Mackinac (May 29) with a force of 20 soldiers, 60 traders, and 200 Indians for the purpose of intercepting Linctot or to "distress the Rebels" in any other way. Captain Langlade was directed to levy the Indians at LaFourche and "Milwaukee," and join Bennett at "Chicagou." Indian scouts sent out by Bennett from St. Joseph's were frightened by reports obtained from other Indians and soon returned. Their fears quickly brought about a general panic. "We have not," wrote Bennett, "twenty Indians in our camp who are not preparing for leaving us, I believe you will join with me when I say they are a set of treacherous poltroons." The return to Mackinac was begun shortly afterwards.

In like manner, a force of six hundred, chiefly Indians, led by Captain McKee, was sent from Mackinac. Forgetting his boast that he would place a pair of handcuffs on every rebel officer left in the country, McKee retreated from St. Joseph's upon hearing the report that Clark was marching towards Detroit.

Early in June, Captain Henry Bird collected some two hundred Indians at the Mingo town. The account brought in by runners of the attack which had been made by Colonel Bowman on the Shawnee town produced a panic among his followers. Some of the savages deserted in order to protect their villages against the American advance which was momentarily expected. Still more of them were anxious to sue for peace.

By August 1, all was confusion at Detroit, for the messages brought by couriers promised the coming of Clark with an army of two thousand Americans and French Creoles.

"Every effort is making to strengthen and complete our new Fort," so wrote an officer who demanded that re-enforcements should be sent, "as we are not equal to oppose the passage of such numbers to this place. Our ditch and glacee will be in a very good state the end of this week. An abatis afterwards to be thrown round the barracks will be ready at the same time. I wish to God I could say the same of our well; it is now upwards of 60 feet below the level of the river, and no appearance of water. Could we only rely on the inhabitants, or had they either the inclination or the resolution to defend their town, there would be nothing to apprehend on that head as we might then take the field."

Clark, as we have seen, had now definitely abandoned his purpose of an immediate movement against Detroit, but he continued to make preparations by collecting supplies for a campaign against that post in the spring. Clark himself reached the Falls of the Ohio, August 26, and there began the establishment of his headquarters. Colonel Montgomery was left in charge of the Illinois battalion.[6]

These events ended American activity in the northwest in 1779. In contrast with Clark's bold and successful dash against Vincennes, with which the year had opened, and the larger plans of 1780, the story of the later months of 1779 has often seemed to historians tame and relatively unimportant. The study will have served its main purpose if it makes evident that in the establishment of peaceful relations with the Indians, in the founding of civil government in the Illinois country, and in the neutralization of all British activity in the northwest by the zeal and publicity with which the proposed expedition against Detroit was promoted, George Rogers Clark and his associates had successfully met the problems which confronted them. In view of these larger events Clark's judgment upon his success in spreading reports may well be given a wider content by the historian, and the summer of 1779 pronounced one that was spent to advantage.

---

[6] Captain John Williams was appointed his aid at Fort Clark (Kaskaskia); Captain Richard McCarty, at Cahokia; Captain James Shelby, at Fort Patrick Henry (Vincennes); Major Joseph Bowman was given the direction of the recruiting parties.

JOHN H. HAUBERG

of Rock Island, Illinois, was an executive in the lumber and timber business. A philanthropist of major dimensions, he founded the Indian Pow-Wow Council and the Black Hawk Museum. He had been a director and president of the Illinois State Historical Society, and a moving force in that organization. His published works about the area in which he lived include *The Black Hawk Watch Tower in the County of Rock Island; Indian Trails Centering at Black Hawk's Village;* and *A Midwestern Family 1848–1948.*

This article appeared first in the *Journal of the Illinois State Historical Society,* volume 44, number 3 (autumn, 1951), pages 231–240.

HARD TIMES IN ILLINOIS IN 1780

JOHN H. HAUBERG

"Talk about hard times," said an old-timer, "people today don't know what hard times are." This paper has to do with a period when times *were* hard, and people endured in the belief that their children and their children's children would one day, in the Illinois country, know a better life.

The War for Independence was in progress. Virginia had sent George Rogers Clark to Illinois where his presence was to divert the attention of the British recruiting agents among the Indians. That was in 1778. By 1780, Clark and his men had been indulged by the Illinois French for a period of two years—long enough for the French to learn that Virginia money had little or no value. The Illinois French were sick of billeting Clark's soldiers in their homes, especially when times were so hard that they could scarcely support their own families.

The year in Illinois had started off with severe cold. It was known as the "hard winter."

> For three months, snow covered the ground and the rivers were frozen to the bottom. Most of the cattle and thousands of buffalo, deer, turkeys and other animals perished. Settlers were reduced to the utmost extremity for want of bread. "One

johnny-cake was often divided into twelve equal parts twice
each day." Corn rose from fifty dollars a bushel in November
to two hundred dollars in March.

The French towns were no longer able to provide subsistence for
the American soldiers in their homes. But the American boys would
eat, nevertheless, and proceeded to kill "before our eyes even, our
pigs and other animals." A Frenchman complained that Major
John Williams had placed a pistol at the neck of one Gagné and
"threatened fiercely to blow off his head, if he did not agree immediately to obey his order and lodge his soldier."

Captain Richard McCarty, formerly of Connecticut, who commanded one of the companies which marched to Rock Island in
June, 1780, is sometimes criticized for having been tyrannical to
the French. But from his letter to Clark, dated at Kaskaskia, October 14, 1780, there appears to have been much provocation:

> Sir:
>   I have so many things to Inform you of I dont kno' Rightly
> where to begin. . . . Our men are very near all Sick, Some
> dies. . . . The whole people here are Sick, a General Murmur
> Children Dieing fast, Number of the Inhabitants goeing off,
> the Enemy having Distroyed their Corn, pumkins, Cattle
> horses &c. . . .[1]
>   The 13th [August]; Sett of to Return to Islenois . . . we
> have nothing to eat but Corn without Grece or Salt. Much
> Murmuring Amongst the Troops, arrived at Caskakia the 20th
> Myself very sick. . . . People in General Seem to be Changed
> towards us and Many things Said Unfitting. . . . My Men
> have been three days without Provisions, and can not procure
> Any for them they have killed hogs in the Commons this
> Creats Bad Blood & c and Some of My Men as well as Capn
> Kellars have deserted . . . Some of our poor Soldiers Died
> purely for want of Subsistance.

There was practically the same tone in Colonel John Montgomery's letter to Clark as early as September 29, 1779, in which he
wrote:

> I have not had a man to desert from this place Since My
> arivel here But I have Beene under the needsatisety of havein
> som of them whipt for their Conduct . . . But Capt M Cartey
> has had a good Meney deserted over to pancore [St. Louis].

---

[1] This was at Fort Jefferson, on the east bank of the Mississippi, twelve
miles below the mouth of the Ohio.

Certainly part of the 35,000 pounds of bear bacon which had been contracted for two years before would have been welcome, but if any of it was ever delivered, none was in evidence now.

The situation with regard to clothing was little, if any, better. In his letter of September 29, 1779, Colonel Montgomery had written to George Rogers Clark:

> Sir,
> I Cant not tell what to do in Regard of Clothing for the Soldiers as the Goods you Wrote to Me about is Gon But I Expect Sir that you will Stope them and I would Be Glad that if it is in your power To Send a Relefe to Me for the Soldiers if it is onley As Much as will Make them A litle Jump Jacote [jacket] and a pear of overalls apeas I think they Mite Scuffle threw.

Captain McCarty had written to Montgomery on September 19, 1779:

> Sir
> Since you left us my men Desert dayly, they are Continually with me to Cloath them or give them there Discharge, that they may Cloath themselves. I have trouble enough with them and have thought could we Contrive a Method by the intermission of Mr. Bourgard to Satisfie them for the present for If Something is not done, they will all leave me Except my English who are the least Clamourous, yet they Complaine, and Colo, Todds Residence here will spoil the people intirely for the Inhabitants no more Regard us then a Parcel of Slaves. Neither do I chuse to do any thing yet Soldiers & people Disatisfied, you may think what a poor life your humble Servt hath. My Schem is to purchase as much Strouds as will make a short jacket, and a pair of long Trowsers to each man. . . . For Shoes we must Shift with Mogasins. . . . It will be A Terrible Price to the State but yet it will be perhaps better to pay then have in a few days no Soldiers which I think will Shortly be the Case If Some Such Method is not taken.

The situation was no better in regard to boats. In his letter, previously referred to, of October 14, 1780, Captain McCarty wrote that news had reached him that the new Fort Jefferson, which Clark had built that spring just below the mouth of the Ohio, was besieged by the Indians and that he had been ordered to proceed with all troops to give aid. But, he said:

> We have only one Boat of the State hear and that impossible, for it to Swim up Unless Mended, no Pitch nor Oak'um.

. . . I got Boat mended with old rags as well as could be, but
was obliged to have it Sunk to try to make it tight. The 5th
had the Boat loaded but was obliged to unload her, it sinking
and was obliged to press all the little Boats to the No of five to
Carry Men & Provisions.

Colonel Joseph Bowman, too, had written to Clark about a year
earlier from Cahokia: "I am afraid that Unless you send up a boat
for the flower [flour] I shall be disappointed. I have had the offer of
severl Bark boats but none of them in order, or strong Enough to
trust A Load in."

In money matters, Illinois could match any traveler's problems
in Europe today. One bill might be figured in English pounds,
shillings, and pence; another in livres and sols; still another in
Spanish milled dollars; or again, in Continental currency, or in
Virginia paper money. A certificate of indebtedness might be made
out in terms of "7 bucks and one doe," or figured in terms of pounds
of tobacco. The Indian always had a good medium—his furs. Their
values stood up very well. And the Yankee urge for gain was a
characteristic which remained at par. "There is great strides taken
for to make Money at any rate."

Mail service was most undependable. George Morgan, on one
occasion, had to send a letter to the East. He wrote, "The Bearer,
Silver Heels, I have promised sixty Dollars to carry this letter to you
and bring your answer." But even rural delivery service at such
prices could not always be depended upon. Colonel Clark wrote on
April 29, 1779:

A few days ago, I received certain intelligence of William
Morris [William Myers], my express to you, being killed near
the falls of the Ohio; news truly disagreeable to me, as I fear
many of my letters will fall into the hands of the enemy at
Detroit, although some of them, as I learn, were found in the
woods torn in pieces.

The Illinois French had accepted and indulged Clark and his
band of frontiersmen when they appeared in 1778 and, the following year, when recruits were wanted by Clark for the Vincennes
campaign, there had been enthusiasm for the cause, not only by
the men, but by the ladies, and Cahokians, who had been solicited
to give a tenth of the cattle they had, volunteered, instead, to give a
fifth for the cause. By 1780, however, all that was changed and
they complained bitterly of "having at our houses a troop of bri-

gands, who, far from being of any use to us, are insupportable and for whose board we are obliged to take in payment notes for lodgment without any hope of being ever paid."

In a memorial of the inhabitants of Vincennes to the French Minister Luzerne, dated August 22, 1780, they list a long line of grievances against the invading Americans, and complain further:

> They bought all our goods, our horses, our provisions with the pretended money; and when we could not furnish them with any more, they had the audacity to go armed into the public mills and into the granaries of different houses to take away by force flour or grain destined for our food.
>
> Not satisfied with this violence, they thought they had the privilege of a different sort of abuse. They went and shot our cattle in the fields and our pigs in the streets and in the yards; and what is worse, they menaced and struck on the cheek those inhabitants, who wished to stop these strange extractions.

Another example of the discouraging situation is shown in a letter of Richard Winston, writing from Kaskaskia to John Todd under date of October 14, 1780. He said in concluding his letter:

> It being so long a time since we had any news from you we concluded therefrom that Government has given us up to do for ourselves the best we can until such time as it pleases some other state or Power, to take us under their protection. A few lines from you would give some of us great satisfaction yet the generallity of the People are of the opinion that this Country will be given up to France be that as it will a few lines from you [will] add much to [our] happiness.

Simply stated, the country was at war and enduring the inevitable hardships of war. The English had brought western Illinois into the Revolution as a result of a letter by Lieutenant Governor Henry Hamilton, the British commandant at Detroit, written in September, 1776. In it he said that there were with him at the time deputies from the Ottawas, Chippewas, Wyandots, Shawnees, Senecas, Delawares, Cherokee, and Potawatomi, ready to go to war against the Americans. Lord Germain, secretary of state for the colonies, took up the idea and sent positive instructions:

> As it is His Majestys resolution that the most Vigorous efforts should be made, and every means employed that Providence has put into His Majestys Hands, for crushing the

> Rebellion and restoring the Constitution it is The Kings com-
> mand that you should direct Lieut. Governor Hamilton to as-
> semble as many of the Indians of his district as he conven-
> iently can. . . . so as to divide the attention of the Rebels . . .
> which cannot fail of weakening their Main Army . . . and
> thus bring the War to a more speedy Issue.

The colony of Virginia accepted that challenge and exactly two
years after the signing of the Declaration of Independence, July 4,
1778, had an army under the command of George Rogers Clark in
the domain controlled by Lieutenant Governor Hamilton. And the
Virginia legislature on December 9, 1778, passed an act establishing the county of Illinois which was to include the inhabitants of
Virginia north of the Ohio River.

The war carried on in this western "county" was more complicated, just as savage, and as uncertain of outcome as the campaigns up and down the Atlantic Coast. There were estimated to be
eight thousand warriors among the Indians alone. When France, in
1778, came into the war on our side her nationals in Illinois hoped
that they would be restored to the rule of France. Spain entered the
war against England in 1779. New Spain extended from the Mississippi River westward to the Pacific Ocean, and from New Orleans,
west and south, embracing Mexico, Central America, and territory
in South America. England claimed everything from the Mississippi eastward to the Atlantic, and from the Gulf of Mexico north
as far as anyone cared to claim anything. But neither was satisfied
with these boundaries. Both lusted for more. Spain lost no time
after entering the war. Before the year 1779 had closed she had
taken Fort Manchac (Louisiana), Baton Rouge, and Natchez from
the English. She had already extended her conquest on the east
side of the Mississippi and was determined to have more of it. In
fact, "Illinois County" was next on the agenda.

In 1780 General Washington, Lafayette, and the French Minister Luzerne sent Colonel Augustin Mottin de la Balme to the Illinois
country, apparently to attempt a union of the Illinois and the
Canadian French in opposing Britain—a good stroke of diplomacy
if successful. But La Balme evidently found that impracticable.
Instead, he proceeded to lead the Illinoisans to conquest on their
own. He exhorted them:

> The Virginians are not the only scourge which afflicts you,
> gentlemen. On their side the English barbarians are giving

abundantly of goods, of munitions of war, and are scattering with profusion burning liquors (the guardian God of the Indians) in order to have your throats, one after the other, cut. . . . shame is a thousand times more unbearable than suffering.

La Balme recommended a force of four hundred Frenchmen, some eight hundred chosen Indians, ammunition and supplies for forty days, a tent to keep the arms and munitions under cover in case of rain, eight large kettles, eight horses to carry the utensils, and some provisions for the Indians. With such a force he was confident that he could lead them to a better day.

Although the French had received La Balme most enthusiastically, they were able to muster only "about eighty French inhabitants and Indians." Off they went, however, about November 1, 1780, to conquer under the flag of France. Detroit was their objective, but they stopped at the Miami post and proceeded, in a high-handed way, to destroy and rob. They were attacked by the Miami Indians, who lost five of their warriors in the brief encounter, while thirty of La Balme's men were killed, including the Colonel himself. About the same time sixteen Cahokians plundered St. Joseph, Michigan, made prisoners of the traders, and robbed them of their goods and furs. Then Indians, friendly to the British, pounced upon them, killed four, wounded two, and took seven prisoners. The remaining three escaped to the woods.

With these two expeditions the Illinois French had made their contribution to the general, over-all confusion of 1780. The British had hoped to end this war in the West. Their plans were comprehensive and covered the upper and lower Mississippi on both sides. A force under Captain Henry Bird was marching south from Detroit to intercept any force which Virginia might try to send to Clark's relief in Illinois.

On May 2, 1780, some nine hundred fifty British traders, servants, and Indians left the portage of the Fox and Wisconsin rivers bent on the proposed conquest of their enemies below—Spanish, American, and French. More Indian warriors were added as they descended the big river until their forces were estimated as high as fifteen hundred. They thought their mission would be comparatively easy. More difficult, they admitted, would be the task of General John Campbell who, on his way up from the Gulf of Mexico, would have to pass New Orleans, with its militant Governor Bernardo de Gálvez, and the former English towns of Manchac, Baton Rouge, and Natchez, now held by Gálvez. But, they hoped the meeting of the two forces, Campbell's from the south and Emmanuel Hesse's from the north, would settle the mastery of the Mississippi Valley.

Professor James, in writing of the undertaking, says:

> This plan for gaining control over the Mississippi . . . for the recapture of the Illinois country, the Falls of the Ohio, and finally Forts Pitt and Cumberland, was one of the most striking military conceptions of the entire Revolution. If successful, the whole region west of the Alleghanies doubtless would have remained British territory, for all communication between Clark and the East would thus have been destroyed.

And, no doubt, we today would be waving the flag of Canada. By the Quebec Act of 1774, Quebec was our British capital.

But the only result of which the British could boast in 1780 was that in these movements they killed a lot of people and livestock and took a good number of prisoners. They lost, in this general campaign, the town of Pensacola, where General Campbell had wintered. Spanish forces from New Orleans, under Gálvez, took over Campbell before he could even leave. Threatened by very superior numbers, Spaniards, Illinois French, and Colonel Clark's Americans stood shoulder to shoulder and thus drove off the British.

Colonel Clark had his difficulties in 1780. There were shortages of food, clothing, and practically everything else that was needed. Virginia could give no help. In fact, as early as January 29, 1780, Governor Thomas Jefferson had written to Clark, "the less you depend for supplies from this Quarter the less you will be disappointed." Now, because of the threat of Britain, Clark was sought most earnestly by the Kentuckians, the people of Cahokia, and the inhabitants of St. Louis. He was the one man looked to as having prestige and the stature to meet emergencies. He actually claimed to have saved St. Louis by his presence; he had reached Cahokia in time to reassure the Cahokians; then he hurried to Kentucky, raised a thousand men and followed the Indians into Ohio. Clark was the man of the hour.

Before leaving for Kentucky, however, he directed Colonel John Montgomery to lead a punitive expedition to Rock Island against the Sauk and Fox who had been among the British forces which

had attacked St. Louis and Cahokia. The mission was successful in
that it proved Clark was not helpless; that the British were unable
to protect their Indian allies. Indian warriors enlisting and marching afar with British forces could not be sure that their villages
would not be attacked and destroyed in their absence. Montgomery
burned the villages and destroyed the crops, as he had planned.

Throughout this military turmoil in Illinois in 1780, there were
people from east of the mountains migrating west in search of new
homes. By February 20, the severe winter had moderated and the
tide of immigration to the west set in. It was reported that during
the spring three hundred large boats loaded with land seekers had
arrived at the Falls of the Ohio (Louisville). And also, during 1780,
20,000 immigrants from the older colonies had arrived in
Kentucky.

Thus concludes our account of the year 1780 in Illinois. Hardship, confusion, and uncertainty were, perhaps, never in her history so heaped up, pressed down, and running over.

THEODORE CALVIN PEASE

was a lifelong member of the history department at the University of Illinois, and was chairman, 1942–1948. He was a founding member of the Society of American Archivists and editor of the *American Archivist,* 1938–1946. He played an important role in the affairs of the Illinois State Historical Society as a director and then president, 1946–47. Among his best known writings are *The Frontier State, 1818–1848; The Story of Illinois;* and *George Rogers Clark and the Revolution in Illinois.*

This article was published first in the *Journal of the Illinois State Historical Society,* volume 23, number 1 (January 1931), pages 664–681.

1780—THE REVOLUTION AT CRISIS IN THE WEST

THEODORE CALVIN PEASE

The Hebrew people had a peculiarly effective way of indoctrinating their children in the religious and national traditions of their race. Again and again, by a ceremonial observance, by a cairn of stones, by a monument, they sought to provoke from youth a query that would give the opening for the lesson in history that they desired to teach. Our presence here this evening at this sesquicentennial of the westernmost battle of the Revolution, reminds us that at last we are learning the educational wisdom of the chosen people, learning that the surest way to imbue the rising generation with a sense of the greatness of the nation's past is to excite their curiosity to learn about it. The value of the lesson once we are able to instill it cannot be underestimated. A quickened sense that this country of the Illinois, in which we live, is the product of a fine historic past, is the best insurance for a reverent attitude toward its institutions. Believe that this western country as we see it today, like Topsy "just grewed," and it will seem merely an opportunity to gratify your acquisitive desires. Learn the story of how men wrought and sacrificed and fought in this land in bygone days that a more equal liberty might prevail in America, and unbridled selfishness will appear the sacrilege it really is.

For years we have been trying to emphasize the great historic past of this land of the Illinois. We have had to overthrow first in our own minds, then in the minds of others, the assumption tacitly instilled by the text books we studied in childhood that the American Revolution is the exclusive heirloom of the East. Again and again we have repeated the truisms that for a century and a half the upper Mississippi Valley was the theatre of the imperial rivalries of France, England, Spain and the United States, till at length at the close of the War of 1812, the last-named power entered on full and undisputed possession of the prize. The late Professor Alvord unfolded for us the history of the British imperial projects in the Illinois from 1763 to 1774. He taught us that the Stamp Act, of which we learned in childhood as of a strange remote thing, had no other end than to finance British imperial ambitions in the West; that the Illinois bulked more important in the minds of British statesmen than half the old thirteen colonies; that the Quebec Act of 1774, was not merely one of the Intolerable Acts of our school texts, that provoked the faroff Revolution in the East, but a climax of British western policy that brought about a Western Revolution at our back doors. Even today it may strike some of you as new, that it would be perfectly possible to claim membership in the Daughters of the American Revolution on behalf of an ancestor, born in the Illinois country, who enlisted in an Illinois regiment and participated in battles on the soil of the state. Even today if one were to allude, referring to Revolutionary history, to the battle of St. Louis, many people might think it a joke comparable to those mythical combats so dear to the A. E. F., the battles of Tours and Bordeaux. That there were military operations, in this year of 1780, at St. Louis, at Cahokia, at Rock Island, we know. But to grasp their influence on the final outcome we may have to pause for a little reflection. Let us remember for a moment that practically the only successful American campaigns in 1780 were the campaign of King's Mountain and the campaign of the Mississippi Valley. And bearing that graphic outstanding fact in mind let us think a little of the situation of the Revolution in the year we are helping to commemorate tonight.

In 1780 it might well have seemed likely to a well informed observer that the British Empire was going to muddle through as it had done before and was to do again. Britain's policy centered around the squat and pertinacious figure of George III. George's life had one central theme—his determination that the great Whig territorial magnates should not appropriate the royal patronage and govern his kingdom with it, as their forbears had done in the reigns of his grandfather and his great-grandfather. To the contest with the Whig magnates he had been dedicated from childhood, and he waged it with general success throughout the portion of his reign in which he retained his reason. Quite often, to his not very clear understanding, it seemed that his natural enemies, the Whig chieftains, in their struggle to dominate him had merely enlisted as allies, first the revolting colonists, then the great Bourbon powers of France and Spain. But against them all George fought on doggedly. He had to govern England and fight his swarming enemies, through tools like Lord North, Hillsborough, Sandwich, Lord George Germaine, Thurlow, and Wedderburn, all of whom were greedy and ignoble, and all of whom except the two last named were more or less incompetent.

Yet for two years back his military and naval forces had suffered no serious defeats. The great mass of the British nation was loyally supporting the war. A proposed ministerial coalition with the less embittered elements of the opposition had come to nothing; and a parliamentary election in the fall of 1780 had yielded what seemed a safe majority for Lord North's ministry. The prospects of Britain's hanging on till the Bourbon powers and America were tired of the war seemed excellent.

For the United States, we remember, 1780 was the nadir of the Revolution. That Revolution had been the work of a bold and determined minority intent on establishing a better order of things on the North American continent. Another, and Tory, minority had clung to the British crown and a much larger majority had swayed in indecision between the two extremes. Thanks to energy, ability, and organization, the revolutionary minority had seized the reins in 1775, and had declared independence in 1776. For two years, with surreptitious assistance from France and Spain in money and munitions, they made head against the full military power of Great Britain. But the French alliance of 1778 and the open entrance of France in the war, by 1780 seemed to have been of negative value. They helped unite the masses of the British nation for war against the hereditary enemy; at the same time thousands upon thousands in America had sat quiet so long as the question at issue seemed one of the British constitution, had even acquiesced in the Declaration of Independence in the hope that it was a maneuvre for advantage and not an irredeemable step; now with the colonies in open alliance with the ancient foe of Britain they could not longer cherish delusions of an ultimate reconciliation between mother country and colonies; and when forced to take sides they chose the side of England. The French alliance, too, had an evil psychological effect, causing men to slacken their exertions in the hope that France would fight their battle. Hitherto, French military and naval cooperation had borne no fruit. Exhausted financially by war, with trade blighted by the British blockade, with the Southern colonies, which had furnished a major share of valuable exports, in the enemy's hands, with men in Congress too weak for the emergency, the treason of Benedict Arnold seemed to presage a general return to the British allegiance.

Prospects were not cheering on the side of America's ally, France. She had entered the Revolutionary War, partly in the hope of recovering the international prestige she had lost in 1763, partly in fear that if she stood aloof till Britain and her colonies made up their quarrel, the first fruit of reconciliation would be a joint English and American attack on the French West Indies. She had pledged the colonies their independence and for two years had put forth her efforts to achieve her various ends; but her efforts had had the most qualified success, and she was near a financial breakdown. In a few months the resignation of her famous finance minister Necker was to threaten a general collapse.

Spain, the other Bourbon power was in better case than France, but her being so promised little in advantage to the Americans. Spain had not adopted the French fashion of enthusiasm for American independence. "The Spaniards," said Vergennes, "like little children, are attracted only by shining objects." But the shining objects which attracted the Spanish into war with England were highly practical ones—the recovery of Gibraltar, Minorca, Florida and other possessions wrested from her by England in the eighteenth century. In 1780 she seemed in a fair way to achieve some, at least, of these ends. To the Americans she was distinctly hostile; she might use them as tools against Great Britain, but she hoped to see them broken, divided, bankrupt and unhappy, an example to her own vast colonial empire of the evil effects of insurrections against the mother country.

Spain, as the possessor of New Orleans and the trans-Mississippi region, acquires peculiar importance from the standpoint of the

West. She was in the midst of her last great era of territorial
expansion. In almost the same years she occupied the west bank of
the Mississippi and the coast of California. As she framed her
wishes for the fate of the West at the peace, she almost influenced
her French ally to acquiesce in the doctrine that, whoever acquired
the trans-Alleghany, the colonies should not. Her commandant at
St. Louis remained on friendly terms with the Virginian, George
Rogers Clark; but under her prompting the French emissary to
Congress urged the United States to refrain from any western
conquests, leaving that area the exclusive prize of Spain. Considering the matter in that aspect, the importance of Clark's conquest of
the country in 1778 becomes apparent. Without open scandal it was
impossible for the Spaniards to expel him from it. But had Clark not
taken Kaskaskia in 1778, there can be no doubt that the Spanish
would have seized it in 1779, exactly as they seized the British posts
in West Florida on the lower Mississippi, immediately on their entry
into the war in that year.

Spanish ambitions in the old Northwest increased in importance
as they coincided with the rivalries of landed and landless states in
Congress, and with the clash of state claims to the western country. We can remind ourselves briefly that eight states had claims,
more or less conflicting, to portions of the region west of the
Alleghenies; that five had none, and were jealous of the undue
expansion of their neighbors, were even ready to see Spain or Great
Britain have the territory northwest of the Ohio rather than have it
go to aggrandize some one state like Virginia. French and Spanish
emissaries intrigued with the delegates of states like Maryland
which entertained such views. Furthermore, both for Kentucky and
the country north of the Ohio there was the rivalry of Virginia,
claiming the whole by her sea-to-sea charter and Clark's conquest,
as against the great land companies which indirectly enlisted the
congressional support of New Jersey or Pennsylvania.

Such is the general political and diplomatic structure of 1780; let
us now glance at the military situation. In North America Great
Britain retained Canada and New York; under an essentially risky
strategy, she was dividing her American armies, with only a tenuous control of the sea to protect the communications of the forces
engaged in the conquest of the South. But unsound as the strategy
was, it was being crowned with immediate success; Georgia and
South Carolina were in British hands, North Carolina seemed

about to fall. These were, from the commercial point of view, the most desirable of the revolting colonies. Their loss had crippled American finance; and if Great Britain retained them from the wreck of her colonial empire, she could count the Revolution not a total loss. They had been the scene of two great triumphs in 1780, the capture of Charleston with General Lincoln and his army, and the rout of Gates at the battle of Camden. The defeat of Ferguson by the riflemen of the western waters at King's Mountain was the sole unpromising omen for Great Britain in the South.

In the West Indies, British and French fleets and armies had campaigned ever since 1778. The loss of several of the smaller British islands, Dominica, St. Vincent, Grenada, was more than counterbalanced by the British capture of St. Lucia, the French island that was the key to the Windward Antilles. Adequately garrisoned by British commanders on the ground in defiance of the orders of the ministry, it was to contribute to the saving of the British empire in Rodney's victory of 1782.

In the region of the Mississippi, things were less propitious. Ever since the British had realized that the Father of Waters was of but limited use to them so long as the Spaniards retained New Orleans and the control of its outlet, they had promised themselves the capture of the Crescent City whenever God should send them a war with Spain. When that blessing at last overtook them in 1779 they were too slow to take advantage of it. General Campbell, despatched to utilize the weak garrisons at Mobile and Pensacola against New Orleans when war should break out, was given tardy advices of the beginning of hostilities. Instead of taking New Orleans, he had to listen to news of the Spanish capture of Manchac, Baton Rouge, and Natchez, the West Florida posts on the Mississippi. He could only hope for results for the ambitious campaign, projected in the upper Mississippi Valley for 1780. To the situation there we must now turn.

In 1778 George Rogers Clark with the authority of Virginia and his own native address had occupied the ungarrisoned British posts at Kaskaskia, Cahokia, and Vincennes, and had received the enthusiastic French inhabitants as citizens of the Old Dominion. Early in 1779 he had broken up the counter attack of the British Lieutenant Governor Henry Hamilton of Detroit by capturing him and his force at Vincennes. Failure of Virginian support had barred him in 1779 from consummating his triumph by the capture of Detroit.

He had, however, by clever diplomacy established an ascendency over both French and Indians. That ascendency was, however, a most unstable one. With the fickle French it trembled as they became aware of the depreciation of the Virginia paper currency they had accepted at par; as bills of exchange drawn for military supplies on the Virginia agent at New Orleans came back protested, as the newly established Virginia county government proved helpless to protect them against the unruly soldiers of Virginia, who seized needed provisions without payment.

With the Indians, Clark's ascendency was partly the fruit of his own masterful personality, and of the Indian respect for so great a warrior. It was continually subject to reversal from the Indian's recurrent need for the white man's goods—blankets, kettles, cloth, and what not. These articles, save for whisky, were not manufactured in America, and could be procured only from European sources. The British blockade and financial difficulties hampered the Americans from importing such commodities for Indian trade. General Frederick Haldimand, commanding for the British in Canada saw clearly that British control of the supply of Indian goods would ultimately outweigh the meteoric personality of Clark. His one aim was to make sure that no Indian goods should be carried where by any chance they might fall into American hands. That done, he waited for the economic needs of the Indian to draw him back to his British allegiance. And in the long run Haldimand was not to wait in vain.

Not content with waiting for economic laws to assert themselves, the British in 1780 were preparing to execute an elaborate plan of campaign against Spaniards and Virginians in the upper Mississippi Valley with the immediate purpose of conquering both the American and the Spanish Illinois. The root of the matter was to be found in Lord George Germaine's despatch to Haldimand of June 17, 1779. Written with definite knowledge of the outbreak of war with Spain it urged on Haldimand an enterprise against the Spanish in the upper Mississippi to coincide with General Campbell's expected attack on New Orleans. By the time the despatch had crossed the ocean and had been transmitted to distant posts at Detroit and Mackinac, it was of course too late to plan anything for 1779. But Sinclair and De Peyster, commanding for the British respectively at Mackinac and Detroit undertook with enthusiasm the execution of measures for 1780. De Peyster planned to despatch Captain Bird with a force, the nucleus of which was to be fifty regulars and a contingent of artillery, to the Ohio river by way of the Au Glaize and the Great Miami, while the Wabash Indians "amused" Clark at the Falls of the Ohio where Louisville stands today. Haldimand in general approved of the project, which was intended partly as a diversion to assist the far more ambitious campaign that Sinclair was preparing at Mackinac. With the assistance of interpreters and traders among the Sioux, the Winnebago, the Sac, the Foxes, and other western and Northwestern tribes he projected two expeditions, with only irregular organizations of French traders as their nuclei. One was to proceed via the Fox-Wisconsin portage to the Mississippi, while the other was to descend Lake Michigan to the Chicago portage and the Illinois river. A certain trader by the name of Hesse, formerly an officer of the Royal Americans, was to command the whole expedition, which was destined to crush the Virginian and Spanish resistance at Cahokia and St. Louis and to garrison those places for the king, laying requisitions on the inhabitants of the villages for the support of the troops. Meanwhile the great Sioux chief Wabasha, with his braves uncorrupted by the white man, was to sweep down the Mississippi river to cooperate with Campbell against New Orleans. Sinclair, of course was blithely unaware of Gálvez's capture of Manchac, Baton Rouge and Natchez, though by March of 1780 this was old news at St. Louis. Recognizing the difficulty of arranging a cipher for correspondence with Campbell, he hit on the bright idea of writing him in Erse, attaching a Scotch Highland private to the expedition to serve as decipherer.

Sinclair was much hurt at Haldimand's lack of enthusiasm for this far flung enterprise, regarding it as a reflection on his ability to execute if not to plan. Haldimand was, however, a sound and able officer and it was not surprising that he estimated the possibilities of the situation more conservatively than Sinclair. He felt keenly the blow to British prestige among the Indians of the Ohio Valley by Clark's capture of Hamilton, whereas Sinclair protested that his undebauched Sioux warriors had scarcely heard of it. The absurdity of any concert of measures in a campaign between forces operating from Mackinac and Pensacola, bases so far apart that the better part of a year would be needed for a message to pass and repass was, of course, apparent. Even the synchronizing of movements between forces operating from Mackinac and Detroit was difficult in the face of an officer so capable of swift decision and movement as George Rogers Clark. The Indian, able wilderness warrior that he was, was not at his best in attacking fortifications defended by white men.

Still the situation had its advantages. The intricacy of the movement promised to bewilder the opponents as to the true point of attack. If secrecy as to preparations could be preserved, the rapid current of the rivers down which the various expeditions would move could give the opportunity of surprise attacks on unfortified settlements. Bird's expedition, which in personnel and equipment promised the best, might succeed in cutting off the Illinois settlements from Kentucky, when their fall would be only a question of time. There was an excellent prospect in one way or another of capturing Cahokia, Kaskaskia, and St. Louis. However wild Sinclair's corollary campaign might be, with the Illinois country in British hands, a surprise attack down the swiftly flowing Mississippi on Natchez or Baton Rouge would be a possibility that might help to divert Gálvez's attention from Campbell's operations in West Florida. More immediately the hold of Virginia and through Virginia of the United States on the West would be definitely broken.

Both Clark and the Spaniards had advance warning of the expedition in reports of suspicious activity of British agents among the Indian tribes. De Leyba at St. Louis, in March began the construction of a block house and intrenchments to protect the hitherto unfortified town. Clark meditated the disposal of his meager forces, charged, we must remember, with the defense of Kentucky as well as Illinois. He had to face the possibility that the Spaniards might allow the English to capture both the American Bottom and the Spanish Illinois in order to reconquer both for themselves. He was already under instructions from Governor Thomas Jefferson of Virginia to construct a post at the Iron Banks a little below the mouth of the Ohio. Governor Henry had had such a post in mind before the occupation of the Illinois villages was ever considered. To Clark the new post had the advantages of making desertions to the receptive Spanish bank less easy, and of checking any northward swell of Spanish conquests east of the Mississippi. At the Iron Banks or at the Falls of the Ohio Clark planned to hold his main force in readiness with a small outpost at Vincennes commanded by Dalton and a larger one at Cahokia under Colonel John Montgomery.

For the ensuing campaign on the Mississippi, peculiarly enough, our main sources of information are British. We have the one Spanish official account transmitted to Gálvez of the Spanish defense. For happenings on the American side our sole narrative source is a justification of his conduct drawn up by Montgomery in 1783. There are bits of American corroborative evidence, naturally; but aside from these our main source is the British military correspondence.

On May 2, 750 men, traders, servants and Indians proceeded down the Mississippi under command of Captain Hesse. So sure was Sinclair of success that he had designated the persons to command at Kaskaskia and St. Louis once these posts were captured. At the outset, luck seemed to be with the British. Their Menominee allies captured an armed trading boat with twelve men, probably belonging to Charles Gratiot; at the lead mines, near the present site of Galena, seventeen Spaniards and Americans. Both captures included quantities of munitions and provisions of which the expedition already stood in much need. Langlade, meanwhile, with Indians and Canadians was to pass down the Lake to Chicago, to make his attack by way of the Illinois River. Another party was detailed to watch the area between the Wabash and Illinois Rivers.

The news of the approach of the expedition preceded it, producing appeals to Clark for assistance both from the inhabitants of Cahokia and from the Spanish commandant. Actually, according to Montgomery, Clark arrived at Cahokia twenty-four hours before the onset. Montgomery's narrative, which, we remember, is our sole connected American source, would imply that, forewarned of Clark's presence the enemy made no serious attack at Cahokia; in that particular it is contradicted by the British report of killing an officer and three men, and capturing five prisoners there. Unless we assume that these men were waylaid outside of the village, their loss would indicate at least a sharp skirmish. However slight or serious the fighting at Cahokia, on May 26 the expedition attacked the Spanish fortification at St. Louis. Interestingly enough one St. Louis historian at least has argued that the attack of 1780 was a myth. His reasoning is unconsciously a beautiful demonstration of the fallacy of the historical argument from silence. Colonel Mont-gomery's narrative is our authority that a high wind prevented alarm signals from St. Louis being heard or responded to from Cahokia. The Spanish account, manifestly not intended to underes-timate the services and achievements of the officers involved, says nothing of the unanswered signals. It recites that while the Lieu-tenant Cartabona with 20 men took post in the commandant's house to protect the women and children, the Commandant De Leyba with the remainder of 29 soldiers and 281 irregulars under-took the defense against 300 regular troops and 900 savages, glo-riously beating off a severe attack delivered at the north end of the town. Sinclair's account of the repulse was that the Winnebago had attacked boldly, losing a chief and three men; but that the Canadians were backward and the Sac, under the treacherous Calvé, interpreter of the British crown though he was, had behaved in such uncertain fashion, that the Winnebago did not dare push on lest they find themselves between two fires. The Spanish ac-count of Indian outrages against hapless settlers in the country nearby is impliedly borne out by English accounts. But it is impos-sible to reconcile British and Spanish accounts of casualties. Sin-clair reported in all forty-three scalps, thirty-four prisoners, black and white, and about seventy killed. The number of prisoners indicated is about the summary of the previously reported captures near Galena and at Cahokia. The Spanish report was twenty-two killed, seven wounded, and seventy prisoners in all.

Calvé, the interpreter, later protested against Sinclair's making him the scapegoat for the failure of the expedition; but it may well be doubted how enthusiastic the French Canadians were in the enterprise. After all, the typical Frenchman in that period is the one Lieutenant Governor Henry Hamilton encountered outside Vin-cennes in 1778 with two commissions in his pocket, one from the British Lieutenant Governor Abbott, and the other from the Virgin-ian George Rogers Clark. Sinclair had believed he had won the devotion of the French traders by promising them the trade of the Missouri River in case of success, but even with such a lure they may well have hesitated at helping to put their fellow Frenchmen at St. Louis under the tomahawks of a horde of infuriated savages.

Once assured the attacking force was retreating, Clark was called away on June 4 by the near approach of Captain Bird's expedition, in a military sense the most formidable of all, to the

Falls of the Ohio. One other British expedition had already proved abortive. Early in May the highly temperamental Pottawatomie had been turned toward Vincennes, when they encountered a Canadian trader, who asked them if they were going against their friends, the French, four thousand strong at Vincennes. The great majority of the Pottawatomie implicitly believed the story and departed hastily. A small remnant went on to reconnoiter and discovered there were but twenty or thirty Virginians at Vincennes. Well might the British fulminate threats against the French at Post Vincennes who did more harm with their tongues than a Spanish army with its swords. By June the Pottawatomie, reassured and reorganized, had been led back toward their goal, when they clashed with their hereditary foes, the Piankeshaw; the ensuing skirmish, of course, ended all hopes of any achievement against the Virginians.

Meanwhile, on June 3, Bird's expedition was reported eight days' march from the Falls of the Ohio, expecting to reach it before Clark could return. Bird had with him about 400 Indians and could count on a total force of 600. The Indian respect for Clark, however, became increasingly apparent as they drew near a place where they might expect to encounter him. On June 11, Bird had to report that after two days' counselling the Indians had decided to give up an attack at the Falls where decisive strategic results might have been obtained, and to attack instead settlements up the Ohio on the Licking and on Limestone Creek; the posts made little or no resistance. To Bird's disgust the Indians insisted on adopting into their tribes the children of the hapless settlers. Early in August, having concealed his cannon and munitions at old Chillicothe, he was back at Detroit with 150 prisoners. Clark was close on his heels.

In March the harassed settlers of Boonesborough and Bryant's station had besought Clark to lead them in a raid on the Indian villages north of the Ohio. With a force of 1,000 men he crossed the Ohio at the Licking near the present site of Cincinnati on August 1. At Piqua, on the great Miami on August 8 he encountered a force of Shawnee, Mingo, Wyandot, and Delaware warriors prepared to receive him. In an afternoon's hard fighting he inflicted on them a decisive defeat, and celebrated his triumph by destroying their villages and crops.

It remains to tell the story of the exploit which your celebration especially commemorates. After their defeat at St. Louis the invading forces retreated rapidly, scattering for want of provisions; part by the Mississippi, part between the Mississippi and Lake Michigan and part by the Chicago portage whence two vessels from Mackinac brought them off.

Under Clark's orders Montgomery with 350 men set out in pursuit, probably a day or two after Clark's departure on June 4. By Montgomery's account they apparently moved up the Illinois as far as the Lake of Peoria and thence to the Rock River, destroying the villages and crops of the Indians before they could rally from the retreating expedition for defense. It is possible that the raid penetrated even farther than Rock Island. Perhaps it can be connected with Sinclair's statement that 200 Illinois cavalry arrived at Chicago five days after his transports left; perhaps it is alluded to in the recollections of the trader Long, sent by Sinclair early in June to bring off furs from Prairie du Chien, who relates that the Americans came to attack them five days after they left.

The raids of Montgomery and Clark ended American activities in the western campaign of 1780. An elaborately widely organized attack, on which the British had expended all their influence and surplus resources from either side of the Mississippi, had culminated in raids on two or three inconsiderable Kentucky settlements. The Americans, thanks to Clark's dispositions and his ability in executing them, had repelled the British attacks and had launched sharp and successful counter attacks on the British Indian allies, to impress forcibly on their minds that American settlements could not be raided with impunity. They had demonstrated that however slightly they garrisoned the region beyond the Ohio, they could repel any British attempt to reoccupy it. A British recovery of the region, a Spanish recapture of it from the British—either one of them would have clouded the clear title of conquest and continued possession which Virginia was finally to quit-claim to the Confederation.

Two remaining operations of 1780 in the region may be briefly mentioned, rather from the significance of the motives that prompted them than for their specific results. I refer of course to the futile expedition of La Balme against Detroit and the raid under the auspices of the Spanish commandant on St. Joseph.

The historian, in all likelihood, will have to surrender to the writer of imaginative fiction the attempt to solve the fascinating puzzle of La Balme. In a little group of papers, whose presence in the Haldimand Collection indicates they were taken from the slain

La Balme by his Indian conquerors, is summarized the story of the man who had been an officer of the King of France, who had come to America to be inspector general of cavalry in Washington's army, and who had finally come west on a strange and, as yet, unexplained mission. Apparently his errand required him to provoke and to receive from the French inhabitants the bitterest complaints against their Virginia masters. Perhaps in this he acted as the emissary of the land companies that were anxious to break Virginia's hold on the western region. Perhaps his errand was the more orthodox one of helping to organize a Franco-American descent on Canada. But why he should raise, under the French flag in the Illinois, an absurdly insufficient expedition that perished under Indian tomahawks before it got even within striking distance of Detroit is an unsolved mystery story. A secret emissary of French ambitions in the western country, a secret emissary of the Vandalia, Illinois and Wabash land companies in which French agents had their financial interest, a secret emissary of Washington, or a self-appointed executive of a wild scheme all his own—the historian relinquishes the puzzle to the novelist.

Of the Spanish expedition against St. Joseph, recruited from Illinois Frenchmen, marching under Spanish auspices across the state of Illinois to take and hold for a day an ungarrisoned post, it is possible to speak more definitely; for whether or not in its inception it was intended to establish a Spanish claim east of the Mississippi, it was used by Spanish diplomats for that purpose in the negotiations for peace.

Indeed as we end our study of the West in this critical year of 1780 it appears to be in little the reflection of the problems and difficulties that beset the path of American independence. Here you find the Frenchman, a dubious friend not to be too far trusted, the Spaniard, an ostensible ally and potential enemy to be trusted still less. In the disaffection to Virginia rule of the elements in Kentucky from the other colonies, in the intrigues of the land companies in the West against the Virginia monopoly are mirrored forth the jealousies between state and state that beset the unhappy Congress. Virginia currency, in seeking the lowest abyss of depreciation, was ahead of the more famous Continental currency, in the complete collapse of public credit. The economic stagnation and distress of the East found its vivid counterpart in the West.

And yet in the face of all these difficulties the soldiers of Virginia in the western country had demonstrated to the British that for 1780, at least, they must forego their expected triumph. Let us repeat once more that only in the West in 1780 did the Revolution achieve military success. In military operations it is impossible to get rid of the effects of success in one field on the situation in others. We remember that George Rogers Clark had reached out for the Illinois that he might the better defend Kentucky; we remember also that Clark considered Kentucky the buckler of the whole frontier against Indian raids—and George Rogers Clark was no mean strategist. If, in 1780, the defense of Illinois and Kentucky had collapsed, could the riflemen of the backwoods have passed over the mountains to break Ferguson at King's Mountain? Without King's Mountain, Greene could hardly have executed that marvelous campaign, in which he accepted defeat in every battle but one, and cleared the enemy from the Carolinas. Without Greene's campaign, Washington's masterpiece, involving the synchronization of three fleets 3,000 miles apart, and widely separated armies, could hardly have culminated in the triumph of Yorktown and the collapse of the First British Empire. We have, it is true, followed but one chain of causation out of many. But I hope it convinces us that the western campaign of 1780 was a measurable contribution to the final achievement.

"And it shall come to pass, when your children shall say unto you, what mean ye by this service?" What shall we say to them? What after all is the lesson that we can draw for ourselves and for the next generation from a commemoration such as this? Shall we not tell them that in this country of the Illinois a hundred and fifty years ago there were, as there are today, many men who sought their own private interests and built their own private fortunes whom we willingly forget? Shall we not tell them that we retain the memory of a few, only in proportion as they sacrificed their private ends and risked fortune and life in the hope that a new and better order of things should prevail on this continent? This western area of the Revolution is measured today in tens and scores of millions of population, millions the way for whose coming was smoothed by the men who strove that the ideals of the Revolution should there prevail in the days when its people were numbered by thousands. Beyond their wildest dreams has the work of their hands been established upon them.

NELSON VANCE RUSSELL

who received his Ph.D. in history from the University of
Michigan, taught at the University of Michigan, and at the
University of California at Los Angeles. He served as chairman of the history department at Coe and Carleton Colleges.
He first organized and then was head of the Reference Division of the National Archives, 1935–1938. Russell served
as president of Carroll College, Waukesha, Wisconsin,
1946–1951. His best known work is *The British Regime in
Michigan and the Old Northwest, 1760–1796.*

This article appeared first in the *Journal of the Illinois
State Historical Society,* volume 31, number 1 (March,
1938), pages 22–53.

THE FRENCH AND BRITISH AT PLAY
IN THE OLD NORTHWEST, 1760–1796

NELSON VANCE RUSSELL

The settlers of the Old Northwest during the British régime found
considerable time for leisure midst a busy life, although it is true
that their energies were mainly devoted to the practical problems
of clearing small areas of the forest for their villages, planting
crops, building homes, trading in furs, and constantly struggling
with the Indians. These people were the pioneers of a new civilization in the vast hinterland which now comprises the populous
states of Michigan, Wisconsin, Illinois, Indiana, and Ohio. Theirs
was to toil and fight, and yet a study of their life shows that there
were many leisure hours to be filled with games and sports of all
kinds. One discovers that despite a large degree of isolation from
the outside world, and the fact that distances were so great from
village to village as to make common exchange of interests and
ideas almost impossible, their social activities were about the same
as they were in the East. Human nature did not vary greatly,
whether in the fur posts of the Old Northwest, or in Puritan Boston
and Quaker Philadelphia.

At the close of the French period there were a number of settlements in the Old Northwest, largely fur trading posts. Among these
were Detroit and Michillimackinac within the present confines of

the state of Michigan, Vincennes on the Wabash River, and several small villages scattered along the Mississippi, extending from the mouth of the Kaskaskia River northward 75 miles to Cahokia.

The leading citizens of these villages were members of three different groups. The first, and by far the most important group, was made up of the old and well-established French families known as the "gentry"—a rather elastic term—among whom there was to be found a considerable degree of refinement and culture. Some of these came from the better classes in Canada and France, and made an effort to surround themselves with all the luxuries that could be brought from Canada and Europe. A few possessed considerable capital before migrating to Michigan and Illinois, and others rose to prominence by industry, astuteness, and good fortune. Among the more prominent were Jean Baptiste Barbau of Prairie du Rocher, the Bauvais, Charleville, Viviat, Janis, and Cerré families of Kaskaskia, and the Saucier, François Trottier, Girardin, and J. B. H. La Croix families of Cahokia. In Detroit, there were the Barthe, Campau, Navarre, Labadie, Drouillard, Legrand, Baptiste, and Jacques Baby families.[1] Gay they were, and light-hearted, yet pious; honest beyond comparison, generous to a fault, hospitable, free, and laughter-loving, with no cares from "ambition or science." [2] They always seemed to enjoy life keenly, being gay even when times were at their worst. Possibly ignorant of books they were, but certainly neither boorish nor unintelligent. Their easy-going ways were doubtless due to their placing no great value on time, of which they had an abundance.

The British fur traders and merchants who came into the country at the close of the Seven Years' War made another social group. They were industrious and energetic, and it was not long before success crowned their efforts, making them clearly the leading force both economically and socially.

Again, there were the military officers at the forts, who found time hanging heavily on their hands, with only the dull routine of garrison duty to perform. They constituted a very important element in the social life, and found plenty of attractive, vivacious

---

[1] Among some of the prominent families at Michillimackinac, though not of the gentry, were the Ainse, Chevalier, Sejournée, Langlade, Bourassa, Cauchois, Cadotte, and Chaboillez families.

[2] Apparently life did not change much, for as late as 1836 a similar description of the French in Kaskaskia was given by Edmund Flagg.

young women for partners at the balls, which were the principal convivial activities of the posts.

Below these groups was the large mass of people: *habitants, coureurs de bois, voyageurs,* and slaves. These were pleasure-loving also, dissipating their energies for the most part in "drinking, gambling, and gossiping; and as irresponsible as children, they were easily turned aside from the pursuit of their real interests." But with all their faults, conspicuous though they were, the *habitants* differed much from the American frontiersmen. The latter had no respect for law and authority, while the *habitants* usually preferred to be guided by law in their intercourse. Quarrels were frequent, but instead of ending them in fights, they went to the courts for settlement; especially in their business transactions, the French sought the aid of a judge or notary. C. F. Volney, the noted traveler who made a tour of the upper Mississippi Valley toward the close of the eighteenth century, was not favorably impressed with these people. He wrote:

> They know nothing of civil or domestic affairs: their women can neither sow, nor spin, nor make butter, but spend their time in gossiping and tattle, while all at home is dirt and disorder. The men take to nothing but hunting, fishing, roaming in the woods, and loitering in the sun. They do not lay up, as we do for winter or provide for a rainy day. They cannot cure pork or venison, make sour kraut or spruce beer, or distill spirits from apples, or rye, all needful arts to the farmer. If they trade, they try by exhorbitant charges to make much out of a little; for *little* is generally their *all,* and what they get they throw away upon the Indian girls, in toys and bawbles. Their time is wasted too in trifling stories of their insignificant adventures, and journies *to town* to see their friends. . . . (Thus they speak of New Orleans, as if it were a walk of half an hour, instead of fifteen hundred miles down the river.)
> The Frenchman, on the contrary, will be up betimes, for the pleasure of viewing and talking over matters with his wife, whose counsel he demands. Their constant agreement would be quite a miracle: the wife dissents, argues, wrangles, and the husband has his own way, or gives up to her, and is irritated or disheartened. Home, perhaps, grows irksome, so he takes his gun, goes a shooting or a journeying, or to chat with a neighbour. If he stays at home, he either whiles away the hour in good humoured talk, or he scolds and quarrels. Neighbors interchange visits: for to visit and talk are so

necessary to a Frenchman, from habit. . . . There is nowhere
a settler of that nation to be found, but within sight or reach
of some other. On asking how far off the remotest settler was,
I have been told, He is in the woods, with the bears, a league
from any house, and with nobody to talk to. . . .

The Frenchman's ideas evaporate in ceaseless chat; he
exposes himself to bickering and contradiction; excites the
garrulity of his wife and sisters; involves himself in quarrels
with his neighbours; and finds in the end, that his life has
been squandered away without use or benefit.

Other travelers seemed to be more or less of the same impression. George Croghan described the French of Detroit as "generally
poor wretches . . . a lazy, idle people, depending chiefly on the
savages for their subsistence." Philip Pittman noted that the male
inhabitants of Illinois were "very superstitious and ignorant." [3]
Victor Collot, after an extended journey through the interior of
North America, described the settlers of the Illinois region as follows:

These people are, for the most part, traffickers, adventurers,
hunters, rowers, and warriors; ignorant, superstitious, and
obstinate; accustomed to fatigue and privations, and stopped
by no sense of danger in the undertakings they form, and
which they usually accomplish.

In domestic life, their characters and dispositions are similar to those of the Indians with whom they live; indolent,
careless, and addicted to drunkenness, they cultivate little or
no ground, speak a French jargon, and have forgotten the
division of time and months. If they are asked at what time
such an event took place, they answer, "in the time of the
great waters, of the strawberries, of the maize, of potatoes": if
they are advised to change any practice which is evidently
wrong, or if observations are made to them respecting the
amelioration of agriculture, or the augmentation of any
branch of commerce, the only answer they give is this: "It is
the custom; our fathers did so: I have done well; my children
will do the same." They love France, and speak of their
country with pride.

The French gentlemen, when entertaining guests and attending
mass or balls, dressed "beyond their means" and loved to appear

---

[3] Jacob Lindley described the French at Detroit as "superstitiously religious,
going to mass more than two hundred days in the year."

"grand abroad." There is an abundance of evidence to be found in the numerous settlements of estates drawn up by the notary clerk and preserved in the Kaskaskia manuscripts, to indicate a luxury of dress that is astonishing; richly trimmed coats, embroidered waist coats with "diamond" buttons, silken hose and silver buckles are among some of the items frequently mentioned for the wealthier inhabitants. Both men and women made an effort to imitate as far as possible the styles of Paris or other European cities. Travelers recorded that stores and shops were well furnished, with every kind of fine cloth, linen in fact, and every article of apparel for men and women. These were sold on the frontier nearly as reasonably as they were in New York and Philadelphia. Descriptions of dances, especially the more elaborate balls, pictured the men as wearing "very fine fur caps" adorned with "Black Ostridge Feathers" and amazingly large "Cockades" of white tinsel ribbon, and again, dressed in "their best bibs & Tuckers." The women at the posts, like many of their sex still, were said to pay too much attention to dressing their heads, and when making social calls decked themselves as though "their parents possessed the greatest dignities in the state." As in every age and clime, the men complained of their improvident attention to the newest fashions, since, in spite of their isolation, the women were not unfamiliar with the best of the day's vogue. Relatives or friends who traveled, advised the frontier women of all the changes of Dame Fashion. One, Archange Askin, second child of Mr. and Mrs. John Askin of Detroit, married Captain David Meredith and shortly after moved to England. Her charming and vivacious letters to her parents and sisters at home kept them well informed on the styles of dress in England.

> Low crowned chip hats [she advised], with large bows of strip coloured ribbon, is the prevailing system, with frilld calico jackets, and broad sashes, and nothing is now so vulgar for either gentlemen, or lady, as to be seen with a silk stocking that appears the least blue.

She was very observant, all which duly affected the styles in the faraway frontier posts.

> I notice [she wrote her mother] that all the ladies are wearing their skirts almost under the arms so as to raise the waist line. Sashes are about the width of a narrow collar and

are fastened at the back with a buckle. Neckerchiefs are very open as formerly and the neckband very narrow. The hair is curled, hanging at the back and arranged in small curls in front, with a piece of ribbon or a band of muslin around the head; even a thin lawn handkerchief arranged for a head-dress, with a white feather in it, is very fashionable in the best society, so there is no need of going to great expense about dressing the hair.[4]

A careful inspection of the contemporary records furnishes data which accords rather poorly with the popular conception of frontier habits and dress. The inventories of wardrobes found in these wilderness settlements show a profusion of rich attire. John Ask-with, a clerk of John Askin, falling heavily into debt, had his wardrobe, which he brought from Montreal, sold at public auction. One item, two pairs of leather breeches, was quite in keeping with the times.

But what manner of life did this recently penniless Detroit clerk lead that should account for the possession of thirty-six other pairs of breeches and trousers? A vest is a conventional article of male attire, but what social functions did Askwith attend which should necessitate the possession of thirty different vests? For the most part these garments are not described, but included in the number was one satin vest (did it match the satin breeches?), one of cassimere, one of white cloth, and one "black vest princess stuff." Among other items of this pioneer Detroiter's wardrobe were a dozen shirts, ten cravats, and fifteen coats. There was "camblet" coat, and a "camblet" cloak, a great coat, a white cloth coat, three black coats, and three flannel jackets.

A "parcel old hose and black tosels" was sold for nineteen shillings. Did the auctioneer arbitrarily lump these things together, or did a Detroit gentleman in those days wear tassels on his hose? If not, to what other use did Askwith put the tassels, and what did the purchaser expect to do with them? In the absence of more detailed information one can only speculate on these matters. But there is no need to speculate over the "parcel of ruffles and 2 black stocks," which was sold immediately after the hose and "tosels."

---

[4] Some of the military men picked their wives from the frontier women, and found upon their removal to England some social difficulties. Captain Henry Bird found himself in such a predicament. He wrote: "The ladies have undertaken to drill Mrs. Bird and do not despair of her coming in and out of a room without being taken for an Indian Lady in less than a year." Bird to William Edgar, January 28, 1785, Edgar MSS.

Then there were silk gloves, shoe-buckles and other articles too numerous to mention. One finds no lack of clothes for every occasion.[5]

The women had other traits of Mother Eve, aside from their interest in clothes and styles. One traveler recorded:

> One of the first questions they propose to a stranger is, whether he is married. The next, how he likes the ladies in the country, and whether he thinks them handsomer than those of his own country; and the third, whether he will take one of them home with him.[6]

In this game of love, some unusual events occurred. William Edgar, with his "amorous Competitor, C. Barber" broke the heart of the "once admired Miss Gouin." James Bannerman thought this passion contagious at Detroit, "where its operations" seemed "in general singular and sometimes whimsical." John Hay longed to be back at Detroit, for he detested New York. This, he admitted, was because of the rumor that "fair Ellen [was] murdering people by dozens." He was not surprised, for he acknowledged she had "charmed enough to captivate many."

But, as in all other phases of life, love was not without serious problems, for even the frontier had a code of morals. Captain Bird complained to Edgar of his serious loss when Mrs. Schieffelin left Detroit:

> I was deprived of the happiness of her Society some months before her departure, some illiberal transactions of her very unworthy Partner, banished him from every Gentleman's company and I (from the arbitary exactions of hard hearted custom) was reduced to the situation of Tantalus, and endured an intellectual famine in sight of a Rational banquet.

He asked Edgar to see his friend and tell her that "no man admires her more, that I even love her as much as I ought." [7] Neither did

---

[5] Askin wrote from Michillimackinac for a piece of silk with the "trimmings." Askin to Isaac Todd and James McGill, May 8, 1778, and later he mentioned his great need of waistcoats and breeches, and six or eight yards of fine white cloth and suitable "trimmings." In May, he ordered twelve pairs of shoes for Mrs. Askin, and a wedding gown of "french fashion" for Kitty. The next month he sent a request for a gold thimble.

[6] This was typical of the frontier, it seems. Askin, in 1778, congratulated Sampson Fleming upon the birth of a boy. "Perhaps," he wrote, "he may one Day become my Son in law, I have Girls worth looking at."

[7] He began: "Mrs. Schieffelin whose figure and genius you and I have so often admired."

love go smoothly for William Maxwell, for his Sally "eloped from her bed and board" to live in a "house of her own." But he seemed, after living with her a year, to be glad of the change. "She tired me heartily," he claimed, "I mean with her tongue and hands." To his friend he confided: "I believe on the whole Socrates need no more be quoted for his patience with his wife where my story is known." [8] Nevertheless, in spite of all difficulties, these people were jovial and light-hearted, ever seeking pleasure in racing, hunting, dancing, lavish entertaining, card playing, and the various winter sports.

Most of the gentry lived comfortably and well. One account states that François Trottier at Cahokia was "grandly Housed" and that his home had a "great furnished hall." The property of the Jesuits at Kaskaskia was described as being divided "into many low apartments" and in addition there were "cow sheds, Negro cabins, a barn, a stable, a weaving room, a horse mill [and] a dovecote." One journalist described the houses of Kaskaskia as "well built mostly of stone," and he further noted that the inhabitants lived "generally well." [9] No doubt these villages presented to the visitor a peaceful and orderly appearance, with an air of permanency unusual on the frontier. Most of the houses had pointed roofs, thatched or bark, extending over the "galleries" or porches.

> At one end of the building, and sometimes at both ends, was the large chimney of the generous fireplace. The houses stood close to the street for sociability's sake, and the yard around was protected by a whitewashed picket fence, within which were a flower garden, a small orchard of fruit trees, a vegetable garden, slaves' cabins, and a barn.[10]

An inventory of the property of the Jesuits at Kaskaskia listed sixty-eight Negroes trained as farmers, blacksmiths, carpenters, brewers and masons. Some of the wealthier families were even

---

[8] On August 4, 1768, he wrote that all was going well again. Fleming wrote to Edgar: "Kiss all the ladies for me that will let you and I'll do the same for you." Edgar must have been the Don Juan of Detroit. Apparently doctors advocated a change of clime when a youth suffered a "melancholy disorder" from love affairs. This was Donald Campbell's impression. Sterling sent Lt. John Wynne, at Fort Erie, a barrel of 900 good onions. "Enough" he wrote, "to spoil your kissing for one Winter."

[9] Thomas Hutchins described the houses of Kaskaskia as "well built; several of stone, with gardens, and large lotts adjoining."

[10] In Detroit, the houses were of "Log or frame Work, shingled," and with the orchards adjoining, gave the settlement a "very smiling" appearance. Again, the buildings were described as "low, being mostly a story and a half," and "the farms fertile."

better off and owned numerous slaves. A member of the Bauvais family in 1765 owned eighty slaves and furnished the royal magazine at one time with 86 thousandweight of flour—which was only a part of one year's harvest. While no Detroit or Michillimackinac family had as many slaves, nevertheless, Indian or Negro slaves were common in all the more important families in the Old Northwest.

The settler was especially fond of horses, and horse racing was one of his favorite pastimes.[11] With the coming of the English, more and more horses were introduced and efforts were put forth to improve the breed; in the last decade of the eighteenth century almost everyone had at least one horse, while the more prosperous merchants and traders possessed several.

During the winter months, pony racing on the ice was indulged in, with every young man of the village testing out a pony of uncertain speed. An individual might challenge the whole village, or the village might challenge him, and then things began to happen. When the ice was solid, these races would take place along the edge of a river or lake; at Detroit they were held most frequently upon the River Rouge, a small stream below the main settlement, which, having a sluggish current, furnished excellent ice in season. This made an ideal place for that kind of sport, especially on account of the circuitous channel which allowed spectators to spread out considerably and have an unobstructed view.

> Every Sunday after mass the crowd gathered at the appointed place and the fun was on. The challenged and the challenger brought out their ponies and scored for a start, while the crowd sized up the animals and the betting was furious. There was no starter, no jockey, no book-maker, no drawing for the pole. Each driver handled the reins over his own animal. He maneuvered for position and took his chances with his adversary. And when at last the ponies were off for the mile stretch down the river, the excitement among the multitude on the bank was something tremendous. If ever violence was done to the French language, it was upon such occasions, when individual opinions were struggling for utter-

---

[11] A census in 1767 listed 216 horses at Kaskaskia and 260 at Vincennes. Thomas Hutchins mentioned the fine breed of horses. Lindley noted that the French at Detroit were seen after mass "frolicking and horse racing in the road passing the worship house."

ance from hundreds of throats. Large sums of money changed
hands, considering the financial resources of the town.

Races often ended in severe altercations, sometimes leading to
blows; disputes were commonly settled in court.

Not less popular in the winter were the sleighing and skating
parties. When the autumnal rains came, submerging the lowlands,
the wintry frosts soon followed, converting the flooded areas into
miniature seas of glass. Detroit was especially fortunate in this
respect, for about three or four miles above the fort was a large
marsh, called by the French, *Le Grand Marais*. Here, when the
winter weather was favorable, the inhabitants of the fort and
village gave themselves unrestrainedly to the pleasures of dancing
and other festivities. In the fall the young men of the town would
build a long, narrow, log hut, with a fireplace at each end, for their
parties. Rough hewn tables, which were easily taken down, were
placed here and there. Early on Saturdays, young and old would
come in sleighs, and after a sumptuous meal of wild turkey, bear
steak and venison, washed down with quantities of wine, the rest
of the day was spent in games of various kinds, but principally in
dancing. These activities continued until the evening gun warned
the party that:

> The evening shades might be but 'vantage ground
> For some fell foe.

Next day, Sunday, the gentlemen would go back after mass and
spend the day in carousal, feasting on the remains of the preceding
day's feast. Sleigh-riding on the ice, and balls and parties in town
furnished entertainment for the rest of the week. "The summer's
earnings scarce sufficed for the winter's waste." [12] Indeed, one
"French official wrote in 1737 that the inhabitants of the Illinois
were burdened by debts as a result of their excessive drinking and
gambling."

The people of the Illinois region were not usually so fortunate as
those farther north, in having winters severe enough to furnish
sufficient ice for skating or sleighing parties. However, the winter
of 1783 was an exception in that the Mississippi froze from bank to
bank at Cahokia and the ice held for an entire month "which gave

---

[12] Entertaining was very common and there was genuine hospitality. One
writer mentioned a ball which he attended at Fort de Chartres "given by a
Gentleman of the Army, to the French Inhabitants who made a very droll
appearance." Hutchins also noted the politeness and hospitality of these folk.

the Créoles and the Spanish The pleasure of visiting." The crust of snow which had formed was strong enough to bear men and boys who were able to kill the deer with a "Stroke of the Hatchet" in the surrounding region.

Descriptions of the parties of that day were found in the poetry of the period too, for even the frontier did not lack its poets. One of the best known of all the post officials was Col. Arent Schuyler de Peyster, who settled at Dumfries, Scotland, after the War of American Independence. Here he became a close friend of his neighbor, Robert Burns. De Peyster was somewhat of a writer, and several of his short poems related to his life at Michillimackinac, Detroit, and Niagara, where he was commandant during the stirring years of 1775–1783. In one of his poems he pictured the canoeing and racing on the River Rouge. He enumerated those who were present, and described the festivities, the dancing, the races, and of course the drinking. All who had horses were present. The manager of the festivities for the occasion was Guillaume La Mothe, a Frenchman who was an officer in the Indian Department. An elaborate frontier feast followed the race, which was greatly enjoyed by the officers of the post, their wives, and their guests. So much drinking was indulged in that the party became boisterous and hilarious. With unusual license, the poet had the wild bears and deer come from the nearby woods and watch the pleasure-seekers in their hilarity.

The *habitant* was especially fond of a wedding, and kept up its festivities several days. The banns, announced at mass [13] on three preceding Sundays, formed the main subject of conversation in the ensuing days, for marriage was a lifelong contract of serious import, divorce being unknown. At the betrothal, the marriage contract was signed by both parties, their relatives, and their friends. The bride also furnished a dowry, the amount depending upon the position of her father.[14] The ceremony took place soon after the betrothal. After the signing of the certificate and the church register, a great celebration followed, lasting for many hours, or until all were fatigued. Sometimes the party took place at the *Grand Marais*,

---

[13] Sometimes this could not be done, as the "Mackinac Register" shows. The priest, under unusual circumstances, failed to announce the banns. At Vincennes, the banns were published for three Sundays, but no doubt there were many irregularities. Marriages between Catholics and Protestants were not unknown.

[14] When James Sterling married Angelique Cuillerier, her father gave nearly a thousand pounds in dowry consisting of horses, money, and peltry. Sterling Letter Book, February 26, 1765.

or, with dancing and feasting, at the home of the bride. The menu
was in strange contrast with our modern feasts:

> The *coup d'appetit* was passed around, brandy for the gen-
> tlemen, some mild cordial for the ladies; then followed the
> repast. Soup, *poissons blanc* (whitefish), *poisson doree* (pick-
> erel), pike, roast pig, with its dressing of potatoes, blood
> pudding, partridges, wild turkey, ragouts, venison larded,
> pates of *pommes de terre* (potatoes), sagammite, a dish of
> porridge made of cracked corn, eaten with cream and maple
> sugar, . . . *praline* was dried corn, pounded fine and mixed
> with maple sugar; . . . *galettes au buerre, crocquecignole* (a
> sort of doughnut), *omelette soufflee*, floating islands, pears,
> apples, raspberries, grapes in summer. Coffee ended the
> feast.[15]

Other diversions were shooting, hunting, and fishing.[16] Every
man had his gun and knew how to use it. Indeed, his life very often
depended upon his proficiency in the use of this instrument. The
neighboring woods abounded in partridge (grouse), wild turkey,
hare, deer, and what not, while the waters were filled with fish such
as trout, whitefish, and sturgeon. Record after record tells of fishing parties on the Great Lakes in the winter. Holes were cut in the
ice, in which were set lines and bait. Nets were dexterously placed
under the ice for whitefish weighing 3 to 7 pounds, which were
used as bait to catch trout weighing from 10 to 60 pounds. Now
and then this sport ended in stark tragedy, for many a fisherman
never returned. In summer, the weather was so hot and the air so
filled with mosquitoes and black flies as to be a "counterpoise to the

---

[15] Vegetables, fruits and meats of all kinds were found in abundance. See
especially "Augustin Grignon's Recollections," and the accounts of officials
such as Henry Hamilton, Robert Rogers, John Bradstreet, Edward Abbott and
Richard Dobie, and various travelers such as Johnathan Carver, Isaac Weld,
John Lees, Alexander Henry and the Quakers who visited Detroit in 1793.
Even delicacies from the outside world were not unknown. Capt. Dederick
Brehm sent a keg of olives to some friends in Detroit, and wrote: "They were
extremely good when I got them and I hope will arrive sound and good to your
place." Brehm to Edgar, April 29, 1722. George Morgan, at Fort de Chartres,
wrote his wife that he had "two Years Provisions in the House consisting of
Salt Petred Gammons, Rounds of Beef, Buffaloe Tongues, Vennison & Bears
Hams &c &c" and a large house containing 200 "couple" of pigeons. Morgan
also mentioned, in another letter, receiving tea "of a very bad quality," choco-
late, coffee, sugar, rice, salt, etc.

[16] Fleming described his pleasures in hunting on the *Grand Marais* at Detroit. When leaving Montreal for Ireland to shoot ducks, September 9, 1782,
he requested a small bag of wild rice from the *Grand Marais*, "cost what it
will."

pleasure of hunting" and fishing. Nevertheless, Alexander Henry related his pleasure in shooting large numbers of wild pigeons at Sault Ste. Marie. The marshes and swampy areas along the Mississippi, the Illinois, the Rock, and other rivers were a hunter's paradise in the fall when great flocks of wild geese and ducks stopped to feed before going farther south.[17]

During the spring, summer, and early fall, boat races were very popular. Every male was trained early in the management of the canoe, for boats were objects of necessity on the frontier. Rivers and lakes were the main roads in summer, and the only vehicle was the canoe. Nevertheless, travel was not always by water, for at a very early period a road was built to connect the Illinois villages. It followed the American Bottom from Kaskaskia to St. Philippe, where it divided, one branch continuing along the lowland to Cahokia, and the other along the top of the bluffs to the same village. From these villages, trails led in many directions. The canoes used by the inhabitants were made of the bark of trees, birch being preferred; for the longer boats, trunks of trees were dug out or burned by slow fire. Great care had to be taken in all cases to see that the wood was perfect, for a boat which leaked was a great annoyance. Besides races, on a warm summer evening, the rivers and lakes along the settlements were filled with canoes in which young men and women enjoyed each other's company.

Nowhere can one find a lovelier picture of hardy frontier folk whose livelihood depended upon the waterways, than in those descriptions of the boatmen or *engagés,* who were noted for their songs. As they pulled across the placid waters of lake and river, labor was lessened by the chorus of voices that kept time to the strokes of oar and of paddle.

> Faintly as tolls the evening chime,
> Our voices keep time, and our oars keep time,
> Soon as the woods on the shore look dim,
> We'll sing at St. Ann's our parting hymn,
> Row, brothers, row! the stream runs fast,
> The rapids are near, and the daylight's past.

Thus one might hear a hundred voices, rising and falling in unison, as the boatmen passed over the waters of the Old Northwest.

---

[17] It was recorded that the plains along the Mississippi were well stocked with buffalo, and "all Sorts of Game." Clark wrote Mason, November 19, 1779, that the Illinois area was "covered with Buffaloes and other Game." Hutchins made a similar observation.

These *engagés* were picturesque, dressed in "gaudy turbans, or
hats adorned with plumes and tinsel, their brilliant handkerchiefs
tied sailor-fashion about swarthy necks, their calico shirts, and
their flaming worsted belts" which circled their waists, holding
their knives and tobacco pouches. Rough trousers, leggings, and
cowhide shoes or gay moccasins completed their outfits. Whenever
a burial cross appeared, or a stream was left or entered, these
rough "sons of the woods" removed their hats, and made the sign of
the cross while one of their number uttered a short prayer; and
again they were off, their paddles beating time to a rollicking
French song:

> Dans mon chemin, j'ai rencontré
> Trois cavalières, bien montées;
> L'on, lon, laridon daine,
> Lon, ton, laridon dai,
>
> Trois cavalières, bien montées,
> L'un à cheval, et l'autre à pied;
> L'on, lon, laridon daine
> Lon, ton, laridon dai.

In all social life, French characteristics predominated, even
throughout the British régime. During the summer evenings,
though they were given much to drinking and gambling, the dance
was the favorite amusement, and to this frolic came the men and
matrons, young men and maidens; even the parish priest graced
these festive occasions.[18] The careless, pleasure-loving *coureurs de
bois* and *voyageurs,* returning to the settlements, gave added color
to these celebrations, at which all danced until the early morning
hours or even daybreak, with little appearance of rowdyism or
vulgarity to mar their simple festivities. The Sunday evening dance
was particularly popular, attended by all—young and old, rich and
poor. Every description which the records have furnished us of
these festive occasions mentions the good behavior and fellowship
that existed. Everyone joined happily in the church festivities, of
which there were many—possibly too many for the good of the
farmers; at least so some complained. In Illinois, the Mardi Gras
was very popular; the evening was passed at one of the large

---

[18] Cards were played incessantly, not always for money. To prevent abuses
and disorders caused by "red or black slaves," Clark provided that they should
take "their recreation in dancing on Sundays and feast days . . . during the
daytime" and then only when they had a permit "signed by their masters."

homes, where the main contest was the flapping of pancakes, after which there was dancing. The charivari which followed most of the weddings of the day was also good fun, for it had not degenerated into the vulgar exhibition of more recent days. There were no age restrictions at these parties. Alexander Grant, Commodore of the Royal Navy on the Upper Lakes, wrote to his friend, John Askin: "We hop and bob every Monday night at the Council House." Later, at the age of seventy-one, he felt himself growing quite hearty again: "Danced fifteen couple down the other night," he wrote. By this time, in addition to his strenuous life on the frontier, the Commodore had reared a family of twelve children (eleven of them were girls). His home, known as the Grant Castle, was always the scene of much gay life and hilarity.[19]

One of the outstanding characteristics of frontier society was its openhanded hospitality. Isolation from the outside world caused the people to welcome visitors, even total strangers, to their homes. Traveler after traveler testified to this trait, nowhere better pictured than in the warm reception and parties given Sir William Johnson when he visited Detroit in 1761.

It was a glorious September day when Sir William arrived. "Acutely aware that he appeared better on a horse than off," Johnson sent George Croghan ahead to procure mounts. A few miles below the settlement he met his deputy and mounted for his entry. The Indian villagers ran out to salute him; in reply he had the Royal Americans return three volleys from their boats. The naïve delight of this great man in the warmth of his reception in the heart of New France is evident in these lines of his diary:

---

[19] "We have endeavoured to make the Winter pass as agreeably as we could, by having a Dance every week," wrote Askin to Grant, April 28, 1778. This seemed to be general. Richard Cartwright wrote: "I am glad you are so gaily and agreeably amused at Detroit, and tho we cannot pretend to vie with you in Brilliancy yet we have our little Entertainments for which we are entirely beholden to the Gentlemen of the Garrison. We drink tea at the Fort every Saturday Evening, after that have a Concert, and then dance till about 12 o'clock, when we go to Supper." Cartwright to Edgar, February 17, 1780. In the early part of 1780 the following dancing bills were paid by:

Major de Peyster	£ 14/9/11
Captain Britton of the Navy	12/12/7
Captain Grant of the Navy	14/9/1
Captain Burnet	14/9/1
Mr. Forsythe	20/12/7

See Macomb Account Books in Burton Library. In 1780, the dancing bills amounted to £ 556/6/2. The records also mention "Country Dance Books," and fiddles.

All along the road was met by Indians, and near the town, by the inhabitants, traders, &c. When I came to the verge of the fort, the cannon thereof were fired, and the officers of the garrison with those of Gage's Light Infantry received me, and brought me to see my quarters, which is the house of the late commandant Mr. Belestre, the best in the place.

His time, when he was not in Indian Council, was spent in wining and dining, almost as feverishly as in modern Detroit. Sir William greatly enjoyed the sustained sociability, for he was never happier than when reveling in the table talk of men and the tea talk of ladies. Let Sir William tell of these delights:

> *Sunday* [September] *6th.*—A very fine morning. This day I am to dine with Captain Campbell, who is also to give the ladies a ball, that I may see them. They assembled at 8 o'clock at night, to the number of about twenty. I opened the ball with Mademoiselle Curie—a fine girl. We danced until five o'clock next morning. . . .
>
> *Saturday 12th.* . . . This morning four of the principal ladies of the town came to wait on me. I treated them with rusk and cordial. After sitting an hour, they went away. . . .
>
> *Sunday 13th.*—Very fine weather. . . . At 10 o'clock, Captain Campbell came to introduce some of the town ladies to me at my quarters, whom I received and treated with cakes, wine and cordial. Dined at Campbell's. . . .
>
> *Monday,* 14*th.*—Fine weather. This day I am to have all the principal inhabitants to dine with me; . . . I took a ride before dinner up toward the Lake St. Clair. The road runs along the river side, which is all thickly settled nine miles. . . . The French gentlemen and the two priests who dined with us got very merry. Invited them all to a ball to-morrow night, which I am to give to the ladies.

Here again he met the beautiful young lady, evidently by appointment, for he wrote:

> *Tuesday,* 15*th.*—Fine weather. This day settled all accounts. . . . In the evening, the ladies and the gentlemen all assembled at my quarters, danced the whole night until 7 o'clock in the morning, when all parted very much pleased and happy. [I] promised to write Mademoiselle Curie as soon as possible my sentiments; there never was so brilliant an assembly here before.

Mademoiselle appeared no more in the diary. Might one raise the query whether this short-lived gaiety, with folk of his own kind, seriously tempted Sir William to marry a woman of his own class?

We cannot answer; we only know of the "polite flutings of an elderly gallant a long way from home and enjoying what must, after all, be considered a butterfly flight in the fading sunlight." At least it was a strenuous life. But it would have been far more strenuous if his wife (his housekeeper, he called her), Molly Brant, had known of his doings at Detroit. It was well for her peace of mind, and possibly also well for Sir William's personal safety, that she was kept in ignorance, for there is little doubt that Molly's influence was very great with the Indians, and she was devoted to Sir William.[20]

The hospitality continued even through the departure. On September 17, Sir William went downstream to a village of the Hurons, where he visited the priest. When the officers from the fort arrived, he treated them and the Indians, and was carried in a chair to Captain Jarvis' for breakfast; the good captain had three of these luxurious conveyances to prove the leadership of Detroit in transportation. "Officers prancing on horseback, Sir William and Captain and Mrs. Jarvis carried in their sedan chairs," the party went through three merry miles, stopping here and there to bid adieu to various citizens, who no doubt entertained them with the best their conditions afforded. "Dined with the company out of doors. Parted [from] them all at this place," he wrote. Probably there were "adieus, good-bys, Godspeeds, much fluttering of handkerchiefs, perhaps a furtive tear. After all, it had been a splendid visit, both in solid accomplishment and the hospitality offered by a cultivated French society, the more remarkable because of the leagues of wilderness which hemmed it round."

Another charming picture of life on the frontier is given by Henry Hay who, as a young fur trader, visited the post of Miamitown (now the teeming city of Fort Wayne, Indiana) during the winter of 1790. Hay spoke particularly of the hospitality of these simple folk. He related that he had only been at the post a few days, when a Mrs. Adhamer manifested her politeness and attention by begging him to send his clothes and linen to her home for her Pani slave to launder, as it was most difficult to get clothes washed in such an out-of-the-way place.

From his journal one might gather the impression that life was all play, feasts, and dances, for all kinds of ceremonies followed

---

[20] Molly was Joseph Brant's sister, and she possessed great influence among the Six Nations, especially the Senecas.

each other in almost kaleidoscopic succession. The ringing of three cowbells by three boys running through the village "making as much noise as twenty cows would" called the settlers to midnight mass, and also to morning and evening prayers on Sunday. Musicians played their instruments on all occasions—drinking bout, dance or mass—and sometimes went "reeling from the one to the other." On one occasion, a joke was played on Mrs. Adhamer by stealing her pig, which was her "only support when the fresh meat" was killed; and the journalist added: "What hurt her more was, that she intended to kill it tomorrow." The excuse given for this fun was that she was a woman who was "amasingly fond of playing her jokes upon other people; . . . for which they were fully determined to play her this one, which we premeditated upwards of three weeks ago."

Temperance reform or an age of sobriety certainly had not made any appearance at the forks of the Maumee. On Christmas night, Hay and his companions became "infernally drunk"; so far gone were they that one of the traders gave our journalist "his daughter Betsy over the bottle." The next morning, they found themselves "damnation sick" and unable to eat any breakfast. Nevertheless, they "went to mass and played as usual," first partaking of a cup of coffee to settle their heads. This did not keep them sober long, for the following evening all except the author became "very drunk"; one, being too drunk to leave, had to stay at the home of his host all night. The very next evening, the celebrants were "damned drunk" and the writer added that upon visiting some ladies the following morning he found his companions there imbibing again, but he refused their invitations to partake "at so unseasonable an hour as 11 o'clock in the morning"; however, he promised to join them in the afternoon.[21] On New Year's day, he made the rounds of the "Principal families" kissing all the "Ladies young and Old." [22] The gay French spirit is evident in many places in the diary. On one occasion, after a flood, the ladies were "taken for a row on the river

---

[21] These people indulged in heavy drinking, as did all pioneer communities and contemporary society in general. When the *voyageurs* returned, there was much drinking and merrymaking, mingled with some lawlessness, for these men were noted as the most reckless class of the communities. In Kaskaskia in 1779, Jean Girault protested to the magistrates that some of the inhabitants became so drunk that they discharged their guns and endangered the lives and property of the citizens.

[22] Calls were generally made on New Year's day, when it was customary for the hostess to present her cheek to the departing guests for a goodbye kiss.

to the accompaniment of fiddle and flute," even before the high waters had subsided.

Alexander Fraser got a similar impression of frontier life. He wrote that the French folk of Illinois had a passion for drunkenness and were "for the greatest part drunk every day while they can get Drink to buy in the Colony." He further stated that the Negroes were obliged to "Labour very hard to Support their Masters in their extravagant Debaucheries."

One does not find the same hospitality manifested toward the close of the century. The incoming horde of Americans was regarded by the old French stock much as the cultivated Romans regarded the invading Germanic barbarians. Thomas Bentley found life particularly difficult at Kaskaskia. He addressed a letter to his enemies on September 5, 1780, in which he stated:

> I know that most of you are mortified to see me struggling to overcome the difficulties which you yourselves, conjointly with that rascal Rocheblave, Cerré, and others, have brought upon me. I am persuaded that there are not ten amongst you in this village who would not like to see me crushed under the load of my misfortunes. I know that it is a crime for a damned Englishman to attempt to stay among you; Irishmen suit you better; they are equal to you in perfidy; as for lying, flattering, and drinking trafia, they can do it as well as any of you.

Again this situation is well illustrated by a letter which Frederick Bates, a young Virginian (and neighbor and friend of Thomas Jefferson), who had recently come to Detroit to seek his fortune, wrote to his sister. Bates may be regarded as a fair representative of the Virginia planter aristocracy of the time, and both in Detroit and in St. Louis (to which place he removed) he held numerous important public offices. At the time of writing this letter, Bates was twenty-two years of age, and a comparatively recent arrival at Detroit. He wrote:

> I make but little progress with the french girls. They are not very apt to think favorably of the Americans. They think them a rough unpolished, brutal set of people. The pleasure of walking on a sunday evening, is almost counter-balanced by the trouble attendant on that parade & ceremony with which the salutations of the French must be returned. The Miss Grants daughters of the Commodore of the British Squadron on the upper Lakes, are the finest girls in this country. Their mother is a Canadian and they are Roman Catholics. Last

Christmas I went early to the midnight mass, and seated
myself in their Pew. They came, and with the most obliging
good nature, requested me to make room,—I rose—apologized
for my intrusion—& seated myself in the Pew next to them,
Determined to be diverted at my expence, they beckoned to
me as many as three times to move, as I was in the seat of a
lady who was coming in. After mass, I remonstrated with
them on their cruelty in taking such pleasure in my embarras-
ment. They thought it a cruelty, which they might very innocently exercise. Their father altho' in the British service lives
on this side the Strait, on one of the best Farms in the
Country. Their mother (which is a singular circumstance
among French Ladies) superintends the farm, the produce of
which, supports the Family very decently. The old Gentleman's salaries as Commodore and privy Counsellor, are
funded, as portions for the girls.

Even an election day was a holiday for old and young, voter and
voteless. They were occasions "to meet, to smoke to carouse and
swagger," though the records leave one in doubt as to whether they
ended in drunken brawls. A leading candidate for the provincial
legislature of Upper Canada, in the election of 1792, was David W.
Smith of Detroit, who has left considerable correspondence concerning this campaign.

Perusal of these records leaves no doubt that neither human
nature nor the methods of politicians have altered materially since
1792. Smith was willing to spend money freely, although even as
with candidates today, there could be no hope of ever securing its
return unless by indirect means. The inducements to the voters
took the form of free tavern entertainment, accompanied by lavish
dispensing of liquors. "Should I be returned without an undue
Election or the appearance of party or bribery, I shall be most
happy," wrote Smith on July 26, "& in that case I beg an Ox may be
roasted whole on the common, & a barrel of Rum be given to the
mob, to work down the Beef."

With the passage of time, the candidate's ideas concerning entertainment of the voters became more expansive, and in a letter to
John Askin on August 14, he presented this captivating picture:

The french people can easily walk to the Hustings, but my
gentry will require some conveyance; if boats are necessary
you can hire them, & they must not want beef or Rum, let
them have plenty, and in case of success I leave it to you,
which you think will be best to give my friends a public
dinner, & the ladies a dance, either now, or when I go up. If

you think the moment the best time You will throw open
Forsyths Tavern, & call for the best he can supply. I trust you
will feel very young on the occasion, in the dance, & I wish
that Leith and you should push about the bottle, to the promotion of the Settlements on the Detroit. The more broken heads
& bloody noses there is the more election like, and in case of
Success (damn that if!) let the White Ribbon favors be plenti-
fully distributed, to the old, the Young, the Gay, the lame, the
cripple & the blind—half a score cord of wood piled hollow,
with a tar barrel in the middle, on the Common, some powder,
pour tirer, & plenty of Rum. I am sure that you will preside
over & do ev[er]ything that is needful, as far as my circumstances will admit. there must be no want & I am sure you
will have ev[er]ything handsome & plentiful.

Elliot I am sure will give you a large red flag to be hoisted
on a pole near the Bon fire, and some blue colored tape may
be sewn on in large letters E S S E X. . . . Have proper booths
erected for my friends at the Hustings, employ Forsyth to
make large plumb Cake, with plenty of fruit & ca & be sure let
the Wine be good & plenty. Let the peasants have a fiddle,
some beverage & Beef.

It would be easy to add numerous descriptions of the many other
sports which tempt one to linger, but one can only mention other
phases of social activity which more than filled the hours of leisure.
Running, wrestling, rowing, bowling on the narrow streets, arrow
shooting, quoits, and especially card playing during inclement
weather, are only a few of the many ways in which the inhabitants
of the Old Northwest enjoyed life to the fullest.

So happy and carefree was life in the western wilderness that
those who moved elsewhere were inclined to yearn for the pleasures of the posts. "I cannot but repeat again our Inclinations and
wishes are to be with you. . . . [My wife's] [23] mind is occupied with
reflections of the many happy hours passed at Detroit, it is to be
hoped that sometime or another we shall have a renewal of the like
pleasures," wrote Lieutenant Mercer to John Askin.[24] De Peyster
was most happy during his stay in Michigan. "A sore heart it gave
us to leave Detroit," he informed a friend, "had we but some of our

[23] Refers to Phyllis Barthe, wife of Lieut. Daniel Mercer.

[24] Mercer to Askin, Reading (in Berkshire) April 29, 1790. Askin's daughter,
Madelaine, wrote her father she was sure that she would not have as pleasant
a winter at Queenstown as she had had at Springwells, "but I may have the
pleasure of talking about them with the ladies of the 5th. I assure you they
regret leaving Detroit." Madelaine Askin to John Askin, October 15, 1792.
From Plymouth, England, John Burnet wrote Askin of his "many happy days"
at Detroit. Burnet to Askin, March 6, 1787.

relations there, I could have spent my life in its little society."
Richard Cartwright, Jr., described the people of Detroit as "gaily
and agreeably amused" and admitted that the social life at Niagara
could not pretend to vie with Detroit in its brilliancy.

Not long after the War of Independence with its ravages, and
the continued uncertainty which prevailed concerning trade at the
western posts, social life lost much of its thrill and charm. In
Illinois there was a period of anarchy and confusion which began
before the close of the war and continued for some years. Tyranny
followed tyranny, bringing disorder and chaos. John Edgar, who
used his influence to promote peace, wrote to Major John Hamtramck in September, 1789:

> The name of an American among them [the Indians] is a
> disgrace, because we have no superior. Our horses, horned
> cattle, & corn are stolen & destroyed without the power of
> making any effectual resistance: Our houses are in ruin &
> decay; our lands are uncultivated; debtors absconded & ab-
> sconding; our little commerce destroyed. We are apprehensive
> of a dearth of corn, and our best prospects are misery and
> distress, or what is more than probable an untimely death by
> the hands of savages.

Father Gibault at Vincennes well summed up conditions when
he said: "In Canada all is civilized, here all is barbarous. You are in
the midst of justice, here injustice dominates. . . . Everybody is in
poverty, which engenders theft and rapine. Wantonness and drunkenness pass here as elegance and amusements quite in style."
Some found the winters long and tedious, and hoped to move away.
"This place once the gaiest and most sociable known has under-
gone surprising changes," wrote Anthon to Edgar. "Numbers of
people ruined," he continued, "old Acquaintances Dead and gone, a
gloomy Aspect in all most every ones face, great demands and
small remittances, seizures and Executions in Abundance, and I
am afraid a Universal Bankruptcy will ensue among the Trading
people here." [25] These conditions did not last long, however. The
depression was temporary, and soon life was as gay and brilliant as
ever, and continued so to the close of the British régime.[26]

---

[25] September 26, 1785, he mentioned Detroit people who put money in the
Bank of North America as "broke and undone."

[26] Donald Campbell wrote: "For my own part I am heartily tired of Detroit,
tho' the best frontier Garrison I begin to know the People too well, I do not
think they improve on a long acquaintance." Campbell to Bouquet, July 3,

One is inclined to dwell longer and in much greater detail upon the social activities of these past romantic days. Life in the harsh conditions [27] of the wilderness, when intercourse with the outside world was so uncertain, was not one of seclusion, or of toil only, but was interspersed with all the hilarity and joymaking that could be obtained in such a situation. Human nature was far from being suppressed, and the picture left is one of charm and gaiety, often of passion unrestrained. Those were happy days. It was a simple life with simple pleasures, possibly a life which cannot be found in the tumult and shouting of this ultramodern age.

1762, another comment: "You talk of your place [Detroit] being duller than ever. &c. believe me it cannot be put in competition with ours [Michillimackinac] for dulness jealousy & envy with all the etceteras mentioned in your's. Where Society is thin, I agree with you, They should make the most of it." Duggan to Selby, June 3, 1796.

[27] Life was hard and there was much unhealthiness, especially along the Mississippi lowlands. George Morgan claimed that no French native of Illinois was known to have lived "to an old Age." There was a period of great disorder and confusion in Illinois following the war. John Edgar wrote to Major Hamtramck, October 28, 1789: "An attempt has been made to steal my property & slaves, & the life of my wife, as well as that [of] Mrs. Jones was in the most imminent danger. . . . Every day we are threatened with being murdered, & having our houses & village burnt; the Pianakeshaws steal our horses, & take them to the Spanish side, where they live, & where we dare not, even allowing we had sufficient force, follow them; so that truly speaking, our situation is desperate & even pitiful."

PART II

PART II

The Frontier State

1820-1845

I N 1803, two years after Governor William Henry Harrison arrived at Vincennes, the capital of the Indiana Territory, Fort Dearborn was erected by federal troops on what is now the intersection of Michigan Avenue and Wacker Drive in Chicago, on the south bank of the Chicago River. Over the following years the various Indian tribes ceded their lands in Illinois and left the state. New settlers continued to arrive in Illinois and the area's first United States land office was opened at Kaskaskia in 1804. The Illinois Territory (which included Wisconsin) was established in 1809, with Kaskaskia as the capital and Ninian Edwards as the first governor of the territory, which had a population of more than 10,000.

Although the War of 1812 made settlers apprehensive of Indian attacks, the only serious action in Illinois occurred two or three miles southeast of Fort Dearborn on August 15, 1812, when Indians massacred the soldiers and civilians who had evacuated the post and were en route to Fort Wayne. After the war the line of settlement inched northward, generally along the rivers. (Two important immigrants at that time were George Flower and Morris Birkbeck, who founded the famous English Settlement in Edwards

County.) In April 1818, the Illinois Enabling Act was passed by the Congress, and by August the state constitutional convention adopted a constitution and chose Kaskaskia as the capital. Shadrach Bond was inaugurated first governor of Illinois in October and President James Monroe, on December 3, 1818, signed the act that made Illinois the twenty-first state of the Union. Two years later, when Illinois had a population of 55,000, the frontier had moved farther north and Vandalia was made the capital.

Most of the settlers in the first great wave of immigration came from the South (less than 13 per cent came from New England and abroad) in search of farmland, and as the land in the far south of Illinois was settled the newcomers followed a northward-moving farming frontier—along the rivers and into the wooded areas that dotted the prairies. They had to have wood for shelter and fuel, and the prairies themselves were treeless. Besides, breaking the prairie sod was a man-killing job. Only later would they discover the amazing fertility of the prairie soil.

Slaves had been held in Illinois since 1720; although never in large numbers. The Ordinance of 1787 seemed to end slavery in the Illinois country, but in fact, those Negroes who had been slaves before 1787 continued their lives of bondage. The introduction of new slaves was discontinued, but the practice of binding Negroes to long-term indentures made it possible to evade the intent of the ordinance. Although the Illinois constitution of 1818 had prohibited slavery, the issue was hotly debated until 1824 when the people voted against calling a convention to legalize slavery.

In the next ten years settlers reached all areas of the state. A land office was opened in Springfield, Galena became a major city, and the General Assembly became obsessed with canals and other internal improvements. By 1830—the year the Lincoln family moved from Indiana to Illinois—the population exceeded 150,000.

The 1830s saw a tremendous surge of immigration that tripled the population to more than 475,000 by 1840. The Erie Canal, which opened in 1825, not only brought newcomers to Chicago and northern Illinois by way of the Great Lakes, it also accelerated the rate of settlement and changed its pattern: most new Illinoisans came now from the northeast United States and from abroad.

The complete defeat of the Sauk and the Fox in the ignoble Black Hawk War of 1832 put an end to the Indian menace in

Illinois, and in 1833 the remaining Indian lands were ceded to the federal government—the same year that Chicago began its legal existence as a town. In 1837 the General Assembly passed the grandiose Internal Improvement Act, providing for a network of canals, railroads, and roads throughout the state, again voted to move the capital farther north, this time to Springfield, and approved a city charter for Chicago. In the little northern Illinois town of Grand Detour (named for the "Big Bend" on the Rock River), John Deere invented the first successful self-scouring steel plow, which had a profound effect on prairie farming. As the thirties came to an end, Mormons fled from Missouri and founded the town of Nauvoo, 45 miles north of Quincy on the Mississippi.

In 1829, near the center of the state, the village of New Salem was founded; it prospered for four or five years, declined rapidly, and was a ghost town by 1840. It is remembered today as the place in which the young Abraham Lincoln worked as storekeeper, postmaster, and surveyor, and which—as a state assemblyman and self-educated lawyer—he left in 1837 to seek the greater opportunities offered in the new state capital.

In the 1830s and 1840s, Illinois's days as a frontier state were drawing to a close. Its population reached 850,000 in 1850. Permanent settlers, either absorbed or displaced the earlier self-reliant, individualistic hunters and trappers. In the 1840s the first steam railroad in Illinois (the Northern Cross) was completed, connecting Naples on the Illinois River with Jacksonville, and later, Springfield. The state furnished soldiers for the Mexican War, adopted a new constitution, and completed the Illinois and Michigan Canal.

The greatest source of internal dissension at mid-century was the growing Mormon town of Nauvoo, which had received a charter from the General Assembly that enabled the Mormons to be all but independent of state authority and to have their own army, the Nauvoo Legion. Soon Nauvoo was the largest city in Illinois and Joseph Smith, the Mormon leader, began to wield significant political power. It was Smith's capricious use of this power, rather than the Mormon religious belief and practice, that brought the fear and hatred of many Illinoisans upon him and his followers. Indeed, Smith's continued political activity, compounded by rumor, speculation, and half-truths, created conditions that made violence inevitable. After Joseph and his brother Hyrum Smith, were murdered at Carthage, a state of open warfare seemed likely, and in 1846 Brigham Young, newly come to power, led most of the Mormons from Illinois on their epic trek to Utah.

Life in Illinois was still crude and rough; money was hard to come by; transportation was unbelievably bad; disease was rampant; and the quality of public education was rudimentary at best. Haphazardly, the land and its climate produced bountiful crops and floods, droughts, and plagues of insects. There were then, as now, days and seasons that could not be improved upon, but the long, unbearably hot and humid days of midsummer and the paralyzing cold and deadly blizzards of deep winter were grievous in their effect. Many immigrants, nevertheless, as though immune to extremes of weather and the rigors of Illinois pioneer life, were able to improve their situations in the prairie state.

Although agriculture was the major occupation in the state, it soon became difficult for small farmers to acquire land on terms that would permit them to succeed. As early as the mid-thirties, speculators had begun to acquire large tracts of prairie, particularly in central and eastern Illinois, and this activity accelerated in the 1840s and 1850s. Some speculators acquired thousands of acres of arable land and became known as "agricultural Napoleons." Thus the practice of tenant farming was developed, similar to the feudalism of the Middle Ages. Many tenant farmers were treated decently but many were ruthlessly exploited. The large landlords, together with the railroads, controlled so much land that it became difficult for the undercapitalized immigrant to buy his farm. Indian removal and post-pioneer civilization had made farming safe, but all too often the farmer's life was filled with long hours of hard labor and grinding monotony on another man's land.

RAY A. BILLINGTON

received his Ph.D. in history from Harvard in 1933,
taught at Clark University, Smith College, and Northwestern University. Since 1963, he has been Senior Research
Associate at the Huntington Library, San Marino, California.
He served as president of the American Studies Association
of the Organization of American Historians and of the Western History Association. He was a member and director of
the Illinois State Historical Society. Among his best known
works are *Westward Expansion; United States History,
1865–1950; The Far Western Frontier, 1830–1860;* and as
editor, *Histories of American Frontiers Series.*

This paper was presented at the 49th annual meeting of
the Illinois State Historical Society. It was published in the
Journal of the Illinois State Historical Society, volume 43,
number 1 (spring 1950), pages 28–45.

THE FRONTIER IN ILLINOIS HISTORY

RAY A. BILLINGTON

The historian who attempts to isolate the unique characteristics of
the people of any American region must search for clues in both
their imported traits and the environmental influences operating
upon them. Of the latter, none has been more influential than the
impact of the frontier; in the continuous rebirth of civilization that
occurred during the settlement process both men and institutions
were "Americanized" as inherited practices or traits were cast
aside. This mutation followed no set pattern, for in no two regions
of the West were the ingredients of the new society—man and
nature—blended in identical proportions. At times man was so
influenced by tradition that he refused to bow completely to the
forest environment; thus the Massachusetts Bay Puritans were too
united by religious ties to respond to the centrifugal forces of
wilderness life. At other times the environment was sufficiently
overwhelming to create utterly distinct behavior patterns; the Mormons who settled the deserts of Utah exhibited few of the traits
usually found on the frontier. In relatively few areas were the two
ingredients sufficiently balanced to create a completely typical result. One favored spot where this occurred was Illinois.

This can best be realized by restating several general propositions concerning the frontier process, then applying them to the
early history of the state.

First, the frontier was an area where man's inherited institutions
were significantly altered by natural conditions. Illinois offers a
unique example of this transformation, for within its borders are
two differing soil areas, each of which influenced not only the
settlement process but subsequent economic developments. These
resulted from two of the glaciers that ground their way southward
during the Pleistocene Age. One, the Illinoian Drift, covered the
state as far south as the Ohio River, leaving behind as it receded a
rugged hill country littered with glacial debris, and a compact clay
soil marked by the absence of such essential elements as sulphur,
potassium, carbon, and nitrogen. At a later day in geological history a second ice sheet pushed slowly down from the north—the
Wisconsin Drift. Grinding down hills into smooth prairies, this
glacier left behind a level countryside and a light loam soil rich in
both the humus and chemicals needed for fertility. The Wisconsin
Drift, however, did not benefit all parts of the state equally. The
extreme southern limit of its advance was marked by the clearly
defined Shelbyville Moraine, the most important natural boundary
in all Illinois. Pioneers were quick to notice the difference between
lands lying north and south of this dividing line. Above the moraine the countryside was level, the soil deep, and the swamps
numerous—swamps that could readily be drained to form humus-
rich fields of immense productivity. Below, the rugged hills and
glacier-strewn waste discouraged frontiersmen.

For a century both land prices and agricultural yields confirmed
the judgment of the first settlers. In 1904, for example, lands just
north of the moraine sold for from $75 to $125 an acre; those to
the south for $30 an acre. In the same year fields in Coles County,
lying in the glaciated area, yielded 36 bushels of oats or 40 of corn
to the acre; in Cumberland County, just to the southward, only 28
bushels of oats or 30 of corn were produced. Higher yields, in turn,
allowed a greater degree of population concentration; a typical
county north of the moraine contained 42 per cent more people
than another to the south. This reflected a more advanced stage of
urbanization, on which depended cultural progress. The counties
north of the Shelbyville Moraine, with more taxable wealth, could
support better schools, colleges, libraries, and similar intellectual

agencies. Although twentieth-century industrialization has lessened the effect of this natural boundary, Illinois's early history provides an outstanding example of that impact of nature on man, which typified the Americanization process.

Secondly, the frontier was an area where men of all sections and all nations met to form a new society, enriched by borrowings from many lands. In few other areas of the West did the accident of migration result in such a thorough blending of many racial strains as in Illinois. From the Southeast, from the Middle States, from New England, from older states of the Northwest, and from Europe came the state's pioneers, each contributing new flavor and new strength to the social order that evolved.

The first settlers were from the South. Some came from the seaboard regions, but more left homes in the uplands of the Carolinas, Virginia, Tennessee, or Kentucky, where a mingling process had already produced a mixed population from Scotch-Irish, German, and English strains. Skilled in the techniques of conquering the wilderness, these sturdy woodsmen were crowded from their old homes by the advance of the plantation frontier during the first quarter of the nineteenth century. Moving northward over Kentucky's Wilderness Road, or drifting down the Ohio River on flatboats, they reached such embarkation points as Shawneetown by the thousands, then fanned out over the trails that led to the interior: some along the Great Western Road through Kaskaskia and Cahokia to St. Louis, others along the Goshen Road toward Alton, still others northward through Carmi to Albion after that town was founded in 1818. Filling in the rich bottom lands of the Ohio and Mississippi first, they soon spread over the forested portions of southern Illinois, seeking always the dense timber that testified to good soil. There they girdled the trees, planted their corn, raised their log cabins, split rails for their worm fences, shook through regular attacks of malaria, and steadily extended their civilization over a widening area.

The predominantly southern character of Illinios's early migration cannot be overemphasized. In 1818, when the first rough survey was taken, 38 per cent of the settlers were from the South-Atlantic Seaboard, almost 37 per cent from Kentucky and Tennessee, 13 per cent from the Middle States, 3 per cent from New England, and 9 per cent from abroad. Thus 75 per cent of the people were from the South, as opposed to 25 per cent from all the

rest of the United States and Europe. Nor did this ratio change
during the next decade; as late as 1830 observers believed that
Illinois was on its way to becoming a transplanted southern commonwealth, with all the institutions—including slavery—of its sister states south of Mason and Dixon's Line.

Then the tide turned. The Erie Canal was responsible. The opening in 1825 of that all-water route between the Hudson River and
Lake Erie shifted the center of migration northward as New Englanders and men from the Middle Atlantic States found the gate-
way to the West open before them. Now the Great Lakes, not the
Ohio River, formed the pathway toward the setting sun. From
Buffalo and New York, steamboats carried pioneers to new towns
that sprang up as embarkation points: Cleveland, Toledo, Detroit,
and Chicago. In 1834, 80,000 people followed this route westward;
eleven years later the number reached 98,000. Michigan and Ohio
attracted some, but Illinois, which was scarcely settled north of
Alton, was the mecca of more. As they landed on the Chicago
wharfs, that frontier hamlet blossomed overnight into a booming
city. Such was the demand for buildings to house the newcomers
that lots which sold in the spring of 1835 for $9,000 fetched
$25,000 four months later. Most stayed in the cramped city only
long enough to lay in supplies for the overland trip to the farm at
the end of their rainbow. As they flooded over the countryside the
statistics of the government land offices told a dramatic story: a
quarter of a million acres were sold in 1834, two million in 1835,
almost four million in 1836.

The newcomers were as predominantly northern as the earlier
immigrants were southern; fully 75 per cent were from north of
the Mason and Dixon Line. Some came in groups from their native
New England, fully equipped with pastor, schoolmaster, and eastern ways of life. Rockwell, Tremont, and Lyons were planted in
this way between 1833 and 1836; a year later Wethersfield was laid
out by Yankees whose childhood had been spent in the shaded
streets of that old Connecticut village. More came as individuals or
in families, bringing with them the habits of their native New
England and an insatiable thirst for land that did not, as one
advertiser put it, stand on edge. As they came they transformed
northern Illinois into a replica of the Northeast, just as southern
Illinois was a duplicate of the Southeast. "Each of these two foun-
tains of our civilization," wrote the editor of the *Democratic*

Monthly Magazine in 1844, "is pouring forth its columns of immigrants to the Great Valley, forming there a new and third type that will reform and remold the American civilization."

Yet no frontier state could be typically American without the invigorating impact of European migration. Illinois benefited from the transfusion of this fresh blood during the 1840's. First to come were Irish peasants who drifted westward as laborers on canals and railroads; many eventually settled along the path of the Illinois and Michigan Canal. They were soon joined by German pioneers who had been driven from their homes by a devastating potato famine. Taking advantage of the cheap transportation offered by returning cotton ships, they reached New Orleans, then traveled up the river to the cheap lands of Missouri, Illinois, and Wisconsin. With them came a sprinkling of intellectuals fleeing the political tempests of 1848. Few in numbers but large in influence, these leaders injected German customs and thought into the Illinois social order to a degree rarely equalled in other states.

If an Illinoisan had paused to take stock of his state at the close of the settlement period he would have been proud of what he saw. In few commonwealths was acculturation so complete. Here in 1850 lived 334,000 native sons, 138,000 born in the South, 112,000 from the Middle Atlantic States, 37,000 from New England, 110,000 from the other states of the Old Northwest, and 110,000 foreign born. Each group contributed something to the composite whole; each made Illinois more completely American. "The society thus newly organized and constituted," wrote a Westerner, "is more liberal, enlarged, unprejudiced, and, of course, more affectionate and pleasant, than a society of people of *unique* birth and character, who bring all their early prejudices, as a common stock, to be transmitted as an inheritance in perpetuity."

Illinois's good fortune was in marked contrast to the fate of its neighbor, Indiana. When the settlement of the two territories began, they seemed destined to follow a parallel course. To Indiana, as to Illinois, came the southern migratory stream, to fill the southern third of the state in the first quarter of the nineteenth century. If the frontier process had operated normally, New Englanders, men from the Middle Atlantic States, and Europeans would have moved into its northern portions. That they failed to do so was due to two unhappy circumstances.

One was the state's bad reputation. Travelers who entered Indi-

ana from the northeast were forced to cross the elongated morass
along the Maumee River known as the Black Swamp, then thread
their way across the swampy tablelands of the upper Wabash
where drainage was so poor that water frequently covered the trails
even in periods of normal rainfall. They never forgot this first
impression. In books, in newspaper articles, and in conversations
they always referred to "the swamps and bogs of Indiana"—a
phrase soon indelibly associated with the name of the state. In vain
did Hoosiers protest that the prairies of Illinois were no drier; for
decades northern pioneers passed over poorly advertised Indiana.

An even more effective deterrent to settlement was the activity
of land speculators, of whom a Hartford businessman, Henry L.
Ellsworth, was most prominent. Impressed with the beauty and
richness of Indiana's prairies while on a western trip in the 1830s,
Ellsworth moved to Lafayette in 1835 and promptly began amass-
ing land until his holdings totaled 18,000 acres. He farmed them so
profitably, even after the Panic of 1837, that other Easterners
made similar investments. Ellsworth encouraged this; in his little
book, *The Valley of the Upper Wabash* (1838), he promised to
farm prairie land for any investor, paying the owner 8 or 10 per
cent, and taking his own profit from half the remaining surplus.
Numerous easterners entered into such contracts with Ellsworth;
others were persuaded to buy Indiana lands by his advertising.
Within a few years their holdings blanketed the central and northern portions of the state, effectively discouraging settlement by the
$5.00-an-acre price demanded for resale. Not until the 1850s did
mounting taxes force the speculators to unload; then purchasers
were principally younger sons from southern Indiana who moved
northward in search of land. Ellsworth's propaganda and poor
advertising, by closing the gates to pioneers from the Northeast
and Europe, deprived Indiana of that population blending that so
benefited Illinois.

Third, the frontier was a region where mechanical ingenuity was
highly developed in the never-ending battle between man and nature. In Illinois settlers were forced to display a higher degree of
adaptability than on most frontiers, for they faced a natural barrier
that would have proved insurmountable to men of lesser stature:
the vast central grassland. This was a forbidding obstacle to pioneers trained by two centuries of experience in the technique of
clearing wooded areas. They had learned to judge the fertility of

land by the density of its forests, to build their homes and fences from the plentiful wood supply, to secure their fuel from the wilderness, to obtain water from springs or streams, and to depend for shelter on the bands of timber left standing when fields were cleared. The habits of woodland pioneering were so deeply engrained in the average pioneer that any deviation was difficult if not impossible.

Yet that adjustment had to be made before Illinois could be settled. In the northern portions of the state vast fields blanketed by six-feet-tall grass were interlaced with forest lots or crisscrossed by the bands of timber that followed every stream, but in central Illinois the prairies stretched away to the horizon on every side. Every instinct told the pioneer to avoid these grasslands. How could soil that would not support trees grow crops? Where could he get wood for his cabin, his fences, and his fuel? How could he obtain drinking water in a region where sluggish streams were thick with silt? How could he farm fields that were turned into swamps by every rainfall? And, most important of all, how could he bring the prairies under cultivation when tough sod shattered the fragile cast-iron plows which had proved adequate in timbered areas? Those were the problems that had to be solved before central and northern Illinois could be settled.

Little wonder, in view of these obstacles, that the shift from forest to prairie was made slowly. Farmers in the wooded areas along the Fox and Rock rivers first began pasturing their cattle on nearby grasslands, then experimentally turned under some of the sod. When the land proved productive, others imitated their example, until a ring of farms surrounded the open grassland. Each year the cultivated fields were expanded until eventually they met. By 1850 all the grasslands of Illinois were under the plow save the central portions of the Grand Prairie. Not until the Illinois Central Railroad penetrated that region five years later was the last unsettled area occupied.

No simple account of the settlement of the state reveals the inventiveness, ingenuity, and boldness displayed by the Illinois pioneers. They overcame one of their most deep-seated prejudices when they learned that a soil's richness could not be determined by the density of its timber. They discovered that "stone coal" could be brought in more easily than wood for heating. They learned how to sink wells, and developed both well-drilling machinery and windmills to ease the back-breaking task of providing water. They discovered that cooperative efforts were necessary for drainage. And they invented special plows, pulled by from four to six oxen, to break the tough sod. The expense involved in the use of these cumbersome contraptions, which could be hired from a local operator at a rate of from $2.00 to $5.00 an acre, created a demand for more efficient equipment which sent inventors to their drafting boards; one landmark was passed in 1837 when John Deere gave the world the steel plow. They learned to plant a "sod crop" by cutting upturned furrows at intervals with an ax, then dropping in a few kernels of corn. Although these fields could not be cultivated, the good Illinois soil produced yields up to 50 bushels to the acre, while the roots helped break up the rotting sod.

Learning new techniques and inventing new implements, the Illinois farmer not only solved one of the most troublesome problems faced in the conquest of the continent but by his very ingenuity stamped himself as a typical product of the American frontier.

Fourth, the West was a region where democratic theory was enshrined and democratic practices perpetuated. Living in a land where all men were reduced to equality by the greater force of nature, conscious of the economic opportunity that promised to make the poor rich, and impatient of restraints from uninformed Easterners who knew nothing of western problems, the frontiersman insisted that each man's right to rule himself was as fundamental as his right to good land. The Westerner made few contributions to the mechanics of democracy, for in the realm of theory he was imitative rather than inventive, but he did show a marked tendency to adopt the most liberal practices of the East he had left behind. Illinois, as a typical frontier state, exhibited this tendency admirably.

Its people's democratic faith was first reflected in the Constitution of 1818. At this time Southerners predominated; in the constitutional convention twenty-one were from the South, two had been born in Illinois of southern parents, five came from the Middle Atlantic States, and only one from New England. Despite this influence toward conservatism, despite even the perpetuation of slavery—in the form of indentured servitude—the Illinois constitution was a model of democratic practice. Based on the frames of government already adopted in Ohio, Tennessee, and Kentucky, but going beyond them in the direction of popular rule, it vested virtually sovereign power in the legislature, while reducing the governor to a mere figurehead. True, the chief executive, together with the justices of the state Supreme Court, constituted a council of revision empowered to veto acts of the assembly, but as laws could be passed over the veto by a mere majority vote, this meant nothing. Property qualifications for voting and office holding were swept away, and all adult males who had lived in the state for six months were allowed to vote. Mounting western nationalism was reflected in a provision that the governor must have been a citizen of the United States for at least thirty years.

The Constitution of 1818, democratic as it was, only paved the way for still more liberal changes during the next years; eventually even the state judges were popularly elected. Illinois, a frontier state, believed, even before Lincoln's classic statement, in rule of the people, by the people, and for the people.

Fifth, the frontier was a region of optimism, of boundless belief in the future. The Illinois frontiersman shared with his fellow Westerners an exuberant faith in progress; like them, too, he had a rambunctious confidence in his ability to make his dreams come true. One manifestation of this spirit was his willingness to support colleges. Although primary education was not fully established until the passage of the school law of 1855, institutions of higher learning began to multiply a quarter-century earlier, many of them church-supported schools dedicated to the task of producing intelligent congregations and learned ministers. By 1840 the thinly settled, poverty-ridden Prairie State boasted no less than twelve colleges. Pioneers unable to read and write were anxious to contribute time and money to assure their children a better opportunity, their community a richer culture. In few other states were frontiersmen willing to invest so heavily in the future.

On a less elevated plane, frontier optimism in Illinois found expression in speculative land buying. In no other wilderness commonwealth were so many acres engrossed by jobbers, so many "paper towns" laid out, so much absentee capital invested, in the years before 1850.

They were legion, the starry-eyed speculators who gobbled up the forests and prairies of the state. Many were farmers who bought more land than they could use, hoping to sell off the remainder to later comers; in 1850 seven million acres of Illinois land that had been sold but not improved was largely held by such purchasers.

Others were local businessmen or politicians who accumulated strategically located lands against the price rise they believed inevitable. Still others were wealthy Easterners or Southerners whose careers were devoted to speculation. Men of this ilk engrossed six million acres in Illinois between 1847 and 1855 by buying up soldiers' warrants at from 50 cents to $1.00 an acre; others of the same fraternity bought seven million acres of rich countryside near Springfield between 1833 and 1837. A favorite occupation of all these speculators was the accumulation of prospective town sites. Scarcely a bend or fork of a stream deep enough to wade in, scarcely a bay on Lake Michigan that would shelter a row-boat, scarcely a spot on any imagined canal or railroad that might conceivably be built in the future, that was not grabbed up by some land jobber. Most of these never got beyond the "paper" stage—where maps were drawn to induce gullible Easterners to buy town lots—yet in one northern Illinois "town" that had only one house, lots sold for $2,500 each, while a Chicago observer, witnessing the mad scramble for town sites, seriously proposed reserving one or two sections in each township for farming!

Finally, the frontier was an area where opportunism, rather than an enduring belief in any one theory or system, shaped the character of economic life and thought. Students of the westward movement, failing to recognize this, have frequently insisted that the West was a region of economic radicalism, of *laissez faire*, of rugged individualism. True, the frontiersman was an economic radical on occasion, but he was just as likely to be found among extreme conservatives; he was an individualist if such a course seemed feasible, but he did not hesitate to embrace the cause of collectivism if that path promised greater profits. He did believe in *laissez faire*—some of the time—but he was ready to demand national or state aid, and even governmental ownership of essential services, if such a course seemed wiser. The frontiersman, in other words, was a practical realist who believed in following the path that promised greatest immediate returns, regardless of past precedents. An opportunist rather than a theorist, he showed no embarrassment when forced to shift his thought with the changing times. The Illinois pioneer reflected this point of view. His vacillating opinion on the question of state-operated transporation facilities and on matters of finance illustrated how well he fitted into the frontier mold.

He first became aware of the transportation problem in the 1820s and 1830s when accumulating agricultural surpluses in interior Illinois brought home the need for highways to the main trade arteries of the West: the Mississippi River system and the Great Lakes. Statisticians were everywhere present to demonstrate the profits that would go to the pioneer if these could be built. A bushel of corn, they pointed out, sold in the interior for from 12 to 20 cents; at Chicago or on the Ohio River that same bushel fetched 50 cents. As the average farmer produced 60 bushels to the acre, lead-pencil engineers needed only enough ciphering paper to prove the stratospheric profits that would be the farmer's with better outlets. For every 100-acre farm the increased return would be $1,800 a year; for the ten million acres soon to be in production the saving would be $180,000,000! Roads and canals would transmute Illinois's povery into luxurious affluence. So all agreed, and they were equally sure that these outlets could only be built by the state government, which alone boasted resources and credit adequate for the giant task. By the beginning of the 1830s all Illinois was advocating an important experiment in state socialism.

Thus was the stage set for the fabulous internal improvement program launched during the next decade. An approving populace watched delightedly as the legislature authorized construction of the Illinois and Michigan Canal, secured a land grant from Congress, and placed the credit of the state behind the canal bonds that were marketed in the East and England to finance the project. This simply whetted the popular appetite for more. The canal benefited only one corner of Illinois; why should the rest be neglected when state-constructed railroads and canals would not only pay for themselves and enrich shippers but assure such profits that taxes could be abolished? Swept along on this wave of enthusiasm, Illinois adopted its famous Internal Improvements Act of 1837. This fantastic measure pledged the 400,000 poverty-ridden inhabitants of the frontier state to spend more than $10,000,000 on a network of railroads and canals which would crisscross in every direction. If the program had been less grandiose, and the times more auspicious, Illinois's dreams of a state-operated transportation system might have been realized. Instead the mere magnitude of the plan, the lack of managerial skill among those entrusted with its administration, and the Panic of 1837, brought a speedy end to the whole project. By 1841 work was at a standstill.

The effect of this debacle on public opinion was great. As Illinois farmers viewed the visible remains of their wrecked hopes—half-completed road beds, untidy slashes that marked the beginning of canals, a $15,000,000 state debt, a 50 per cent increase in land taxes, debt repudiation—a feeling of revulsion against state ownership swept across the state. During the next few years the one completed railroad, the Northern Cross, which had cost $250,000, was sold for $21,000 without a voice being raised in protest. The people wanted no more public control; private enterprise could run the risks in the future. For the next generation the citizens of Illinois advocated *laissez faire* as strenuously as they had governmental ownership a few years before.

Their frontier-like tendency toward opportunism was even better illustrated when two panics during the pioneer period brought them face to face with an age-old question: what banking and currency system would assure security and prosperity for their state? Twice they tried to solve the problem, and each time their answers differed.

The issue first arose in the era of hard times following the Panic of 1819. What was needed to stem the downward trend, all agreed, was more money. This could best be provided by local banks, backed by the faith and credit of the state, which could issue paper currency. On the crest of this pro-bank sentiment, the legislature in 1821 chartered the Bank of Illinois, capitalized at $300,000 to be subscribed by the state, and authorized to issue bank notes in small denominations to the full extent of its capitalization. The notes were made legal tender for all public and private debts; any creditor who refused to accept them was prohibited from seizing property pledged as security for at least three years. This, in other words, was an inflationary measure, designed principally to increase the amount of circulating currency. Popular meetings in Illinois and elsewhere went even farther along the path toward inflation by demanding a complete paper currency bearing no relationship to specie.

The inflationary trend was accentuated during the prosperous 1830s when money was in great demand for land speculation, business expansion, and the internal improvement program. By this time the State Bank of Illinois, with headquarters at Springfield, had joined the Bank of Illinois in catering to the state's financial needs. Both of these institutions were called upon to aid the public works program that was launched in 1837. This was done by increasing their capitalization, turning over to them state bonds in return for shares of bank stock, and then borrowing back the bank notes issued on the basis of the state's own securities. Officials honestly believed that this flimsy process would not only supply money for internal improvements but eventually pay for all construction, as the bank stock was expected to pay annual dividends of from 8 to 10 per cent. These returns, plus tolls from canals and railroads, would soon retire the entire investment and provide so much income that taxes could be abolished! This was the talk, not of wild dreamers, but of sober businessmen and state leaders.

Illinois learned its lesson when the Panic of 1837 tumbled down its speculative house of cards. With hard times anti-bank feeling swept across the state. Farmers who owed money to the banks grumbled that they could not continue their payments. Others who were paid for their produce in the depreciated notes of the two institutions complained that they were being swindled. Still others lost heavily when the banks finally collapsed. More were convinced that there was a direct connection between the banks and the panic. The depression, they told themselves, was a product of the wild currency fluctuations that followed the overissue of state bank notes. These might benefit eastern capitalists, but every fluctuation drove the poor man, who could never understand such financial mysteries, deeper into debt. His only protection was to abolish banks and paper money, returning to the security of a solid gold and silver currency. "A bank of earth is the best bank," wrote one, "and a plow share the best share," while another declared: "Banks to help the farmer appear to me like feudal lords to defend the people." The Illinois farmer of the post-panic era was the most conservative of all Americans on financial questions.

The reaction of the state's pioneers to the panics of 1819 and 1837 demonstrated the opportunistic nature of frontier economic thought. In one case they moved leftward along the road to inflation; in the other they swung so far to the economic right that the nation's business leaders and bankers seemed financial radicals by comparison.

Reactions such as these stamped the Illinois frontiersman as typically American. He was typical, too, in his optimism, his democracy, his ingenuity, and his faith in progress. Molded by the frontier environment and strengthened by contacts with fellow pioneers from all the western world, he served as a perfect answer to Hector St. John de Crèvecoeur's famous query: "What then is the American, this new man?"

JOHN W. ALLEN

affectionately known as "Mr. Southern Illinois," had been a
teacher, school administrator, lecturer, and curator of the
Museum at Southern Illinois University, Carbondale. He was
a past president of the Illinois Folklore Society, and director
as well as president (1956–57) of the Illinois State Historical Society. He was known also for his newspaper column
titled "It Happened in Illinois" and for *Randolph County
Notes; Pope County Notes;* and *Legends and Lore of Southern Illinois.*

This article appeared in the *Journal of the Illinois State
Historical Society,* volume 42, number 4 (December 1949),
pages 411–423.

SLAVERY AND NEGRO SERVITUDE IN POPE COUNTY, ILLINOIS

JOHN W. ALLEN

A great deal of interesting information lies unnoted in the county
records of southern Illinois. In searching for data concerning the
history of various counties, the author has found numerous refer-
ences to slavery and to other forms of Negro servitude in this
section of the state. The most valuable information is, of course, to
be found in the records of the older counties. For instance, the first
four deed books of Pope County contain many recordings concerning Negro slaves and servants. A part of the information gathered
from these books is presented here in the belief that it will prove
helpful to those interested in the history of slavery in southern
Illinois, for the Pope County records are typical of those in other
older counties of this part of the state.

These records reveal that the practices relating to slavery and
Negro servitude in southern Illinois did not conform to the statutes
enacted for their regulation. It is also evident that public officials
were aware of the inconsistency and even participated in the eva-
sions. Before presenting the information from Pope County, it
might be well to review briefly the general history of slavery in
Illinois—with such an outline in mind, the Pope County story may
be better understood.

It seems that the first Negro slaves of Illinois were those brought from San Domingo by Philippe François Renault. Several hundred of these people reached Illinois about 1720, perhaps in the latter part of 1719. Some of them were used in Renault's mining ventures in northwestern Illinois and in Missouri. Others were used in farming operations about the now-vanished village of St. Philippe in Monroe County. In addition to the imported slaves, a number of Indians were also held in bondage. However, the total number of slaves in the territory seems to have shown little increase after 1720. According to the *Jesuit Relations,* records of missions established by the Jesuits, there were only 300 Negroes and 60 Indians held as slaves in Illinois in 1750.

In 1763 when this territory was ceded to the English, the latter did not interfere with the practice of slavery. Hence, when it came into the possession of Virginia at the end of the Revolutionary War, nothing was done to restrict the existing practice. When Virginia ceded the territory to the newly formed federal government, the French, Canadians, and other inhabitants of Kaskaskia, with those of other villages in the territory, assumed that they would be allowed to retain their properties and "ancient privileges." The Ordinance of 1787 provided that there should be no slavery nor involuntary servitude "otherwise than in the punishment of crime, whereof the party shall have been duly convicted." However, Governor Arthur St. Clair, of the Northwest Territory, and Governor William Henry Harrison, of the Indiana Territory, maintained that this did not affect slaves held prior to 1787, and both agreed that additional slaves could not be brought in. The law barring the introduction of more slaves was evaded by indenturing Negroes brought in after the ban had been placed.

Indiana Territory, of which Illinois was then a part, legalized this practice by action of the Governing Council and by action of the Territorial Legislature, in 1803, 1805, and 1807. By these acts it was legally permissible to indenture Negro males up to thirty-five and Negro females up to thirty-two years, though indentures were generally for longer terms, on some occasions for as long as ninety-nine years. These regulations were adopted by Illinois Territory upon its separation from Indiana in 1809.

The Illinois Constitution of 1818 forbade slavery, but it did not specifically regulate against the slavery already established. To evade this provision of the new constitution, the practice of indenturing was continued, but it was legal to indenture a servant for only one year. In some instances the constitutional provision against slavery was simply ignored. Children born to an indentured Negro woman could be indentured, the boys until they were twenty-one years old, and girls until they were eighteen. Indentures already in force were not interfered with in any way. Few paid heed to this limit of time.

The legislature of the new state, in March 1819, re-enacted the principles of the earlier territorial laws. These laws passed by the first General Assembly became known as the "Black Laws." Under the provisions of this act, a Negro could not become a resident of the state unless he had a certificate of freedom from a court of record. Without such a certificate the Negro could be sold for one year. Should he have the required certificate and be admitted to the state, he still could not bring suit, testify in court when a white person was concerned, or vote; nor could he travel except in very restricted areas. The whole plan seems to have been intended to drive free Negroes into voluntary indenture. The Negro's plight was indeed a sorry one.

Travelers crossing the state with their slaves and other property often expressed a desire to settle here, but some hesitated to do so because of the ban on slavery. This situation led those citizens of Illinois who favored slavery to demand a convention to amend the state constitution and make slavery legal. A vote for such a convention was authorized by the legislature in 1823. In the general election that followed, August 2, 1824, there were 4,972 votes cast for a convention (for slavery) and 6,640 cast against a convention (against slavery). Pope County cast 273 votes for and 124 against.

This election did not end slavery in Illinois. In some counties, principally in the southern part of the state, indentured servants and slaves were held after 1824. This is shown by numerous certificates of freedom executed after that date. Though the institution of slavery was definitely disappearing the general attitude toward the Negro could hardly be termed favorable.

In 1862 the people of Illinois voted, by a majority of 107,650, to refuse admission to Negroes. At the same time they voted by a majority of 176,271 to prohibit Negroes from voting or holding office. In 1862, a Negro in Hancock County was arrested for being in the state ten days and intending to remain permanently. He was found guilty and fined. Interested citizens appealed his case to the

State Supreme Court, which in 1864 upheld the verdict of the lower court.

Such incidents as these perhaps more clearly reveal the general feeling toward Negroes than does the fact that the legislative acts of 1865 ratified the Thirteenth, Fourteenth, and Fifteenth Amendments to the United States Constitution and repealed the "Black Laws" of 1819 and similar ones enacted in 1853.

The foregoing brief outline of the general history of slavery and the treatment of Negroes in Illinois furnishes a background for a more detailed study of Negro servitude in Pope County. The first entry concerning a Negro servant in the records at Golconda is a document filed on June 25, 1816, about six months after the formation of the county. By this indenture, Silvey, a Negro woman about twenty-four years old, on June 22, 1815, bound herself to serve John Morris of Gallatin County, then including portions of Pope, "for a term of forty years next ensuing." Silvey received "$400.00, in hand, paid, receipt of which is hereby acknowledged." She was also to receive "good and sufficient meat, drink, lodging and apparel together with all other needful conveniences fit for such a servant." Silvey pledged herself to "faithfully serve, obey, not absent herself from her work, and to not embezzle or waist [sic] her master's property." With this indenture, a bond was filed, signed by John Morris and one surety, guaranteeing that Silvey would not become a public charge of Pope County. Except for length of service pledged, this indenture complied with the law of Illinois Territory at that time. In its form it is typical of such contracts.

In the majority of indentures recorded, an entry similar to the one where Silvey acknowledges the receipt of a certain sum of money "in hand, paid, the receipt of which is hereby acknowledged" will be found. It is to be seriously doubted whether the Negroes actually received the money.

The second entry noted was a "Bill of Bargain and Sale" that states, "Know ye all men by these presents that I, Jessie Jones, of the State of Kentucky and county of Caldwell, have this day bargained and sold and delivered unto Thomas Ferguson of Illinois Territory and County of Johnson, a certain Negro Man named Jeffery about thirty years of age, and for consideration of the sum of five hundred and twenty-five dollars." This bill of sale was filed in the office of Joshua Scott, recorder of Pope County, on November 28, 1816. Since this document is an outright bill of sale, it did not conform to the legal requirements of Illinois Territory.

The next entry concerning a servant is an indenture acknowledged before William Greenup, county clerk of Randolph County, and dated December 17, 1810. It was not recorded in Pope County until November 28, 1816. By this indenture, similar in form to the one between John Morris of Gallatin County and the Negro woman named Silvey, George, a "Negro Man" about twenty-one years of age, for a consideration of "five hundred dollars, lawful money of the United States," bound himself to serve David J. Black for the term of sixty years.

The next entry points to a method approximating outright slave trade in the Illinois Territory, since the consent of the servant is not indicated as having been secured. In this case, Louis LaChapelle of Randolph County had Isaac, a Negro man about twenty-three years of age, bound to him for a period of forty years for an indicated consideration of $500. This indenture was acknowledged before William Greenup, county clerk of Randolph County, Illinois, on February 3, 1815. LaChapelle then made a notation on the indenture as follows: "—for value receive [sic] I asign [sic] over all my write [sic] to the within indenter [sic] unto Thomas Ferguson and hath this day delivered the above indentere [sic] servant as the above indenters [sic] calls for as witness my hand and seal this 7th day of June 1815. L. LaChapelle."

Another record indicates the outright purchase of a slave by Thomas Ferguson, a citizen of Pope County. This slave, Toney, had been purchased by Richard Thomas Porter, of Edgecomb County, North Carolina, for "200 pounds currency of North Carolina." Porter was "to have and hold forever." Then, on April 26, 1809, the following transaction was recorded: "For value received, I, Richard Thomas Porter—do assign over all my write [sic]—to Thomas Ferguson." Porter also "will warrant and defend title." This transaction evidently took place in Pope County, since it was acknowledged before Joshua Scott, who was serving as county clerk.

David Black then appears with a "slave" named George, whom he had purchased of Thomas Dunkerson, of Christian County, Kentucky, on November 19, 1810, for $400. This slave was sold to Thomas Ferguson on April 2, 1811. In the next recorded transaction, Wiley Davis of Eddyville, Kentucky, assigned his interest in Letty, a slave about twenty years old, and son about one year and ten months old, to Ferguson. In the following entry Ferguson bound a Negro man named Anthony for thirty years in return for "a certain lot numbered 163 in Sarahville, now Golconda." Anthony was to have immediate possession and "enjoy the rents and profits" during his term of servitude. The value of the lot must have been negligible, since lots 161 and 168, fully as well located, sold within a year from the time of Anthony's indenture for $3.00 each. On July 7, 1816, Jeffery, mentioned in the second entry on the county records, and previously referred to in this discussion as having been "bought" from Jessie Jones by Thomas Ferguson, voluntarily bound himself to Ferguson for a period of thirty years for lot numbered 167. This lot was not transferred to Jeffery until December 1, 1821, more than five years after he had signed the indenture. On July 27, 1816, Lettie, or Lettice, a Negro woman about twenty-eight years old, was bound to Thomas Ferguson for a period of thirty years for a lot numbered 166 in Sarahville. The lot mentioned was not transferred to Lettie until December 1, 1821. We next find a bill of sale whereby John Ditterline on December 18, 1816, transferred his rights to Mary, "a slave for life," to Ferguson for a consideration of $500. This transaction took place in Pope County as evidenced by its acknowledgment before Joshua Scott, county clerk.

In April 1817, Anthony, Lettie, Jeffery, and George agreed to go to Missouri Territory with Ferguson. If this trip was made as indicated, it would appear that Lettie and Jeffery were later safely returned to Illinois since lots numbered 166 and 167 were transferred to them on December 1, 1821, but no later mention of either Anthony or George was found on the records.

Other indentures followed. Betty, a Negro woman about twenty-two years of age, bound herself to Samuel Langdon for a period of sixty years for a consideration of $400. This indenture was acknowledged before Robert Lacey, judge of the county court, on February 8, 1817. Nancy Williams, a Negro woman from Missouri Territory, bound herself to Jacob Robinson for a term of twenty years for a consideration of $500. This indenture was executed before Joshua Scott, county clerk of Pope County. In April 1817, Daniel and Vina bound themselves to Joshua Scott, county recorder, for forty years. The consideration named in each case was $400. These indentures for Daniel and Vina were acknowledged before Joshua Scott, and both indentures were witnessed by Prudence M. Rose and Polly Pankey.

On August 20, 1817, Anny bound herself to Isom Clay for sixteen years for a consideration of $400. One week later David Turner and Millie, "late out of Jefferson County, Virginia," bound themselves to David Cowan for fifty years. A consideration of $400 is named in each case. On January 6, 1818, Judith, about seventeen years old, "last [sic] of the Territory of Missouri," bound herself to William Wilson, of Pope County, for a period of ninety-nine years. For this term of service she is supposed to have received $400. On February 13, 1818, Linda, a Negro woman about nineteen years old, "last [sic] out of Missouri Territory" likewise bound herself to William Wilson for a period of ninety-nine years for a named consideration of $400. This indenture would have expired on February 13, 1917.

A Negro boy named Anthony, about eighteen years old, was sold on December 14, 1820, by John Henry, of Pope County, to Elizabeth Henry, of Logan County, Kentucky, for the sum of $612. This bill of sale was certified by Craven P. Hester, a justice of the peace for Pope County. This would definitely indicate the sale as taking place in Illinois. Anthony had not previously appeared in the records of the county as a slave.

According to tradition, and occasionally by implication, other outright sales of slaves occurred in Pope County after the admission of Illinois to statehood. An outright sale was made in the settlement of the estate of Larkin Kesterson, who died on May 25, 1829. In his will, Kesterson provided "that his said executor shall sell his two Negro men, Macklin and Frank, together." This provision of the will was carried out by Robert Kesterson, father of the deceased and executor of his estate, when the Negroes were sold in November 1829, for $325. Neither Macklin nor Frank was previously recorded in the circuit clerk's records of slaves.

These instances of unrecorded slaves held by Kesterson, as well as the case of Anthony cited in the previous paragraph, coupled with unverified traditions, would seem to indicate that there were numerous other slaves owned in Pope County. Negro indentures were not found on the deed records in the circuit clerk's office after this date, though they are referred to in other county records.

A new turn of affairs is indicated in the next group of entries dated August 19, 1823. At that time William Beams emancipated and issued certificates of freedom to twelve slaves as listed below:

Abraham .... about sixteen years old
Martin .... nine years old
Gilbert .... about twenty-one years old
Cunningham .... about eight years old
Sam .... about twelve years old
Thomas .... nine years old
Hetty .... six weeks old
Lotty .... about seventeen years old
Nelly .... about forty-five years old
Rody .... about thirteen years old
Luckey .... about twenty-two years old
Nancy .... about sixteen years old

These are the first emancipations found recorded in Pope County. The certificates are signed by Beams, with his mark, and are witnessed by Edmund Richmond.

The next recorded emancipations were made on February 13, 1830, when Wiley Jones granted freedom to "Chaney a woman of color twenty-six years old of low stature" and to her children, Anne, Judah, James, and Alfred. All this was "for and in consideration of faithful service." The emancipations made by Beams and Jones were evidently of slaves or servants held in Pope County.

The record of Fannie Mac, "a woman of color," is somewhat singular. Fannie Mac purchased her son, Caesar, a slave, from Stephen Smelser, of Calway County, Kentucky, on September 14, 1835, for the sum of $550. One hundred and fifty dollars was paid in cash and the balance by a note with security. On January 29, 1836, she, "for love and affection," emancipated Caesar. Fannie Mac thus held, for a short time, her own son as a slave.

A slightly different case was that of a slave named Lewis, brought from Arkansas to Pope County for the express purpose of emancipation on March 15, 1838. The next year a somewhat similar case is found when Eli Roden, of Pope County, formerly of Arkansas, emancipated "Mary Ann, a woman of color, a slave," and her children, Melvina about four years old, Margaretta about three years old, and Henrietta about one year old.

David A. Smith, on March 22, 1817, secured the approval of an Alabama court and freed his slaves, William, William's wife, Isabel, and their six children. These certificates of freedom were filed for record in Pope County on November 22, 1838.

Other certificates of freedom for former slaves appear on later Pope County records. Thus, on May 10, 1845, "Moses, a man of color," after extended and complicated legal procedures, establishes the fact that he had purchased his freedom, along with that of his wife and son, from their Tennessee owner for $1,450. In these proceedings Moses was represented by "next friend" John Stephenson. These certificates were filed in Pope County and indicate that these Negroes became residents there.

On the same date, May 10, 1845, "Jerry, a colored man," filed his certificate of freedom in Pope County after he had failed to secure passage to Liberia from Hardeman County, Tennessee. On May 27, of the same year, Winnie, who, after involved court procedures in Missouri and in Kentucky, won her freedom, filed the certificate in the office of the recorder in Pope County. The records in this case cover about ten pages and indicate that Winnie had been illegally in slavery for some years.

Slaves were evidently held until a comparatively late date in Pope County. This is indicated by the fact that Lucinda, and her eight children, named as slaves, were freed by the will of William R. Adams, which was dated December 28, 1846.

One of the most interesting certificates during this period is that filed for Matthew Scott on September 22, 1846. In this certificate, the freedom of Scott and his family, consisting of a wife and nine children, is established along with the fact that Scott had received a military discharge from the "company of Captain William McCalley in the General Jackson War."

On July 31, 1850, Patsey, who had been born free in Virginia, established the fact in this county by registering her certificate in the recorder's office. On the same day, Theodore Mundle, through an affadavit filed by Robert T. Leeper, established the fact that he was a free Negro and had lived with his mother in the county for the past five years.

In the inspection made, no later records of certificates of freedom were found on the records for Pope County.

In all cases concerning the freeing of slaves, a somewhat detailed description is given. This procedure was used so that the one emancipated could be readily identified. In the case of slaves or servants brought into the state and indentured, it was required that bonds be furnished in order to guarantee that such Negroes would not become public charges of the county. Laws of the period also required that similar bonds be filed for Negroes being emancipated. In some instances this requirement was fulfilled. In other instances no record of a bond occurs; it was in compliance with this demand that William Beams, on August 19, 1823, filed bond for $13,000 with the county court.

The foregoing instances are cited as being indicative of the course of slavery and Negro servitude in a typical southern Illinois county. Other uncited records of slaves and indentured servants are to be found in various Pope County records. A careful search fails to reveal the later disposition of those bound to a term of service. The records do not show that these servants and slaves were freed when the periods for which they were bound expired. Tradition likewise fails to provide an answer.

BENJAMIN P. THOMAS

the noted Lincoln scholar, received his Ph.D. in 1929 from the Johns Hopkins University. He taught history and then became executive secretary of the Abraham Lincoln Association, Springfield, Illinois. He was editor of the *Abraham Lincoln Quarterly,* 1940–1953, and an editorial advisor to the *Collected Works of Abraham Lincoln* edited by Roy Basler, 1945–1953. Among his publications are *Lincoln's New Salem; Portrait for Posterity; Lincoln and His Biographers,* but his best book is the incomparable *Abraham Lincoln: A Biography.*

This article was published first in the *Transactions of the Illinois State Historical Society* for 1934, pages 61–75.

LINCOLN AND NEW SALEM

BENJAMIN P. THOMAS

Until recent years, Lincoln's heredity and the different environments in which he spent his boyhood, youth and early manhood were looked upon as drab, sordid, uninspiring and as obstacles that he in some mysterious manner succeeded in surmounting. Recent research has traced his family back for generations and revealed him not as rising from the dregs of society, as some had supposed, but as the product of decent, sober, respectable, if unlearned and unambitious parents, and of a line of typical American pioneer ancestors.

The work of Frederick Jackson Turner and his school of historians has given us a better understanding of the influence of the frontier in shaping American institutions, characteristics and life. With this comes a better appreciation of the part the frontier played in shaping Lincoln. We are beginning to realize that, while Lincoln's early environment was hard and crude in some respects, it was also a powerful developer of self-reliance, independence and energy.

Lincoln had less than a year of formal schooling, for the rest, he was self-made. He learned, he was not taught. What he read he mastered, but he did not read widely. He learned principally by mingling with people and discussing things with them, by observation of their ways and their reactions—in short, from his environment. Carl Sandburg, in the preface to his *Abraham Lincoln: The Prairie Years*, says that Lincoln was "keenly sensitive to the words and ways of people around him. Therefore those people, their homes, occupations, songs, proverbs, schools, churches, politics, should be set forth with the incessant suggestion of change that went always with pioneer life. They are the backgrounds on which the life of Lincoln moved, had its rise and flow and was moulder and moulded."

With this conception New Salem assumes a new importance as a factor in Lincoln's development. No other period of his life lends itself so readily to intensive study of his environment as do his six years there. His physical surroundings have been recreated. The names and occupations and something of the character of most of the inhabitants of the village are known. Information on the village life is available in letters, newspapers, reminiscences of residents or their descendants and miscellaneous sources.

New Salem was founded in 1829, by John M. Camron and James Rutledge. Its beginnings were a mill, a store and a saloon. At first its growth was slow; then, in 1832, expectation of the Sangamon River's being made navigable for light-draft steamboats and anticipation of New Salem's becoming a thriving river town caused a boom in it and the surrounding country. But navigation of the river proved impracticable, and by 1833 or 1834 New Salem's growth had stopped. By 1836 it had begun to decline. Its inaccessibility, a conviction that it had no future as a river town, and restriction of its trading area by the growth of other towns induced its residents to try their luck again somewhere else. In 1839, when Menard County was set off from Sangamon and Petersburg was made the county seat, New Salem received its final blow. Its few remaining inhabitants moved to the more promising town, some of them taking their houses with them. By 1840, New Salem did not exist.

At the height of its prosperity it contained about twenty-five families and at least thirty log or frame structures, among them a combination saw and grist mill, a tavern, three or four stores, a "grocery" or saloon, a carding machine and storehouse for wool, a cooper shop, a blacksmith shop and a tannery. Among its residents were a shoemaker, a hatter, a wheelwright, a cabinet maker, and two doctors.

Most of the buildings were log houses rather than cabins. The frontiersman distinguished between these types of structures. Peck's *New Guide for Emigrants* (1837) says: "A *log house,* in western parlance, differs from a cabin, in the logs being hewn on two sides to an equal thickness, before raising; in having a framed and shingled roof, a brick or stone chimney, windows, tight floors, and are frequently clapboarded on the outside, and plastered within. A log house, thus finished, costs more than a framed one."

New Salem was the center of a prosperous agricultural region. Within a radius of 10 or 15 miles were scattered farms and smaller settlements—Clary's Grove to the southwest, Little Grove to the west, Rock Creek to the south, Sand Ridge to the north, Sugar Grove and Irish Grove to the northeast, Indian Point and Athens to the east. From all these places the village drew trade and visitors. In August 1834, C. J. F. Clarke described conditions in the New Salem neighborhood to his friends in the East.

> He wrote: I have been requested by all those that I have rec'd letters from to write what the people live in, what they live on, etc. I will tell you. I should judge that nine tenths of them live in log houses and cabbins; the other tenth either in brick or framed houses. The people generally have large farmes and have not thought so much of fine buildings as they have of adding land to land, they are now however beginning to build better houses. Many a rich farmer lives in a house not half so good as your old hogs pen and not any larger. We live generally on bacon, eggs, bread, coffee. Potatoes are not much used, ten bushels in a large crop and more than is used in a family in a year. Sweet potatoes are raised here very easy. The wheat crop is very good, corn is very promising. Mother wishes to know what kind of trees grow here. We have all kinds except pine and hemlock. Houses are built of white oak, black walnut, white walnut, and some linn. Almost all kinds of fruit grows here spontaneously; among them are the crab apple, cherry, two or three kinds of plums, black and white haw, gooseberrys, etc., etc. The black walnut is a beautiful tree, the wood of which is very much like mahogony. There is a considerable quantity of cotton raised here but none for exportation. Tobacco grows well here, etc. etc.

Most of New Salem's inhabitants were young, enthusiastic, full of hope and confidence. They were of the third wave of migration, having been preceded by the roving hunters and trappers and the restless squatters. They were homebuilders, most of them with some stock and capital, who bought land or hoped to do so soon.

They, too, were restless, however, and many of them moved on in search of something better. Courage, persistence, ingenuity were the requisites of success. Wealth, "kin and kin-in-law didn't count a cuss." Government was of, by and for the people, with public opinion as its principal sanction.

There were two elements in the place. One was a rough and roistering, happy-go-lucky crowd known as the Clary's Grove boys. They lived in and around the community of that name, but came to New Salem to drink, gossip, trade and play. Their hangout was Clary's grocery; for Bill Clary, owner of the grocery, was a brother of John Clary, the founder of Clary's Grove. Physical strength and courage were their ideals. In individual and free-for-all fights they had demonstrated their superiority over the boys from other settlements, and they ruled the town when they chose to. T. G. Onstot recorded that "they trimmed the manes and tails of horses, cut bridles so that but a little remained to break at the first pull; cut girths, put stones under saddles so as to cause riders to be thrown mounting."

Less picturesque, but more important in the life of the village, were men of a more serious turn like Dr. John Allen, Dr. Francis Regnier, James Rutledge, the tavern keeper, Mentor Graham, the schoolmaster, Henry Onstot, the cooper, Joshua Miller, the blacksmith.

But the fact that we can distinguish two types of inhabitants does not mean that social lines were drawn or social distinctions made. Doctor and laborer, preacher and ne'er-do-well took part together in the village life. Grocery keeper and temperance advocate, Yankee and Southerner, rubbed elbows with each other. Diverse types were represented in the groups that idled at the stores. Discussions in such groups brought out differences of opinion and divergent points of view. Men learned what other men were thinking.

The majority of the settlers in and around New Salem were Southerners. The Rutledges and Camrons came from Georgia and South Carolina, stopping in Tennessee, Kentucky, and southern Illinois before arriving at New Salem. Peter Lukins, the cobbler, and his brother Gregory were Kentuckians. The Grahams and Onstots came from Kentucky and Tennessee; the Chrismans from Virginia; the Berrys, who lived on Rock Creek but took a prominent part in New Salem life, came from Virginia by way of Kentucky and Indiana. Thus, here, as well as in his former homes in Kentucky and Indiana, Lincoln lived in a Southern pioneer atmosphere. His contact with these people helped him understand the Southern temperament and point of view.

Interspersed with the predominant Southern element were some Yankees and a few settlers from the Middle States. Doctor Allen was a native of Vermont and had some of the characteristics of the New England reformer. He organized a temperance society and a Sunday School in the village. He was a strict Sabbatarian, giving all Sunday fees to the church, and having all his Sunday food cooked on Saturday. Sam Hill, the storekeeper, came from New Jersey; John McNamar, his partner, came from New York. C. J. F. Clarke and Mathew S. Marsh, who lived on nearby farms, were Yankees. The Southerners usually came by families; the Easterners were individuals who had separated from their families and had come west to seek health, wealth or adventure.

Most of the people in the community made their living from the soil, or with their hands; but the place was not devoid of intellectuality. James Rutledge is said to have owned twenty-five or thirty books. He was organizer and president of the New Salem Debating Society. Jack Kelso, a lazy, dreamy man, who was an expert fisherman and marksman, brother-in-law of the blacksmith, could quote long passages of Shakespeare and Burns. Doctor Allen was a graduate of Dartmouth College Medical School. Doctor Regnier and Rev. John M. Berry of Rock Creek, who often preached in New Salem, were fairly well educated. T. G. Onstot, son of the cooper, said that Berry did as much as any man to "civilize and Christianize the central part of Illinois." William F. Berry, son of John M. Berry and Lincoln's partner in business; David Rutledge, son of the tavern keeper; Bill Greene, who clerked with Lincoln in Offut's store, and Harvey Ross, who carried the mail to and from New Salem, attended Illinois College at Jacksonville, thirty miles from New Salem. According to C. J. F. Clarke, that institution was "doing more for this country than any eastern man could expect," and its students "almost astonish the old folks when they come home."

New Salem had no church, but services were held in the schoolhouse, across Greene's Rocky Branch to the south of the village, and in the homes of the inhabitants. The strongest religious sects were the "Hardshell" Baptists, Cumberland Presbyterians and Methodists. Strange new sects were continually forming, however, as the self-reliant pioneer—usually with untrained mind and faulty logic—exercised the prerogative of interpreting the Scriptures for himself. Clarke noted that besides the denominations mentioned there were many others that "deserve no name."

Every year camp meetings were held at Concord and Rock Creek. The famous Peter Cartwright, whose home was at Pleasant Plains, ten miles from New Salem, labored in the New Salem district and preached often at these meetings, which were of the old-fashioned emotional sort. Sometimes members of the congregation, overcome with hysteria, would be seized with the "jerks." "Usually persons taken with the jerks," wrote Onstot, "to get relief would rise up and dance, some would try to run away, but could not, some would resist, and on such the jerks were very severe." The women especially were addicted to this hysteria. The first jerk would loosen bonnets, caps and combs "and so sudden would be the jerking of the head that their long, loose hair would crack almost as loud as a waggoner's whip."

Besides the church members there were some free thinkers in the community who read Thomas Paine's *Age of Reason* and Constantine de Volney's *Ruins of Empire,* and who questioned the pronouncements of the preachers. The church members had little hope for them. The Baptists, Clarke observed, "preach the hardest election doctring that I ever heard. They say they were created for Heaven (the church members) and such as die in their sins were created for Hell, or in other words, God made a part of mankind for eternal happiness and the ballance for endless misery. This is a kind of doctering I cant stand."

The Methodists and Baptists looked askance at preachers who were college trained. Preachers of the old school suspected college men of having no religion in their hearts and knowing nothing about it except what they learned at school. Written sermons were taboo; and even preparation was frowned upon by some. A true preacher got his inspiration directly from the Lord as he spoke.

Deeply concerned with creeds and the externals of religion, church members despaired not only of unbelievers and skeptics but of those of different faiths as well. Julian Sturtevant, coming from Yale to teach at Illinois College, wrote: "In Illinois I met for the first time a divided Christian community, and was plunged without warning into a sea of sectarian rivalries, which was kept in constant agitation." Methodists and Baptists argued endlessly "about the way to heaven, whether it was by water or dry land," while both scorned the "high toned doctrines of Calvinism" and the "muddy waters of Campbellism." Peter Cartwright told of a mother of another denomination who, at one of his revivals, forcibly tore her two daughters from the altar to prevent their becoming Methodists.

Yet religion was a potent force for good, and in some respects an intellectual stimulus. Sermons, poor as they often were, gave many people their only examples of creative mental work, while discussions of salvation, baptism, morals and faith provided a sort of intellectual free-for-all. According to Herndon, Lincoln, during the New Salem period, was a free thinker. He must have entered with zest into the theological arguments, and profited by the niceties of thought, the subtle distinctions and the fine-spun argument that they necessitated. Yet while he enjoyed them as a mental exercise, and while he eventually attained to a deep faith, the emotionalism and excesses of the frontier religion and the bitterness of sectarian rivalry must have been repellent to him, and were probably a cause of his lasting reluctance to affiliate with any sect.

Lincoln came to New Salem in late July 1831. Long, lean, awkward, with big frame and coarsened hands, he was a typical youth of the American frontier. His total schooling did not amount to a year; but principally by his own efforts he had learned to write a clear, distinctive hand, and to read and cypher "to the rule of three." He had made his living as a laborer and river man. He came to New Salem to work as a clerk in Denton Offut's store and to run the mill, which Offut had rented. His first contacts were with the rougher element, with whom he speedily established himself. His courage and physical prowess commanded their respect, while his honesty and truthfulness soon won their confidence. The Clary's Grove boys became his staunch admirers, and followed and supported him in anything he did. As time passed he won the respect and admiration of the better element as well.

In the spring of 1832, when he had been in New Salem less than a year, the Black Hawk War broke out, and Lincoln and many of the other young men of the community, immediately volunteered. Already his popularity was such that he was elected captain of his company. He served for eighty days, enlisting as a private when the term of enlistment of his company expired and it was mustered out. He saw no fighting, but from this, his only military experience, he learned something of soldiers and the soldier's life, the value of leadership, discipline, morale. Around the campfires he enhanced the reputation for story telling that he had already made. He wrestled with champions of other companies and won still greater admiration of his strength and athletic skill. His experience supplied him with a store of anecdotes. He met men whose friendship was valuable to him—John Calhoun, who later appointed him deputy surveyor; John T. Stuart, who became his law partner; John J. Hardin, and other rising young Illinois politicians.

Returning from the war, Lincoln found himself out of a job, for Offut's store had failed. Before enlisting he had announced himself as a candidate for the state legislature, and he now plunged into his campaign. But he was not elected. He had lived in New Salem only a year, and was still relatively unknown outside of that community.

Lincoln pondered over what he should do. He thought of becoming a blacksmith, but decided against it; thought of studying law, but was afraid that with his deficient education it was useless to attempt it. Eventually he bought a half-interest in a store on credit. Soon he and his partner, William F. Berry, bought out one of their two rivals in the mercantile business and merged their two stores. But neither Lincoln nor Berry was cut out for a business career. The store failed, Berry died, and Lincoln was left with a burden of debt from which he was not free for fifteen years.

He was greatly discouraged, and in his autobiography, written in 1860, said that he was reduced to the elemental problem of securing bread to keep body and soul together. The easy way out would have been to move away and make a fresh start somewhere else, leaving his debts unpaid. But Lincoln remained. He did not blame the town for his failure, as many men would have done. He believed that if he could succeed anywhere he could do it at New Salem. He had no intention of evading his obligations, and he wished to remain with his friends.

Biographers and historians have accepted the idea that he had serious difficulty in making a living at New Salem. But this could hardly have been so. Except for the harassment of debt he was not bad off; for with his strength and skill and reputation for honesty he could have had no serious trouble getting work. Travelers in Sangamon County in the early thirties remarked time and again about the scarcity of laborers and the good wages paid to them. Patrick Shirreff, a Scotsman, for example, stated that "labor is scarce and highly remunerated. A good farming help obtains $120, an indifferent one $100 a year, with bed and board." He calculated that this was equivalent to 80 acres of land a year, and in proportion to the cost of living and land, about 800 times as much as English farm laborers got. Under such circumstances Lincoln could have had no difficulty earning a living, and certainly he could not have been in want. It is significant that in 1837, when he left New Salem, he owned a part interest in a forty-seven acre tract of land and two lots in Springfield.

Lincoln could make a living, but he was not content to remain a laborer. He was looking for a chance to better himself. In his spare time he took advantage of the opportunity to improve his education. In 1832, during his last months in Offut's store, he studied grammar. Mentor Graham, the schoolmaster, told him that John Vance, who lived north of New Salem, owned a copy of Kirkham's *Grammar,* and Lincoln walked six or eight miles to get it. He studied it assiduously, and with Graham's help mastered it. He studied history at New Salem, and his interest in literature, especially Shakespeare and Burns, was stimulated by Jack Kelso, at whose home he boarded during part of his residence. During the winter of 1832 he became a regular attendant at the meetings of the New Salem Debating Society. Back in Indiana he had sometimes stopped work to make extemporaneous speeches to stumps and corn stalks, and in Macon County, where he lived before coming to New Salem, he had discomfited two visiting politicians by an impromptu reply to their speeches. His efforts at New Salem were his first attempts at formal debate. The members of the society, who had expected only humorous remarks from him, were amazed at his ability.

By the spring of 1832, when he announced his candidacy for the legislature, he had already acquired the knack of terse and lucid statement which characterized his later style. J. G. Nicolay and John Hay, his war-time secretaries and biographers, who were more familiar with his later writings than anyone, said that the circular which he addressed to the voters in this campaign was written almost precisely in "the style of his later years. The errors of grammar and construction which spring invariably from the effort to avoid redundancy of expression remained with him through life. He seemed to grudge the space required for necessary parts of speech. But his language was at twenty-two, as it was thirty years later, the simple and manly attire of his thought, with little attempt at ornament and none at disguise."

On May 7, 1833, Lincoln's ambition was gratified to some extent when he was appointed postmaster at New Salem. He held the position until the removal of the office to Petersburg on May 30, 1836. As postmaster he could read all the newspapers that came to the village, and at this time formed the habit of newspaper reading. This broadened his outlook and, continued through life, furnishes a partial explanation of his ability to understand the public mind. Financially the job was not much help to him. His salary depended upon the gross receipts of the office, which were small. No figures are available for the New Salem office; but from the receipts of some of the other Illinois offices at that time we can estimate that Lincoln probably received twenty-five or thirty dollars a year. He supplemented this by doing all sorts of odd jobs—splitting rails, helping at the mill, working in the fields, serving as local agent for the *Sangamo Journal,* tending store for Hill. On election days he often made a dollar by serving as clerk, and sometimes returned the poll book to the courthouse in Springfield for which service he was paid at the rate of twenty cents a mile, coming and returning.

In the autumn of 1833, he was appointed a deputy to the county surveyor, John Calhoun. Calhoun assigned him to the northern part of the county—what is now Menard and the southern part of Mason County. He continued as a surveyor probably until he left New Salem in 1837, certainly until December, 1836.

His positions as clerk, storekeeper, postmaster and surveyor gave him a wide acquaintance in the community, and in 1834, when he ran for the legislature a second time, he was elected easily. He was re-elected in 1836. During his second term his Whig colleagues made him the minority floor leader. At Vandalia, the state capital, his ambition was further stimulated. There he saw wealth, education, breeding, charm, things relatively unknown to him. He met skillful politicians, able lawyers, distinguished men from all parts of the state. He heard good speeches and listened to arguments before the State Supreme Court and the Federal Court for the District of Illinois. His experience there was a liberal education, of the type he could not get from books. Small wonder that at the end of his first legislative session he returned to New Salem with his ambition fired, and renewed his studies with such determination that his friends were concerned for his health.

Before going to Vandalia he had decided to become a lawyer. For years he had been attracted by the law. Back in Indiana he had read the *Revised Statutes of Indiana,* and at New Salem had read the *Laws of Illinois.* In 1833 he bought a book of legal forms with the aid of which he drew up mortgages, wills and other legal instruments for his friends. He had even argued minor cases before the local justice of the peace. During the legislative campaign of 1834 John T. Stuart, a young lawyer in Springfield, encouraged him to study law and make it his profession. After the campaign he decided to do so, and as he said, "went at it in good earnest." At an auction in Springfield he bought a copy of Blackstone's *Commentaries.* Other books he borrowed from Stuart, walking or riding to Springfield to get them. In December, 1836, he applied for a license to practice, and in March, 1837, the Supreme Court granted him a certificate of admission to the bar.

When Lincoln returned to New Salem from the legislative session of 1837 the decline of the village was well under way. He realized that there was no chance there for a legal or a larger political career. It was expected that the legislature would soon set off the northern part of Sangamon County as a separate county and that Petersburg would be the county seat. Several New Salem families had already moved there, or were planning to do so. Lincoln might have gone there too; but Springfield, twenty miles southeast of New Salem, which had just been chosen as the new state capital, offered even larger political and legal opportunities. Lincoln had many friends there. He had taken a leading part in having Springfield made the capital, and this action had increased his popularity. John T. Stuart was willing to take him as his law partner. On April 15, 1837, astride a borrowed horse, and with all his personal possessions in his saddle bags, Lincoln moved to Springfield.

In his six years at New Salem Lincoln had gone far. He could justly take pride in his progress. He came there at twenty-two, an aimless pioneer youth. When he left at twenty-eight he was a recognized political leader not only in the village, but in the state. He had made valuable friendships in the county and the state at large. He had learned to think for himself, and to express himself with force, clarity and individuality. He had equipped himself to make a living with his brain instead of his hands.

At New Salem Lincoln found himself. His coming there freed him from the retarding influence of his family. The community was more diversified, more complex, more stimulating than those places where he spent his boyhood and youth. The activities and contacts of his New Salem years revealed the possibility of betterment and gave him some conception of his own capacity.

Lincoln's success as politician and President was largely due to the fact that he knew how the common man would think. This he learned in no small measure at New Salem, where, during part of his residence at least, he worked on common terms with the humblest of the villagers. He learned how and what the blacksmith thought, how the storekeeper, the saloon keeper, the farmhand, the cobbler viewed things. At no other period of his mature life did he have such intimate contact with the common people. And he took away with him an abiding understanding of them.

The rural background of Lincoln's New Salem years and of his boyhood and youth left a lasting impression on him. Many of the similes and metaphors which enrich his literary style smack of the countryside. His jokes and anecdotes had the flavor of the soil. Often in later life he clarified his ideas with rural analogies drawn from his New Salem experiences. "The horse, the dog, the ox, the chin fly, the plow, the hog, . . . became interpreters of his meaning, solvers of his problems in his great necessity, of making men understand and follow him."

The New Salem environment, typical of that of the West in general, offered opportunities which Lincoln would not have had in an older community. Humble origin and lack of schooling were no handicaps, for they were common deficiencies. A newcomer had no difficulty in establishing himself; for no one had been there long, no propertied class had emerged, and social castes were unknown. Equality of opportunity was in large degree a fact, and democracy and nationalism were the political ideals.

Lincoln accepted these ideals, and benefitted by the opportunities that the frontier afforded. But at the same time he avoided the frontier's weaknesses or at least outgrew them with time. He became self-reliant without becoming boastful and without overestimating himself, analytical and conservative rather than opportunistic and impulsive. In a region where men sometimes made their

own law, where informality prevailed, and where people were concerned with the present and the future rather than the past, he
realized the value of law, and was respectful of form and traditions. At New Salem as in his later life his individuality stands out.
Yet while becoming a leader of his fellows Lincoln never lost touch
with them. He grew beyond his associates, but not away from
them.

GRANT FOREMAN

born in Detroit, Illinois, received his law degree from the
University of Michigan and was admitted to the Illinois bar
in 1891. He was a recognized authority on Indians and western history, and among his better known works are *Indian
Removal, The Emigration of the Five Civilized Tribes; Marcy
and the Gold Seekers,* and *A History of Oklahoma.*

This article appeared in the *Journal of the Illinois State
Historical Society,* volume 34, number 3 (September 1941),
pages 303–333.

ENGLISH SETTLERS IN ILLINOIS

GRANT FOREMAN

We are accustomed to think of the pioneer days of Illinois as days
of spartan simplicity, hardship and often privation that challenged
the fortitude of the stoutest hearts. While there was another side to
the picture, one can never know the full joy of life rural Illinois
afforded in those remote days unless he sees it through the eyes of
the immigrant translated from the poverty and oppression of English servitude to the opulence of the prodigal young American state.

To the English immigrant of a hundred years ago, the privilege
of living in this country was a boon indeed. Life was simple and
often hard, but the immigrants found it a paradise. The miracle of
abundant food, of meat every day, was indeed something to write
home about. And they wrote voluminously to their relatives and
friends of this and other wonders of the vastly more abundant life
they found here. Let the person who is dissatisfied with his lot and
the way things are run in this country read the letter of the young
English immigrant girl at Kaskaskia who grew lyrical over the new
life that yielded her $1.00 a week and her keep.

In the early part of the nineteenth century, Birkbeck, Flower,
and other Englishmen had made southern Illinois known to England, and it was only natural that with the agitation following the
Poor Laws, the Chartists, and the Corn Laws, when Englishmen
scattered over the world, many should direct their course to Illinois. Birkbeck's settlement, however, was the destination of only a
small part of the Illinois immigrants. From Perry and Randolph

counties, from Kaskaskia, Albion, Alton, Jacksonville, Nauvoo, Canton, and Pekin, they wrote letters back to their relatives and friends in England and these were printed in British newspapers. Examination of files of these papers in the British Museum has brought to light interesting accounts of Illinois of a century ago that localize these English settlements.

The potters of England, in an effort to reduce unemployment in their craft, organized a society to promote the acquisition of land in the United States and the financing of emigration to that remote country. The society established a paper that published many letters from English immigrants in Illinois, Wisconsin, Iowa, and Ohio. [1] A copy of this paper came to the notice of William Lee D. Ewing, auditor of public accounts for the state of Illinois, who on July 30, 1844, wrote the society a long letter from Springfield detailing many advantages of emigration to the state, and soliciting employment in securing land for it. This letter was printed in full in the *Examiner*.

Ewing gave much interesting information. He described the geography of the country; explained what the word "prairies" meant:

> Plains without trees and covered during the proper season with a thick sward of good grass for the feeding of cattle. . . . The opening of a farm in this country is comparatively of little cost. Material for building cheap; say for instance first rate pine boards at fifteen dollars or nearly £5 [*sic*] for 1,000 feet. I have surveyed several hundred thousand acres of land in Illinois, and am therefore intimately acquainted with its location, and profess to know something about its various rich soils.

He said that he could not secure as much as 12,000 acres in one body desirably located, which was what the potters wanted, and for lack of which they finally located their colony in Wisconsin. But he said that he could get land in smaller tracts from individual owners at from $2.00 to $3.00 an acre within 45 miles of St. Louis, "a city situate on the great Mississippi river and containing a population of 35,000 souls and within 25 or 30 miles of Alton, on the same river—population about 6,000."

---

[1] *Potters' Examiner and Workmen's Advocate*. The first issue appeared Dec. 2, 1843. It was published weekly and circulated in the pottery towns of Staffordshire. The first nine issues were printed at Hanley, and later publication was at Burslem.

Concerning the expense of improving the 20-acre farms they contemplated, he said:

[One can] procure the building of a comfortable log house, such as the mass of our population live in, with two rooms, and a passage between them, two doors, one in each room, two windows in each room, one chimney in each room, with a good floor, a stable, such as we have in this country on the most of our farms, for four horses, a corn-crib, or rather, a house wherein to secure Indian corn, a well dug and walled up with brick or rock, with windlass and bucket. All these, I say, I can procure the building of, for 450 dollars, or perhaps less. I can have ten acres of ground ploughed for 25 dollars. I can have it put under secure fencing for about 100 dollars, and perhaps less. In some situations I know for less. The first year, you plant your ground in Indian corn on the tough prairie sod, which will produce you about twenty-five bushels of corn to the acre *without cultivation*, worth forty-five cents or twenty-pence per bushels. Thus you can procure a home, land costing about two and a half dollars per acre, for less than 625 dollars. The production of the ten acres of Indian corn would be, on an average, worth to you about sixty-two dollars, independent of the production of the garden.

After the first year, your land would produce, according to cultivation, from fifty to seventy-five bushels of corn (Indian) per acre, or twenty-five to thirty-five bushels of wheat, sixty of oats, thirty to forty of rye, three hundred to five hundred bushels of potatoes (Irish). For your own subsistance you can purchase pork at one and a half to two dollars per 100 lbs.; beef, ditto; mutton, ditto; poultry at half a dollar to three quarters per dozen; butter ten to thirteen-pence per lb.; flour, at three and a half to four dollars per barrel, or 196 lbs., with the barrel; work horses (good) can be had from forty to fifty dollars per head; good milch cows, from eight to twelve dollars; sheep, at one and a half to two dollars per head; best Berkshire hogs very low—at what particular price I cannot say.

. . . Come to our country! Its government is mild and parental. It is boundless in extent, the fertility of its soil incomparable. Its health in such places as I and others can select, as good as any in any part of the world. . . . Clay for porcelain and earthenware is found in great abundance in this state. . . . The title of the Chief Magistrate is Governor, and not President. The name of the present Governor of Illinois is Thomas Ford.

Scores of letters written by English immigrants in Illinois were discovered and read. They were all addressed to parents, brothers,

and sisters back in England and reproduced in provincial English
newspapers, for the contents had an irresistible appeal to land-hun-
gry and food-hungry tenantry. They all told of the abundance and
cheapness of food in Illinois, a subject the writers never tired of,
and which they knew would hold spellbound the incredulous readers they hoped would follow them to this land of plenty. There was
little money in circulation. The country had not recovered from the
crash of 1837 and the closing of banks throughout the country—
banks issues were of uncertain value. But when there was no
money, food commodities would answer as a medium of exchange.

A potter who shared with some others the reprehensible habit of
signing his letter with only his initials for publication, wrote from
Alton on November 1, 1841:

> My brother Thomas went down to town today, and bought
> the hind quarter of a cow eighty-seven pounds weight, for one
> dollar and twenty-five cents. Last week, I bought one ham,
> twenty-six pounds weight, for one dollar; and twenty chick-
> ens, for one dollar and ten cents.

Then, as if to tax the credulity of the family in England:

> We can afford to put two or three of the latter into each pie
> we make; but my wife is almost tired of chickens and eggs.
> We made nine pies today of different sorts, for we never think
> we have had our meals if there should not be two or three
> pies, either of chickens, beef, pork, or apples, on the table. We
> begin to feel very dainty;—we often say, when we are sitting
> down to a good cup of tea, that if we were to return to
> England, we should not know how to make three pounds of
> beef last through the week, for we generally have here from
> fifteen to twenty pounds of beef per week, and ten pounds of
> ham, two pounds of butter, three ounces of tea, three pounds
> of sugar, one peck of potatoes, one stone of flour, and apples
> and fruit in abundance! We often have wild ducks, partridges,
> pigeons, rabbits, venison, and many other good things that we
> never expected to have ever tasted in England. We are very
> comfortable, and should be much more so if our parents were
> with us. We want you to be here, to partake of our hams. We
> intend buying six of the best we can find in town this winter,
> and curing them ourselves. We have each bought a cow, and
> also two horses for the family. . . . From its drawing toward
> Martinmas we thought proper to take stock, when we found,
> that the value of our goods, at the factory, amounted to about
> eight hundred dollars.

And surely this opulence would astound father, mother, sisters
and brothers, and envious neighbors when they heard the news:

We are worth about four hundred dollars in clear property!
Tell William he may sell my violin, and appropriate the
money towards defraying his expenses in coming to us, for we
want him to be here, as soon as he can make it convenient to
come. Tell him that Thomas and Sarah want him to assist
them in fetching the cows up, and to go with Mr. Robinson's
boys into the woods, to gather grapes and nuts; and tell little
Henry that his sister wants to see him, and that when he
arrives here we intend presenting him with a calf. . . .

Mr. Robinson and Mr. Goodwin and families, Mr. Barris-
ford and Mr. James came all in good health; and the day after
their arrival, we had a goose for supper—and a joyful time we
had. . . . We have engaged Mr. Tams to work for us. I
informed you we had bought two horses last week. T. Olivant
went into the woods to fetch a load of wood with one of them.
On returning back, my brother Thomas in taking it to the
stable, was thrown out of the waggon, and received a bit of a
shaking, but no serious injury. The accident was caused by
the reins breaking, and the horse taking fright.

The first time we drew our kiln, I wish you had been here to
have seen the sight. It was such a one that I never expected to
see. There were three potsellers, with their waggons, waiting
for the ware, as it came out of the kiln. All the ware was
drawn, packed, and sold before dinner! The weather is milder
now than it was at this time last year, for we were obliged
then to cease work, from the frost being so severe, but now we
are busy as we can be. Give our love to my father, mother,
brothers, and sisters; and tell them all, they must come as
soon as they can, for we want them to be with us. Tell my
father that he must not think of farming for the first twelve
months after he comes here, as he will do better by potting,
for we often want his assistance. If he were with us, we
should do much better than we are doing, although we are in
as good circumstances as could be expected, from our being
but young men, and in a strange land.

Hoping you will make yourselves as happy as you can, and
that the time is not far distant when we shall all meet together at Alton, believe us to remain your affectionate Son
and Daughter.

Benjamin Berrisford, another English potter, came to Illinois
also by way of the Mississippi River. He located at Alton with some
fellow countrymen, and on December 19, 1843, wrote to his wife in
England that he would send for his family as soon as he could get
the money, which was very scarce.

But of meat *there is more than can be eaten!* Beef I can buy
at one half-penny per pound; pork such as you would make

sausage of, at one farthing per pound; deer I can buy a whole carcass for two shillings-and-six-pence or three shillings. Hens are two pence halfpenny each; pigs I could buy eight or nine for about twelve shillings which would be worth £9 in England. I went to the pork house this morning, for some spareribs and I bought for two-pence-half-penny as much as I could carry home; so here is the place for cheap living.

He enclosed a separate letter to the children: "Be careful, my dear children, and save all that you can, for, most likely, I shall send for you towards the latter end of the summer." He had brought from England a quantity of clay pipes hoping to turn them at a profit, but could do little with them, "as the people here smoke cigars." He was curious to know how the potato crop at home had turned out. Reminded of some of the oppressions in England, he regaled the children with the difference in Illinois:

My children, I have never seen Old Gibbs, with his Poor's Book, nor Hilton with his Blue-Bottle Book, since I have been in this country; for instead of policemen, we have pigs to guard our house at night. We can leave anything out at night, and find it there next morning. We have had as much flesh meat hanging under the porch of our house as any butcher in the Potteries stands market with.

I believe from what I can see of the country, it is likely to become a fine place in the course of time. Alton is a terrible place for pig-slaughtering; there are about two thousand killed here every week, for about five months in the year. Wages run from three to five shillings per day; so wages are pretty good considering the price of provisions. Flour is but one shilling per stone, and butter from fourpence to sixpence per pound; lard from 2½ to 3d per pound; sugar 4d to 5d; coffee 5d, tobacco 5d to 6d per pound; cheese from 3d to 4; soap 4d; tea, best 4s per pound.

The anonymous potter again wrote from Alton, September 12, 1843, of the progress of their pottery:

We have built our new kiln, and a very pretty one it is, too; and, as the Americans say, "I guess it will shine when it is fired full of glost ware:" which circumstance will not be long before it takes place; and then I should like for the whole of you to be here, that you may see the reward of persevering industry. Our old slip kiln, not being large enough for our present purposes, we have built another this week, which is 21 feet long by 5 feet wide. We have engaged a sagger-maker, a dish-maker, a hollow-ware presser, a man to throw coarse ware, and now we are going to send to St. Lewis for a slip

maker. I will now tell my brother B. a few of our prices, so
that if he thinks he can earn at those prices sufficient to
purchase a little bread and a few potatoes, we should like him
to come, as we will undertake to find him plenty of beef and
pork to them; although, perhaps, when he comes here, we
shall find him something else to do. For ewers we pay 4s. per
dozen; for chambers, 4s. 6d; for cover-dishes, 3s. 3d.; for 4's
jugs, plain 3s. 3d. per dozen; and 12's French, 2s. 11d.; for
round nappies, 12's 5d. per dozen; 11's 4½d.; 10's, 4d.; 9's,
3½d.; 8's, 7's, 6's, 2½d., per dozen; and for plates, twifflers,
and muffins, 4s. 2d. per score. Such are our prices!

We were very sorry to hear of our mother and sister being
ill, but we sincerely hope they are better again. We wish they
were here to taste some of our fruit. Talk about fruit, indeed!
My wife says she is wearied of the sight of it, for we have
never been without apples, plums, peaches, and a number of
others too numerous to mention, since we came to America.
Sarah says you must try to come as soon as you can, to taste
some of our preserves. While I am writing, the kettle is over
the fire full of plums! When you sent us word you were
getting ready to come with James . . . we were full of joy, but
it did not last long, for we soon learned that Mr. G. was
coming without you.

But we must be drawing towards a conclusion. We are now
in a brick house, which contains four large rooms. Mr. Williams . . . has left Mrs. . . . and is coming to work with us.
You must excuse my not writing sooner, as I have been
waiting for the finishing of our kiln. We expected it to have
been finished sooner, but we have put off the business, week
after week, 'till now. You shall have another letter in about a
month after you receive this. We feel anxious to hear from
you. You must let us know how trade is with you when you
write next.

While running this series of contemporary letters, the *Examiner*
came into possession of one written long before the potters' movement was inaugurated. It bore the date of February 11, 1831, and
was written by John and Elizabeth Kilham to their brothers and
sisters. They arrived and settled, July 24, 1830, four miles west of
Jacksonville, a village of 700 inhabitants. Their letter was filled
with accounts of the many blessings they enjoyed: they had purchased for 5s. 7½d. per acre, 510 acres of land, 190 of timber and
320 of prairie; game was plenty, and they could hunt to their
hearts' content with no fear of being charged with poaching; there
was no tithe nor tax on the land until after five years, and then only

one penny per acre; they could make their own candles or soap, and grow tobacco or anything else without paying a tax to the government; there were no excisemen nor other inspecting officers such as they had been accustomed to in England. They had four yoke of oxen, steers, milk cows, and pigs.

They were all prospering; brother William had cleared $110 in eight months, besides being furnished with meat, washing, mending and lodging. They cut all the wild hay they needed on the prairies, and found wild plums and berries; but they requested numerous items from home: plum seeds, pears, cherries, black currant berries, onion seed, strawberries, "potatoes, ash tops, early rounds, apple potatoes and different sorts;" red clover seed, six good rough topcoats, six darkcolored waistcoats, two hare shag coats, two hoppers, one wheat riddle, and one oat wire riddle, a recipe for making fire bricks.

Their neighbors included Englishmen named William Hall, William Kilham, John Leach, Adam Allison, John Lembrough, John Lazenby, and others whose names were not given. W. H. Sykehouse and Mr. Gelders of Moorends and Mr. Barker of Pontefract were on the way. There was an urgent demand for tradesmen, tinners, wireworkers, brickmakers, millwrights, and stonemasons, as all the arriving artisans had turned farmers.

Mary Harvey, a young English emigrant girl, wrote in January 1844, at Kaskaskia, the historic town long since swept away by the raging Mississippi:

> We are now all comfortably situated, and all as happy as we possibly can be, separated from our dearly-beloved mother! We had a pleasant voyage to New Orleans. From New Orleans to this place is about 1,450 miles. It is one of the oldest settlements in this part of the continent, founded in the same year as Philadelphia. We met some gentlemen on the steamboat, as we were going up the river, who engaged us all, and promised us all situations.
>
> Harriet got married the day after we arrived here. We are at the residence of one of the finest ladies in the place. She is the daughter of the richest man in this part of the country. There were present a number of the finest gentlemen and ladies in the city. Such is the equality with which strangers are received here. Harriet and her husband live on a farm about a mile from the city, and are well and comfortably situated, he is very kind to her, and she says she is very happy. They so far have rendered perfect satisfaction to his employer (for there

are no masters here except over negroes), he does not receive much wages yet, as he is not accustomed to the country and the kind of work that he is engaged in. I spent a few weeks with them before I got a situation. Now I will give you a specimen of the manner of living. The first evening of marriage they had prepared for them a large pot of broth, made from five fat hens;—a great dish with the folks here,—it is called "borgoo."

In her enthusiasm Mary could not resist making the mouths of mother, father, brother, and sister water by the incredible account of luxuries surrounding her: On Christmas day she, Alfred and Harriet sat down to five fat roasted suckling pigs; on New Year's day they dined on a large fat turkey stuffed with sage and onions; and equally incredible, they had *tea and coffee at every meal.*

Meat of every description in plenty; our tables they are loaded with beef, mutton, pork, and bacon, at every meal. We have had wild turkeys, venison, pheasants, partridges, and rabbits in abundance. Wild ducks and geese are as plentiful here as the partridges. A good hunter will kill more game in a few hours than he can carry home.

But though, my dear mother, I am living in a finer country than ever my imagination had pictured to me as existing in this world, I can never be happy until I see you, and find my bosom beating against yours. If you can only make up your mind to come here, I will send you the money. I should then be as happy as I can be in this life. I cannot, my dear mother, express the love I feel for you; nor can words express the desire of my heart to see you again. Disquietude will attend my nights until I feel your embrace, and fold in my arms my dearest mother. You can live happily here, with the pleasure of seeing your children happy and comfortable; growing in wealth and honor as long as they are industrious and honest.

I am out at service by the week. I have one dollar per week, every thing found me except clothes. There are but three in the family, the doctor, his wife, and child. I go to see Harriet every Sunday on horse-back. Last week I went to a ball, three miles from this place in a rig with a young gentleman. We had a very pleasant party. Plenty of good-looking gentlemen, and all of them elegant dancers. They dance a great deal here, and enjoy themselves in every innocent way.

Tell Eliza not to fall in love in England, as the beaux are in plenty here; good-looking, rich, polite and attentive, and treat all young ladies with the greatest decorum, let them be ever so poor, and as perfect equals. There is no distinction here, except what is called by money and learning. The poor marry the rich, and the rich marry the poor. A labourer's son is as good as the governor's son. The young gentleman that took me to the ball, told me that nearly all the great officers of this state had been poor friendless boys, without much money or education when they started in life. The United States Senator, the greatest man in the State, was a mechanic's son. The governor [2] was a wood-chopper when he was twenty years of age. . . . Kiss Eliza, Ellen, Elizabeth, Ann and Sarah for me: Tell them not to forget me in their evening and morning prayers. I never close my eyes, my dear mother, without beseeching the Almighty to grant that I may see you all in this happy and fruitful country. . . .

I cannot picture to you the treasures of this country, or the advantages, as nobody, that is industrious, can help becoming rich! Beef costs two farthings per lb.; Pork two farthings per lb.; Potatoes four-pence a bushell; Chickens four shillings a dozen; fine Horses one pound sterling, that would cost five or six in England; four-year-old Horses, unbroken, two pounds; cows from one to two pounds. . . . I just now saw the leg of an eagle, that would fly off with a large lamb. Every man can shoot whatever game he sees; be it where it may; no matter whose land it is on. My paper will compel me to conclude, but I could write for a week, as I have much to tell. One mile from the house where Alfred lives, flows the great Mississippi river, two miles wide, and the water running along at ten miles per hour; and which you will have to come up, if you come to this country. On the other side is the beautiful river Kaskaskia, flowing along so sweetly, like the favoured river of Canaan, through a land of milk and honey! for this is one, if there be such on this terrestrial globe! To conclude; you must picture us as happy as we can possibly be without your being here, and having nothing to desire but your presence with us, to make us happy! There is not a single person in this country but who can always get plenty to eat, let them be never so idle; as it is in such abundance, and so exceedingly cheap. Everything is cheap, except such things as they bring from England. Advise all friends that come, to bring plenty of clothes, shoes, pots, and such things as are very cheap. These are useful here. Harriet and Alfred send their love to you and all friends. I am grown so lusty that my clothes will hardly hook on me. Harriet's cheeks are as red and plump as ever, though she is not so stout as she was. I must conclude, my

---

[2] Thomas Ford was Governor, Sidney Breese of Carlyle and James Semple of Alton were United States senators from Illinois at that time.

dear friends, by assuring you that health, peace, happiness, prosperity for you, is the prayer of my mother's devoted daughter,

Mary Harvey.

Direct: Kaskaskia, Illinois, United States of America.

Another Englishman who identified himself only by the initial "S" came to Albion in Birkbeck's settlement. Writing to his father, mother, brothers, and sisters in the spring of 1844 he admitted that he had been ill, but he said:

> If you would give me my former situation, and pay my passage back, we are all in one mind, we would not return. We met with our inconveniences, but what of that? As to our travels, I think I have related them up to New York; from there to Albany we proceeded in a tow boat, one hundred and sixty miles, paid 1 dollar each, luggage free; from Albany to Buffalo, three hundred and sixty-three miles, 3 dollars each, luggage free, five days on our passage; from Buffalo to Erie, on the Lake Erie, ninety miles, 1 dollar, 50 cents each, luggage free. If you come this way, and the wind be high, you will find it unpleasant as the sea; a steamboat leaves every morning, they told us. There was a canal cutting from Cleveland to Cincinnati, some said it was finished, but others said not; I should think if it be completed when you come, it would be the best way, as we found water conveyance to be a great deal cheaper, and much pleasanter, than land. At Erie we engaged a waggon and six horses, bearing seventeen bells, for 3½ cents per lb.; 2 dollars 50 cents for each woman, one hundred and sixty miles to Pittsburgh; but the man, for his own interest, took us a way that brought us to Beavers, thirty miles below Pittsburgh, and here we had to stop three days waiting for a boat, and being weary we bought an old ferry boat, and got some pine and fitted it up so we could lodge in it, and we ran down near a thousand miles in fifteen days, and lay by at nights, and stopped at Mount Vernon, and then sent G. Curtis to Mr. Lambert's, for we could not engage a team, and Mr. Lambert was so kind as to come eighty-six miles, and brought us up here, and only charged expenses, and we arrived on the 10th of July.
>
> Land, with or without wood, is 1 dollar 25 cents per acre, and we are in hopes it will drop to 75 cents; meat 2 cents per lb.; flour 2½ cents. I bought a cow and a calf for less than 8 dollars, and I think they would be worth as many pounds with you; a poor man must work all summer with you for a cow, but here he may earn one in a few days, and have the summer's run for nothing, as many hogs as he pleases, and

plenty of deer. I intend to have another cow or two as soon as possible, and have bought some India corn for winter fodder; I have three acres of land, two of which I have sown with corn, which is coming up well.

As to trying to entice people to come, I have seen so much dissatisfaction in W. C.[3] that it keeps me from it. Those who come here to do better than their means will allow, get disappointed; they that come to do as well as they can, get on best. There is an old man lives here, who, some time ago, had scarcely a single dollar; now, most of his seven children have farms of their own, and the others, as they rise, will have the same chance, which, in England, not one of them would have had. All that come with industry and economy may soon fare well. There are many who choose a place and build a log house, and there live until they save as much as will buy eighty or a hundred and sixty acres of land; these make themselves a happy people. Poor men that come here may enjoy the ancient privileges of Old England; and all that come and make themselves at home will do well. Do not think it to be a place of sickness, because we have been sick; for Mr. Lambert's have all missed, and the old settlers told us there had not been such a summer for dryness and sickness, and J. Charlesworth says he has not seen a place or part he likes as well as this.

As for luggage, a little will do for a single man that does not know where he is to settle; but if I had to come now, I would bring my iron crow, chisels, hammer, wood team, and a many more such; some of them I sold for 1d. or 2d. per lb., and here I must give 25 cents; iron is 2½ cents per lb.; and the smith charges 12½ cents for working it. If you sell your best traces for so high a price as 8d. per lb., that perhaps will be all; then judge about it. I don't say bring any sort of lumber but such as is most useful. If you buy an iron spade or two at Liverpool to bring with you, you should use them a little to make them look old, that they may pass free from duty; bring also a cutting knife or two, and give G. S. 1s. for the frame saw irons; they may never be of any use to him. Get my uncle, W. B., to get me a well-finished lathe spindle at Doncaster, as cheap as he can; one here will cost more than with you; and a set of turning chisels and gauges, from a hardware shop, 5 Stringdale-street, Liverpool. Bring two or three dozen of hand-saw files, and your solid irons with you; they are 50 cents or more here. I believe all cast work, clear of rough or polish, is as cheap at Pittsburgh or Cincinnati, as it is with you. Don't

---

[3] London is divided into eight postal districts, of which the West Central is one. Mail originating in that district usually bears the designation of "W. C."

bring a shot gun with you, for they are good for nothing here; rifles are all used here; and if you have bought a gun, sell it, for it will not be worth as many dollars here, as pounds with you. Bring your feather-beds with you; bring us a pair of strong iron candlesticks; bring your sound and useful pots. A set of china here is 8 dollars, such as you may get for 2 dollars, and all other pots accordingly. We give 12½ cents for a basin, such as you may get for 2d. or less. Tin-ware is dear and bad; fire irons are dear. We feel a great want for iron ovens. But side-ovens require wide ranges; there is not a range in all this settlement. There is a sheet-iron oven or two, but they make them hot with a fire to themselves. Bring no plough irons. All this is different advice from others, but believe it is right.

I shall now give you a definition of the money in the New York States: they say 8s. to the dollar, and in this State but 6s. You must be aware of the Yankees, lest they cheat you. You must always recollect there are 100 cents. in a dollar; and to be safe, always reckon by cents. The least piece is 6¼ cents., and has upon it two pillars with a crown between them; the next is 12½ cents., next 25, then 50, then 1 dollar; and all these are Spanish coin, and bear the same impression. There are some 9 cents. pieces, and some 18, but these have no pillars on them. There are also Mexican coins, that look like dollars, but are 6¼ cents. short. The United States' coins are 10, 25, and 50 cents. and 1 dollar. As for bills, if you take any, mind and take United States Bills. Bring no sovereigns here; at New York they are worth 4 dollars and 75 cents.; and 4 dollars 80 cents., at the silversmith's facing the Exchange.

We think you had better come by New Orleans. Your baggage will be to shift from the ship to the steamboat, and then you run at once to Shawnee-town or Mount Vernon. If it be wet, don't come to Mount Vernon, as there are some muddy rivers to cross. If you come this way, by New Orleans, I mean, you will perhaps have to be nine weeks on the sea; but then you will have more room in the ship, and less trouble in shifting your things; and when you do shift them, mind and look if you have your number, for there were some people on the canal, through carelessness, lost two boxes. It would be well to paint your name upon them, and number them. I dare say that by Orleans, if you mind at Liverpool, will be the cheapest way to come, and in the shortest time. To all this you may adhere, but come the way you please; if by Orleans, try if you can find a ship bound to Orleans, and endeavor to see the captain yourself, (but mind it is him,) and agree as low as you can; and mind that your births are made secure. All the way as we came we found our own provisions, and laid on our beds, and had a room to ourselves; this is the cheapest way. Ten of us paid perhaps twenty-five cents. for one night; this was on land. The iron oven I mentioned came from Birmingham. . . .

I wish my father to bring me a pair or two of fustian trowsers, and for winter wear some for themselves; they would not be amiss. Nothing but trowsers are worn. I have seen a waist-coat and a tradesman's fustian coat bought in at a sale for 8 dollars. I could have bought as good at Liverpool for little more than three dollars; for there is plenty of clothing of all sorts made up there. Bring with your blankets a web of fustian, and some plaided stuff for the females. I think I have mentioned all of that description you need care for. A mattress full of good hay seeds, carraway seeds, some marygold seeds, celery, both sorts of cabbage, brocoli, lettuce, carrots, radishes, cresses, mustard, some peas and beans of a good sort, some plum stones of a good kind, and various others; seek them under the trees, if you cannot get them without. John's father, if he pleases, will bring two or three pounds of turnip seeds, from Marris's, Hatfield. We want some camomile, and any other seeds you think proper; but be sure to bring all the seeds I have mentioned, knives, forks, as many dozens as you please, and any other kind of cutlery ware you may think of, for all sorts are very dear with us. Cotton balls, needles, tapes, laces, if you have a good lot. Bring Isabella and Eliza a small plain work-box; hide them with your raffled cotton, and if the custom-house officers want to put a duty upon them, you can easily tell them your business, and that they are your own things, and for your own use. Pins here are very bad. You two females should go to James Holmes, and get him to learn you to cut out. Bring some patterns for waistcoats; and some good sized iron wedges. Baskets are dear. Iron is about 6¼ cents. per lb. at Orleans, and will cost 1 or 1½ cents. to bring it here, and then the store-keepers charge 12½ cents. If you come by Orleans, bring one barrel of sugar, for it may generally be bought at 6¼ cents. per lb., and is the same price as iron, and the storekeepers charge 12½ cents. Bring what other groceries you may think proper; coffee is most used, and is here 20 cents. per lb. We would like you to bring some good pear pippins, Yorkshire green apples, and, if you can, some berry slips, black currants, and some good grafts; we would try to make them grow; if corked tight up in a bottle, I think they would do; sea air and water kills trees. I would like you to bring me a dozen or two of good gimblets and a spikes ditto or two, for I have bought too few. One day, a little time ago, a man came to me for a gimblet, which I bought in Liverpool for about 2d., and he sent in return, last Saturday, a dozen of eggs, and a pair of fowls; the pullet is just at laying. Young fowls I can buy at 1 dollar per dozen, about 6½ cents.

Job Rigby and William Brunt came together, and on November 15, 1842, began the ascent of the Mississippi River at New Orleans on a steamboat that seemed to them so large as to suggest comparison with a moving city. When within three miles of Chester, the boat ran aground, and after remaining fast for two weeks the travelers left it and found hospitality in the home of one of the former settlers a few miles from the river. Job wrote the next May 13, of their adventures. He was a shoemaker, but found the business poor. While they got a room for 25 cents a week, his work commanded only "50 cents for making pegged shoes; and if bound 75 cents. They found all their own leather."

Job liked the people in the community. He wrote:

> It is not here like it is in England; they do not respect a man from his dress, or external appearance. They look at his actions; and if he be an honest man he is respected. . . . There is plenty of wild game, such as wild deer, turkies, rabbits, geese, ducks and many other kinds. But I must tell you, America never was in a worse state than it is respecting money, at the present time. The people have property to sell, but cannot get money for it, so they trade with each other. Job has become a farmer, and he inventoried his seven hens and a cock and the prospect of thirty chickens in a few days.
>
> We have a sow and seven young pigs, which cost us a dollar —4s. 2d. We shall buy a cow very soon, as Eliza will soon be able to milk.
>
> You wish to know the cheapest way to come after us. You must come by the Anderton Carrying Company to Liverpool, and along with the Latter-day Saints to New Orleans. It will cost £3 15s. per head—under fourteen years, half price. If you come you must land at Chester; it is about twenty miles from Chester to this place. Be very careful with your luggage. Bring with you some pots, viz., cups, twifflers, dishes, &c. You can get a dollar's worth of food or live stock for six printed twifflers, but no money for them; flesh 1d. per lb., flour, 12s. per 2 cwt., sugar 5 cents per lb. Get some prints to make some bonnets; some leather hemp, and thread. Direct for Job Rigby, Steel's Mill, Randolph County, Illinois.

Brunt found at Six Mile Prairie another young Englishman from Leeds, Yorkshire, named Hodgson, who helped him find a tract of "Congress land." Then he and Rigby engaged three wagons, returned to the Mississippi River, hauled their baggage and household goods and Brunt's family to the "Prairie," and temporarily lodged both families in a two-room house. Squire Short, another hospitable settler, found a horse for Brunt and accompanied him on the twenty-six mile ride to the land office at Kaskaskia, where he entered 160 acres. He gave the following description:

> It is partly wooded and partly Prairie. . . . I paid 200 dollars, about £41 5s. in English money. This is as good an estate as any in England of the same extent. I have now a hewed log house, 18 feet by 22, a large kitchen, a barn 18 by 24, but which is not roofed. My residence is named by the old farmer, "Mount Pleasant." I have about 20 acres cultivated in Indian corn, wheat, oats, and potatoes. Our stock consists of one prime yoke of oxen, three good horses, three good cows, and calves, one yearling calf, eleven hogs, one sow pig, twenty-two cocks and hens, fourteen chickens, a hive of bees, two canaries, two dogs, Captain and Winter, and three kittens; all of these, together with our family, in good health.
>
> The neighbours here are chiefly Americans, and very kindly disposed. They are all true lovers of liberty! I will relate one instance. After having heard me, in conversation, describe the condition of the labouring population of Great Britain and Ireland, at a public meeting-house in the Prairie, a subject which would have been treason in England, was proposed for discussion, viz., "Who are the real producers of Wealth?" and "Would, or would not, the people of England be justified in rebelling against the Government?" . . .
>
> Money is scarce, but the necessaries of life abound. All kinds of provisions are very cheap. Clothing is generally dear. I advise any who come to bring their old clothes, and strong and stout for winter, and very light for summer. Stout blankets and the common kind of blue bed-covers. Bring a crate of ware, consisting of cups, saucers, twifflers, 6 and 4 inch muffins, coffee cans, half-pint mugs, a few 10 and 14 inch dishes, flats; let them be all good, printed seconds; china seconds as well, and they will sell. They must be the kind I have mentioned; viz.: cups, twifflers, and saucers, are the most in request. It would be well to bring the entry of them with you. Some double-bladed knives, but let them be good ones.
>
> The best landing-place for this settlement, and the nearest, is Chester, Randolph County, Illinois. Thence there is a tolerably good road to, and but 25 miles from our house. This is considered the most healthy part in the county. We have game in abundance, from the squirrel to the deer, the par-

tridge to the turkey. We have killed and eaten of them three
times a day. We never sit down to food without pork, eggs,
milk, coffee, butter, &c. &c. on table. In fact, an individual
trained in America, and living under its laws, cannot starve!
as they do in England. If an Englishman comes here, he will
never go back. Poverty, and the fear of it, seems to be unknown here!

We are anxious to know how all old friends are. For ourselves, we unite in saying, God bless you every one! Jump off
at Chester, and be sure to ask the Captain of the steamer to
allow you to do so.

Direct—William Brunt, New Settler from England, Six Mile
Prairie, Perry County, Illinois. To be left at Steel's Mill Post
Office.

Thomas J. Filcher, an intelligent potter from Henley, settled at
Nauvoo. On April 16, 1843, he wrote the *Examiner* in answer to
inquiries of the preceding September, and gave considerable information concerning the country: reason for sickness in the river
bottoms, the climate, etc.

This Winter the Mississippi which is more than a Mile
across, has been frozen over five weeks, so that teams could
cross on the ice all the time; but this Winter has been the
most severe one that has been known for many years.

With respect to the dipression in the monitary system of
this country, I would just remark, that the amount of real
specie in this country is almost as much as it has been for a
[great] many years past. But during the time that the United
States Bank was in vogue the Proprietors of that Bank issued
a great amount of Paper Money, more than they had of real
capital; many followed the example, and Banks soon became
very numerous and money plentiful. This produced good
times and increased the value of property; but the Proprietors
of Banks became so notorious in the issuing of Paper Money,
as to create a suspicion, in the minds of the people; demands
were then made upon the Banks, which they could not meet;
and the Banks went down. Thus property, which had been
purchased when times were good, and money in plenty, became reduced in value, and those who had it in their possession suffered in consequence; and many of the Merchants
became Bankrupts. Since I have been in this country four
Banks have gone down in this state.

With respect to five or six individuals, such as you describe,
coming to this country, it is my opinion, that it would be a
good speculation, and you would meet with great encourage-
ment. I know of neither clay, nor coals, in this immediate

neighborhood. But at Centerville in Knox County, joining to Warren County, there is clay that makes Tobacco-pipes, and plenty of coals on the spot. Knox County is as healthful as Warren County, but the land is not considered so fertile.

If you come at all, I would not advise you to leave your family, as I feel confident that you would do well! With respect to what you should bring with you, what you have named would do very well. Remnants of calico and good second-hand clothes are good property here, and pay no duty on importation. If you could bring away some good seconds earthenware with your goods, you would do well; such as Twifflers; seven-inch Muffins; 24 Bowls; 12 and 24 Jugs; and 24 Mugs; these things fetch a high price, in this country, and sell well. Do not stay in any large town except you could get a situation to suit you, as your goods will not fetch so much as they will in small towns and in the country.

Filcher wrote again in the fall of 1843, to George Mart:

Sir,—I received a letter from my parents, on the 12th of October, containing your respects to me, with a request that I should send you a particular account of the state of this country, to which request I cheerfully respond. I am living in the city of Nauvoo, to which city numbers of people, from all parts of the United States, are gathering; many of whom, I have the opportunity of conversing with almost daily. This enables me to know something of the state not only of this State, but the United States.

The Americans, in general, are great people to speculate in all kinds of business. Many have established Banks, and issued a large amount of notes, when they have had a very small amount of real capital. Thus, when their Banks have been run on, they have been unable to cash their notes, and they have consequently gone down. This State of things has caused the money markets in this country to be very unstable; but, I rejoice to inform you that we do not depend upon a monied currency for subsistence, as you do in England. I have now been in this country near 12 months, and have a half of an acre of land in one of the principal streets of the city; a Brickhouse upon it, 17 feet by 15; a good cow; 2 hogs; and 8 fowls; and have not yet received a dollar, in cash, for my labour. And notwithstanding Banks are breaking, and merchants failing, there is still a superabundance of the necessaries of life which may be obtained for labour. Wheat is now selling for 1s. 6d. per bushel; Indian corn and oats are selling for 6d. per bushel; beef and pork is one penny per pound; potatoes from 6d. to 1 s. a bushel; a good cow from £2 10s. to

£3 10s.; butter 6s. a pound; all food in proportion. Clothing is generally rather high, but every industrious man can obtain not only the necessaries, but the comforts of life; and can breathe the pure and wholesome atmosphere of REPUBLI-CANISM. Since I have been here, I have had the pleasure of voting at a General, August Election, and I went in for Pure Democracy. We have now coming in office a Democratic Governour [4] and Lieutenant Governour; and we have a major-ity of Democrats both in the House of Representatives and the Senate. In fact, this is a Democratic state, and six months residence constitutes a voter in it.

Perhaps you might have some idea that you shall, sooner or later leave the contest in which (according to my knowledge of you) you have been faithfully engaged, and come to this country. You have nobly and manfully stood forward to assist in striking the death-blow to the prosperity of tyrants; they have already staggered from the blow and ultimately must expire. But if they should be so long in dying, that you cannot wait to see them expire, you can leave Mr. John Richards to preach their Funeral Sermon, and Mr. Samuel Robinson to sound their Funeral Knell; and if you should leave Jeremiah Yates to be sexton tell him to see well to their interment, and put his seal upon their tomb, for fear there should be a resur-rection from the dead. This being done, you may come to this country, place yourself in the midst of plenty, and enjoy, through life, those blessings you have so long contended for.

. . . If you come to this country . . . bring with you as much earthenware as you can; and there is a very great profit upon secondhand clothes a short distance from any large trading cities, and also gray calico and haberdashery. Bring as much of these goods as possible; situate yourself in a small town, where there is a good share of country business; get some live stock as soon as possible, and prepare for getting upon a farm. Do not be discouraged at the change of business; almost any body can farm in this country; and when you have gotten 20 acres of land of your own, fenced in and cultivated, you will be as independent as any of the great ones in Eng-land. It will not occupy half of your time; and will produce for you all you need; but be sure to get some Timber-land for fencing and firing. This being done, you can live in the enjoyment of every privilege vouchsafed to man by his Crea-tor! You will not be compelled to support a constabulary force, nor the religion of State, by paying Church-rates against your will. Poor-rates, Magistrates' rates, and Church-rates will sink into eternal forgetfulness, as there are no Paupers, and no

---

[4] Gov. Thomas Ford.

hired Magistrates nor Police wanted. You can choose what religion you like; and pay what you like for it! . . . I have lived in six different houses since I came in this country, and not any of them had any locks or bolts, to the doors. The Americans are not mean as to commit petty thefts, or to rob the poor. . . . I have known carpenters to commence a building, and scarcely ever collect their tools until the completion of the job. So much for American honesty! Before I conclude, I would say the disordered state of the currency has much affected the Mercantile Business of this country. There is, therefore, no certainty in anything else, but FARMING. Land is from 1¼ to 5 dollars an acre. Here you may find sweet employ and live a life of Peace and Joy!

Joshua Garside had lived four years at Canton when he decided that his observation of Illinois pioneer life would interest the readers of the *Manchester Examiner and Times,* his home paper, by means of which he and his neighbors kept in touch with events in England. Accordingly he set down many things that occurred to him, and incorporated them in two long letters dated July 29 and October 7, 1851, to the *Examiner and Times.*

The Great Exposition at Hyde Park was under way, and Garside enjoyed the description of the Crystal Palace and its contents; but he resented the patronizing tone of the English press concerning the modest contributions to the exposition sent over by Garside's new countrymen. Passing over that subject, he launched into an account of the new country:

Illinois—the beautiful, ever-prolific Illinois! Could I at this beautiful season of the year transport some of your readers from the streets of your smoky city, and place them on one of the wide, boundless prairies, stretching like a sea farther than the eye can reach; could I place them in a position where they could command a view of the rich, wide, extensive corn fields, the yellow fields of grain now ripening into harvest, and orchards with trees laden with fruit, what a sight would be presented to their bewildered imaginations! Illinois will eventually become the greatest fruit-raising country in the world. I will mention one instance, in order to give this statement additional weight. Messrs. Overmans, who own a nursery some four miles from this place, sold this spring some twenty thousand young fruit trees, and mostly all to the farmers of this county; and this is but a solitary instance. There are other nurseries in this and the adjoining counties that have done a more extensive business than this. Illinois is destined

to become one of the richest and most powerful states in the
union. Everything at present points that way. With a liberal
state government, like the one we now have, nothing but mad
speculation can prevent this state from becoming the granary
of the world—she has within herself all the requisites for
boundless wealth. Her minerals, such as coal, lead, and iron,
are inexhaustible; bituminous coal is found within three feet
of the surface of the earth, and that too of a very good quality;
her soil is rich and the climate is good, and the state, as it
becomes more settled, becomes more healthy.

The magnificent grant of land made by congress to the
state of Illinois, for the purpose of constructing a railroad
through the centre of the state, has given a new impetus to
business, and has been the means of causing a greater influx
of emigrants from the eastern states than ever. The legislature, at the last session, consummated the contract for the
construction of the railroad, with a company of eastern capitalists, and the undertaking is to be completed in four years.
The length of the road will be some 600 miles; when the road
is completed, and in full operation, the company pays to the
state seven per cent of the nett proceeds. The stock has all
been taken up, and the company for constructing the road
take possession of the land granted by congress (which is a
strip six miles wide, the full length of the road), as the road
progresses. The road will commence at Chicago, at the head
of Lake Michigan, and terminate at Cairo, on the Mississippi
river. A strong body of surveyors are now in the field, and it is
intended to push the work forward with all possible speed. It
is a bold and noble enterprise; it will not cost the state
anything; but will when in operation, be a fruitful source of
revenue. The Illinois canal, which connects the waters of
Lake Michigan with Illinois river, was completed in the summer of 1848. The traffic in that direction has now become
immense; it has opened new sources and new avenues of
trade with the Lakes and the Midland States. Something,
however, appears to be wrong in the construction of this
canal; so many breaks occurring, obstructing navigation in
the best season of the year. Indeed, nearly all the public works
in this country appear to be constructed in too great a hurry.
There is a want of finish about them to which the eye of an
Englishman is accustomed; but, of course, this must be attributed to the newness of the country, and the desire to go ahead
in as quick time as possible.

The roads in this section of the state, owing to the rich
alluvial soil, are, on the breaking-up of winter, and in very wet
weather, almost impassable. To obviate this, plank roads are
coming into general use, and good roads they are indeed. The

cost of making a plank road—taking the cost of one now in course of construction from Canton to Liverpool on the Illinois river, about twelve miles long, and now nearly completed —is about 3,000 dollars (£200) [sic] a mile. The planks are laid across the road, on three rows of sleepers. The width of the plank road is about eight feet, and the earth is thrown up at each end of the plank, and the road will, it is supposed, last some seven or eight years.

The legislature of this state at the last session, among other liberal acts, passed what is called the Homestead Exemption Law, allowing every citizen to hold property to the amount of one thousand dollars, to be exempt from execution for all debts contracted after the 4th July, 1851, on which day the law came in force. How this law will operate remains yet to be seen; it does not altogether meet the approbation of the merchants. A law similar to this has now been in operation for some time in New York, and one or two other eastern states, and seems to work well enough. There is one law just come in force which very forcibly reminds me of home, and that is the new cheap postage law. Taking into consideration the extent of the country, the enormous length of the mail routes, and the rather imperfect manner in which the postal arrangements are carried out, it is, I consider, a most liberal concession on the part of the American government. The mail system here has not yet arrived at that perfection which it has reached in England, but it is improving. There only now wants one thing to carry out this grand cheap postage scheme, first adopted by Great Britain, and the example now followed up by the United States—one link is wanting to make this noble scheme perfect—and that is, the *ocean* penny postage; I trust, ere long, to see it adopted; it will bind closer together the ties of brotherhood between the two greatest nations, speaking the same language! and it will strengthen the good feeling which now exists between England and the United States. One very important thing in this country is the system of telegraphic communication. This is carried on to a greater extent, and made more subservient to public convenience, than it is in England.

Respecting the political institutions of the country, I have but very little to say. The Americans have just and good reason to be proud of their country, and of that band of heroes whose names are imperishable on the pages of history, whose bravery and indomitable energy laid the foundation of this great republic. Could you but witness the enthusiasm which is manifested on each return of the nation's birthday —could you but witness the intense interest with which that bold declaration of independence is listened to, and behold the

manifestations of joy and patriotism exhibited on the return
of each succeeding 4th of July, you would almost wish yourself an American. They are justly proud of their Washington
and of their country; a manly pride pervades each breast. I
wish the working people of England knew a little more of this
country than they do. Wofully ignorant are they of almost
everything that relates to its history; particularly the history
of the war of independence. Indeed many newspaper editors
in England, and even members of parliament, when they
attempt to describe anything relative to any particular state,
make the most egregious blunders. Is it, therefore, to be
wondered at that the humbler classes are so ignorant on the
subject? But I hope a better day is coming. I trust that the
taunts and sneering allusions made about the paupers of
England, about the ignorance of the lower classes of English,
about the crime and intemperance of England, will ere long
be without foundation.

The system of public schools in this country is carried out
admirably, but I am not so well acquainted with its organization and ramifications as to give you any particular description. It is a very rare occurrence to find among the Americans
a man or woman who cannot read and write. The good effect
of these public schools is visible in the intelligence of the
people; it is visible in their everyday duties and business; and
if the good effect of these public schools is so visible in the
new settled state of Illinois, how must it be as regards Massachusetts, New Hampshire, Connecticut, and other eastern
states, where the system has been long in full operation?

To those working men in England intending to emigrate to
this country, particularly to those who intend purchasing
land, I would just say a few words. *Do not by any means buy
or contract for any land from any company, society, or agent
in England, who pretends to offer great inducements and
advantages to emigrants.* It is all humbug to say the least of it,
if not downright imposition. Many a poor emigrant has been
swindled out of his money by these land-sharks.[5] The Potters-
ville scheme in Wisconsin turns out to be a failure. Expectations are held out which it is impossible ever to realize. It only
excites the *pity* and not a little contempt and derision of the
American farmers to think that the English (who generally
boast of being more than commonly shrewd) should be so
easily seduced into such wild-goose schemes. If a person
intending to emigrate has means sufficient to buy land, let
him hold on to it; let him come out direct to the farming

---

[5] Systematic robbery of the emigrants landing from the ships that brought
them across the ocean had become so notorious that societies were organized
to furnish them protection against swindlers.

districts; let him hire himself out to some farmer for one or
two years; and in the meantime be listening to all he hears,
and he will have many opportunities for buying farms, as
there are always some for sale. Don't be in a hurry. He will be
sure to succeed in the end. But the idea of buying a piece of
land as soon as he gets out (or in some cases before he starts)
is preposterous; for if a person is unacquainted with the
nature of the title of the land, he is very liable to be taken up
on some bad title, and probably, before many years roll over,
he will have his farm to buy over again. There are various
kinds of titles, such as congress title, patent title, tax title, and
some others. A residence among the farmers for about two
years will make him acquainted with the nature of these
titles, and then he can purchase accordingly. There are a good
many English in this county, from the neighbourhood of
Manchester, Hyde, Dukinfield, Oldham, and Stockport. Some
follow farming who but a few years ago were cottonspinners,
powerloom weavers, or dressers; and now most of them own
pretty good farms of from 40 to 160 acres, and are doing very
well. Others are engaged in mechanical pursuits; or whatever
else they can get to do, for a person coming out here must not
be particular in what or as to what he does. He must be able
and willing to turn his hand to anything and everything, and
then he will be sure to succeed. It is a very great change for a
person to come from the cotton factory and to go on to a
farm; the new kind of labour, the difference in food, mostly at
first corn meal, or what is more properly called "pork and corn
dodger," the entirely new mode of living, and the comparative
loneliness which the transition from town to country brings
upon them, often discourages many; and it is only by steady
perseverance and a firm determination to overcome these
difficulties, that he may expect to succeed in his new undertaking.

. . . The cholera is very prevalent in the western states. A
number of deaths have taken place at St. Louis, Missouri. It
has again appeared in this vicinity, and at the most of the
towns on the Mississippi, Illinois, and Missouri rivers, but not
in quite so epidemical a form as it did in 1840.

In his second letter, Garside rejoiced in the change of tone of
some of the London newspapers towards Americans and their
contributions to the "World's Fair." He declared:

The laughs and sneers have been turned into something
like surprise at the "rugged utility" of the American contributions. McCormick's reaping machines, which are used by almost every farmer in this section of country, have made

English farmers scratch their heads with wonderment and
surprise, at the first display of its labour-saving power. Any
quantity of orders are given on the first display of the superiority of American over English ploughs. Hobbs throws consternation into all who have hitherto trusted in the infallibil-
ity of Bramah's celebrated patent locks; and lastly, and by no
means the least important, the yacht *America* throws down
the gauntlet to the world, and carries away the palm. So much
for the "rugged utilities of the Yankees." "John Bull Whipt
again," has often been sung in my ears since the above facts
became known here, and many are the jokes (all received in
good humour) which have been cracked at my expense. It is
pleasing and gratifying, however, to see the good results arising from these triumphs of American skill; it proves that the
English are willing to take a few lessons even from their
transatlantic brethren, and that we are not quite so stupid as
some of the press in this country would fain represent us to
be.

This has been a remarkable year for Illinois; it has been the
stormiest season ever known by the oldest settlers. The Illinois
river has overflowed its banks, causing the river in some
places to be from four to six miles wide; and being a somewhat slow, sluggish stream, it does not get within its banks in
a hurry. We have had storms and tornados in their most
terrific force. You in England have no idea of the fury and
strength of a storm in such a flat prairie country as Illinois.
No mountains or hills to intercept its fury; houses turned
over, fences prostrated; dreadful havoc indeed does it make
sometimes. Some fifteen years ago a tornado passed over this
place (Canton), destroying nearly every house in town, and
killing many persons. Dry goods from the stores were found
miles distant; the traces of its destructive course are yet
visible in the form of tall, dead trees—the trunks still standing—with all the limbs twisted off—monuments, as it were,
of this terrible hurricane. This is the greatest drawback I
know of to this prairie country. Aside from this, a more
desirable farming country than Illinois cannot be found on
the surface of the globe.

The crowning glory of the seasons in this western climate
comes on just about this season of the year; the almost
insufferable heat and dust of mid-summer being past, that
beautiful season known as the "Indian summer" comes to our
relief; the white frost begins to touch the earth slightly; the
leaves of the forest begin to assume their many and varied
hues, so pleasing and so beautiful, adding a charm and splen-
dour to the fall of the year; the days are warm—the nights
cool—the skies blue and cloudless—and oh! what glorious

sunsets! I have often read the eloquent and glowing descriptions given by travellers of the magnificent sunsets of the classic lands of Italy and Greece. If they can at all compare with the beautiful evenings we enjoy here, when the sun retires in the west, they must indeed be glorious to look upon. This kind of weather continues until towards the middle of November, and then we bid farewell to it with feelings of regret, as its departure is the sure sign that stern winter with all its rigors will soon set in. Now is the time for sport and pigeon shooting—now is the time for lots of game, and that, too, for shooting, without the dread of being set down as poachers. Such a word as poaching is unknown here; it cannot be found in the American vocabulary. . . . Towards the beginning of December, when winter begins to spread its snowy mantle over the prairie, will be the time for wild geese and duck shooting in the river bottoms; then will be the time when the peculiar sharp ring of the rifle will startle many a deer from its covert—and then will be the time when we can buy (we who have no time to spare in shooting) a good haunch of venison for about forty cents, less than two shillings (this, I suppose, would be considered very cheap with you!); then we can have all kinds of game very cheap. The Illinois river abounds in the finest quality of fish of every kind. A person who loves to indulge in such field sports need never want for opportunity or occasion to supply his table with animal food, without much trouble. . . .

Emigrants coming out west, and more particularly those coming from the eastern states, seem to have an idea that everyone coming here is sure to have an attack of the fever and ague—that they are obliged to have a good shake before they get acclimated. When they arrive here they generally find that fever and ague are very bad a little "farther west." I have now been here over four years, and not yet have I seen one real case of fever and ague. I have often heard that it is somewhere in the neighbourhood. It is, I suppose, most prevalent on the river bottoms, particularly in such seasons of overflow as we have had this year. Such seasons as this bring on myriads and myriads of mosquitoes.

I have often remarked, that the eastern people have an idea that when they get out here they will find the residents a sort of half-barbarian, half-Indian class of people; but they are greatly disappointed on finding that the residents in the west are just as smart, if not smarter, than themselves. . . .

The taxes here are light, comparatively speaking, to what you have to pay in England. Property is assessed at two-thirds its value, and yet I hear a good deal more grumbling by those who pay taxes than ever I heard in England. I could not help but laugh the other day when the collector informed me, that of all those who paid taxes, he always found the English the most willing to pay, and that they grumbled the least. "I suppose," says he, "that you have been so used to being taxed in England, that it comes, like bread and butter, quite natural." I am indeed proud to say, that there is less cause of complaint made against the English for misconduct or unruliness than against any other class of emigrants. Many are the rows and disturbances created by the Irish with all around them, caused by too great a love and indulgence in the "dear craythur."

The Germans, or rather a portion of them, and Americans, in St. Louis and New Orleans, have got to loggerheads. It appears that some of the Germans have come to the determination to form a "Native German party," in order to enforce some of the doctrines of the democratic party. There is a great feeling of prejudice and aversion manifested by the Americans against the formation of any native party whatever. Look at the disastrous results arising from the collision of Irish and American native parties that took place in 1844, in the city of Philadelphia. Governor King, of Missouri, has administered a scorching rebuke to the Germans. It appears that a military company had been organized by the German party, when application was made to the governor for arms from the state arsenal.

Governor King [6] not only refused to supply them, but as a sort of sweetner to the bitter pill, administered the following home thrust, which I extract from his letter: —"I do not hesitate to inform you that I cannot send you the arms for that occasion, and I take the responsibility of saying further, that I shall not send them until I am satisfied there is a greater disposition evinced amongst those who are to use them, to observe the moral restraints imposed upon all good citizens; to say nothing of what I consider to be the absolute legal enactments upon the subject. I am one of those who have ever been willing to open wide the doors, for the reception of our foreign population, who have sought a home and an asylum in our happy country, yet when they come, I think it evinces a much better spirit on their part, to set about Americanising themselves, adapting their habits to our institutions, our moral, social, and lawabiding habits. As American citizens, our habits, our social, moral, and religious restraints, are based upon the principles handed down to us by the fathers of the revolution, and we profess to know more of

---

[6] Austin A. King, a Democrat, became Governor of Missouri in 1848, and served until he was succeeded by Sterling Price in December 1852.

the influences which have served to elevate us as a people to a high rank among the nations of the earth, than it is possible for those foreigners to know who have just come among us."

Some of the Americans have often complained to me that so few of the regular stout English farmers come out to this country. They complain that too many come from the manufacturing districts. They want to see more come out from the agricultural districts of England. It is very rare that I come across an Englishman who follows farming here that followed the same occupation in England; they are generally from the manufacturing districts. However, the same system of farming in England would hardly pay here. We had about a year ago in this vicinity a first-rate specimen of an English farmer —a tall, stalwart, well-built man—his name was Thomas Critchlow, from the neighbourhood of Ashbourne, Derbyshire. He came out alone, a year ago last spring, for the purpose of choosing a location. During his stay, about six months, he gained the confidence and esteem of a good many influential farmers around here. He decided upon returning to England for the purpose of fetching his family. He left here last November for New Orleans, on his way home. On arriving there, and about three days before the ship sailed, he was seized with the cholera and died.

There are a good many able farmers in this country, whose kindness to new comers is worthy of the highest praise, and I think I cannot do better than mention a few names, among which are Elijah Capps, Esq., D. Vittam, Esq., and S. C. Nelson, Esq., Messrs. Overmans, Messrs. Ingersolls, merchants, and a good many others.

My opinion has often been requested as to which of the two ports, New York or New Orleans, I would recommend emigrants to embark for. I would say New York all the time, as I consider that emigrants coming from Great Britain come from too northern a latitude to land in New Orleans with anything like security from sickness; and a sick person has a poor chance of recovery on board the over-crowded steamboats. Too often, alas! does many a poor emigrant, after escaping the perils of a sea voyage, find his grave on the banks of the Mississippi River. I consider it healthier to land at New York by all means. I may, however, revert to the subject again some future time; want of space will not allow more at present.—I remain, sir, your obedient servant.

GEORGE R. GAYLER

of Macomb, Illinois, after serving in the Air Force in World
War II, received his bachelor's degree from Western Illinois
University and his Ph.D. in history from Indiana University.
He has published articles on Mormon and English history,
and is now a professor of social science at Northwest Mis-
souri State College, Maryville, Missouri.

This article was published in the *Journal of the Illinois
State Historical Society,* volume 49, number 1 (spring 1956),
pages 48–66.

THE MORMONS AND POLITICS IN ILLINOIS: 1839–1844

GEORGE R. GAYLER

The Mormon problem in Illinois during the 1840s resulted not
from any single phase of the settlement of Nauvoo and its
outlying districts, but from a combination of characteristics of
the Mormons and especially of their leader Joseph Smith. The
distrust and hate which came to dominate the citizens of Illinois in
relation to the inhabitants of Nauvoo can be traced to the Mormons' attitudes and actions in local and national politics, more
than to talk of polygamy or their economic and religious views.

In many respects the Illinoisans created the situation which they
were later so vigorously to condemn. They were certainly not unaware of the political possibilities of the Mormons when the latter
first entered and settled within the state. The reception offered
them and the generous charters making the city and the Nauvoo
Legion practically independent of the state government serve as
ample proof of that. Whigs and Democrats attempted to outdo each
other in securing the support of the new group, and the Mormons
were certainly not sufficiently naïve to fail to recognize and to take
advantage of this situation.

After Joseph Smith's arrival in Illinois late in 1839 he was too
busy with other matters to turn his attention immediately to politics. First he had to care for his followers, secure a place of
settlement, and acquire the necessary lands. Then the Prophet

journeyed to Washington, seeking federal aid in obtaining redress for injuries suffered by the Saints in Missouri. He presented his petitions to Congress, but was disappointed in an interview with President Martin Van Buren. The famous charters were also being acquired at this time. These endeavors occupied most of Smith's time for the first months of the settlement, and had their effects upon his political feelings. His reception in Washington and especially his treatment by Van Buren soured Smith against the Democratic Party for many months, and definitely influenced his stand in the elections of 1840 and 1841.[1]

In the Illinois gubernatorial election of 1838 Thomas Carlin, Democrat, led his Whig opponent, Cyrus Edwards, in Hancock County by a vote of 633 to 436. The closeness of this race explained in part the preliminary welcome extended the Mormons by both parties in 1839. Within a year the newly arrived Saints were already beginning to give hints of their influence in state and local politics. The presidential election of 1840 showed that the apprehensions of many Hancock County Gentiles as to Mormon political influence were not unfounded.

As the Mormons' political power grew in Hancock County, anti-Mormon activity also increased. In an editorial published on May 19, 1841, the *Warsaw Signal* denied the accusation "of having, for political effect, flattered the Mormons" and declared:

> We believe they have the same rights as other religious bodies possess. . . . But whenever they, as a people, step beyond the proper sphere of a religious denomination, and become a political body, as many of our citizens are beginning to apprehend will be the case, then this press stands pledged to take a stand against them. . . . It is bound to oppose the concentration of political power in a religious body, or in the hands of a few individuals.

Similar views were set forth in the resolutions adopted at a mass meeting at Warsaw, one of which stated: "There exists serious grounds of apprehension that the leaders of the Mormon body design, so soon as the numbers of their church constitute a majority of the votes, to control the officers of this county." On June 19 a meeting was held at Warsaw to select delegates to a convention to

---

[1] Smith wrote the High Council from Washington: "We do not say the Saints shall not vote for him [Van Buren], but we do say boldly . . . that we do not intend he shall have our votes."

be held at Carthage, the county seat, on June 28 to nominate candidates for the next election who would be "in opposition to Mormon influence and dictation," and the address adopted by this convention called upon the citizens of Hancock County to "lay aside former party feelings and oppose, as independent freemen, political and military Mormonism."

The reaction initiated against their political activity after only one election was to have grave consequences for Joseph Smith and his followers. The Mormons swelled the Hancock County vote to 1,976 in the 1840 presidential election—nearly double that of 1838. The Whig candidate William Henry Harrison received more than twice the vote of his Democratic opponent Van Buren (1,352 to 624).[2] Smith's intense dislike of Van Buren was definitely evidenced in these results, for he had apparently had no previous party predilections. The *Western World* of Warsaw seemed already to be aware of this in its initial issue (May 13), since it commented that the Mormons were "for Harrison" in the November election. Governor Thomas Ford explained this vote by indicating that the Mormons were especially bitter toward the Democrats because, after supporting the party in Missouri, they had been driven out of that state by a Democratic governor.

This Mormon boycott of the Democrats continued in the election for Congress the following year. Undoubtedly also influenced by Whig support in the passage of the Nauvoo charters, the Mormon vote made possible a decisive victory in Hancock County for John T. Stuart, Whig, over James H. Ralston, Democrat (1,201 to 523). Hancock County politics, however, were by this time dividing along Mormon and anti-Mormon rather than Whig and Democratic lines. William H. Roosevelt, a prominent Democrat, had predicted that "the [Gentile] Democrats . . . with scarcely an exception, will vote the Anti-Mormon Ticket." The anti-Mormon candi-

---

[2] At Warsaw, Harrison led Van Buren 142 to 78 and at Carthage 219 to 162. Two hundred Mormons scratched off the last name (Abraham Lincoln) on the Whig electoral ticket, substituting the name of Democrat James H. Ralston. The *Quincy Whig* of Nov. 7, 1840 called this "something connected with the vote at Nauvoo precinct, which needs explanation. . . . Rumor says that the Hon. *Richard M. Young*, of the U.S. Senate, and the 'little giant,' Stephen A. Douglas, who wants to go to Congress, were present at this election, and of course their names are freely used in connection with this little petty trick." This was done, according to Linn, "to keep the Democrats in good humor." John C. Bennett, the principal Mormon lobbyist for passage of the Nauvoo charters in Springfield, wrote that despite this Lincoln "had the magnanimity to vote for our act, and came forward after the final vote and congratulated me on its passage."

date for school commissioner won by four votes and the candidate for county commissioner by eighty-four.

A change in Mormon political attitudes took place in the winter of 1841–1842. On December 20, 1841, the Prophet in an open letter to his "friends in Illinois" stated:

> In the next canvass, we shall be influenced by no party consideration. . . . We care not a fig for Whig or Democrat; they are both alike to us, but we shall go for our friends, our tried friends, and the cause of human liberty, which is the cause of God. We are aware that "divide and conquer" is the watchword with many, but with us it cannot be done—we love liberty too well—we have suffered too much to be easily duped—we have no catspaws amongst us. . . . [Stephen A.] Douglas is a master spirit, and his friends are our friends. . . . [Adam W.] Snyder [3] and [John] Moore are his friends— they are ours. These men are free from the prejudices and superstitions of the age, and such men we love, and such men will ever receive our support, be their political predilections what they may. Snyder and Moore are known to be our friends; . . . they have served us, and we will serve them.

Orville F. Berry, taking Smith at his word, de-emphasized the role that politics played in creating the later unpopularity of the sect. The Prophet and his brother Hyrum, according to Berry, "were ready to go to either [party], where they thought it would work to their advantage." Events, however, notwithstanding Smith's own words, demonstrated otherwise. Most observers recognized the invalidity of his explanation that no persons had been more instrumental in securing the passage of the Nauvoo charters than the Democrats, for the charters had passed the legislature without a single dissenting vote from either party.

It is not difficult, however, to explain Joseph Smith's unwise actions. Stephen A. Douglas, as a justice of the Supreme Court, had rescued the Prophet at Monmouth from the first attempt of Missouri authorities to extradite him,[4] and more than any other political figure of the time Douglas influenced the thought and actions of the Mormon leader. Smith himself stated in 1841: "Judge Douglas

---

[3] Snyder, as chairman of the Senate Judiciary Committee, had a large part in the parliamentary procedure of passing the charters.

[4] The Missouri authorities' claims for Smith's extradition rested, first, on alleged "crimes" committed by the Mormons during their residence in that state, and second, on the attempted assassination of ex-Governor Lilburn W. Boggs in May, 1842 by Orrin P. Rockwell, one of the "Danite" band of Mormons. Rockwell's act was publicly approved by the Prophet, though he disclaimed any personal connection or responsibility.

has ever proved himself friendly to this people, and interested himself to obtain for us our several Charte[r]s." The "freedom of the city" was conferred on Douglas, and he "became a welcome guest at Nauvoo and in the Smith home." Ford also declared that Smith "inclined to esteem his discharge as a great favor from the democratic party."

This reversal on the part of the Prophet was a major political blunder. "If Smith had been a man possessing any judgment," said William A. Linn, historian of the Mormons, "he would have realized that the political course which he was pursuing, instead of making friends in either party, would certainly soon arraign both parties against him and his followers."

On December 1, 1841, the *Signal* lamented the low attendance at a Democratic meeting in Carthage:

> Politics *are* dead in this county, and will continue so, unless one of the parties will consent to the degradation of uniting itself to a corrupt and degraded church, and suffer Joe Smith to become sole Dictator. To this, we trust neither party will consent.

The death, in the midst of the campaign, of Adam W. Snyder, Democratic nominee for governor whom the Prophet praised in the letter quoted above, and the substitution of Thomas Ford in his place did not alter the Mormon vote for the Democratic Party; Ford received 1,748 votes in Hancock County to 711 for his Whig rival, ex-Governor Joseph Duncan. The wrath of the Whig press of Illinois knew no bounds. The *Sangamo Journal* of Springfield was especially bitter in its attacks on the Mormons; an editorial on January 14, 1842, accused Smith of forsaking religion for politics, and its issue of June 10 charged a collusion between Democrats and Mormons in state politics. The *Warsaw Signal* said:

> One of our Representatives [William Smith] is a Mormon, and a brother to the Prophet—our Sheriff [Jacob B. Backenstos] is in fact and heart a Mormon. . . . The whole ticket was a mongrel affair, made up by agreement between Joe Smith and some anxious office-seekers, of one of the political parties [the Democrats].

Ford later stated in his *History*:

> The whigs, seeing that they had been out-generaled by the democrats in securing the Mormon vote, became seriously

alarmed, and sought to repair their disaster by raising a kind of crusade against that people. The whig newspapers teemed with accounts of the wonders and enormities of Nauvoo, and of the awful wickedness of a party which would consent to receive the support of such miscreants.

Niles' National Register estimated that the Saints had

about six thousand votes under their immediate control, sufficient to give them the balance of power between parties in the state. It is alleged that they have found out how to make a profitable market of this power. . . . They are now accused of having contracted to support the [Democratic] party . . . in consideration of which the city of Nauvoo had a charter granted to it with very extraordinary powers. . . . Legislative powers [are] conferred upon its officers equal to those possessed by the legislature itself.

Smith's invasion of Illinois politics had thus already borne fruit and had set the stage for the grave consequences he and his followers were so soon to suffer. The Prophet did not aid his situation by tongue-in-cheek declarations made obviously for a front, which fooled no one, such as his public statement on the eve of the 1842 election that he did not intend to vote either the Whig or Democratic ticket, but that the Mormons "would go for those who would support good order, &c."

He was also reported to have said, early in July 1842, that he would throw "the weight of his church in favor of those who may come out as opponents of the Anti-Mormon convention candidates." The Mormons then "proceeded to nominate a full ticket of Mormons for Hancock County offices." Their strength was sufficient to influence elections, even those of the principal officers of the state. Their weight, though still felt only on a local level, was instrumental in turning the bulk of the citizens of western Illinois violently anti-Mormon.

By the end of 1842, Joseph Smith had totally alienated the Whigs of Illinois, and though seemingly catering to the Democrats had done little to prove his political reliability to that group. By the time of the next major political contest, the congressional election of August 1843, the Mormon vote had so gained in strength that "Every one conceded that Smith's dictum would decide the contest." Following the familiar pattern, the Prophet publicly stated in January 1843, in a letter to the Nauvoo *Wasp:*

> I have of late had repeated solicitations to have something to do in relation to the political farce about dividing the county; but as my feelings revolt at the idea of having anything to do with politics, I have declined, in every instance, having anything to do on the subject. I think it would be well for politicians to regulate their own affairs. I wish to be let alone, that I may attend strictly to the spiritual welfare of the Church.

Had Joseph Smith followed these words of wisdom, the next two years of the history of his sect in Illinois might have been different.

The attempts by Missouri authorities during the summer of 1843 to extradite Smith greatly affected Mormon political activity; what would normally have been a routine legal procedure took on in that election year a greatly magnified political emphasis. Governor James Reynolds of Missouri called on Governor Ford in June 1843 for armed assistance in arresting the Prophet. Soon thereafter Sheriff Backenstos brought word to Nauvoo that Smith need not fear that the Illinois governor would consent to extradition so long as the Mormons continued to vote the Democratic ticket. Ford later admitted that such a pledge had been given by a prominent Democrat (whom he did not name), but without his (Ford's) knowledge.

Smith was finally arrested on a visit to his wife's sister in Lee County. His friends "obtained a writ . . . returnable . . . before the nearest competent tribunal, which 'it was ascertained was at Nauvoo.'" Both the Whig candidate for Congress, Cyrus Walker of Macomb, and his Democratic opponent Joseph P. Hoge of Galena defended Smith in the extradition hearing—though the verdict of Smith's own Municipal Court could hardly have been in doubt. Smith said:

> Walker . . . told me that he could not find time to be my lawyer unless I could promise him my vote. He being considered the greatest criminal lawyer in that part of Illinois, I determined to secure his aid, and promised him my vote. He afterwards . . . joyfully said, "I am now sure of my election, as Joseph Smith has promised me his vote, and I am going to defend him."

The coming election seemed to be settled, for experience had shown that as the Prophet indicated, so voted the Mormons en masse. "The Mormons follow Smith's wishes in politics," wrote an observer late in 1843, "like a sheep following the bell sheep over a wall." By this time the Saints had gained so much in numerical strength that they could outvote most of the rest of the county or congressional district.[5]

Had matters ended in this way, the repercussions for the Mormons would not have achieved their later intensity. But suddenly, on the Saturday before the August election, Hyrum Smith (Patriarch of the Church and brother of the Prophet) announced before a large mass meeting at Nauvoo that he had received a "revelation" directing the Mormon population to vote for Hoge. This "revelation" was immediately challenged by William Law, a prominent Mormon leader, and finally Joseph Smith was brought in to decide the issue. He stated:

> I am above the kingdoms of this world, for I have no laws. I am not come to tell you to vote this way, that way or the other. In relation to national matters, I want it to go abroad unto the whole world that every man should stand on his own merits. The Lord has not given me a revelation concerning politics. I have not asked Him for one. . . . Mr. Walker . . . is . . . a high-minded man. . . . I voluntarily told him I should vote for him. . . . He withdrew all claim to your vote and influence if it would be detrimental to your interests as a people.
>
> Brother Hyrum tells me this morning that he has had a testimony to the effect it would be better for the people to vote for Hoge; and I never knew Hyrum to say he ever had a revelation and it failed. Let God speak and all men hold their peace.

Hoge carried Hancock County by a margin of 2,088 to 733. The Mormons had once again by a last-minute switch of their vote completely alienated the Whigs and stirred up another outburst of antagonism against themselves. Every Whig paper was loaded with accounts of the wickedness, corruption and enormities of Nauvoo. "From this time forth the Whigs generally, and a part of the Democrats, determined upon driving the Mormons out of the State; and everything connected with the Mormons became political." [6]

---

[5] *Sangamo Journal* (quoting the Rock Island *Upper Mississippian*) on Feb. 9, 1841 estimated Nauvoo's population at 3,000. Ford stated that by 1842 there were 16,000 Mormons in Hancock County alone. The total population of Hancock County in 1840 was only 9,946.

[6] Every possible derogatory incident concerning Nauvoo or Smith was reported by the Whig press. Even a minor rift between Smith and his wife in April, 1844 was reported in a manner greatly out of proportion to its significance. *Warsaw Signal,* April 17, 1844.

Ford throws further light upon the Mormon actions in this election:

> In the Quincy district, Judge Douglas was the Democratic candidate, O. H. Browning was the candidate of the Whigs. The leading Mormons at Nauvoo having never determined in favor of the Democrats until a day or two before the election, there was not sufficient time, or it was neglected, to send orders from Nauvoo into the Quincy district, to effect a change there. The Mormons in that district voted for Browning. Douglas and his friends being afraid that I might be in his way for the United States Senate, in 1846, seized hold of this circumstance to affect my party standing, and thereby gave countenance to the clamor of the Whigs, secretly whispering it about that I had not only influenced the Mormons to vote for Hoge, but for Browning also. This decided many of the Democrats in favor of the expulsion of the Mormons.

The *Quincy Whig*, however, considered that the Mormons voted for Browning "we suppose, because they considered him, by far, the most talented of the two candidates."

The furor caused by the unwise Mormon political activity was not long in asserting itself in other sections. On September 2, 1843, *Niles' National Register* carried the following article:

> We learn by a gentleman from Warsaw, that a meeting of the people of Hancock County, to be held at Carthage, was called today [August 16] to take into consideration their relation with the Mormons. It is said that a good deal of excitement exists against them, and apprehensions of a serious riot and outbreak were entertained. The people of that section of the state are as heartily tired of the Mormons as ever the citizens of Missouri were, but they have suffered them to obtain so strong a foothold that no power can exist which can deprive them of their positions, or induce them to abandon their present residence.

The same paper four weeks later reported that Gentile citizens of Hancock County had resolved "to refuse to obey the officers elected by the Mormons, who have complete control of the county." Ford reported similar mass meetings at Warsaw where resolutions were passed to expel or exterminate the Mormon population. "This was not a movement which was unanimously concurred in. The county contained a goodly number of inhabitants in favor of peace."

Joseph Smith would naturally have been expected to recognize and take heed of the serious situation into which his unwise political activities were leading him. This, however, was not the case. The Prophet continued to direct his flock steadily toward the imminent destruction of his Illinois settlement, and into a period of chaos and disaster that within less than a year would cost him and his brother their lives.

As early as October 1, 1843, the Mormons, intent upon remaining in the political picture, began looking ahead to the next presidential election. On that date an editorial appeared in their organ *Times and Seasons* urging Mormons to consider in the selection of the president a man who would be most likely to give the Saints aid in securing redress for their grievances, which they had hitherto failed to obtain. To this end Joseph Smith on November 4 addressed letters to Henry Clay and John C. Calhoun—two of the chief aspirants for the nomination the following year. In these letters he cited in detail the history of Mormon persecution in Missouri and their failure to receive redress in either the courts of Missouri or Illinois or in Congress, and also asked what stand each candidate, if elected, would take on this issue.[7]

Clay answered on November 15, 1843, stating:

> Should I be a candidate, I can enter into no engagements, make no promises, give no pledge to any particular portion of the people of the United States. If I ever enter into that high office I must go into it free and unfettered, with no guarantees but such as are to be drawn from my whole life, character and conduct.
>
> It is not inconsistent with this declaration to say that I have viewed with lively interest the progress of the Latter-day Saints; that I have sympathized in their sufferings under injustice, as it appeared to me, which have been inflicted upon them; and I think, in common with other religious communities, they ought to enjoy the security and protection of the Constitution and the laws.

Clay's reply excited Smith to anger. After waiting "in the fond expectation, that you would give . . . to the country, a manifesto of your views," he answered at great length on May 13, 1844, employing the type of language which had become characteristic of

---

[7] Smith also addressed the same letter to Van Buren, adding: "Also whether your views or feelings have changed since the subject matter of this communication was presented to you in your then official capacity at Washington, in the year 1841, and by you treated with a coldness, indifference, and neglect, bordering on contempt." Smith made no mention of any reply from Van Buren.

him. Pouring wrath upon Clay's head, the Prophet's reply read in part:

> In your answer to my questions, last fall, that peculiar tact of modern politicians, declaring "*if you ever enter into that high office, you must go into it free and unfettered, with no guarantee but such as are to be drawn from your whole life, character and conduct,*" so much resembles a lottery vender's sign, with the goddess of good luck sitting on the car of fortune, a-straddle of the horn of plenty, and driving the merry steeds of beatitude, without reins or bridle, that I cannot help exclaiming; O frail man; what have you done that will exalt you? Can any thing be drawn from your *life, character or conduct* that is worthy of being held up to the gaze of this nation as a model of *virtue, charity and wisdom?* . . .
>
> Your "whole life, character and conduct" have been spotted with deeds that causes a blush upon the face of a virtuous patriot; so you must be contented in your lot, while crime, cowardice, cupidity or low cunning have handed you down from the high tower of a statesman, to the black hole of a gambler. . . . Crape the heavens with weeds of wo; gird the earth with sackcloth, and let hell mutter one melody in commemoration of fallen splendor! for the glory of America has departed, and God will set a flaming sword to guard the tree of liberty, while such mint-tithing Herods as Van Buren, [Lilburn W.] Boggs, [Thomas Hart] Benton, Calhoun, and Clay, are thrust out of the realms of virtue as fit subjects for the kingdom of fallen greatness; *vox reprobi, vox Diaboli!*

Calhoun's reply, received December 2, 1843, followed a vein similar to Clay's:

> If I should be elected, I would strive to administer the government according to the Constitution and the laws of the union; and that as they make no distinction between citizens of different religious creeds I should make none. As far as it depends on the Executive department, all should have the full benefit of both, and none should be exempt from their operation.
>
> But as you refer to the case of Missouri, candor compels me to repeat what I said to you at Washington, that, according to my views, the case does not come within the jurisdiction of the federal government, which is one of limited and specific powers.

On January 2, 1844, the Prophet wrote Calhoun a lengthy and venomous retort not unlike that received by Clay, including, besides a myriad of personal insults, a lecture on the content of the federal Constitution and a history of religious persecution in the United States.[8]

As a result of these responses from Clay and Calhoun, Smith determined to publish his own personal political views. A long address prepared by the Prophet was read for him on February 7, 1844, setting forth his views of national politics, including such startling recommendations as the following:

> Reduce Congress at least one half. . . . Pay them two dollars and their board per diem; (except Sundays,) that is more than the farmer gets, and he lives honestly. Curtail the offices of government. . . .
>
> Petition your state legislatures to pardon every convict . . . blessing them as they go, and saying to them . . . *go thy way and sin no more.* . . . When they make laws for . . . any felony, . . . make the penalty applicable to work upon the roads, public works, or any place where the culprit can be taught more wisdom and more virtue; and become more enlightened. . . . Murder only can claim confinement or death. Let the penitentiaries be turned into seminaries of learning. . . .
>
> Petition also, ye goodly inhabitants of the slave states, your legislators to abolish slavery by the year 1850, or now. . . . Pay every man a reasonable price for his slaves out of the surplus revenue arising from the sale of public lands, and from the deduction of pay from the members of Congress. Break off the shackles from the poor black man, and hire them to labor like other human beings. . . . Abolish . . . court martial for desertion. . . . More economy in the national and state governments. . . .
>
> Let Congress shew their wisdom by granting a national bank, with branches in each state and territory. . . . And the bills shall be par throughout the nation. . . .
>
> Give every man his constitutional freedom, and the president full power to send an army to suppress mobs. . . .
>
> When we have the red man's consent, let the union spread from the east to the west sea; and if Texas petitions Congress to be adopted among the sons of liberty, give her the hand of fellowship; and refuse not the same friendly grip to Canada and Mexico.

It seems almost incomprehensible that the promulgator of such political views, under the conditions of the time, could have taken

---

[8] The *Warsaw Signal* of June 5, 1844, criticized Smith's violent attitudes toward Clay and Calhoun, and termed the former's answer to Smith "very courteous, yet frank and firm."

himself seriously. Smith was, however, in deadly earnest, and so were his multitude of followers in Illinois.[9]

Smith's announcement was received with mingled scorn, ridicule and anger by his Gentile neighbors. The *Warsaw Signal* declared the Prophet's views "confoundedly dull" and "altogether impenetrable to our intellect," and ended by remarking: "Joe . . . you are a greater dunce than nature ever intended you to be, and that you have about as much knowledge in your cranium of the relative limits and structure of our governmental polity, as there is essential moisture in a January corn stalk." A week later the *Signal* commented: "As a *General, Legislator,* and *Jurist,* Joe cant be beat—except by a *jackass.*"

The reception of the Mormon leader's views by his followers in Nauvoo was far different. Immediately after the announcement the *Times and Seasons* and *Nauvoo Neighbor* answered the question they had previously asked in their editorials, "Whom shall the Mormons support for President?" Formal announcement of Smith's candidacy soon appeared in both papers, and the proclamation "FOR PRESIDENT, GENERAL JOSEPH SMITH" was kept on the editorial page until the Prophet's assassination the following June 27. Sidney Rigdon became the Mormon candidate for Vice-President.

This was not the first time the idea of the presidency had come into Smith's mind. As far back as July 7, 1841, the *Signal* had asked in a series of rhetorical "Questions for the 'Times and Seasons' ":

> Did Joe Smith . . . say, that if they [the anti-Mormons] did not stop their blab about him, he would be President of the United States, (God would give him the office if he wanted it,) and then he would show them what a Bonaparte could do?

Now, however, in election year, the Prophet seemed almost apologetic for permitting his name to be interjected into the national political arena. On February 8, 1844, addressing a political rally in Nauvoo, he declared:

---

[9] The complete text of Smith's speech appears in *Times and Seasons,* May 15, 1844. A short time afterward Smith gave evidence of his sincerity in making these startling pronouncements by stating at a Nauvoo City Council meeting: "My opinion is that the officers of the city should be satisfied with a very small compensation for their services."

I would not have suffered my name to have been used by my friends on anywise as President of the United States, or candidate for that office, if I and my friends could have had the privilege of enjoying our religious and civil rights as American citizens, even those rights which the Constitution guarantees unto all her citizens alike. But this as a people we have been denied from the beginning. Persecution has rolled upon our heads from time to time, from portions of the United States, like peals of thunder, because of our religion; and no portion of the Government as yet has stepped forward for our relief. And in view of these things, I feel it to be my right and privilege to obtain what influence and power I can, lawfully, in the United States, for the protection of injured innocence; and if I lose my life in a good cause I am willing to be sacrificed on the altar of virtue, righteousness and truth, in maintaining the laws and Constitution of the United States, if need be, for the general good of mankind.

Immediately Mormon representatives, selected from among the ablest and most loyal of Smith's followers at Nauvoo, were sent out to campaign for their leader. These campaigners included such members of the top Mormon hierarchy as Brigham Young, Heber C. Kimball, Orson and Parley P. Pratt, Orson Hyde, and John Doyle Lee. The absence of these men was a great disadvantage to Smith when he was arrested and imprisoned at Carthage a few months later. These missing Apostles were then hurriedly recalled, but arrived at Nauvoo too late.

The Apostles went immediately about their religious and political mission in many sections of the United States. One incident related by Lee casts light on the evident lack of seriousness that prevailed toward the new candidate's appearance in the field. Lee held a "poll" on a boat bound for St. Louis and the Prophet won 75 to 50. "This," commented Lee dryly, "created a tremendous laugh." The *Nauvoo Neighbour* reported another "poll" taken on May 16, with 29 votes for Smith, 8 for Clay and 2 for Van Buren. "There is a wonderful shrinkage in Henry Clay, but the General is going it with a rush. *Hurrah for the General!*" Incredible as it may appear, the Mormons seemed to take such polls with absolute sincerity.[10]

In many places, however, the news of Smith's tossing his hat into the ring did not bring such amusement. Governor Ford termed

---

[10] Lee was one of the most trusted followers and henchmen of Joseph Smith and later of Brigham Young. He was executed in 1876 for his part in the infamous "Mountain Meadows Massacre" in Utah in September, 1857.

the Prophet's candidacy the act "to crown the whole folly of the
Mormons," and the famous Methodist circuit rider Peter Cartwright claimed that "almost every infidel association in the Union
declared in his [Smith's] favor." *Niles' Register* reported on March 2
that meetings were being called in Carthage and its vicinity "for the
purpose of organizing opposition to the encroachments and usurpa-
tions of Joe Smith. . . . They talk openly of the extermination of
the Mormons as the only means of securing their own safety." [11]

Smith himself reported the organization of "wolf-hunts," and
that February 17 had been set aside as a day of fasting and prayer
by Hancock County Gentiles for his destruction. A vicious editorial
in the *Signal* condemned Smith's entrance into politics and Mormon control of county elections. The Prophet, however, either
could not or would not heed the ominous warnings, and proceeded
blindly toward his own destruction and that of his Illinois
community.

The Mormon state convention was naturally called for Nauvoo.
The date set was May 17, 1844. Delegates from twenty-seven states
and ten Illinois counties were in attendance. The ticket headed by
Smith and Ridgon was formally adopted, and thirteen resolutions
were passed attacking Tyler's administration and setting forth
Smith's concepts of government as their platform. The convention
adjourned on the same day, after resolving to hold its national
convention in Baltimore on July 13. Mormon conventions in Boston and in Dresden, Tennessee, ended in riots, brought about by
the extremely hostile attitudes of non-Mormons. The delegates to
the Baltimore convention "assembled in a gloomy spirit . . . having just received intelligence of the murder of the man they all
contemplated to have named as their candidate for the presidency.
They met and resolved to adjourn 'sine die.' " [12]

How serious a political disturbance Smith's campaign would
have created is, of course, impossible to ascertain. Judging, however, from the troubles in Illinois, Massachusetts and Tennessee

---

[11] No mention of this was made in Hancock County newspapers of the day,
although the *Warsaw Signal* of February 14 announced another anti-Mormon
county convention.

[12] At least one newspaper was started to promote Smith's candidacy:
"FUNNY—A paper has been started in Belleville, Ills. which supports Joe
Smith's claims for the Presidency. It is Edited by Fredrick Snyder, (son of
Adam W. Snyder deceased, late candidate for Governor,) and entitled the
'Politician.' " *Warsaw Signal*, May 8, 1844.

due largely to the announcement of his candidacy, the United States may have been saved from the bloodiest election in its history by the death of the Prophet. In the election of 1844, with the Mormons once again voting the Democratic ticket, James K. Polk carried Hancock County over Clay by a vote of 1,399 to 747.

Had Joseph Smith possessed the foresight to realize the results of his unwise political actions, he would undoubtedly have employed moderation. Too late the Prophet found he had instigated a reaction, the intensity of which he had theretofore never been forced to face. The Mormon inhabitants of Nauvoo, by their unwise political maneuvers, had lighted the conflagration that in a few weeks snuffed out the life of their leader and brought disaster to their proud city.

Paul W. Gates

received his Ph.D. in history from Harvard in 1930, taught first at Bucknell and then at Cornell University where he was chairman of the history department from 1946 to 1956. He has been a consultant and expert appraiser for Quapaw, Chippewa, and Pottawatomie claims for the U.S. Department of Justice. He was active in professional organizations, serving as president of the Agricultural History Society, 1949–1950, and of the Mississippi Valley Historical Association, 1961–1962. His books include *The Illinois Central Railroad and its Colonization Work; Frontier Landlords and Pioneer Tenants; Fifty Million Acres; The Farmer's Age;* and *Agriculture and the Civil War.*

This article was published first in the *Journal of the Illinois State Historical Society*, volume 38, number 2 (June 1945), pages 143–206.

FRONTIER LANDLORDS AND PIONEER TENANTS

PAUL W. GATES

Not all frontiersmen were pioneer farmers struggling to create homes for themselves in the wilderness or on the prairie, or lonely cowboys watching over their charges on the boundless plains, or fur traders and trappers penetrating the most remote areas in their search for the beaver, the mink, and the otter, or miners optimistically wrestling with nature for the yellow nuggets. There were other frontier residents whose history is not so romantic but whose influence in shaping the emerging social and economic pattern was quite out of proportion to their numbers. The Indian agent with his power to disburse thousands of dollars of annuities, to contract for quantities of supplies, to hasten or delay Indian removal, to control allotments of land and the transfer of allotments, was a marked figure wherever he was stationed. The army officers at their lonely posts at Fort Dearborn, Fort Snelling, Fort Scott, and Fort Riley played their part in building western America many years before their presence was made unnecessary by the onrush of settlers and the establishment of local government. The frontier editors who early appeared in every ambitious little community and started papers filled with stale news of European wars and with congressional harangues lifted bodily from the *National Intelligencer* and the *Congressional Globe* are worthy of attention. The territorial officials, the United States land officers, the lawyers whose services were in demand before there was a legal title to a piece of land in the area, the note shaver, the moneylender or banker representing eastern capitalists are types found on every frontier.

Transcending all these non-farmer pioneers in importance were the great landowners. To anticipate the settlers, they moved with, sometimes ahead of, the vanguard of frontiersmen, following closely the footsteps of the surveyor. Great holdings of land, sometimes running to a quarter of a million acres and more, were acquired by them for resale to other speculators or to actual settlers, or to rent to tenants. At every government land sale these men were in attendance; at every land office town they maintained conspicuous offices; their advertisements provided much of the patronage of the struggling frontier newspapers and in not a few instances the newspaper was simply an adjunct of the land business.

These landowners expressed their supreme confidence in the future of the West by sinking great sums—in part borrowed capital —in the purchase of wild land, frequently retaining little or nothing for taxes, interest, fees, development costs, and other expenses connected with land ownership. If the expected profits did not materialize within a short period, their taxes remained unpaid, tax titles of dubious value issued, and patronage was thereby created for lawyers and the courts, and further financial aid given to the newspapers in the form of the much-fought-over "tax delinquent list." The tales widely bandied about in the West of crippling losses sustained by some of these landowners and the tremendous extent of the tax delinquent list, which at times seemed to indicate that few absentee, or even resident, owners were able to meet their taxes, have led some writers to conclude that no profits were made in the western land business. It is true that most holders of western land at one time or another complained about being land poor but it is also true that in practically every town, large or small, the local squire, the bank president, the owner of numerous mortgages, the resident of the "big house," the man whose wife was the leader of "society," got his start—and a substantial start—as a result of the upward surge of land values in the nineteenth century.

ROMULUS RIGGS—A PIONEER LANDLORD

Having made their plunge, which for the moment gave them nothing but a cold shock and threatened to engulf them entirely, some of these owners of great estates looked for means by which they might make their investments profitable. Thus Romulus Riggs of Philadelphia, who had acquired 256 quarter-sections of land in the Military Tract of Illinois during the thirties, first tried to secure sufficient return from his land to meet his taxes and then to add something for current income. When he discovered the Illinois Suckers' propensity for hooking or stealing timber from nonresident or speculator-owned land he decided that action was necessary or else his investment might become worthless. Legal action, he soon learned, was not the proper step to take as it aroused frontier prejudices and generally proved ineffective. Riggs found it possible to make agreements with squatters upon his land whereby they undertook to prevent unauthorized cutting on a number of sections in return for the right to use the land. A little later he induced squatters to agree to pay the taxes. Then, when their improvements such as a one-room log house, a little fencing, and a few acres of cultivated land represented sufficient labor and investment to put them in a receptive mood, Riggs demanded a cash rent in excess of the taxes. Thus was tenancy born on the frontier.[1]

HENRY L. ELLSWORTH INVITES PRAIRIE LANDLORDISM

It was in the prairie counties of central Illinois that frontier landlords and pioneer tenants were most numerous, as in these same counties today are found the largest of the estates and the highest proportion of tenancy. Long avoided by settlers and speculators, the prairie counties began to attract attention in the late thirties to some degree but more largely a decade later. One of the first persons to recognize the possibilities in prairie farming on a large scale was Henry L. Ellsworth, who, in 1835, acquired 18,000 acres in Vermilion and Iroquois counties, Illinois, and Benton County, Indiana, which he developed with the aid of laborers and tenants. As federal commissioner of patents he used his influence to interest men of capital in making investments in prairie lands

---

[1] This brief statement of the management of the 40,000-acre estate of Romulus Riggs is based on a study of the extensive collection of Riggs Papers in the Library of Congress.

which, he promised, would become highly profitable when tenants were established on them. Ellsworth advertised the prairies and the opportunity for investments in them in government documents, emigrant literature, and newspapers. Tenants, he maintained— and here he is supported by much contemporary evidence[2]—could easily be secured for absentee-owned estates provided some improvements were made; and on a crop-share basis the returns to both tenants and landowners would be large. Ellsworth's own advice on renting land is interesting:

> It is customary to rent land (once broke and fenced) for one-third of the crops, delivered in the crib or barn. At this rent the tenant finds all.
> I would advise to employ smart, enterprising young men, from the New England States, to take the farm on shares. If the landlord should find a house, a team, cart, and plough, and add some stock, he might then require one-half the profits of the same. I would advise to allow for fencing or ditching a certain sum, and stipulate that the capital invested should be returned before profits were divided. A farmer could in this way earn for himself from $700 to $1,000 per annum, on a lease for five years. . . .
> If it be asked, what are the profits of cultivation? I answer, if the land is rented for five years, the profits accruing during this period will repay the capital advanced in the commencement, with 25 per cent. interest per annum, and leave the farm worth $20 per acre at the expiration of the lease. Probably the profit would be much greater.

Ellsworth's great faith in the prairies and the alluring descriptions he gave of them induced many eastern capitalists to buy wild land in Indiana and Illinois. Dozens of people invested through him sums ranging from a few hundred to ten and twenty thousand dollars, and the total area that came under his control in this way ran to seven or eight townships. Other persons who were induced by Ellsworth to invest in prairie lands kept the management of their estates in their own hands. Possibly John Grigg, whose large land business is described below, was one of them.

---

[2] In an article of 1852 directed "To Western Emigrants," Solon Robinson said, "No matter if you have no money, you can rent land very low, and will soon be in a condition to let land instead of hiring it." James Caird, who toured Illinois in 1858, observed that share renting was "very common in Illinois." In reading the prairie newspapers of the forties and fifties one is struck by the number of notices offering farms for rent and, less frequently, advertisements calling for farms to rent.

Ellsworth undertook to establish for himself and his family a great patriarchal estate which he hoped to have well developed by tenants before advancing age required handing it over to his children. Part of the land was held as speculation, the proceeds to be used to finance improvements on the remainder. Hired laborers and tenants were used to construct fences, dig ditches, cultivate the land, and manage the livestock. As early as 1845 Ellsworth was offering to lease unimproved lands for one-half the crops for two or three years, at the end of which period a fee title would be given without further payments. A considerable amount of land was thus brought into cultivation but Ellsworth failed in his attempt to establish a profitable, well-managed, and modern estate like that of the Wadsworths of New York. Inadequate capital, the high cost of drainage and fencing, expensive and impractical experiments, and declining health, together with the crushing effect of the panic of 1857, defeated him. His estate, after some litigation, passed into the hands of more practical and hardheaded frontiersmen like Edward C. Sumner, Adams Earl, and Moses Fowler, who were to achieve the goal that Ellsworth had sought.

While Riggs, Ellsworth, and other frontier landlords succeeded in establishing tenancy at an early date on their holdings they were not able to obtain much rent until the middle of the century. The panic of 1837 and the resulting period of hard times, the scarcity of money on the frontier, and the poor demand for farm products made it difficult to collect rents or to sell land for anything like the prices anticipated, although it was not difficult to secure tenants. In the late forties the tide turned; immigrants by the tens of thousands began coming to Illinois annually, bringing with them some capital; Eastern capitalists again bought land by the section and even by the township; agricultural prices recovered and, of course, land values skyrocketed.

GOVERNMENT LARGESS ENCOURAGES SPECULATION AND LANDLORDISM

In the midst of this land boom which lasted from 1847 to 1857, the federal government adopted several policies which further stimulated land speculation and hastened the end of the public domain in Illinois.

Military bounty land warrants covering more than 60,000,000 acres were granted to soldiers and officers of the Mexican War and to veterans of previous wars. These warrants were dumped on the market, where they dropped as low as sixty cents an acre, thereby doubling the amount of land which speculators could acquire through the use of these rights. At the same time, the wet, over-flowed, or swamp lands were donated to the states in which they were located in the hope that they would be drained. Little was done to drain these swamp lands at the time; instead the lands soon found their way, in huge tracts, into the hands of speculators. Finally, the long discussed project for a central railroad to extend through the heart of Illinois received the blessing of the government, together with a grant of 2,595,000 acres of land to aid in its construction. The completion of this railroad, the longest as yet undertaken, together with the impetus it gave to the building of other prairie railroads, aided in bringing most of the prairie country within easy reach of modern transportation. As a result of these factors the era of the public domain was brought to an end in Illinois prior to the adoption of the Homestead Act.

Railroad Land Policies

Second only to federal land policy in permitting as well as encouraging the establishment of large estates in Illinois was the land policy of the Illinois Central Railroad. As part of its efforts to sell its land grant the railroad invited capitalists to purchase land without limit and assured them, as Ellsworth was doing, that tenants could be secured to farm their land who would bring them high returns in the form of rents. A considerable part of the early sales of the railroad was made to colony promoters and landlords who were planning the creation of huge estates or bonanza farms. The Malhiot estate, subsequently the Vandeveer estate in Christian County, the Sullivant estate in Ford and Champaign counties, the Funk and Gridley estates in McLean County, and the Danforth estate in Kankakee and Iroquois counties, were established in part from purchases of railroad land.

Landlordism and tenancy were also encouraged by the high prices the Illinois Central charged for its land. Few settlers were able to pay the $5.00, $10, or $20 which it charged per acre and if they were tempted by the optimistic descriptions of prairie farming to make a try at it they had to buy on time. Only advance interest was charged the first two years; in 1859 it was made the first four years. The principal payments proved to be hard to meet, few purchasers being able to complete payments on schedule. Lenient treatment by the railroad could not get around the fact that overdue payments resulted in added interest, and an increased debt. After long delays the Illinois Central encouraged settlers to surrender their contracts and take title to a small part of the whole, the payments on which had been completed. Some settlers in this way became owners of tracts too small to farm economically. Others never could complete their payments on the land to which their improvements had given increased value. Some, when pressed by the railroad, borrowed money on the security of their land, took title and mortgaged it to their creditor. From this mortgaged status some were to emerge as full owners, others were to be defeated and to have their farms foreclosed. Tenancy or emigration were open to them.

To the speculators and landlords of the thirties who, like the owners of the Riggs estate, had managed to carry their holdings through the dark days after 1837 was now added a new crop of frontier landlords who were looking for the chance either to rent their land or to sell it at enhanced prices. Over one-third of the area of Illinois was in the wild state, being held by the railroad, which was asking from $5.00 to $20 an acre for its well-located tracts, or by John Grigg, Solomon Sturges, or the numerous other speculators —all eager to sell at prices which were beyond the means of most immigrants, or to rent at a price equivalent to the government's charge for its land. True, the railroad and many speculators granted long credit but some down payment was required and few immigrants could even provide that. Furthermore, it must be remembered that prairie land, which comprised the bulk of the holdings of both the railroad and the speculator landlords, needed artificial drainage, that it was difficult for the man of small means to break up his land without the employment of expensive breaking plows and numerous yoke of oxen, that fencing and building materials were not easy to obtain without the expenditure of considerable money. It seemed, then, that only men with some capital could contract for and meet the payments on railroad or speculator-owned land. In fact, the Illinois Central Railroad was careful in its advertising literature to warn the poorer class that they could not begin prairie farming without $1,000 or more for necessary expenditures.

THE LAND SALES OF JOHN GRIGG

The experience of John Grigg in selling his great 124,000-acre estate in central Illinois is important as showing the rising value of unimproved land.[3] Grigg was not bothered by the lack of capital that so harried many of his contemporaries. His lands became encumbered neither by mortgages nor tax titles and when conditions improved he was in a position to take advantage of rising land values. By the middle forties he was selling land at $3.00 an acre, a price which was not exceeded, except for scattered forties, until 1851 and 1852 when prices ranging upward to $6.00 an acre were received, although $4.00 and even $3.00 remained more common. In the later fifties he received as high as $9.00 and $10.00 an acre, but somewhat lower prices were the usual thing. In the three counties of Sangamon, McLean, and Logan, Grigg's sales, mostly in the forties and fifties, were as follows.[4]

County	Acres	Price Rec'd.
Logan	3,378	$ 21,831
McLean	8,639	36,121
Sangamon	26,532	128,727
Christian	16,910	87,370
Total	55,459	$274,049

Grigg apparently neither planned to withhold his land for higher prices nor to rent to tenants. His policy was to push the land into buyers' hands as rapidly as possible and he was content with an average price of $5.00 an acre. Had he been willing to retain his land for a few years longer or had he attempted to secure tenants he doubtless would have fared better.

---

[3] Information on the entries of public lands is compiled from the abstracts of entries in the National Archives, Washington. Duplicates of these records for Illinois are on file in the State Auditor's office, Springfield. Most Illinois counties have a volume of abstracts of original entries in the recorders' offices.

[4] Data concerning purchases, sales, and leases of land other than original entries have been compiled from the deed, mortgage and miscellaneous records of the various counties covered by this article. Since much of the data here given is collected from many volumes it has not seemed wise to give more than this general reference, except in cases of specific information when the volume and page are cited.

CORCORAN DEVELOPS HIS ESTATE

A major beneficiary of the rising land values and the growing demand for farm rents was William W. Corcoran, the well-known Washington banker and patron of the Democratic Party.

Over many years the federal government had come into the possession of a vast quantity of property through defalcations of treasury officials who had speculated in western land and whose investments and those of their bondsmen had been forfeited to the government. Greatest of these defaulters and absconders was Samuel Swartwout, collector of the port of New York, who had misappropriated more than a million dollars for speculations in western lands. In 1847 the time was deemed right for the government to sell these forfeited lands which had not been restored to the public domain and to which the government's title was not entirely clear. Corcoran, through his friend, Robert J. Walker, was sufficiently informed of the matter to be able to bid low but successful prices ranging from 37 to 41 cents an acre. Choicest of these lands were 22,199 acres in Illinois that were bought for 38 cents an acre. This land was widely scattered, one-half being in Grundy, Macon, Coles, McDonough, Bureau, Fulton, and Will counties. In 1853 Corcoran added to his Illinois investment by a joint speculation made with Congressman Orlando B. Ficklin whereby 3,000 acres were acquired in Coles, Douglas, and Cumberland counties.

Corcoran's investments in Illinois being scattered, he was obliged to place them in charge of a number of agents who gave him a good deal of trouble by the lax manner in which they conducted the business, their inability to collect the rents when due and to pay the taxes before penalties and tax titles had encumbered the property. Corcoran was unable to give the business the close supervision that it needed, especially after 1861 when he was forced by circumstances to leave the country on account of his alleged pro-Southern sympathies. Despite these difficulties and the fact that confiscation proceedings were brought against some of his lands, the estate developed in a most profitable way. Coal was early discovered on the Grundy and Rock Island land and Corcoran's royalties were large for years.

Absentee ownership and nonresident agents seemed to make necessary the cash rent system for the farming land. Corcoran gave leases for as much as five years but reserved the right to sell the land at any time. By means of partial remission of rents or direct financial assistance, he encouraged his tenants to build fences and to erect houses and barns. If the property were sold before the expiration of the lease, improvements put on the land by the tenants might be removed. Rents in the fifties ranged from merely nominal sums plus taxes and stipulated improvements to $1.00 and $2.00 an acre for well-developed farms. Gradually the rents were increased until in the nineties, after the larger part of the estate had been sold, or lost through title deficiencies, they brought as much as $8,000 and $10,000 a year to Corcoran's heirs.

Both Riggs and Corcoran found that they had underestimated the difficulties of managing lands that were located in remote areas. For many years they were subjected to a constant stream of petty annoyances over timber-stealing, squatting, difficulties over tax payments and the collection of rents, and repeated demands by tenants for capital improvements to be made at the expense of the landlord. Their correspondence reflects rank pessimism and thorough disillusionment with the western land business despite the increasing returns it yielded.

Ellsworth was more typical than were Riggs and Corcoran of the great nineteenth-century prairie landlords because he knew intimately the details of farming, gave the land and farming business his close personal supervision and identified himself completely with the development of the prairies. His generation witnessed the emergence of numerous estates ranging from 5,000 to 45,000 acres in central Illinois and northwestern Indiana that were owned, developed, and operated by agricultural Napoleons possessing Ellsworth's vision and optimism plus the energy, shrewd judgment, faith in and capacity to drive themselves as well as their laborers and tenants to such a degree as to make successful their spectacular enterprises.

These prairie landlords followed a fairly common agricultural pattern based on livestock and grain-raising with greater or less emphasis upon the one or the other, but varied widely in their rental policies, their financial practices, and their use of hired labor. It was in Sangamon, Logan, De Witt, Piatt, McLean, Livingston, Grundy, Ford, Champaign, Vermilion, Iroquois, and Kankakee counties that these large estates were located. The Vandeveer estate in Christian County, the Gillett estate in Sangamon and Logan counties, the David Davis and Asahel Gridley estates in McLean County, the C. H. Moore estate in DeWitt County, and the Hoge, Holderman, and Collins estates in Grundy County are well worth study but only the more significant historically can be given attention here.

ISAAC FUNK, A LAND AND CATTLE KING

To most residents of Illinois mention of large estates calls to mind the Funk family. Isaac and Jesse Funk, who were among the pioneers of McLean County, early engaged in the livestock industry, fattening great herds of cattle and hogs for market. One report has it that the Funks bought, fattened, and drove to market 6,000 hogs in a single season. From their cattle and hog business the Funks won high profits which were invested in land. By 1841, Isaac Funk had acquired 5,760 acres in Funk's Grove where his operations were centered. Included within this acreage was a considerable quantity of heavily timbered land which, being surrounded by treeless prairies, was certain to be in demand when these open spaces attracted population. In the early fifties, when the Chicago and Alton and the Illinois Central railroads were being built through McLean County and when there was a rush to secure the remaining public land in the state, Funk began buying on a scale much larger than before, both from the government and from the Illinois Central Railroad, whose holdings in McLean County were large. The profits he was making from the livestock business and from the sale of his timbered land and small pieces of choice prairie land made possible the purchase of some 22,000 acres, the bulk of which was in Funk's Grove.

On his huge estate of 27,000 acres Funk established a bonanza farm as spectacular as, and certainly more successful than, the great farms of the Red River Valley of a later time. In 1861, for example, he was reported to have 1,000 beef cattle, 200 cows with calves, 400 stock cattle, 500 sheep, 500 swine, 240 horses and mules, and 60 colts grazing on his land. Such gigantic operations called not only for large pastures but also for a good deal of corn for fattening the stock. Funk rented the land not required for pasture to tenants who paid him two-fifths of the grain they produced if they provided the farming utensils and teams; but if Funk provided the tools and the teams his share of the grain was one-half. Under the share rent plan Funk also provided housing accommodations, and such barns and cribs as were necessary, and set out the hedge fencing.

Like other cattle kings who invested their profits in large estates, Funk employed hired labor, generally easy to find on the frontier where land values were pushed up rapidly and where considerable funds were necessary even to buy a small tract from the government at its minimum price. Many laborers paused only for a short time on such jobs as Funk offered and then, with funds accumulated, bought land in the vicinity or, perhaps, moved farther west where it could be acquired more easily and cheaply. Other laborers moved up into the class of tenants, some of whom likewise made good and were able subsequently to become owners. Still others, however, found it difficult, if not impossible, to become owners and were to remain as tenants.

Funk bought land partly for development as pastures and for rent to tenants and also for resale at a later time. Funds derived from such sales were to make possible the improvement as well as the enlargement of the estate. Between 1842, when his first sales were made, and 1865, when he died, he sold 2,127 acres for $17,455, some small timbered tracts bringing as high as $90 an acre. In the four years after his death his heirs sold 3,467 acres for $106,761.

Isaac Funk's estate passed into the hands of his numerous children. Much of it is still held by descendants of the third and fourth generation. In fact, the ownership map of Funk's Grove Township even today gives the appearance of a family controlled township as it did in 1855. Unlike some other families whose fortunes were made in holding and developing prairie real estate, the Funks have remained in McLean County, where they have taken a leading part in the great hybrid seed industry, banking, city improvement and other economic activities, in addition to their management of thousands of acres of farm land.

MICHAEL SULLIVANT: THE WORLD'S LARGEST FARMER

No description of frontier landlords of Illinois would be complete if it did not include Michael Sullivant. The Sullivant family had early settled in central Ohio where it had acquired 53,000 acres through the location of military warrants given to veterans of the Revolutionary War. A tract of 5,000 acres near Columbus had been cleared and made into a highly productive farm on which

2,300 acres of corn and 250 acres of wheat were grown, and herds of sheep and 200 to 300 mules were pastured. Tiring of this venture, Michael Sullivant and his brother, Joseph, rented their Ohio farm to tenants on a share basis and undertook to carry their large-scale farming and ranching operations westward into Illinois and later into Kansas.

Attracted by the deep rich soil of the Grand Prairie of east central Illinois at a time when that area was still largely untouched by white settlers, the Sullivants bought from the government, from the Illinois Central Railroad, and from speculators who had preceded them at the land office at Danville, 80,000 acres in Champaign, Ford, Livingston, and Vermilion counties, paying for the railroad land $5 and $10 an acre. A compact tract of 22,000 acres in Champaign County was chosen for the big farm which Sullivant proposed to develop. In February 1855, the Sullivant party left Columbus, Ohio, for Illinois with nine heavy wagons, thirty horses, and thirty-five men, the wagons being designed to serve as tents until suitable buildings could be constructed. The party arrived on the land in time for spring plowing, additional laborers were recruited, and great herds of horses and mules were employed to break the prairie, seed it to corn, and fence the land—now appropriately called Broadlands. From 1855 to 1866 Sullivant conducted operations at Broadlands on a scale that is reminiscent of the great plantations in the South. Between one and two hundred laborers were employed in the summer, vast fields were planted to corn, and great herds of cattle were pastured. In one year 1,000 tons of hay were sold. Later, when the estate was better developed, it was said to have 1,800 acres in corn, 340 acres in other grain, and to be pasturing 5,000 cattle and 4,000 worn-down government horses. Two hundred horses and mules and a large herd of oxen provided the motive power for the plowing, harrowing, seeding, and cultivating.

Despite the large number of laborers he employed, Sullivant had mechanized his farm to a degree that surprised a correspondent of the *Cincinnati Enquirer* who wrote:

> Almost all of Mr. S's farming is conducted by labor saving machinery, so that it is estimated that, throughout, one man will perform the average labor of four or five as conducted on small farms. He drives his posts by horse-power; breaks his ground with Comstock's "spade"; mows, rakes, loads, unloads

and stacks his hay by horse-power; cultivates his corn by improved machinery; ditches any low ground by machinery; sows and plants by machinery, so that all his laborers can ride and perform their tasks as easy as riding in a buggy.

Sullivant's land purchases were financed by loans made by various banks and by the generous credit terms allowed by the Illinois Central, his debt being at the outset $225,000. Heavy interest charges, together with other costs involved in breaking, ditching, fencing, planting, and harvesting his crops, soon raised his total debt to half a million.[5] For a time during the Civil War, Sullivant fared well, his net profit in 1862 being $80,000, which was invested in additional improvements. Less favorable years followed, however, and the high interest charges on his debt obliged him to sell part of his 80,000 acres as he had originally planned to do. Unfortunately, unimproved prairie land in Champaign, Ford, and Livingston counties had not as yet attained the level for which he was holding. Circumstances therefore dictated the selling of Broadlands in 1866—22,551 acres for $270,000. It was stated that the sale of the stock, grain, hay, and farming implements on the estate added nearly $100,000 to the purchase price. Sullivant then turned to a still larger tract of 40,000 acres in Ford and Livingston counties, which was more remote from transportation facilities and in one of the least developed portions of Illinois.

In the next ten years Burr Oaks became the best-known farm in America, so widely published were the stories about its vast operations. Like Broadlands under its new owner, and the great farms of Jacob Strawn, Benjamin F. Harris, John Sidell, and Edward C. Sumner, all on the Illinois prairie, Burr Oaks was a true "bonanza farm" experiment in which individual fields of thousands of acres were plowed, harrowed, seeded, and harvested by the greatest array of farm machinery as yet assembled. A reporter of *Harper's Weekly*, who visited the farm in 1871 in quest for pictures and information, was impressed with the size of the farm, the 16,000 acres in grain, the nature of the management, the specialization and division of labor, the meager buildings and few improvements but especially with the quantity of the labor-saving machinery in use. He wrote:

---

[5] In 1857 Sullivant gave a trust deed to cover a mortgage of $150,000 on his Ford County land. The debt was owed to banks and individuals in Ohio, Indiana, Kentucky, and Virginia.

The machinery in use at Burr Oaks would handsomely stock two or three agricultural implement stores: 150 steel plows, of different styles; 75 breaking-plows; 142 cultivators, of several descriptions; 45 cornplanters; 25 gang harrows, etc. The ditching-plow, a huge affair of eighteen feet in length, with a share of eleven feet by two feet ten inches, is worked by sixty-eight oxen and eight men. These finish from three to three and a half miles of excellent ditch each day of work.

Perhaps the largest crop produced on Burr Oaks with the aid of this great array of farm machinery was that of 1871 when the output of corn amounted to 600,000 bushels.

Tenancy was not introduced on Burr Oaks at first but unmarried laborers, mostly Swedes and Germans, ranging in numbers from 200 to 400 were employed from April through January, being housed in rough barracks. Thus by constructing the fewest and most inexpensive improvements Sullivant was able to make his capital go a long way in buying land and in raising corn from it year after year.

Sullivant's second venture in large-scale farming fared well until the panic of 1873 set in motion a downward movement of prices. To compensate for this reduced income the area in cultivation was enlarged until there were 23,000 acres in corn, but this in turn greatly increased the burden of debt the estate was carrying. The panic also knocked the props from under the real estate market and Sullivant was again cheated of the opportunity of selling his surplus and unimproved lands to aid in carrying the remainder. In 1871 Burr Oaks was mortgaged for $478,000, more than half of which was owed to Hiram Sibley, of Rochester, New York. This money was borrowed at 10 per cent interest and 5 per cent commission, not high rates for Illinois at the time but high enough to make the enterprise hazardous without a combination of good crops and satisfactory prices.

Sullivant found it increasingly difficult to keep all the details of the farming business in his own hands and divided the estate into large units over which overseers were appointed. Division of authority was not a panacea; other and more fundamental difficulties had to be surmounted. Drainage of the prairies was essential but it was costly and Sullivant proceeded slowly, too slowly for his own good. In 1870 it was reported that nothing as yet had been done to drain the tract. Dependence upon his corn crop put the "patroon," as Sullivant was called, in a dangerous position when that crop was light, but little was done to diversify save to pasture considerable numbers of cattle and hogs.

Continued financial worries and inability to sell surplus land forced a change in plans. Laborers on the estate and farmers in the vicinity were invited to become tenants of Sullivant, who was still reluctant to give up his well-earned title of "Corn King of America." In 1874 Sullivant advertised several thousands of acres to rent on shares in tracts of 80 acres or larger. He also wanted several "good farm bosses" to take charge of gangs of fifteen to twenty men with teams, the compensation to be according to ability.[6] This policy of establishing tenants on the land, which brought satisfactory returns to other large landowners in the sixties and seventies, was adopted too late to save Sullivant's estate. A series of poor harvests and an ever-mounting interest burden, together with continued management difficulties, forced an assignment in 1877 and foreclosure two years later.

Although the local press had commented approvingly when Sullivant first came to Ford and Livingston counties to develop Burr Oaks it soon changed its tune. When he was forced to sell part of his land, and later when Burr Oaks was divided into small tenant holdings, the newspapers expressed gratification. These counties already had a very high percentage of land cultivated by tenants or hired laborers, much of which was absentee owned, and the disposal of the Sullivant interest, coming at the same time that the Jacob Bunn estate in Livingston County was being liquidated, was regarded as a step in the right direction. In Monticello, the *Piatt County Herald* called large land holdings "a great drawback" to a region since the majority of the owners were land poor, unable to pay their debts, and kept out small farmers who were much more desirable.

A Modern Landlord

Somewhat reluctantly, it appears, Hiram Sibley, principal creditor of Sullivant, took over the larger part of Burr Oaks, now renamed Sibley Farms. Already experienced in large farming operations on his Howland Island estate in Cayuga County, New York, Sibley threw aside the whole Sullivant plan of operations and

---

[6] In 1876 Sullivant announced that he had "come to the conclusion that I monopolize more territory" than he should and was ready to sell 20,000 acres.

began anew. The 40,000 acre estate being considered too unwieldy for efficient administration, one-half was offered for sale in 1879, part being sold in large tracts and part being divided into small holdings. Sibley reserved 17,640 acres that he divided into 146 tenant farms ranging in size from 80 to 320 acres. In the short space of four years he built on Burr Oaks 134 houses and barns in which were established as many tenant families, who were now largely displacing the migratory labor that Sullivant had employed. All the houses, barns, ditching, tiling, fencing, and other improvements were put on the land by Sibley and they seem to have compared well with other tenant improvements in the same area.

Sibley struck immediately at the drainage question, being determined to have most of his land cultivated. Where his predecessor had left the wetter parts in permanent pasture with native grasses, Sibley began an elaborate program of ditch construction. Very soon he learned, as most owners of prairie farms did, that ditching was not a satisfactory solution; only tile draining would make possible the successful cultivation of wet areas. By 1877, 376 miles of tile had been laid on Burr Oaks, in itself no small investment.

As was common practice, the Sibley lands were rented on a share basis. At the town of Sibley huge corncribs and warehouses for small grains were erected to receive the landlord's share of the crops. A practical and efficient system of supervision was established on the estate including the employment of a general manager, a superintendent and executive officer, an overseer of hands, two overseers of tenants, an overseer of teams, and a foreman of repairs. In line with good farm practice it was the Sibley policy to feed the grain on the farms, and purebred beef and dairy cattle were introduced by the landlord. In 1879, 500 purebred calves were shipped to Burr Oaks from Sibley's New York farm. The system of rotation and the farm practices to be employed by the tenants were closely prescribed. The lease in use on the Sibley farms today is undoubtedly the result of long experience gained in reconciling the divergent views of landlord and tenant. It prescribes among other things how corn is to be planted and how frequently it is to be cultivated, the methods of dividing the crops, the care of the ditches, and the elimination of burrs and weeds, and even states that when mechanical corn pickers are used the tenant "shall glean the field picking up all the ears missed, when requested. . . ." The enlightened policy of a modern landlord and perhaps the greatest justification for tenancy may be seen in the following statement of principle that is included in the livestock and grain lease of the Sibley estate:

> One major way in which maximum profit in farming . . . can be obtained is by maintaining a balanced, all-year program which includes livestock as well as grain production thereby helping to maintain soil fertility and to secure large crop yields. Good soil, adequate buildings and fences combined with a system which includes limestone, legumes and livestock can produce the maximum profit through the co-operation of all parties concerned.

The fact that Sibley was rapidly improving his estate and settling tenants upon it who would have, in the ordinary course of events, higher incomes and more purchasing power than the laborers formerly employed by Sullivant won for him commendation in the local press. Sibley succeeded where Sullivant had failed; his system of rotation and diversification not only built up or conserved soil qualities, but it made for better results, on the average, than Sullivant's system with its heavy dependence upon corn as a crop. A rich section of Ford County which previously had had but slight development, now, under the benevolent management of Hiram Sibley and his representatives and tenants, became a prosperous and thriving area. By 1887, when the pressure for rent lands was heavy in Illinois and when the Sibley policy of providing relatively attractive improvements and giving fair treatment to tenants had become well known, it was reported that "a great many applicants" for rents were being turned away. Since that time the Sibley family has sold a part of the estate and has encouraged tenants to enlarge the size of their tracts until today the 13,600 acres remaining to it are divided into forty-three farms ranging from 160 to 960 acres. The red barns and rusty yellow houses, the great fields of hybrid corn, the herds of Brown Swiss milking cattle and Hereford steers are familiar sights to residents of east central Illinois.

BROADLANDS

Sullivant's chief rival to fame as the farmer of vast tracts of land was John T. Alexander, who took over Broadlands in 1866. Like Isaac Funk and Samuel Allerton, Alexander was chiefly interested in the buying and fattening of cattle for market. On his

5,000-acre estate in Morgan County he pastured great droves of cattle that were bought in Texas and Kansas. The possession of Broadlands, which he enlarged to 26,500 acres, permitted him to increase his operations to such an extent that he was pasturing 5,000 cattle in addition to 500 hogs and many draft animals on his two farms, and was planning to double his herds of cattle. Five thousand acres were planted in corn and 660 acres in other grains. Alexander continued Sullivant's policy of managing Broadlands as a single farm divided into large operating units, the labor being provided by Scandinavians under the charge of overseers. Dwelling houses were kept at a minimum and were found by an observer to be in dilapidated condition. Mortgages in excess of $153,000 and a debt to the Illinois Central Railroad of $89,000 so heavily encumbered the farm that, despite his good fortune in some years, the interest burden, together with management problems, defeated Alexander as it was defeating Sullivant on Burr Oaks. In 1871 the trustees to whom the property was assigned sold two sections to Charles Ridgely and the remainder was deeded to the principal creditor, Augustus E. Ayers, a banker of Jacksonville. Ayers managed Broadlands for some time but he had no such grandiose ideas as Sullivant and Alexander and only waited for an opportunity to unload without sustaining any loss. In 1875 it was reported that Ayers had sold 10,000 acres to 100 farmers and two years later it was said that 1,000 people were living on Broadlands. Even then, some of the land remained available for rent or sale.

OTHER CATTLE KINGS OF THE INDIANA-ILLINOIS PRAIRIE

George Ade has preserved some of the flavor and romance of this phase of frontier history in an arresting article entitled: "Prairie Kings of Yesterday." Here is set forth as nowhere else the era of "Cattle Kings," the huge ranches and farms they established, their lavish way of living and the gradual breakup of their estates. The locale of the story is northwestern Indiana, especially Benton, Warren, Jasper, and Newton counties where estates ranging in size from 4,000 to 30,000 acres were established by Adams Earl, Moses Fowler, Edward C. Sumner, Cephas Atkinson, Parnham Boswell, Lemuel Milk, Alexander J. Kent, and Hiram Chase. Some of these great landlords like Milk, Sumner, and A. H. and G. W. Danforth operated as extensively in Illinois as in Indiana. Milk came to Illinois in the early fifties where he entered the livestock industry.

Profits from the sale of cattle and sheep provided funds to purchase 10,000 acres of land in Iroquois and Kankakee counties and at least 12,000 acres in Newton County, Indiana. In 1880 the "Nabob," as Ade calls Milk, had 50 farms in Iroquois County ranging in size from 80 to 640 acres that were rented to tenants on a share basis, as well as a large farm which he managed directly through laborers. Milk, Sumner, and the Danforths, whose holdings amounted to 80,000 acres, drained great areas first by ditching and then by tiling, fenced and subdivided their estates into small farms which were let to tenants. Gradually their holdings were reduced by sales and today the Milk estate has left some 4,500 acres, the Danforth estate 3,500, and the Sumner estate 6,200 acres.

MATTHEW SCOTT'S LAND BUSINESS

While the large-scale farming operations of Sullivant, Alexander, and other owners of big farms who relied on hired labor delayed the introduction of tenancy for a short time they made sure its widespread adoption, once the estates were broken up, for by then land values had risen so high that few immigrants could do other than rent. Tenancy came earlier on estates which the landlord did not choose to farm himself through hired laborers, but elected to rent instead. Much information on the beginning of tenancy in the Corn Belt may be gleaned from the story of the land business of Matthew T. Scott, Jr.

The Scott family had been prominent in the annals of early Lexington, Kentucky, and it was to leave its mark upon the development of Illinois. Matthew T. Scott, Sr., president of the Northern Bank of Kentucky, with his seven sons, James, Isaac, Joseph, John, Matthew T., Jr., Joseph M., and William, and his three daughters, Mary, Margaret, and Lucy, for themselves and others with whom they were associated, purchased a total of 42,000 acres of land, mostly in Livingston, Grundy, McLean, and Piatt counties in the years from 1836 to 1855, in addition to 5,600 acres in western Iowa. For many years the investment remained dormant, the owners waiting until increasing settlement made possible either sale or rental of the land. Proper attention seems to have been given to the investment for, unlike many other such estates, the Scott holdings did not become involved in tax titles and squatter claims. Eventually Isaac Scott came to Piatt County to develop a number of thousand acres in that section. He settled tenants upon his land, built them homes "better than tenants usually have," constructed an elevator in Bement to house the share grain he received, and became one of the influential men in the community.

After some experience in Ohio managing the family's lands, Matthew T. Scott, Jr., came to Illinois in 1852 to enter land, and three years later to settle. In the midst of a large block of the family land in southern Livingston and eastern McLean counties, he selected a site on the Chicago and Alton Railroad which was planned as a center of operations for his extensive farm business and on it he laid out the town of Chenoa. In an advertisement calling attention to the "Great Sale of Lots in the Town of Chenoa," Scott related numerous advantages the site held, promised a credit of two years to lot buyers with remission of interest to those who within six months would build houses worth four or five hundred dollars, offered to take a quarter-interest in a steam mill and to furnish one-half the money to build it. Inducements were also offered to attract mechanics.

These were the usual efforts made by the town platters on the frontier, but Scott could add to them the construction of great corncribs and warehouses to receive the quantity of produce he was shortly to get from his numerous share tenants. Although Chenoa was too close to Bloomington to become an important city, it did become a considerable agricultural center in which Scott was able to sell town lots for a total in excess of $15,000, at little cost to himself. It was soon apparent that real estate values in Chenoa would always be modest and Scott, more hardheaded and practical than many western landlords, turned his attention to the development, sale, and rental of the large family estate in wild land.

Matthew Scott planned to make the estate in his care a permanent and profitable investment. To accomplish this without undue delay it was necessary to attract settlers by constructing tenant houses, barns, and fences, and by draining wet areas. The cost of such improvements was to be met by selling those portions of the family's holdings, improved or unimproved, for which there was a ready demand. The income from sales, judiciously invested in additional improvements, would raise the rental or the sales value of the remaining land, and would thereby assure a steadily rising income of a permanent character.

The Scott land was not pushed on the market; distress sales were avoided; and only when prices were satisfactory were tracts sold. Study of the deed records shows that a minimum of $6.00 or $7.00 was maintained and few tracts were sold for less than $10.00 an acre. Nor did Scott have to wait long for acceptable prices. The prosperity of the years 1855, 1856, and 1857 and of the Civil War years sent land values up at an unparalleled rate and well-located tracts with only slight improvements brought good returns. In the sixties most sales were made for $10, $11, and $12 an acre and in the seventies for $20 and $25 an acre. Thereafter the price rose to $30, $40, and $50 in the eighties, and to $60 to $90 in the nineties. One tract of 160 acres was sold in 1909 for $200 an acre. A tabulation of Scott's land sales, exclusive of town lots, in the four counties of Ford, Livingston, Logan, and McLean, shows 13,289 acres for which $265,367 were received. These prices, of course, include improvements put upon the land by Scott or his tenants. Funds derived from these sales, together with some capital he brought with him from Kentucky to Illinois, made it possible for Scott to finance extensive improvements on the land he planned to retain.

Both to attract immigrants to his land, either as purchasers or tenants, and to aid them in getting farming operations under way the first year, Scott undertook to build modest, inexpensive "cottage houses" upon the forty or eighty acre tracts into which he was dividing his land and to break the prairie preparatory to the first crop. During his first year in Illinois he built ten or a dozen such houses and broke up and seeded to wheat and corn more than a thousand acres.[7] Since his improvements were in a part of McLean and Livingston counties that was still quite untouched by settlers and unused by cattlemen he did not find it necessary to start fencing at the outset. In 1856 Scott was advertising for "Farmers, Prairie Breakers and Laborers" to aid in developing the twenty quarter-sections that were already considerably improved. Thereafter, Scott rapidly enlarged his land operations and agricultural improvements, building between 160 and 200 tenant houses, setting out 275 miles of hedge, digging 250 miles of ditching, and tiling 5,000 acres.

---

[7] The *Bloomington Pantagraph* watched with much approval the vigorous way in which Scott applied himself to the task of improving his land and the success he had in bringing in settlers, and urged other large landowners to follow his example.

Scott's Rental Sales Contracts

Without fanfare Scott put into operation a plan which was to aid in bridging the gap between the buyer and settler of land and to provide in theory, if not in practice, a ladder from tenancy to ownership. The plan called for contracts whereby Scott agreed to deed a piece of land in six, seven, eight, or nine years in return for one-half the crops for that period. An examination of forty contracts, embracing 3,500 acres, reveals a common pattern in the conditions of the sale with, however, wide variations in terms. In general, Scott provided housing accommodations, although in some instances the buyer had either to erect his own house or to provide the labor or its equivalent for construction; taxes were to be paid by the buyer who was to drain all wet areas, at least share in the cost and labor of fencing, exterminate noxious weeds, bring one-half the land in cultivation the first year and the remainder the second year, and keep all buildings and fences in good condition. Scott allowed the buyer to retain all the first or sod crop, but thereafter required that his half should be hauled by the tenant to his cribs at Chenoa or other focal points.

The crop sharing system required close supervision at harvesting time and did not prove entirely satisfactory to Scott, so in many of the contracts a clause was substituted that worked something like a cash rent. Instead of requiring one-half the crops Scott commuted his share to sixteen bushels of corn per acre, multiplied that by the number of years the contract was to run, and allowed the purchaser to make payments toward the total quantity as fast as he desired. For example, Stephen Casey contracted in 1866 for the S½ SW ¼, Sec. 16, T 26 N, R 4 E in McLean County, of which 70 acres were to be planted to corn. One thousand one hundred and twenty bushels of number-one corn were to be delivered to Scott yearly from 1868 through 1875, and one-half of eight crops of timothy hay—which was to be raised on the remaining 10 acres—was to be baled and delivered to Scott. Payments in excess of the required 1,120 bushels would be credited toward the total of 8,960 bushels for which the contract called, thereby making it possible to hasten final deeding of the property. Another contract, made with James L. Sheppard for 160 acres in Sec. 30, T 29 N, R 7 E in Livingston County in 1864, called for one-half of six crops of corn, rye, oats, flax, and timothy hay; when the aggregate of the crops grown on 477 acres had been delivered to Scott the property would be deeded to Sheppard.

Under Scott's system of making sales on what amounted to a rental basis most of the risk was borne by the purchaser. Scott, it is true, provided the materials and sometimes the labor for the houses, set out part of the fencing, paid for part of the cost of ditching and breaking the prairie, and tiled some of his land, but much of the labor involved in these improvements was provided by the purchaser or tenant. All such improvements added to the value of the land, whether held for sale or rent, and in case the tenant failed to fulfill the terms of the contract everything reverted to Scott. The interests of the landlord were also carefully safeguarded by stipulations requiring that his share of the crops should be assured to him through a lien on all crops and property of the tenant. Some of the contracts did state that full payment of the landlord's share for one or more years would entitle the buyer to a fraction of the land if he did not wish to farm the entire tract any longer. Furthermore, it should be pointed out that the buyer was not held for the high rate of interest on delayed payments that was required of frontier debtors, and that he was not encouraged to borrow from others because of the difficulty of providing collateral, his interest in the land neither being assignable nor subject to mortgage. On the other hand, when there was a poor harvest and the landlord exacted his share despite the smallness of the crop, or in lieu thereof extended the period of the contract to compensate for the failure, the tenant or buyer might either have inadequate supplies to carry him to the next harvest or he might become discouraged at successive failures and throw up his equity. A succession of poor crops or low prices, accompanied by marketing difficulties, put many of Scott's tenants into a frame of mind that induced them to abandon the struggle to acquire title to their farms.

That many of the settlers on Scott's land failed to fulfill their contracts is evident from a study of the deed records. Some gave up the first year, one piece of land having three successive settlers in as many years, while others clung tenaciously to their tracts for a number of years despite drought, poor crops, and low prices, only to lose their homes at a later time. A considerable number succeeded in meeting the terms of their agreement and in securing title to their homes, but the high rate of turnover among settlers and the frequent releases of contracts show that the terms were difficult for many to meet. This was also the experience of numerous buyers of Illinois Central land who struggled in vain to fulfill contracts in money. There is no evidence that Scott was harsh in his treatment of settlers, whose welfare and success meant much to him. Yet when settlers were forced by circumstances to give up their homes he found it easy to sell or rent at higher prices than were previously obtainable, for the improvements put upon the land with the labor of former tenants had definitely made it more attractive. In this way Scott established a successful land business which, at no great expense to him, became highly productive and could be counted on to net good rents or to bring attractive prices at sale. In 1862, only seven years after he had first undertaken the development of his land, Scott sold a part of the corn and wheat he had received on fourteen contracts, amounting to 20,000 and 2,000 bushels, respectively, for $3,500—a net return of more than $2.00 an acre. Meantime, the unfortunate settler whose contract had been voided for failure to fulfill its terms found that land values in Illinois had gone far beyond his capacity to purchase and the choice of tenancy or trying life anew in central Kansas or Nebraska, to which the great tide of immigration was now flowing, alone remained to him.

THE ALLERTON ESTATE IN PIATT COUNTY

Another great landlord of Illinois who deserves attention is Samuel Allerton. Unlike his contemporaries—Funk, Sullivant, Grigg, and Scott—Allerton did not buy his land directly from the government. Instead, he came into the market late and had to pay the high prices that land was bringing during and after the Civil War. It was in buying and selling cattle in the Chicago market, to which he came in 1860, that Allerton was to lay the foundations for his fortune. Quick financial success made possible the purchase of blocks of land in Piatt and Vermilion counties, on which he planned to pasture and fatten the droves of cattle he was buying in the West. In 1863 he made his first large purchase of 1,280 acres in Piatt County, for which he paid $10 an acre. Slowly the estate was enlarged until he and his children had acquired 11,655 acres in Piatt County and 3,660 acres in Vermilion County, in addition to extensive holdings in Henry County and in Nebraska.

TABLE OF PURCHASES BY SAMUEL ALLERTON IN PIATT CO.

Year	Seller of Land	Acres	Price per acre	Amount
1863	William Martin	1,280	$ 10.00	$ 12,800
1865	Williams & Henderson	160	18.75	3,000
1866	Ainsworth and Ater	80	10.00	800
1866	H. C. McComas	6½	20.00	130
1867	Illinois Central R.R.	314	10.00	3,140
1871	John Matsler	80	46.87	3,750
1873	Watts and Bodwell	600	20.00	12,000
1874	D. Williams	40	37.50	1,500
1879	B. F. F. Yoakum	240	31.66	7,600
1880	W. Voorhies	2,000	30.00	60,000
1880	E. J. Clark	240	20.83	5,000
1880	Williams and Dempsey	1,797	35.19	63,241
1881	James Clark	120	30.00	3,600
1882	W. O. Dooley	120	33.33	4,000
1885	James F. Vent	40	35.00	1,400
1885	Horace R. Calif	480	35.00	16,800
1885	Reid and Wilson	479	57.03	27,320
1891		40	112.50	4,500
1892	W. F. Stevenson	1,187	58.97	70,000
1893		162	72.22	11,700
1894		100	70.00	7,000
1899		48	70.00	3,360
1901	Asler C. Thompson	1,080	50.00	54,000
1901		70	80.00	5,600
1902–1918	11 small purchases totaling	892		130,227

Samuel Allerton divided the larger part of his estate, including the broken land bordering on the Sangamon, into pastures which were seeded to cultivated grasses, while that well suited for cultivation was tiled and planted to corn. Extensive operations with emphasis upon pasturing cattle and the use of hired labor left room for only a handful of tenants and as late as 1880 there were only three houses on the estate.

In the division of the Allerton estate, Robert Allerton, a son, came into possession of the Piatt County land. Robert Allerton, unlike his father, disapproved of absentee landlordism and decided to build a home for himself in the midst of his 12,000 acre tract. Consequently, near Monticello, he built an elaborate manor house which is one of the show places in Illinois. Robert Allerton was a modernist with regard to farm practices and soil conservation and through his farm manager was to prescribe carefully the operations of the seventeen tenants on the estate. He and his father rented their land on the share basis; the improvements were owned by the Allertons and the tenants were encouraged to make stock raising an important feature of their operations. In the twentieth century a large part of the estate has been conveyed, or is promised to state and county governments for an old folks' home, a tuberculosis sanitarium, a model farm on which soil conserving practices can be taught, and for a forestry project.

Land being the favorite investment that it is in Illinois, no self-respecting banker, lawyer, or newspaper proprietor in the small towns and cities of the downstate counties can hold, it would seem, a proper position among his fellow men unless he owns a few farms and can talk intelligently about hybrid corn, the chinch bug, yields per acre, crop rotation schemes, farm machinery, and tenant problems. One has only to spend a short time in such flourishing communities as Pontiac, Paxton, Dwight, Morris, Lincoln, Monticello, or larger cities like Bloomington, Springfield, Decatur, and Champaign-Urbana to realize how intimately the fortunes of many city people are tied to the soil through farm ownership. Samuel Allerton had hundreds of imitators, large and small, who, as their fortunes grew, invested them in the purchase of farm after farm. Thus the Oughton and the McWilliams estates were being acquired in the eighties and nineties, farm by farm, and in the same way were numerous other larger or smaller estates being erected in what has generally been regarded as one of the surest and safest types of investment the country offered.

IRISH LANDLORDISM EMIGRATES TO ILLINOIS

Outranking all other estates of Illinois in acreage, in value, and in the public attention it attracted, was the Scully estate which was first established in 1850 but enlarged at a later time. No frontier landlord in the entire country caused as much unrest among his tenants and was the object of as much ill feeling and political agitation as William Scully. Few men of the time were as harshly condemned and as ruthlessly caricatured as he was during 1887 when the campaign against him was at its height. Sullivant, Sibley, Scott, and Alexander generally enjoyed a favorable press but Scully was belabored in this country and in Ireland. His difficulty was that his career as an Irish landlord had been unhappy, to say the least, and that he introduced into America some highly unpopular features of the Irish land system just at the time when they were being modified in Ireland.

Scully was a member of a prominent land-owning and "moneyed" family of Tipperary County, Ireland, which in 1875 was found by a British parliamentary commission to own or hold on long term leases 14,520 acres with a rental value well in excess of $57,000. William Scully himself held at that time 3,344 acres with a rental value of $10,000 or more. Since he had invested substantial sums in America prior to 1875 it may be that his holdings in Ireland were much larger prior to his first undertakings in this country.

The term Scullyism, as used by historians of nineteenth-century Ireland, meant rack renting or extortionate rents, and evictions of tenants without due cause, frequently under distressing circumstances. In the sixties a series of clashes between Scully and the tenants on his Ballycohey estate culminated in a murderous assault on the former when he was attempting to serve eviction notices. This desperate action resulted in the wounding of Scully and the deaths of two men who were aiding him. Condemnation of the act was immediate, but the accounts, even in the conservative *London Times*, showed that the guilty parties had been driven to such measures by Scully's treatment of his tenants. One historian maintains that Scully's "despotism," which arrayed against him "every voice" including "his brother landlords and magistrates" and which was condemned by the coroner's jury, provided the "decisive impulse to public opinion," that led to the Irish land act of 1870. Among other reforms, this act sought to make evictions more difficult and to require that ousted tenants be compensated for their improvements. It was the first of a series of reform measures which have transformed the insecure downtrodden and thoroughly discontented tenant population of Ireland into a class of peasant proprietors. While Irish tenancy was thereafter slowly to diminish, Illinois tenancy was gradually, if not rapidly, increased, and William Scully was an important factor in this development.

SCULLY'S LAND PURCHASES

It may be that Scully's entrance into the western land business was an indirect result of an act of Parliament of 1849 which provided for the creation of the encumbered estates court. Passed to permit the sale of encumbered estates, the act led to the transfer of some 3,000 estates worth £25,000,000. Within a year after the adoption of this act Scully journeyed to America where, after some preliminary inquiries, he proceeded to Illinois. Here, according to the oft-told story, he made a tour of the prairies, taking with him a famous spade with which he dug into the tough prairie sod to determine the nature of the soil. How extensive his search was it is impossible to say but that it bore fruit in wise selection of land none can deny. Having satisfied himself that the prairie soils of Logan County were rich and potentially valuable, Scully appeared at the federal land office in Springfield on October 11, 1850, and located 54 quarter-sections with Mexican bounty land warrants of the act of 1847. Between then and July 5 of the following year he located 133 additional quarters of which two were later suspended because of a conflict. In 1852 Scully located in the Chicago land office 55 quarter-sections in Grundy County, thereby bringing his total acquisitions to approximately 38,000 acres. By using bounty warrants Scully acquired a large tract for a very modest sum. For 792 additional acres in Logan County that were bought from private individuals between 1852 and 1857 he had to pay an average of $6.43 an acre.

It was Scully's plan to keep these lands permanently and to lease them to tenants in much the same way that he and his family had owned and rented lands in Ireland. Possibly, at the outset, he contemplated using part of the land for a large stock farm as Sullivant, Alexander, and others were doing. There is an intriguing advertisement in the *Bloomington Pantagraph* for August 8, 1855, which lends support to this supposition. Circumstances, whether economic necessity or the death of his wife it is not clear, led to an alteration in Scully's plans for in the advertisement he offered 1,200 sheep and 30 head of cattle for sale. He was also busy selling land.

The terms of Scully's sales contract remind one of the Scott contracts. A cash payment of $1.00 an acre was required to bind the bargain, the balance being due in equal payments at the end of the third and fifth years. Improvements worth $100 or $200 were to be put upon the land within the first two years or the contract would be voided and the advance payment would be regarded as rent for the land and not subject to return to the settler. Interest on the amount due ranged between eight and ten per cent and taxes from the time of purchase were to be paid by the buyer. For persons fully paying for the land in one transaction, of course, no such terms were included.

The sale in the fifties of 6,200 acres for an average price of better than $9.00 an acre with 8 or 10 per cent interest on delayed payments—land that had been acquired for 70 cents an acre five or seven years earlier—provided quick returns that might have satisfied the most greedy speculator. True, fifteen of the forty settlers to whom Scully made sales in this period failed to meet their payments and their contracts were forfeited, but Scully had at least collected the $1.00 an acre advance payment which was sufficient rent for a couple of years. Furthermore, the improvements the purchasers made added to the attractiveness of Scully's land and were shortly to make it possible for him to rent tracts for $1.00 an acre. These sales, together with a few tracts sold in the sixties and one piece of 152 acres sold in 1888 for $50.00 an acre, amounted in all to some 4,000 acres, part of which, it is interesting to note, Scully was to buy back at many times the price for which he sold it.

It is unlikely that Scully ever intended to dispose of all his land. Probably the sales of the fifties were for the purposes of tiding him over until paying tenants could be secured. During the Civil War he leased tracts for $1.00 an acre and soon after he was able to secure tenants for all his land. These rents were shortly to provide Scully with a net income of $80,000 and more, which, contrary to the statements made by some of his detractors, was not to be spent entirely abroad but was largely invested in additional land purchases.

Another source of funds for these purchases was the income from rents and from the liquidation of a part, at least, of the Irish estates. In 1868, the year of the Ballycohey tragedy when public opinion in Ireland was running strongly against Scully, pressure was brought to bear to induce him to sell that estate, on which were settled twenty-two tenant families. When, therefore, a local landlord offered to purchase Ballycohey for its "improved value" Scully agreed to sell. In the words of the *London Times* of September 28, 1868, this was a "welcome deliverance for the people." Irish landlordism was coming more heavily under attack at this time, partly because of the excesses to which some owners went in increasing rents and in making evictions, and thoughtful people were beginning to feel that reform was necessary, whereby tenant rights of fixity (or security) of tenure, fair rent, and free sale (the right to sell improvements put upon the land), should be guaranteed by the government. In 1870, Parliament passed a land act which took the first halting steps in this direction, thereby making landlordism in that distracted country less attractive. Scully was doubtless distressed at the success of the reformers in pushing through Parliament the act of 1870, as were most Irish landlords, and, with funds now well in hand, he turned away from his own country and began investing in a larger measure than before in America where the laws gave all the traditional protection to property rights that was characteristic of England.

Only in Kansas and Nebraska were there still available for purchase public lands that were at all comparable to the Logan and Grundy County land. Consequently, Scully turned to these states for investment. In June, 1870, he purchased at the Beatrice, Nebraska, land office 41,420 acres in Nuckolls County which is in the southern tier of counties about 130 miles west of the Missouri River. The following month Scully purchased of the federal government 14,060 acres in Marion County, Kansas, and 1,160 acres in Dickinson County, Kansas, being located about 150 miles from the Missouri River. These purchases of Scully's were among the last of the large aquisitions of farming land by individuals or companies. By 1870 the unrestricted public lands that were still open to private entry were about gone, except for some rich tracts of timberland in the Lake States, the Gulf States, and California, and an area of grazing land that was subsequently to be sold in Colorado. Henceforth, any additional tract that Scully might want would have to be bought from land-grant railroads, from large speculators who had seized upon the agricultural college scrip of the state to acquire tracts of great size, or from pioneer settlers who were having difficulty in meeting mortgage payments or were too restless to stay anywhere for long.

By now the Illinois rents and the liquidation of the Irish estates were producing sums sufficient to make possible a rapid expansion of land buying and for the next decade Scully's agents were scouring Kansas, Nebraska, Missouri, and Illinois in one of the largest individual land buying campaigns in American history.

The greatest volume of purchases being made by Scully's agents was in Marion County, Kansas. Here was bought land owned by persons living as far away as Waterford and New York City, New York; Lenawee County, Michigan; Grant County, Wisconsin; Umatilla County, Oregon; Skowhegan, Maine; Ouray County, Colorado; Brown County, Texas; and Ontario, Canada. Scully bought of John Williams, a well-known banker, railroad promoter, and land speculator of Springfield, Illinois, 9,440 acres in Marion County, Kansas, for $2.00 an acre. These lands had been purchased by Williams at the Junction City land office a little earlier for the government minimum price. From the Santa Fe Railroad, which in this transaction as well as in others showed no disinclination to sell to speculators and large buyers, were acquired 8,622 acres for $38,008. A part of the famous Christie ranch, consisting of 2,560 acres, was bought at forced sale for $13,240 which was about two-thirds of the appraised value. In forty-one other transactions Scully acquired 19,824 acres for $90,048. Finally, 960 acres of tax-delinquent land were purchased for $621. Altogether, Scully acquired 55,666 acres in Marion County at a cost of $179,197. In Butler County, just to the south of Marion, he bought in the eighties 8,605 acres for $77,410.

In 1881 Scully turned his attention to two fertile counties just north and south of the Kansas-Nebraska line. In Gage County, Nebraska, he acquired 22,288 acres for $290,254 and in Marshall County, Kansas, he acquired 5,115 acres for $55,252. Of the sixty-three persons from whom the land in Gage County was bought only nineteen were residents of the county, while eighteen were residents of Illinois and nine were residents of Ohio. In both of these states, but especially in Illinois, were numerous individuals who had accumulated small fortunes from the rise in land values of the fifties and sixties, and who, in the late sixties, began investing heavily in Kansas and Nebraska lands. Illustrations of individuals who carried their land business westward as the frontier advanced from Illinois into Kansas and Nebraska are John and Robert Niccolls, Asahel Gridley, E. B. Munsell, and John Williams.

The price paid by Scully for tracts in Kansas and Nebraska indicates that a considerable proportion of them were improved. A summary of the land he acquired there between 1870 and 1886 is shown by the following table:

SCULLY'S PURCHASES IN KANSAS AND NEBRASKA

Location	Acres	Cost
Marion	55,666	$179,197
Dickinson	1,120	1,400
Butler	8,605	77,410
Marshall	5,115	55,252
Gage	22,288	290,254
Nuckolls	41,420	51,775
Total	134,214	$655,288

About the same time 42,000 acres were acquired in Bates County, Missouri, which probably cost about $200,000. In 1941 the Bates County land was sold to the Farm Security Administration for $1,078,000.

Most profitable among Scully's many investments were his Illinois lands and naturally he was ready to purchase more of them. Money invested in Illinois, however, acquired much smaller acreages, so rapidly did land values rise in the twenty years following the Civil War. Where attractive land in Kansas and Nebraska could be acquired for $5, $10, and at the most $20 an acre, it was necessary to pay from $30 to $50 an acre for prime land in Illinois. Thus in 1875, a depression year, Scully paid $47 an acre for 824 acres in Logan County. The following table shows his purchases in this county together with the number of persons from whom the land was bought and the price paid.

LATER PURCHASES OF SCULLY IN LOGAN COUNTY

Year	Number of Settlers	Acres	Amount of Purchase Money	Ave. Price Per Acre
1875	4	824	$ 39,082	$47.73
1877	2	263	10,303	39.17
1878	10	1,662	67,750	40.16
1879	3	751	25,000	33.28
1880	1	160	6,200	38.75
1883	1	80	3,600	45.00
1885	1	188	4,938	26.26
1886	1	114	4,290	37.71
Total	23	4,042	$161,163	$39.88

In Sangamon County, Scully made but one purchase, but it called for the largest payment and one of the highest per acre prices of any of his contracts. The purchase included 4,161 acres in two townships that had been entered in May 1836, by John Berry of Bath County, Kentucky, for the estate of Archibald Hamilton in the great speculative boom of the middle thirties. The land remained in the hands of Berry until 1876 when the court ordered that it be conveyed to the Hamilton heirs with reasonable expenses to the Berrys for their management during the preceding forty years. A year following, in 1877, James C. and George H. Hamilton sold the land to Scully for a total price of $215,297.40, or an average of $51.75 an acre. This was a depression year when the price of land, as well as of commodities, was abnormally low.

About the same time Scully pushed into Livingston County which in the fifties had a larger proportion of its area in the hands of speculators than any other Illinois county. Here Solomon Sturges had acquired 40,000 acres, Alexander Campbell 11,000 acres, Bronson Murray 8,120 acres, and Michael Sullivant 13,920 acres. In addition the 70,000 acres of Illinois Central land, the 27,000 acres of canal land, and the 39,360 acres of "swamp" land had been in part acquired by speculators. Many of these large owners like Murray, Sullivant, Jacob Bunn, William H. Osborn, and Matthew T. Scott, were developing their tracts either with hired labor or through tenants and there early appeared a high proportion of tenancy in the county. The breakup of the Sturges, Campbell, and Osborn estates was favorably regarded by the residents of the county and the financial embarrassment of Sullivant and the sale of his Livingston County land was locally approved. When, however, Scully began buying in the county in 1876 his action was subjected to unfriendly criticism. Only two important purchases were made: one in 1876 when section 14 in Round Grove Township was bought for $17,920 and the other in 1887 when the Cayuga lands amounting to 1,500 acres were acquired for $45 an acre.

This constitutes the whole of Scully's land purchases aside from 27,000 acres in Louisiana, which do not appear to have been bought as farming land, and some tracts in Grundy and Logan counties which he had sold and which he later repurchased, paying in some instances five times what he had sold them for. In the four states of Illinois, Missouri, Kansas, and Nebraska, Scully had amassed an empire of land amounting to 220,000 acres at a cost to him of $1,350,000.

SCULLY'S RENTAL POLICY

Scully's rental policy, while differing sharply from that of most frontier landlords, did not embody the worse features of the Irish system as was later charged.[8] Historians generally are in agreement that one of the chief causes of Ireland's misery was that, outside of Ulster, tenants had no right in improvements on the land. When evicted they had nothing to sell, nothing for which to claim compensation. Hence they abused the land through improper farm practices and erected the very poorest hovels in which to live. Scully even tore down tenant homes as part of the process of making evictions on his Tipperary estates and his tenants had no legal redress. From the very beginning of his leasing in America, however, Scully provided that improvements, such as fences, houses, barns, and other buildings, were to be constructed by the tenant and, more important, that they were to be subject to removal or sale by the tenant. The concession of tenant right was probably necessary in America in order to attract settlers, but Scully's refusal to aid them in getting started, as Scott, Sibley, and other landlords were doing, had the effect of delaying settlement of his land for a decade. It was to farms already somewhat improved or on which the landlord would provide part of the cost of building and fencing that the first persons looking for rents naturally went. Isaac Funk, David Davis, Asahel Gridley, and Jesse Fell were accumulating and improving their thousands of acres of prairie land through hired laborers and tenants, and scores of smaller owners were also improving and offering for rent 80- and 160-acre farms on a share rent basis. In the fifties "For Rent" advertisements were becoming common in the prairie newspapers and once in a while there also appeared such advertisements as: "Wanted. Farm for Rent." Landlords with improved farms were having little difficulty in securing tenants, but Scully's policy of using his available funds for the purchase of land and not for improvements, while permitting him to buy a large acreage, delayed the expected income from the land by a decade and explains in part why the Scully improvements were among the poorest in the West in the frontier period.

---

[8] It is not the common practice to record leases as deeds and mortgages are recorded, and yet in the Miscellaneous Records and sometimes in the Deed Records of western counties may be found scattered leases that for one reason or another have been recorded.

Scully's policy with regard to security of tenure was definitely more liberal than was the custom in Ireland. His early leases were for periods of five or six years and with satisfactory management were fairly certain to be renewed. The concession of what amounted to tenant-right encouraged tenant improvements and that in turn made for more contentment on the part of the renter who, so long as he farmed his land properly, paid his rent and taxes at the appropriate time, and did nothing to antagonize Scully or his agents, would be assured of the right of continued occupation. Nevertheless, the exacting rents combined with poor times in the seventies and in the eighties made for restlessness among tenants and frequent moves.

Taxes on the Scully farms were the obligation of tenants. In practice they were paid by the landlord, added to the cash rent and collected at the same time. In this way any danger that the titles would be placed in jeopardy through non-payment of taxes was avoided. There was sound reason for Scully's tax policy. With such a large group of tenants as he was to have it would have been possible for them to vote, in local tax districts, heavy appropriations for roads, schools, and other public buildings and as loans for local railroads, and to have the burden carried by the landlord. It is only necessary to read frontier newspapers of the time to realize that this was common practice in states like Illinois, Iowa, Kansas, and Nebraska, where large quantities of land were owned by absentees. For example, an advocate of township subsidies to aid railroad construction in Piatt County urged that such a subscription "compels the lordly speculator, who holds thousands of acres of land in our county at such prices as to prevent its settlement and improvement, to bear his just proportion of the burden of building the road. . . . In no other way can these speculators be reached; they have already induced our Legislature to shield them from the burden of school tax, and I say now tax their land to build the Railroad. . . ." Another observer, writing from Thayer County, Nebraska, said: "The speculators are getting tired of building school houses, so that they are offering their lands for sale very low and on reasonable terms." By requiring that the tenants should pay the taxes and all local assessments, Scully not only made certain that they would, as a group, be cautious in voting for expensive buildings or road construction programs but that they would constantly exert a moderating influence to keep costs of local government and taxes at the lowest possible level. This tended to produce within the Scully area poorer roads and inferior school facilities than were being provided elsewhere.

In the twentieth century the farm management practices in operation on the Scully farms are enlightened and progressive. The requirements that clover shall be planted on every part of the land once in four years, that corn shall not be planted more than two years in succession, and that a proper system of rotation shall be followed to make sure that soil depletion does not occur are well known. The supervision given to the tenants assures better farm practices than are generally followed on owner-operated farms. Such controls may at times irk the tenant but they certainly work to the mutual advantage of landlord and tenant. Had Scully attempted to include such requirements in his early leases he would have been laughed to scorn by frontier farmers who had no idea that the prairie soils of Illinois could be exhausted by planting them to corn year after year. Nor was it expedient for Scully to prescribe in the early period, as is done today, that "all burrs, thistles and other weeds and willow bushes" shall be destroyed. Good practice requires that farmers, whether tenants or owners, do these things, but experience was to show that tenants were inclined to neglect them.

The appearance of weeds and brush in the fields as well as in the hedgerows was characteristic of tenant farms. A Livingston County paper complained that there was such a high turnover among tenants on the neighboring farms that the burrs were rarely eradicated. It urged that a law be adopted to compel the owners to have weeds destroyed. A campaign for compulsory weed eradication was directed at tenant-operated farms, particularly the Scully farms. It was stated:

> Rented farms can always be identified by the dilapidated state of the buildings, the tumble-down fences, the mammoth crop of weeds, the unthrifty general appearance—the air of desolation and destruction . . . all too flagrant not to be observed. The rented farm is free to be plucked in every possible manner. . . . The whole object too, is to secure the utmost drain on the soil—getting everything off without returning any of the fertilizers to make it productive.

It was argued that Scully's policies attracted to his land "the very poorest of farmers, who only take Scully's land with a view of leaving it just as soon as they can" after skimming the cream and leaving the land much depreciated.

In Logan County it was pointed out that the practice of planting corn on the Scully land year after year without any rotation and the continued neglect of weeds was not only impoverishing the land, which was overrun with weeds, but was having a deplorable effect upon surrounding farms. On few farms in Illinois in the nineteenth century could it be said that careful methods of cultivation and husbandry were employed, and Scully's tenants and their farm practices were probably no worse than those on most other rented farms. But attention was focused upon Scully because of the unpopularity of his cash rent policy and the fact that he was an alien who was contributing little to the development of the state.

The most characteristic feature of the Scully leases was the cash rent. Although by no means unknown on the frontier the share or grain rent was more usual. Some landlords, Matthew Scott for example, rented for a stipulated amount of wheat or corn per acre. More common and certainly more thoroughly approved was the share rent which, according to the *Vermilion County Press* of July 28, 1858, was generally based on one of three fairly standard rates: the proprietor who furnished all the stock, seed, and equipment and paid the taxes received two-thirds of the produce, the tenant who furnished everything likewise received two-thirds, and if the stock was jointly owned and other expenses were equally divided the landlord and tenant divided the crops equally.

A principal advantage of the share rent was that, unlike the cash rent, it did not have to be adjusted upward or downward with fluctuating prices and rising land values. On a cash rent basis land generally brought $1.00 an acre in the fifties and sixties, $2.00 an acre in the seventies, and $3.00 and $4.00 an acre in the eighties and nineties and $8.00 and $10.00 an acre at times in the twentieth century. When land values were rising fairly rapidly, upward adjustments of rent were to be expected, but they frequently led to outcries of rack renting when instituted by Scully, regardless of the fact that the new rent might still provide a small return on the sale value of the land. Furthermore, there is evidence that in the nineteenth century Scully was not inclined to be lenient when crops were poor or prices low. Today the Scully abatements are well known and understood in the Middle West and few there are who would complain that rent adjustments have been inequitable, which is tantamount to saying that the policy of the family is more sensitive to the needs of the tenants than it was in the nineteenth century.

Somewhat less supervision is necessary under the cash rent system than under the share rent, and perhaps it avoids some of the suspicion and ill will that has characterized landlord-tenant relations in certain areas. But to make certain that he received his rent, Scully found it advisable to require rent payments before the crop was sold—certain to involve the tenant in great hardship especially as he could not borrow upon his crop. He also informed shippers and buyers in the vicinity of his land that his lien on the crop of his tenants came first under the terms of the lease and under the tenant laws and that he could and would recover damages from anyone who bought grain before his rent was paid.

No feature of the landlords' policies in the seventies and eighties was more disliked than the cash rent. The drop in agricultural prices after 1873 was not reflected in land values to the same degree and was not followed by rent adjustments. Not only were prices low but weather conditions were unfavorable for corn in 1876, 1877, and 1878 in much of the prairie section and there were partial crop failures or light crops. Farmers were caught between the upper millstone of rigid costs such as taxes, freight rates, rent or interest, and the nether millstone of diminishing income. Share renters and mortgaged owners, of course, were seriously affected. Many mortgages were foreclosed and the previous owners either depressed into tenancy or were forced to emigrate elsewhere. The cash tenants at the same time were actually being asked to pay higher rents, despite the trying times. In the neighboring state of Indiana it was said that work in cities was so scarce that laborers were anxiously looking for farms to rent, even though the "extorionate and heartless" landlords were charging as high as $4.00 and $5.00 an acre. Such rents, while high, were not unknown in Illinois.[9]

Tenant Unrest

Discontent and unrest began to appear among tenant farmers and were reflected in the rural press. For example, in 1876 the

---

[9] In 1870 the University of Illinois, which had come into possession of the Griggs farm, was renting seven tracts at prices ranging from $2.80 to $5.00 an acre. The McFee farm near Bloomington was advertised for rent in 1876 for a cash rent of $5.00 an acre.

Farmer City Journal published a "pitiful story" of two cash renters who had leased a farm for $700, did their best to make a success of it, but, failing, were faced with the loss of their crops, horses, and farm utensils. Finally a compromise was reached by which they paid $200 and gave up their entire crops for the year. The writer said:

> What a sad comment this and similar cases is upon the cash rent system in such a variable climate as central Illinois. Paying $200 for the privilege of toiling all season with three teams, the wear and tear of farm machinery, board and incidental expenses, then to crown all, donate the crop and have nothing left.

The *Pontiac Sentinel* of August 10, 1876, warned that few renters were able to meet the terms of their leases without beggaring themselves and their families and many of them were abandoning their farms. Tension between landlord and tenant reached serious proportions. In one case a landlord was attacked and badly mauled by an outraged and disillusioned tenant. Scully, whose three hundred-odd Illinois farms were now tenanted on a cash rent basis, came under attack perhaps for the first time in his experience in America. The *Chicago Times* wrote of his "very exacting terms and high rates" which were being continued despite the lightness of the crops in recent years and the arrears into which tenants had fallen. When Scully announced that he would "allow no tenant to sell any of his crop of this year until the rent has been paid up in full" the tenants became highly indignant. They held a protest meeting at which a committee was appointed to visit the Governor to ask him to intercede for them. "Scully's actions savor much of the tyranny of the absentee landlords of Ireland," said the *Chicago Times*. "All over central Illinois a strong feeling is growing up against such immense estates, especially when operated by persons outside the State." Another mass meeting of renters was held at Saybrook in February 1879, at which resolutions were adopted declaring cash rent unjust and discriminating in favor of the landlord. The participants pledged themselves to pay grain or share rents only, unless the landlords would lease their farms for a "cash rent of $2.00 per acre and that only for cultivated lands." It was about this time that a measure was introduced into the Illinois legislature at the request of those who found Scullyism repugnant to American principles, to impose an extraordinary tax on absentee and alien owners of land.

The tenant unrest in the prairie counties of Illinois, which came to a head in the late seventies, failed to win political attention for the problems of the renter. Illinois was being immensely stirred by agrarian unrest that was directed against the malpractices of the railroads and the deflationary policies of the federal government. But Grangerism was a landowners' movement and did not concern itself with the problems of the tenant. Being the poorest educated and most foreign of the rural population, the tenants were unable to dramatize their grievances sufficiently to win the attention of the agrarian parties. In fact, tenants were dealt an additional blow during the height of their unrest by the action of the legislature in authorizing landlords, under certain circumstances, to "institute proceedings by distress" before rent was due. This legalized a practice which Scully in effect had required his tenants to sanction. Their cries being ignored, the tenants had an outlet still open to them: that was to abandon their farms and to migrate to the new frontier in central and western Kansas and Nebraska.

When the discontent of the tenant farmers was at its height the Burlington Railroad seized the occasion to advertise its Nebraska land in the papers of central Illinois. Young men were urged not to rent in Illinois when they could own in Nebraska; "Life is too short," the advertisement stated, "to be wasted on a rented farm." About the same time the Santa Fe Railroad, in advertising its Kansas land, claimed that there were "no lands owned by speculations" in the area of its grant, in contrast to the huge acreage of speculator-owned land in Illinois. Discontent and the attractions of a newly developing frontier induced many thousands of tenants, as well as unsuccessful farm owners, to join the western trek. Farmers operating tracts smaller than 100 acres were finding it increasingly difficult to compete with those working larger units of land and in the decade of the eighties 17,000 of them were forced to give up their homes to their more successful competitors.[10] In Ford County, where tenancy and large-scale farms predominated more than in any other county in the state, a series of meetings was being held as early as 1872 by a group which was organized as a homestead colony and was planning to move westward. Six years later another group of 121 people was organized, consisting mostly of renters from Ford and Vermilion counties, who were going as a colony to Kansas with their seventeen carloads of freight.

---

[10] The census of 1890 reported 17,087 fewer farms of less than 100 acres than were reported in 1880.

Throughout the prairie counties a similar movement of population was under way. Renters, dispossessed owners who had been unable to meet the high interest charges on their mortgages, and agricultural laborers who had failed to get the much desired piece of land, all were moving, the goal being Kansas, Nebraska, Iowa, and Missouri. In the decade of the seventies 175,000 people who were born in Illinois migrated to these four states in addition to many thousands of others who came to Illinois from the East or from Europe and then moved farther west in search of land. Many were to succeed in the new country but others were to find conditions in the younger states not materially different save in degree from those in Illinois. If they tried life anew in Marion, Butler, Marshall, or Dickinson counties, Kansas, or in Nuckolls and Gage counties, Nebraska, they found the best land in private hands, owned by the railroads who were looking for purchasers at high prices, or held by William Scully and other large landlords who were looking for tenants on the same conditions as applied in Illinois though at lower rents. Emigrants from Illinois, arriving in the humid section of Kansas, were faced with notices, "Wanted: Farms to Rent," indicating that their search for land was again to be frustrated. Frequently it was the experience of these landseekers that no matter how far they proceeded in their search they were certain to be anticipated by the railroad, the speculator, or the frontier landlord. When the futility of their search for land which they could not own became apparent, their feelings were crystallized into keen resentment against those who had forestalled them.

Western attitudes toward large-scale land speculation and frontier landlords were not always consistent. Absentee owners were thoroughly disapproved of but the resident owner generally escaped criticism. "You are a curse to our country," said an indignant writer of nonresident landowners of Livingston County. Careless cropping methods, the one-crop system, poor housing accommodations, inadequate fences, the existence of weeds and brush, and poor roads and school facilities were all blamed on the absentee owner, not on the renter.

THE ATTACK ON SCULLYISM

William Scully was not only an absentee landlord but also an alien who had no inention of settling in Illinois or, for that matter, in any part of the United States. As if that were not enough of a challenge to frontier mores, Scully refused to improve his own land but waited for tenants to do that, and the nature and quality of their improvements were not to win for him good feeling. A fourth count against Scully was his system of cash renting that seemed to many who were accustomed to share renting an alien institution. Finally, at a time when powerful monopolies were extending their control over many fields in America, it was natural that the huge land-buying program of Scully should arouse indignation. One of his purchases, 1,500 acres in Livingston County, acquired in 1887, was particularly ill-timed, coming as it did when anti-Scully feeling was strong in Illinois and Kansas. It was called "very unfortunate" for the community which was certain to be "injured generally" by it.

Resentment against the Scully leasing policies accomplished nothing in the seventies but a decade later it had become deeper and more dangerous in all four states in which the Scully farm lands were located. Journalistic vituperation of the rankest kind was heaped upon Scully, anti-alien landowner bills directed at him were passed by three of the states, and in the legislatures of these states and in Washington Scullyism became a major issue, the principal question being how best to strike at it.

Westerners were troubled that Scully was deriving a handsome income from their area and paying no taxes, since his leases required his tenants to assume this obligation. Had it been argued that the total rates charged tenants were determined in part by the productivity of the land and in part by the demand for rent land, and that Scully's rents plus taxes could not have been materially higher than those other landlords were charging, the westerners would not have been convinced. In their opinion Scully was evading taxation by requiring his tenants to pay assessments for him, thereby adding to their burdens. The people of Logan County became so incensed against Scully that they tried to tax his rent roll. This he met by contending that the rent roll was owned in England, and, therefore, was not taxable in Illinois. On somewhat different grounds the state Supreme Court invalidated the tax.

Failing in their efforts to tax Scully's income or rent rolls, the anti-Scully forces united in a move to make alien ownership of land illegal. From 1883 to 1888 small-town newspapers of the prairie counties published editorial after editorial condemning alien and absentee ownership of land and demanding either that future alien acquisitions should be made illegal or that all alien-owned land should be forfeited to the states. Successive purchases of land by Scully, who kept doggedly at his task of increasing his domain, were given wide publicity and added fuel to the fire. Soon the *Bloomington Pantagraph,* the *Chicago Tribune,* and other influential papers—even the *New York Times*—joined in the cry against Scully. In Kansas and Nebraska similar journalistic campaigns were under way, the principal differences being that in these two states they were marked by a greater degree of scurrility. Papers that were slow to join the hue and cry were called Scully organs. They soon found that few issues were more popular at the time than the attack upon William Scully and the demand for legislation to curb or end alien ownership, and before long they, too, were making pointed remarks about the undemocratic character of tenancy and the danger of land monopoly.

The newspaper attacks followed a common pattern in their onslaught on Scullyism and alien ownership. Stress was laid on the un-American character of tenancy—despite the fact that numerous westerners owned large tracts of land they were renting to tenants —on the fact that taxes had to be paid by tenants, and above all on the cash rent feature. The term "rack renting" was frequently bandied about, though there is no important evidence to show that Scully's rents were higher than those of other landlords. The safeguards that Scully included in his leases to make sure that his tenants paid their rents were called outrageous. That they were comprehensive and were sometimes harshly enforced is doubtless true, but any person who reads a lease of yesterday or today will be struck by the realization that it was designed—like the modern installment contract—to protect the landlord or the vendor, not the renter or the purchaser. The Scully tenants were described as ignorant foreigners, Bohemians, Scandinavians, and Poles who "are not a class who are desirable neighbors," a "dreary and woebegone" lot of "scarecrow tenants" who "are in a state of absolute serfdom under his heartless alien rule, mostly 'transients' raising nothing but corn, year after year, from the same ground." The Scully lands were described as the "most forlorn-looking estate in Illinois" with dwellings that were "a miserable lot of shanties"— mere sheds, bearing no paint and having little glass. Constant cropping of corn had so impoverished the land, it was argued, "that it breeds burrs and weeds, the seeds of which are carried to surrounding farms. . . ." The poverty-stricken tenants were unable to meet their taxes and public improvements on "Scully land," it was said, were the worst to be found in the entire state of Illinois; roads were execrable, schoolhouses were as poor as the tenant dwellings and the school term was limited to five months.

That there was a good deal of truth to these accusations cannot be denied, but neither can it be denied that much the same kind of thing could be said of tenancy on other estates. True, efforts were made to distinguish between "bad" landlords and "good" landlords who had "good" tenants that employed "good" farm practices, had "good" improvements, and enjoyed "good" treatment, and were prosperous. Among these good landlords were John D. Gillett whose 16,000 acre estate in Logan and Sangamon counties entitled him to rank among the leading frontier landlords, David Littler who had some twenty or more farms in Logan, Sangamon, and Piatt counties, Bronson Murray whose 10,000-acre estate in Livingston and LaSalle counties, now somewhat reduced, was said to have "an excellent lot of tenants," and Bernard Stuvé, the famous historian of Illinois, on whose estate in Piatt County were said to be built "the model tenant houses of the country." Likewise, the tenant policies on the Sibley and Funk farms were generally approved, but the Jacob Bunn farm of 2,500 acres, the Buckingham farm of 2,000 acres, and the Oliver farm of 3,000 acres in Livingston County were unfavorably regarded. The landlord who built homes for tenants, fenced and drained the land, and used the income from it for further improvements, or who lived in the neighborhood of his estate won commendation. That Scully instituted an elaborate and comprehensive system of tile drainage on his Grundy County lands in the eighties seemed to make no difference to residents in the neighborhood. He was an alien who spent his income elsewhere, extorted rack rents from his tenants, and kept them in poverty while casting a blighting influence over the counties in which his land was located. "The Lord Scully tribe of aliens will have to go—so far as Illinois is concerned," said the *Princeton Republican* while the *Pontiac Free Trader and Observer* urged that speedy action be taken to prevent Scully from buying any more land in the United States.

ANTI-ALIEN LANDLORD LEGISLATION

The campaign against alien landlords was associated with the demand for the forfeiture of unearned railroad land grants and for the withdrawal of the public lands from large-scale purchasing. As early as 1884 all national parties had joined in the fight against alien landlordism, the clearest statement being made by the Union Labor Party in 1888:

> We believe the earth was made for the people, and not to enable an idle aristocracy to subsist, through rents, upon the toil of the industrious, and that corners in land are as bad as corners in food, and that those who are not residents or citizens should not be allowed to own lands in the United States.

Until into the nineties the cry against alien landlordism as well as unearned railroad land grants was taken up by all agrarian parties and the demand for confiscation of alien lands and for forfeiture of land grants was vigorously pressed. The platforms of the Farmers' Alliance and the People's or Populist Party stressed these two issues as much as the silver question, the Northern Alliance in 1889 actually giving first place to them. Despite this condemnation of alien ownership and the demand for its end and the flurry of legislation that it precipitated, historians of agrarian movements, without exception, have neglected it and centered their theme around that of silver and the malpractices of railroads. They fail to recognize that fundamentally, but not every clearly, this western discontent was directed at the forces which were making for tenancy and the disappearance of the small farm owner.

The campaign against alien landlords reached its climax in 1887 when the farmers of the West were aflame with hatred of Scully-ism, "land monopoly," absentee and alien ownership of land, and the land-grant railroads. In the newspapers, the state legislatures, and farmers' meetings, William Scully was held up to excoriation as the archetype of alien landlord whose rental policies made mere serfs of his tenants. A barrage of legislation directed chiefly at Scully was adopted. On June 16, two such measures received the approval of the Governor of Illinois and became law. The first prohibited nonresident aliens from acquiring real estate though it did not and could not require, as the most bitter opponents of Scully demanded, that alien-owned lands should be forfeited to the state. The second act was designed to prevent alien landlords from requiring tenants to pay the taxes assessed upon the land they rented. At the same time the anti-Scully agitation in Kansas and

Nebraska produced results. The Nebraska act prohibiting aliens from acquiring land was similar to that of Illinois. Kansas, where the most violent feelings were aroused against Scully, contented itself after considerable legislative maneuverings with proposing an amendment to the state constitution that would permit legislation to prohibit alien ownership of land. Wisconsin, Minnesota, and Colorado likewise adopted laws to prevent alien ownership. Similar laws were adopted by Iowa in 1888, Idaho in 1891, and Missouri in 1895.

To shut Scully and other nonresident aliens out of the territories, Congress in 1887 adopted an act "to restrict the ownership of real estate in the Territories to American citizens." The most vigorous supporter of the anti-alien landowning bill was Lewis E. Payson, representative in Congress of a number of the prairie counties of Illinois including Livingston where Scully at the very moment was engaged in enlarging his holdings. Payson was given active aid by the *Pontiac Sentinel* which called the bill of "vital importance" to the country. Never before in American history had such a barrage of legislation been directed so largely at one man as were the acts of nine states (including Indiana whose law of 1885 anticipated the others) and the federal government.[11]

There were cynics, at the time, who took pleasure in deriding the agrarian radicals and reformers who were sponsoring both the anti-alien landowning legislation and a comprehensive and thorough reform of the entire public land system. They called the reformers demagogues, accused them of seizing upon a popular issue like Scullyism and riding it for all it was worth while neglecting more fundamental issues. They pointed out that the western

---

[11] The federal act of March 3, 1887, was clearly the result of anti-Scully agitation in Illinois, Nebraska, and Kansas and the feeling in other plains states that the great volume of land then being acquired by British cattle interests was dangerous for America. In 1886, when the anti-alien landowning bill was being considered by the House Committee on the Judiciary, it was first reported unfavorably with, however, a minority report urging its adoption in which it was said that if enacted it would "prevent any more such abuses as that of Mr. Scully, who resides in England, and is a subject of the Queen, but owns 90,000 acres in the State of Illinois, occupied by hundreds of tenants, mostly ignorant foreigners, from whom he receives, as rent, $200,000 per annum. . . . This alien non-resident ownership will . . . lead to a system of landlordism incompatible with the best interests and free institutions of the United States. . . . A considerable number of the immigrants arriving in this country are to become tenants and herdsmen on the vast possessions of these foreign lords under contracts made and entered into before they sail for our shores."

radicals were proposing to close the public domain to speculators when the last of the desirable land was gone and to stop alien purchases of land when foreign capital was already tending to go elsewhere. They showed that while the radicals were demanding the forfeiture of the Scully lands, none of the bills that were being seriously considered and had a chance of passage threatened any such drastic action. All the legislation was likely to accomplish at this late date was to stop further purchasing by Scully and then only if he failed to become an American citizen.

One of the most effective of these cynics was a Scotch alien—George Campbell—who objected to the measures being considered by the Illinois legislature on the ground that they did not strike at the real causes of tenant unrest. "If Scullyism exists it exists because it is not inconsistent with existing laws, and there is no proposal now being made to modify the laws in any way, beyond this Alien Land Bill." If the legislature was in earnest in wishing to end Scullyism and rack renting, argued Campbell, it should adopt reforms similar to those that Gladstone was introducing into Ireland which provided for fair rent, freedom to sell tenant-made improvements, and security of tenure.

Another criticism that was made of the anti-alien landowning bills was that they could easily be evaded by the foreign owners' taking out American citizenship. What was needed, the *Bureau County Republican* argued, was an amendment to the constitution that would "positively prohibit any one man from holding over one thousand acres of tillable soil." In Illinois no one seriously pushed such proposals. The legislature was in no mood to deal with tenancy in a constructive way but was blindly striking at Scully, possibly to soothe its conscience for its failure to solve the problems of the tenants. Dozens of landlords had by 1887 attained a state of great affluence in Illinois, among them the Governor, Richard J. Oglesby, and David Littler, a prominent member of the legislature. Another, David Davis, who had died just the preceding year, had been justice of the United States Supreme Court, senator from Illinois, and prominently considered for the presidency. The interests of the landlords were not to be disturbed.

The attack upon Scully had its effect, however, in bringing to an end the purchasing of land by him in Illinois, as well as in Kansas and Nebraska. To meet the provisions of the anti-alien landowning acts, which denied aliens the right of permanently holding land

they acquired by inheritance, Scully took out citizenship in the
United States so that his heirs who likewise would be citizens could
retain his estate intact. This action was taken in the national
capital and there is no evidence that he ever contemplated establishing a permanent residence in Illinois or in any other state
where his lands were located. The Illinois act to prevent landlords
from requiring tenants to pay taxes, of course, made necessary
revising the terms of the leases, but it may be doubted that it
resulted in any reduction in the total cost of the land to the tenant.
It did, however, serve to remove from Illinois one of the major
grievances that the public had against Scully.

The Pattern of Prairie Landlordism

For better or for worse, landlordism and tenancy were well
established in Illinois and in parts of Missouri, Kansas, Nebraska,
and Iowa by 1890. Contributing heavily to this end were the land
speculators like Riggs, Sturges, and Grigg, and the frontier landlords like Sullivant, Alexander, Scott, Allerton, Sibley, and Scully.
In the counties where their holdings were concentrated were found
the highest percentage of farms operated by tenants. Ford County,
which contained the Sullivant, later the Sibley estate, had the
highest proportion of farms operated by tenants, 54 per cent as
compared with the state average of 34 per cent. Logan County, in
which Scully had 225 farms and where many more were owned by
Gillett, Littler, and others, had 52 per cent of its farms tenant-operated. Mason County, where the McHarry and Herget estates—containing respectively 5,000 and 9,200 acres—were situated, had
one-half of its farms in tenant hands. The county fourth highest in
tenant-operated farms was Christian, where the 22,000 acre Malhiot estate lay, much of which was by 1890 in the hands of the
Vandeveer family. Next came Piatt County, where the Allerton and
Scott estates were located, and Grundy County where Scully owned
seventy or eighty farms, the Collins family thirty to thirty-five
farms, the Holderman family sixteen farms, and where the Hoge
family and other large owners had many more. Similarly in Marion
and Butler counties, Kansas, and Gage and Nuckolls counties,
Nebraska, where Scully had between six and seven hundred farms,
were found a high proportion of farms operated by tenants.

It may be argued that landlordism and tenancy were necessary
frontier institutions in the prairie counties where the costs of begin-

ning farming were so much higher than in wooded areas farther east. Certain it is that the capital required to buy land, especially from speculators or from the Illinois Central Railroad, import lumber for buildings, erect or set out fences, ditch, drain, and later tile the wet areas, break the tough prairie sod and seed it to corn, and purchase supplies until the first harvest was ready, together with the extortionate interest rates charged on borrowed capital on the frontier, made it difficult for many settlers to start as actual owners without accumulating a heavy debt. Funk, Scott, Sibley, and Allerton, with their ample resources, could accomplish what poor settlers could not, at least not without long delays. That they were influential in bringing the prairie into cultivation somewhat earlier than small owners could was their service to the state, but tenancy was the result and the cost.

On the other hand, on the Scully estates, where the landlord made few or no improvements except for tiling and that only after the land had already been tenanted, the renters had to provide their own capital for buildings, fences, ditches, and prairie breaking. True, their improvements were wretchedly poor as were the tenants themselves, but the fact remains that here was a substantial group of settlers who brought some 38,000 acres into cultivation with the investment of what little capital they may have brought with them. The only thing they did not have to provide was the $200 with which to buy the quarter-section from the government. Does this suggest that small-farm development by owner-operators might have occurred in the prairies had not the large speculators and frontier landlords anticipated them and got possession of most of the prairie land? It cannot, of course, be claimed that tenancy would thereby have been kept out of the prairies.

The swift rise of tenancy is one of the most striking features of the history of the American prairies. Careful observers had no occasion to be shocked in 1880 at the publication of the first census statistics showing that this rise for tenancy dated almost from the beginning of white settlement. A government land policy that permitted large-scale purchasing by speculators bears its responsibility for this early appearance and rapid growth of tenancy. The rise in land values that set in during and after the Civil War, and, of course, the increasing rents made it difficult for laborers and tenants to acquire ownership while the increasing capital demands of prairie agriculture and the unfavorable prices that produce brought in the seventies and again in the early nineties tended to depress many farm owners into the tenant class. The agricultural ladder from laborer through tenant to owner doubtless worked for many, as evidenced by the biographical sketches that appear in the numerous county histories of Illinois. But it must be remembered that these sketches are generally of those residents who had succeeded, who were now proudly describing their accumulations of property despite all adversity. At a later time the ladder seemed to work among children of owner-operators who started as laborers and worked up to the stage of mortgaged owners. On the other hand, the ladder worked in reverse for many others who, unable to meet the mortgage interest, lost their farms to the banker, the insurance company, or the local money lender.

Nowhere in America at the end of the century was tenancy more deeply rooted than in the prairies. While critics in the twentieth century were to find that prairie landlordism frequently provided expert farm management and the best of farm practices that were not always found on owner-operated farms, they were to confess that the old dream of owning one's farm was coming to be pracically unattainable to a large proportion of prairie residents.

PART III

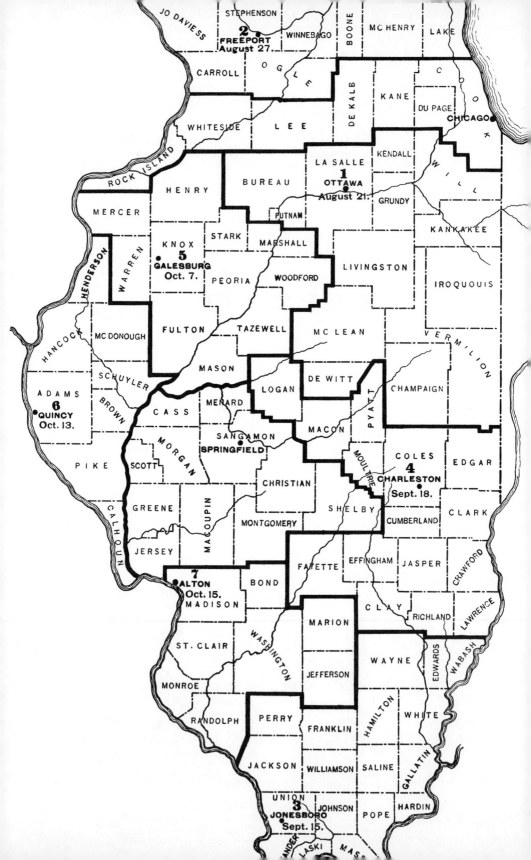

PART III

The Age of Lincoln and Douglas

1848–1865

EVEN AS THE POPULATION of Illinois increased to 851,470 in 1850, political campaigns received the intense personal attention of the electorate. Politics was understood not only as a continuing demonstration of the democratic process but also as a welcome escape from the routine and monotony of daily life. Having at least read extracts from the speeches of the candidates favored by local newspaper editors, every voter could discuss the candidates and the issues with his friends. Best of all, almost everyone had the chance to participate in a campaign. Candidates for state office stumped the state as best they could while their political friends and supporters spoke and worked for them in areas they could not reach. The major political rallies held in Chicago, Springfield, and other urban centers, featured colorful parades with banners and placards by day and torchlight processions by night, glee clubs, marching societies in full regalia, picnics, drill teams and cannon salutes—and above all, *speeches*.

Every speech was replete with fervid praise for the candidate and lengthy exhortations and explanations of a party's and candidate's position on the vital points at issue. At last the officer-seeker would appear to address the enraptured multitude—a Moses afoot on a quick-time march to Canaan or a pied piper hustling followers among his rabble. If the rally was successful, the audience waited to "strike hands" (as Lincoln put it) with the candidate. The whole affair was personalized, intense, and altogether fulfilling.

In the years immediately preceding the Civil War, Illinois supplied some of the principal participants for the political convulsion that would soon rend the entire country. Abraham Lincoln, once a Whig and later a Republican, politically adept and firmly committed to the principle of American unity without compromise, contended with Stephen Arnold Douglas, the nationally known spokesman of the Northern Democratic party, a polished orator and equally dedicated to the preservation of the Union, but a man who believed that only political expediency and compromise could hold the nation together. As Lincoln and Douglas represented different points of view on the major issues that divided the nation, so each represented a large part of Illinois.

The state's earliest settlers had come from Virginia, the Carolinas, Kentucky, and Tennessee, and had taken up land in southern Illinois; the next wave of settlers, who for the most part settled in northern Illinois, had come from New England, the North generally, and from abroad. With few exceptions, persons from southern Illinois had strong ties with the South and would sympathize with that section, while "free soil" and Whig-Republican attitudes were common in northern Illinois. These two points of view met head-on as Lincoln and Douglas contested for the votes of the Illinois legislators in the senatorial campaign of 1858. Douglas, although he won the senatorial race in 1858, lost so much support in the South that he would be denied the presidency in 1860. Lincoln, though losing, gained national prominence on the political stage, which he retained until he was elected president in 1860.

Between 1850 and 1860, the population of Illinois had again more than doubled to exceed 1,700,000. Except for the panic of 1857, the decade was an era of general expansion, exuberance, and progress. In 1850 there had been 110 miles of railroad in the state; ten years later the total was more than 2,800 miles, during which time the Illinois Central, the Alton, the Rock Island and Chicago and North Western railroads became operative. The first state fair was held; the Office of Public Instruction was created; the first free public school system was approved. The mass production of the self-scouring steel plow by John Deere in Moline and the reaper by Cyrus H. McCormick in Chicago made large-scale grain farming possible. In 1856, two years after the party was founded, William H. Bissell was elected as first Republican governor of Illinois.

In May 1860, Lincoln was nominated for the presidency at the Republican National Convention; held in the Wigwam in Chicago, it was the first national political convention to take place in that city. He would be opposed by Stephen A. Douglas, a Northern Democrat, by John Bell of the Constitutional Union party, and by John C. Breckinridge of the Southern Democratic party.

Lincoln has become such a towering figure in history that Americans have regarded him as a national father image, as the embodiment of all that is good in American democracy, and even as a demigod, Christlike in word and deed. And though legend has often made him a person much larger and greater than life, the legends are important as an index of popular opinion and no doubt reflect the ideals in which people want to believe. Conversely, although Douglas was a major politician with a large national following, the subsequent popular elevation of Lincoln has somewhat debased Douglas's deserved stature and made him seem almost a villain. He was, in fact, an energetic, experienced, formidable and worthy opponent who was gravely handicapped by a schism in the Democratic party. In Illinois, Lincoln beat Douglas by only 12,000 votes, but the entire state Republican ticket was elected by a much wider margin.

When the Civil War began, Illinois men rushed to the federal colors to uphold their belief in the inviolability of the Union, but few of them, in 1861, would have joined an army whose primary cause was the freedom of Negro slaves. In the last eighteen months of the war, however, many Illinois soldiers came to recognize the evils of slavery and to concede that it was at the center of the conflict. By the time the war was over, approximately 256,000 Illinoisans had joined the Northern army, and Illinois had furnished 152 regiments of infantry, 17 regiments of cavalry, and 2 regiments and 9 batteries of artillery. More than 34,000 men from Illinois, 16 percent of the state's total force, lost their lives in the war.

During the war, despite the unresolved internal problems presented by those who opposed the Lincoln administration (including the Copperheads), Illinois experienced a growth in population and a booming economic life. In the election of 1864 Lincoln again carried the state, receiving about 30,000 votes more than General George B. McClellan; and General Richard J. Oglesby, a Republican, was elected governor. Then, in May 1865, the body of the martyred president was returned to the quiet prairies, to Oak Ridge Cemetery in Springfield.

In the second half of that troubled decade of the sixties, Illinois became the first state to ratify the Thirteenth Amendment which abolished slavery and involuntary servitude. The University of Illinois was created, and the trade-union movement gained strength. Ulysses S. Grant was elected president and General John M. Palmer, a Republican, was elected governor. In 1870 the population of Illinois exceeded 2,500,000.

born in Kentucky, moved to Carlinville, Illinois, while still
in her teens, and in 1842 married John M. Palmer. Often
alone because of her husband's careers as lawyer, soldier,
and politician, she assumed the responsibility of caring for
several of her own brothers and sisters, and for members of
Palmer's family as well as her own children. When Palmer
became the fifteenth governor of Illinois in 1868, it appears
that she would have preferred the simplicity and quiet of
Carlinville to the demanding official and social duties so
much a part of life in the Executive Mansion; nevertheless,
she was active in church affairs while meeting her additional responsibilities as first lady of Illinois.

This article appeared in the *Journal of the Illinois State
Historical Society*, volume 3, number 2 (July 1910), pages
39–44.

REMEMBRANCES OF TWO SPRINGFIELD WEDDINGS OF THE OLDEN TIME

MRS. JOHN M. PALMER

While pondering the changes wrought by the passing years memory carries me to the early days and its customs with regard to
weddings. I recall as a child the marriage of my eldest sister, Susan
Lamb, in 1848, when to be "engaged" was a sacred event, not to be
lightly regarded as is the custom of some in these days, and the
deep mystery of the preparations, the quiet sewing upon 'white
goods,' the endless yards of cambric ruffling, hemmed by hand and
'whipped' on, sure evidence to a neighbor who had brought her
work to sit awhile that *something* is going on.

There was great secrecy observed when the rich 'rep' silk of the
wedding gown was selected in the nearest city, St. Louis, and made
in the house by Miss Sophia Van Nostrand, the most experienced
"mantua maker" of the town, lest the coming event be surmised.
But few of that wedding group remain. The bride was attended by
my next eldest sister Caroline, a cousin, Mary Johnson, and Miss
Eunice Conn of Jacksonville (whose mother was one of the Swan-
wick family of Kaskaskia); the bridegroom, John Cook, still living,

a grandson of Governor Edwards, and son of Daniel P. Cook, was attended by Lucien Carr of St. Louis, Jacob Bunn and Legh R. Kimball of this city.

The simple ceremony, performed by the Reverend John G. Bergen, was in the old parlor, at whose windows the starry-eyed jessamine and fragrant sweetbriar clambered for admission, and then the quiet staying at home to receive calls the next day, the bride arrayed in the charming blue silk 'second day' dress. For weeks the autumn rain poured in torrents, but put no restriction upon the round of evening parties.

I pause, and a later picture of the "fifties" arises. Another sister was the bride, and time in its progress had modified the extreme simplicity of weddings; yet there was still the same shrinking from taking a curious public into confidence. The engagement is not unexpected and hosts of friends are waiting to bestow best wishes. A new house—on the old site—(now the Court of Honor building, on the corner of Second and Adams streets, Springfield) erected by my father had just been completed, and it was planned to have the wedding something of a 'house-warming.' Invitations were issued two or three weeks in advance, and were vastly different from the elaborate style now in use. A tiny card lies before me with the names of the parents, 'Mrs. and Mrs. James L. Lamb, At Home December 19, 1855' in the center of the smooth, glazed surface, and in the lower left hand corner the names of the prospective groom and bride, William J. Black and Caroline Lamb; accompanying this, another card bearing the names of the wedded couple and her name in the left hand corner.

Amongst the guests present were, of course, many whose names are familiar. Mather, Roberts, Campbell, Opdycke, Prickett, Jayne, Edwards, Remann and Black, for they were 'kin;' Mr. and Mrs. Lincoln also, with no thought of the tragic future, Dr. and Mrs. Wallace, our own physician, Dr. Todd and family, Colonel and Mrs. Williams, and the Van Bergens, the Ulrichs and Vredenburghs, the Hursts, and others of the old Taylor family, the Irwins, and it was on this occasion that Wm. H. Marston, who afterward married 'Lila' Irwin, made his entrance into Springfield society. Mr. and Mrs. Wm. Pope, neighbors and long time friends, were with us, Virgil Hickox and wife, Mr. and Mrs. James C. Conkling, and Mrs. Lawrason Levering of St. Louis, formerly the handsome Miss Spain, a sister of Mrs. Robert Anderson; the Ridgely, Webster and Huntington families were represented, Major John T. Stuart and his wife, Dillers, Ruths and Corneaus were all there, James Barret and his charming wife, and John Calhoun, a name familiar to older people, and his daughter Lizzie. Time and patience would fail to mention all. Many well known throughout the State, among them Hon. O. H. Browning, Robert E. Blackwell and Ben. Bond. Custom decreed that for weeks before the event the bride-elect should be invisible to the outer world—even at church her presence was prohibited, for the 'invitations were out,' and alas! for the young woman who defied public opinion and became the target for idle curiosity during the intervening time.

How well I recall with what inward quaking, yet outward show of bravery a call was made upon an aunt of the bridegroom (Mrs. Young, wife of Judge Richard M. Young) who with her daughter, had come from Washington, D.C., to attend the wedding and was at the Chenery House. It was due her, yes, but how could she! Common sense won the day and together they made the call.

How vividly it comes back to me! The intense cold of those December days—and that recalls an incident illustrative of the close relationship between the servitor of that day and the family.

A faithful retainer, to whom children had been born during his service in the family, anxious to contribute his part to the wedding festivities took the wood-box which it was his daily duty to keep filled in order to supply the air-tight stove, by which the bridal chamber was heated, and, unknown to all, it was prepared, and with pride he bade us witness the result. Very neatly had the box been covered with pure white, the whitest wood had been selected and between each layer, arranged log cabin fashion, had been placed sheets of white paper. The effect—can you imagine? Alas, that such loving labor should end but in smoke.

That winter night! snow, star-light outside the quickly closed doors. 'A bitter chill it was—the owl for all its feathers, was a-cold,' but within was light and gaiety, for youth and happiness made warm the heart and heeded not the lack of furnace fire, while wood stove and open grate shed limited heat. I have a vision of the maiden as she stood before our minister and friend, Reverend Richard Varick Dodge, in her white robe of heavy moire and satin; the plain, pointed bodice laced up the back; the low cut neck and puffed 'caps' forming the sleeve with its handsome moss trimming, the full, gathered skirt, white satin slippers guiltless of heels, while the tulle veil, fastened by orange blossoms enveloped the small, graceful figure like an enshrouding mist.

It was my privilege, as first bridesmaid to throw back the veil when the simple service of the Presbyterian church was ended, and the young husband in black dress suit, immaculate gloves, with white brocade waistcoat and tie, bent to bestow the first caress upon the trusting face upturned to meet his own, and in those eyes shone the love of a lifetime.

There were but four attendants, a cousin, and myself; the gentlemen, Mr. McDowell of St. Louis and again Mr. Kimball. Our gowns were of white English crepe over silk slips, after the fashion of the day, with ample skirt and 'baby' waist—a sash of moire ribbon tied at the back, and gloves and slippers to correspond with those of the bride.

After the congratulations of the many guests, supper was announced; the bridal party preceded others to the dining room proper, for there were three—and paused before a table on which were no flowers—for flowers in December as decorations, were then unknown—but its center piece was an immense white cake, with frosting emblematic of the occasion, with its daintily molded figure of a veiled bride; on either end of this table was a tall pyramid of macaroons, skillfully united by icing, and over which was thrown at the last moment a web of spun sugar, the work of our home 'confectioner,' Mr. W. W. Watson, which process was watched with great delight by the children of the household. Branch candlesticks of silver, with candelabra and old fashioned sconces held waxen candles, whose soft light not only mellowed the beautiful scene, but was sometimes necessary to supplement that of the gas, then a crude production liable to leave us in the darkness, without warning. On the snowy napery were silver cake baskets of various sizes and shapes—not all our own, but loaned by many households of those pleased to be associated in any way with the glad occasion; these were artistic in the arrangement of generous slices of gold, silver, marbled and sponge cakes, with intermingled colors of jelly, composition and dark, rich fruit cake made from a recipe whose excellence had been tested by more than one generation of housewives—not only pleasing to the eye but good to the taste; there, too, were tall, fragile glasses of syllabub, and custards and genuine ice cream manufactured at home and frozen with ice from the subterranean depths of the old ice house, down whose sloping roof the children loved to slide at risk of life and limb. Candied fruits, one of the earlier importations from St. Louis, were a feature of this occasion. In an adjoining room a similar table was spread, save that in its center the pyramid was formed of quartered oranges dipped in boiling syrup and over it the same gossamer web.

For the third room a more substantial feast was provided for those whose masculine taste, or the coldness of the night, demanded different fare. Here were quail, cold turkey, boiled ham, pickles and tongue, with coffee, sparkling and of mahogany color, hot rolls and endless plates of old fashioned bread and butter, sliced to wafer-thinness and appetizing to behold.

No colored servant in evening dress was there, but friendly hands served one another with pleasant jest and repartee. Ah, those were good old days, and the merry company separated, many of them to reassemble on the next day at an elaborate dinner given the bridal party by an aunt, Mrs. Thomas Mather, whose handsome house and spacious grounds, afterwards purchased by the State, have given way to the present Capitol building of Illinois.

For three hours the guests remained at the table, while various gastronomic wonders were supplied by the imported cook, and the cloth was changed with each successive course. It was the most elaborate and formal dinner that had ever been given in our capital city. We parted, to meet in the evening at eight o'clock at a party, to which one or two hundred guests had been invited by the sister of the bride, Mrs. John Cook, whose wedding has been mentioned in this sketch.

And so for weeks the festivities went on, neighbors, relatives and dear old friends vying with one another to honor the young couple.

No wedding journey was taken, or even thought of; for in those days there were no palatial Pullmans to tempt by their luxurious ease, and then, as now, the ice king held undisputed sway from November until April.

Ah, happy, old-time days and customs, ye come not back again! "The old order changeth," and we who remain must bow to present pomp and circumstances, believing that the youth of the heart is always the same and that love is love, abiding and true in all ages and under all skies.

WILLIAM H. SMITH

a graduate of Illinois State Normal University, taught school, served as the McLean County Superintendent of Schools, and was an editor as well as a businessman. He was in demand on the lecture platform, first with "Bill" Nye and then by himself. He wrote a number of books, including *The Evolution of Dodd, Walks and Talks, The Promoters* and *All the Children of All the People.*

This article was published in the *Journal of the Illinois State Historical Society,* volume 13, number 1 (April 1920), pages 23–32.

OLD-TIME CAMPAIGNING AND THE STORY OF A LINCOLN CAMPAIGN SONG

WILLIAM H. SMITH

It was on August 8, 1860, that a "grand rally" of the Republican party was held at Springfield, Ill., to ratify the nomination of Abraham Lincoln, as the party's candidate for the presidency of the United States. Party spirit ran high, and enthusiasm for what the party stood for was at a white heat all over the Prairie State. The result of all this was that great crowds flocked to the state capital, from every county and town in the entire commonwealth, not only to show their loyalty to the party they were pledged to, but especially to do honor to the man who represented all they politically hoped for and believed in. I was but a boy of fifteen at the time, yet the events of that occasion were so emphatic and pronounced that they stamped themselves indelibly upon my memory, many of them in great detail, and it is of some of these and one especially, that I write in what follows.

Railroads were few and far between in Illinois in those days, and only a minor part of those who wished to attend the great meeting could reach the state capital by such means of transportation. But horses were plenty, and there were wagons galore, especially farm wagons, in all the region between Chicago and Cairo, and the rural people of the state (and most of the people of the state were rural at that time. Chicago had less than 100,000 inhabitants, and there was not another city in the state that had a population of 10,000 all told) were used to traveling in their own conveyances, or on horseback. It was in the time of the year when prairie roads were at their best, and so it was that the farmers came by the thousands to attend the "grand ratification." Many came two, and some even three hundred miles in this way, joyfully, gladly, to show their devotion to the cause they represented, the party they were a part of, and the man they loved. They rode or drove by day, camped by the roadside at night, their faces always towards one common point, the state capital, and their hearts filled with great expectations as to what they should see and hear when they arrived at their destination. These facts show something, even at this late day, of the fervor, not to say passion that animated the spirits of the rank and file of the Republican party more than half a century ago.

My father was a farmer who owned and cultivated a section of land, 640 acres, in the southeast corner of Christian county, about 60 miles from Springfield. He was an original Lincoln man, was a member of the state convention which met at Decatur, early in the summer, where Mr. Lincoln was declared as a "favorite son," and where the plans were laid, and the machinery was started, which in a large measure resulted in his nomination a few weeks later at Chicago, and he was also present at the Chicago convention, all the time from its call to order to its *sine die* adjournment. He brought back from Decatur a part of a black-walnut rail that Mr. Lincoln had split years before, and after his return from Chicago he could not speak aloud for more than a week. He had a naturally stentorian voice, which he literally wore to a frazzle in rooting, as it would be called nowadays, for his favorite candidate in the Wigwam where the convention was held in the then, as now, "Windy City" on the lake.

Early fall is the very witching time for sowing wheat in central Illinois, and father had 200 acres to sow that fall. But that could not keep him from attending the grand rally, nor from taking his five hired men with him to help swell the throng that was to greet the great party leader. And I was greatly delighted when he told me that he also wished me to make one of his company that was to attend the great event. Young as I was I had joined the Wide Awakes, the marchers and torch-bearers of the campaign, and it was as one of these that I went on this pilgrimage to the state capital. I was also a member of the Campaign Glee Club, but more of that later.

Father fitted up his largest and strongest farm wagon with a broad platform, or sort of flat deck on top, built over the frame of a hay rack, a plain surface about eighteen feet long and six or seven feet wide, floored with stout oak boards but without any railing around the sides. This was for the use of the Glee Club, some dozen or more young men and boys, who when not in action sat with their feet and legs dangling over the edge of the deck, riding sidewise as the wagon was driven along. When they sang they stood up on the deck-platform with their arms around each other to keep from falling off as the wagon joggled over the uneven roads. Under the platform, and to be got at through a trap door that was cut through the deck, there were stored the "provisions" of the trip, also blankets, torches, oil-cloth uniforms, etc. Father furnished four of his best horses to pull the load, and he drove the outfit most of the time on our four days' trip coming and going. We boys of the Glee Club sat on the uncushioned planks of that oak-floored deck-platform for those same four days, by day, and most of us slept under the wagon during the nights we were out. And that was a part of the way we younger fry did our bit in that memorable campaign.

No sooner were we started on our journey capitalward than we began to be joined at every cross-road by other pilgrims bound for the same goal. Indeed we fell into and became a part of such a procession from the very outset. This procession grew and grew in length as we progressed until before the second night of our encampment it was more than seven miles long, and it was made up almost exclusively of farm wagons and men on horseback. One would see here and there an express wagon with springs under its bed, and there were a very few carriages in all the line. This seven-mile procession was only one of several similar ones coming in to a common center from all parts of the state.

The second night out we camped in a tract of timber, about three miles south of Springfield. We were all up before daybreak on the following morning, and the last star had not been put to bed for the day when we started on the last lap of our memorable journey.

It was five o'clock in the morning when our Glee Club, wagon and all, arrived at the old state house square, then in the very center of the city of Springfield. Just as we came up opposite the front entrance of the capitol building who should come out of its door but the great hero of the day, Abraham Lincoln himself, tall and gaunt, his high plug hat making him look taller than ever. (I have often wondered how it happened that he was where he was so early in the morning of that great day.) His unusual height was specially emphasized as he came out onto the sidewalk by the fact that ex-Governor Wood, a very short and stubby man, was walking beside him. The two together made a very striking appearance as they walked along.

My father knew Mr. Lincoln well, and as he was driving he was the first of our party to recognize him. He called out to him, and when Mr. Lincoln turned and raised his hat in response half a dozen or more of the young men on our wagon jumped to the ground, ran to the sidewalk, picked the tall man up bodily, and began carrying him along the street on their stalwart farmer-boy shoulders! (It was in the month of May, five years later, that I stood in front of the same capitol building and saw the casket which bore all that was mortal of the then martyr president carried out from its front door, borne on the shoulders of eight stalwart soldiers along the same sidewalk where our boys so triumphantly carried him that morning of which I am writing.)

It was several blocks from the state house to Mr. Lincoln's home, but once our boys had taken hold they never let up till they had set their load down on his own doorstep. I have often thought that it must have been a far more honorable than it was a comfortable ride for Mr. Lincoln, carried as he was like a log of wood on the shoulders of those wildly shouting farmer boys.

A part of our campaign outfit brought all the way with us was a small cast-iron cannon, a gun about three feet long, with a two-inch bore. It was regularly mounted on a conventional wheel-carriage, in such cases made and provided, and was drawn by a pair of black ponies. The driver of the ponies and the captain of the cannon gun-squad was an old soldier of the Mexican war. The oufit made quite a telling appearance and the little old gun could make a noise which, as I remember it, was many times what might be expected from one of its size.

Our Glee Club wagon kept abreast of our boys who were carrying Lincoln, and the cannon and its squad were just behind us in the procession. We all halted in front of Mr. Lincoln's home, the cannon was unlimbered and placed squarely before the gate that led up to the steps where he was standing, and a salute of thirteen guns was fired in honor of the day, the occasion, and, above all, of the man whose ear-drums must have been nearly ruptured as he stood leaning against the door-jam, smiling and laughing, as he constantly shook hands with the crowds that jammed into the yard in spite of the cannonade that was going on in front. It was a sight to remember.

As soon as the salute had been fired the captain of the squad went up to Mr. Lincoln, and after shaking hands with him, and receiving thanks for the honor conferred, asked him if he would name the gun.

Mr. Lincoln laughed most good naturedly, and replied: "Oh, I never could name anything. Mary had to name all the children."

The captain was a quick-witted man (or was what he suggested an inspiration) and he immediately came back with: "Why not call the gun 'Mary Lincoln?' May we name it so?"

In reply Mr. Lincoln waved his long right arm, and with a hearty laugh said: "Yes. Let it go that way."

And so it was that our noisy little old gun was christened by the man in whose honor it had spoken its loudest and best that early morning now so long ago.

I am glad to add that this same noisy little old gun is still in the ring, well-preserved and well-nigh worshipped by the second and third generation of those who were present at its baptism. Its home is in the little rural town of Rosemond, Illinois, in the southeast corner of Christian county, of that state. It bears the name of "Mary Lincoln" engraved in letters of brass on its own proper person, and once a year it is almost reverently fired, a single time, "For Auld Lang Syne."

After the tumult of the firing had ceased, and the source of the great noise had been duly named and driven away, our Glee Club filed into the front yard and together we sang the following song for the tall man who stood in his own doorway and listened and laughed and applauded as we sang.

Our leader was a very good singer, as singers were counted in those days. He sang with the spirit and understanding, in a clear, full voice, and he spoke every word so that every one within ear-shot could understand everything he said. He sang the verses of the song and we all joined in on the chorus.

I never saw the words of this song in print, and I have no idea who wrote it, but he was a good song writer whoever he was. I learned the words from hearing our leader sing them again and again, as we sang at one campaign meeting and another that fall. In this way I learned by heart instead of merely committing to memory the words of this old song. Things merely committed to memory very soon get un-committed. What is learned by heart is rarely, if ever, forgotten. This is how it comes about that I can now, more than half a century after I helped sing the chorus of this song in Mr. Lincoln's dooryard, write out the words without any effort to recall them. I merely note this fact in passing.

So here is the song:

AN 1860 CAMPAIGN SONG.

Tune, "Vilkins and Dinah or "Tural-li-a."

There was one Old Abram lived out in the west,
Esteemed by his neighbors the wisest and best;
And if you will only but follow my ditty,
I'll tell you how he took a walk down to Washington City.

Chorus:

Sing tural, li ural, li ural, li a,
Sing tural, li ural, li ural, li a,
Sing tural, li ural, li ural, li a,
Sing tural, li ural, li ural, li a,

His home was in Springfield, out in Illinois,
Where he'd long been the pride of the men and the boys;
But he left his brown house without a sigh of regret,
For he knew that the people had a White one to let.
Said Old Buck: "Mr. Lincoln, your notions I think
Are extremely correct, let us all take a drink;
We've the best of 'J. B. Green Seal' and old sherry,
And I've no objections, just now, to be merry."

Chorus:

Said Old Abe: "As for drinking, please excuse me today,
And you and your crowd have it all your own way;
The people have trusted you longer'n they oughter,
And all that I ask is a glass of cold water."

Chorus:

"Cold water!" said Buck, "We have it, I think,
Although with our crowd it's not a favorite drink;
We partake of our tipple on its own native merits,
And we need something stronger to keep up our sperrits."

Chorus:

The cabinet, well frightened, searched the White House with
   a will,
But they couldn't find water put down on the bill;
Jerry Black made a report, that without any doubt,
The whiskey was plenty, but the water played-out.

Chorus:

Of course, without whiskey the meeting was bum,
And they wished, more than ever, that Abe hadn't come;
So when Old Abe saw they had no more to say,
He took up his hat and wished them "Good day."

Chorus:

So Old Abe he returned to his home in the West,
Leaving Buck and his cabinet greatly depressed;
And if this part of my tale you'll remember,
I'll tell you the balance next sixth of November,

Chorus:

As for the rest of that memorable day its record is a matter of
history, written in many places. I only add a few words just here to
make this particular picture a bit more complete all by itself. A
double procession, many miles in length, and largely made up of
the sort I have already described, marched and counter marched in
front of Mr. Lincoln's house from early morning till well into the
afternoon. Then the ranks disbanded and went into camp, all
round the city, to wait for the evening performance. Our own party
found such a resting place in the old fair grounds, just outside the
city limits.

I think it was about five o'clock in the afternoon when, as we sat
or lounged about, resting up for what was yet to come, a closed
carriage drove into the enclosure, and some one called out that Mr.
Lincoln was inside it. Instantly there was a rush, the horses were
unhitched from the vehicle, and everybody who could get near
enough to lend a hand helped push it towards a platform that stood
near, which had been built for speaking purposes later in the day.

As soon as the carriage reached the platform the door was pulled
open and Mr. Lincoln was pulled out and carried up on to the stage.
There he was stood up on his feet, and the crowd yelled for a
speech. He started to say a few words when the platform on which
he was standing began to sway and to creak, as if about to fall from

the over-burden upon it, and which it had never been built to stand up under. The situation was critical but Mr. Lincoln was equal to the emergency. Raising his hand high, he said laughingly, but in a loud voice: "Get off, get off. This must be a democratic platform to threaten to go to pieces if a crowd tries to stand on it! I won't try to stand on it, and I don't want you should either! You get off, and so will I!"

And everybody got off so quickly that the platform did not fall. In the confusion that followed Mr. Lincoln somehow escaped and got out of the crowd. The horses were brought back and hitched to the empty carriage, later it was driven away. (The fact was that Mr. Lincoln had no intention of going into the crowd, but a zealous and highly influential political friend wanted him to see the throng, and induced him to go out in a closed carriage, with the curtains drawn. But the secret of his trip somehow leaked out, with the results I have told.)

That night there was another endless procession, composed largely of Wide Awakes in uniform, bearing torches and firing Roman candles as they marched along. It was long after midnight before all was over and the tired thousands dispersed and went wherever they could. For ourselves we got our Glee Club wagon into the first open field we came to after we left the city, and stretched ourselves under it and slept the sleep of the entirely exhausted.

We were the better part of two days getting home, and both father and I spoke only in whispers for several days thereafter. Hired men and all, we set to work on the 200 acres of neglected wheat sowing which had waited for its just dues while we were doing our political duties, such as fall to the lot of all true patriots in a genuine democracy. And the acres of wheat we sowed that fall brought forth a bountiful harvest the next summer. What the political seed that was sowed that fall brought forth is a matter of history that all the world knows.

CLINTON L. CONKLING

was the son of James and Mercy Levering Conkling, who were good friends of Abraham Lincoln in Springfield. In later life, Mr. Conkling was a member of the Lincoln guard of honor, a small group of prominent men who organized to protect the body of Lincoln from grave robbers.

This article appeared in the *Transactions of the Illinois State Historical Society* for 1909, pages 63–67.

HOW MR. LINCOLN RECEIVED THE NEWS OF HIS FIRST NOMINATION

CLINTON L. CONKLING

The Republican National Convention met in Chicago, May 16, 1860. The interest throughout the country in the results of the meeting was intense. The general opinion, especially in the East, was that William H. Seward of New York would be nominated, although Horace Greeley and others from New York were opposed to him. The Republican State Convention on the ninth day of the same month had declared Abraham Lincoln to be the first choice of the Republican party of Illinois for the Presidency. Many delegates and politicians thronged the city several days before the convention. Mr. Lincoln's friends were early on the ground working earnestly and effectively to create a sentiment in his favor.

N. M. Knapp, then of Winchester, Illinois, wrote to him from Chicago, as follows:

> TREMONT HOUSE.
> GAGE, BRO, & DRAKE. PROPRIETORS.
> CHICAGO, Monday May 14, 1860.
> DEAR SIR—Things are working; keep a good nerve—be not surprised at any result—but I tell you that your chances are not the worst. We have got Seward in the attitude of the representative Republican of the East—*you* at the West. We are laboring to make you the second choice of all the delegations we can where we cannot make you first choice. We are dealing tenderly with delegates, taking them in detail, and making no fuss. Be not too expectant but rely upon our discretion. Again I say brace your nerves for any result.
> Truly your friend,
> N. M. KNAPP.

Mr. Lincoln was present at the state convention at Decatur but did not go to Chicago. He remained in Springfield, went to his law office as usual, received reports of the progress of events by telegrams, letters and from persons returning from Chicago, visited his friends to discuss the situation and prospects and, occasionally, as was his wont, joined in a game of hand ball, the then favorite pastime of the professional men of the town.

The only wires into Springfield in 1860 were owned and operated by the Illinois and Mississippi Telegraph Company and were called the "Caton Lines" after Judge John D. Caton of Ottawa, Illinois, president of the company, and one of its organizers. Its principal office was at St. Louis. John James Speed Wilson, afterwards known as "Colonel" Wilson, was superintendent of the eastern division with headquarters at Springfield. E. D. L. Sweet was superintendent of the western division with his office in Chicago. These divisions were afterwards called the southern and northern divisions, respectively.

C. F. McIntire, with an operator named J. B. Pierce, was in charge of the local office in Springfield which was then on the north side of the public square (but at what number I have been unable to learn). I have no further information about these operators. A year or two afterwards the telegraph office was moved to the rooms previously occupied by James C. Conkling as law offices, being the second floor over Chatterton's jewelry store, now 121 South Fifth Street, on the west side of the Square, where it remained for some years. The first telegraph office in this city was in the second story over Pease's hardware store, now 506 East Adams Street on the south side of the square.

Upon the absorption of the Illinois & Mississippi Lines by the Western Union Telegraph Company in 1866, Mr. Sweet was appointed superintendent of the latter company, and upon his resignation in 1868, Colonel Wilson succeeded him and removed to Chicago. He continued in that position until 1879, when he resigned to go into other business. He died a few years afterwards. Mr. E. D. L. Sweet is still living in Chicago at the advanced age of eighty-six years. During the convention he had charge of all the telegraphic arrangements. There was only one wire into the "Wigwam" and this was connected in the main office with the eastern wire of the Western Union—it being the general opinion that the nomination would go to an eastern man, Seward being the one most often mentioned in that respect. Mr. Wilson was in Chicago during the convention and divided his time between the main telegraph office, at the southeast corner of Lake and Clark streets, and the convention in the "Wigwam," a building erected for the occasion at the corner of Market and Lake streets. Most of the personal messages from delegates to Illinois points were sent from the convention hall to the main office of the Caton Company by messenger boys.

On Friday morning, May 18, 1860, the third day of the convention, the delegates met at ten o'clock to ballot. James C. Conkling of Springfield who had been in Chicago several days but was called back unexpectedly, arrived home early that morning. George M. Brinkerhoff, Sr., of this city was reading law in Mr. Conkling's office, which was then over Chatterton's jewelry store. About half past eight o'clock Mr. Lincoln came into the office and asked Mr. Brinkerhoff where Mr. Conkling was, as he had just heard on the street that the latter had returned from Chicago. On being told that Mr. Conkling was not in but probably would be in an hour, Mr. Lincoln said he would go out on the street and come back again as he was anxious to see Mr. Conkling. Presently Mr. Conkling came in and later Mr. Lincoln again called. There was an old settee by the front window on which were several buggy cushions. Mr. Lincoln stretched himself upon this settee, his head on a cushion and his feet over the end of the settee. For a long time they talked about the convention. Mr. Lincoln wanted to know what had been done and what Mr. Conkling had seen and learned and what he believed would be the result of the convention. Mr. Conkling replied that Mr. Lincoln would be nominated that day; that after the conversations he had had and the information he had gathered in regard to Mr. Seward's candidacy, he was satisfied that Mr. Seward could not be nominated, for he not only had enemies in other states than his own, but he had enemies at home; that if Mr. Seward was not nominated on the first ballot the Pennsylvania delegation and other delegations would immediately go to Mr. Lincoln and he would be nominated.

Mr. Lincoln replied that he hardly thought this could be possible and that in case Mr. Seward was not nominated on the first ballot, it was his judgment that Mr. Chase of Ohio or Mr. Bates of Missouri would be the nominee. They both considered that Mr. Cameron of Pennsylvania stood no chance of nomination. Mr.

Conkling in response said that he did not think it was possible to nominate any other one except Mr. Lincoln under the existing conditions because the pro-slavery part of the Republican party then in the convention would not vote for Mr. Chase, who was considered an abolitionist, and the abolition part of the party would not vote for Mr. Bates, because he was from a slave state, and that the only solution of the matter was the nomination of Mr. Lincoln.

After discussiong the situation at some length, Mr. Lincoln arose and said, "Well, Conkling, I believe I will go back to my office and practice law." He then left the office.

I was present during a part only of this interview and depend largely for the details of this conversation upon what Mr. Conkling and Mr. Brinkerhoff have told me. In a very few moments after Mr. Lincoln left I learned of his nomination, (just how I do not now remember) and rushed after him. I met him on the west side of the Square before anyone else had told him and to my cry, "Mr. Lincoln you're nominated," he said, "Well, Clinton, then we've got it," and took my out-stretched hand in both of his. Then the excited crowds surged around him and I dropped out of sight.

In my possession are five original telegrams received by Mr. Lincoln on the day he was nominated. All are on the Illinois and Mississippi Telegraph Company form.

The first one sent was from the telegraph superintendent Wilson, and shows signs of haste and bears no date. It reads,

"To Lincoln:
> "You are nominated."
>> "J. J. S. Wilson."

Mr. Pierce, the operator who received this message at Springfield, writes from Young America, Illinois, under date of June 4, 1860, to Mr. Lincoln saying that this was the first message for him announcing his nomination.

A moment after this message was sent a messenger boy brought to the main office in Chicago a message addressed simply "Abe" and which read "We did it. Glory to God," "Knapp." The receiving clerk brought the message to Mr. Sweet, calling his attention to the address, and also to the expression "Glory to God." Mr. Sweet directed that the words "Lincoln, Springfield" be added and that the message be sent at once. This message is probably the first one to Mr. Lincoln from any person who was actively at work in his behalf in the convention and without doubt was from Mr. N. M. Knapp who wrote the letter of May 14.

The next two telegrams are from J. J. Richards who was connected with the Great Western Railroad Company and was its agent for some time at Naples, which was then the end of the road. Owing to the great amount of freight then brought to Naples by boat from St. Louis and other points down the river, and which was there re-shipped to central Illinois points, the position of agent required a man of good business ability, and for this reason he was stationed there. He subsequently went to Chicago.

These telegrams are as follows:

                                                          May 18, 1860.
              By Telegraph from Chicago 18   1860.
        To Abraham Lincoln:
                    You'r nominated & elected.
                                                      J. J. Richards.
                                ————18————
                    By Telegraph from Chicago 18————18——
        To Hon. A. Lincoln:
                    You were nominated on 3rd ballot.
                                          J. J. Richards.

Mr. J. S. S. Wilson followed his first message, probably within a very few moments, by another which reads:

                                ————18————
                    By Telegraph from Chicago 18   1860.
        To Hon. A. Lincoln:
                    Vote just announced. Whole No 466 necessary to choice
        234 Lincoln 354 votes not stated on motion of Mr. Evarts of
        NY the nomination was made unanimous amid intense enthu-
        siasm.
                                          J. J. S. Wilson.

For kindly assistance in compiling this paper I am indebted to Hon. Robert T. Lincoln; Mr. Charles S. Sweet, his secretary; Mr. John W. Bunn and Mr. George M. Brinkerhoff, Sr.

DAVID DONALD

received his Ph.D. in history at the University of Illinois
in 1946, and since then has taught at Columbia University,
Smith College, and Princeton University. Dr. Donald is now
Harry C. Black Professor of American History and director
of the Institute of Southern History at Johns Hopkins University. He has been a fellow of the Social Science Research
Council, Fulbright Lecturer at the University of North Wales,
and Harmsworth professor of American History at Oxford
University. He is the author of *Lincoln's Herndon, Lincoln
Reconsidered, Inside Lincoln's Cabinet, The Civil War Diaries
of Salmon P. Chase,* and *Charles Sumner and The Coming
of the Civil War* (for which he won the Pulitzer Prize for
biography).

This article appeared in the *Journal of the Illinois State
Historical Society,* volume 40, number 4 (December 1947),
pages 377–396.

THE FOLKLORE LINCOLN

DAVID DONALD

I

The Lincoln cult is almost an American religion. It has its high
priests in the form of Lincoln "authorities" and its worshipers in
the thousands of "fans" who think, talk, and live Lincoln every day.
The very name of its founder possesses magical significance—witness its use in advertising everything from automobiles to barber-
shops. Lincoln's birthday is a national holiday, commemorated
with solemn ceremonies. In 1909—the centennial of his birth—Illinois teachers were directed to devote at least half of the day of
February 12 to "public exercises . . . patriotic music, recitations of
sayings and verses . . . and speeches." The school children were to
conclude the celebration by chanting in unison, with their faces
turned toward Springfield, the following ritual:

A blend of mirth and sadness, smiles and tears;
A quaint knight errant of the pioneers;

A homely hero, born of star and sod;
A Peasant Prince; a masterpiece of God.[1]

The Lincoln birthplace in Kentucky, the memorial in Washington, and the tomb in Illinois have become national shrines visited by thousands each week. The Lincoln admirer has his shelf of sacred books—a very extensive shelf, as one judges from the nearly four thousand titles listed in Jay Monaghan's *Lincoln Bibliography*. There are monographs on every subject from *Abraham Lincoln's Chiropodist* to *Lincoln's Favorite Hymn*. For no other American has there been such a constant searching of the auguries to learn *What Would He Do Were He Here Today?*

It was probably inevitable that Lincoln should, as Emerson phrased it, "have become mythological in a very few years." America was badly in need of a hero. By 1865 George Washington seemed so dignified and remote that it was hard to think of him as a man, much less as a boy; he was a portrait by Peale or Houdon bust. Davy Crockett had degenerated from frontier hero into comic legend. Andrew Jackson, Henry Clay, and Daniel Webster were already slipping into the limbo of lost souls—the history books.

The times and the events of the Civil War had made a great popular leader necessary. There had been the emotional strain of war, the taut peril of defeat, the thrill of battles won, the release of peace. Then had come the calamitous, disastrous assassination. The people's grief was immediate and it was immense. Properly to describe it one would need the eloquence of a Whitman or a Sandburg. Men had a lost feeling. "The news of his going," mourned William H. Herndon, Lincoln's Springfield law partner, "struck me dumb, the deed being so infernally wicked . . . so huge in consequences, that it was too large to enter my brain. Hence it was incomprehensible, leaving a misty distant doubt of its truth. It *yet* does not appear like a worldly reality."

Mourning intensified grief. The trappings of death—the black-draped catafalque, the silent train that moved by a circuitous route over the land, the white-robed choirs that wailed a dirge, the crepe-veiled women, the stone-faced men—made Lincoln's passing seem even more calamitous. Over a million persons took a last sad look at the face in the casket and went away treasuring an unforgetta-

---

[1] *The One Hundredth Anniversary of the Birth of Abraham Lincoln: For the Schools of Illinois*, issued by Francis G. Blair (Springfield, 1908). The verse is quoted from "Abraham Lincoln," by Walter Malone.

ble memory. They became of that select group who had seen Lincoln.

II

In those dark postwar decades there was keen interest in the Great Emancipator and Great Martyr—those two phases, always in capitals, keep cropping up in nearly all the correspondence of the period. There were those who speculated on what Lincoln would have done had he lived, and there were more who tried to recall what he had done while alive. An avid audience looked forward eagerly to the memoirs and reminiscenses that began to flood the country. The Monaghan bibliography lists over four hundred and fifty speeches, sermons, and histories of Lincoln which appeared in the year of his death.

To this urgent demand for details on Lincoln's life, few would answer as did George Spears, a friend from New Salem days, who explained the brevity of his recollections by declaring: "At that time I had no idea of his every being President therefore I did not notice his course as close as I should of." Not only persons who knew Lincoln retailed "facts" to the eager world, but also those who had merely met the president, or those who might have met him, or those who wished to have met him. Stories, sometimes without the slightest shadow of factual foundation, were spread by word of mouth, and by mere repetition gained authenticity. Then they appeared in Lincoln biographies and have been handed down ever since as indubitably accurate.

At the time of Lincoln's death there was no single pattern into which the stories and anecdotes about him could fit. In the blurred memories of former slaves there was the shadowy outline of a preternaturally shrewd Lincoln, half Moses, half Yankee. "I think Abe Lincoln was next to the Lord," said one ex-slave. "He done all he could for the slaves; he set 'em free." Then the aged Negro went on to "reminisce":

> 'Fore the election he [Lincoln] traveled all over the South, and he come to our house and slept in Old Mistress' bed. Didn't nobody know who he was. . . . he come to our house and he watched close. . . . When he got back up North he writ Old Master a letter and told him that he was going to have to free his slaves, that everybody was going to have to.

> . . . He also told him that he had visited at his house and if
> he doubted it to go in the room he slept in and look on the
> bedstead at the head and he'd see where he'd writ his name.
> Sure enough, there was his name: A. Lincoln.

Gradually the Negro built up a more emotional image of Lincoln, a perfect man and, in a peculiarly individual way, a personal emancipator. In Negro houses all over the nation one could find "many old pictures of Lincoln pasted on the walls of the sitting room over the mantelpiece. . . . They just had to have Lincoln near them," explains their chronicler, John E. Washington; "they loved him so." "His life to these humbler people was a miracle, and his memory has become a benediction," Dr. Washington adds. "To the deeply emotional and religious slave, Lincoln was an earthly incarnation of the Savior of mankind."

At the other extreme were the stories spread by Lincoln's political enemies, legends which still persist in some parts of the South. To these the sixteenth president was only "a man of coarse nature, a self-seeking politician, who craved high office . . . to satisfy his own burning desire for distinction." He was, so a Southern canard went, of Negro ancestry, or his presumptive parents were immoral, shiftless poor white trash. Unscrupulous as a lawyer, he was unprincipled as a politician. He was a man of low morality, and his "inordinate love of the lascivious, of smut," so it was whispered, was "something nearly akin to lunacy." But today, as Avery Craven has pointed out, "the unreconstructed are few and growing fewer," and most present-day Southerners would agree with the distinguished Louisiana historian, Charles Gayarré, who characterized Lincoln as "humane and pure, kindly disposed toward the South."

III

Naturally the strongest growth of Lincoln legends has occurred in the North. There have been, in general, two opposing schools of tradition. One, essentially literary in character and often of New England or Eastern sponsorship, presented a prettified Lincoln, a combination of George Washington and Christ. Occasionally there were difficulties of reconciling the two ideas, and the resulting portrait looks somewhat like a Gilbert Stuart painting with a halo dubbed in by later, less skillful hands. The problem was to reconcile the standards of democracy in the gilded age with the familiar pattern of the Christ story. Fortunately for authors, consistency is not an essential in folklore.

In eulogies, sermons, birthday speeches, Republican campaign addresses, orations before the G.A.R., and in poems, too numerous to count and too tedious to read, one gets a glimpse of the pattern. This Lincoln has the outlines of a mythological hero; he is a demigod. Born in obscure circumstances, he rose over hardships, became president, was lawgiver to the Negro race, won a tremendous victory, and was killed at the height of his power. By his death he expiated the sins of his nation. After one makes the obvious concessions required by mid-century morality and by the exigencies of a republican form of government, this portrait of Lincoln conforms very closely to the type of ideal hero in classical mythology.

The eulogists had some doubts as to how Lincoln's ancestry should be presented. A mythological hero should spring from unknown parentage (or at least it is concealed even from himself), sent by the gods to save his tribe. There are a series of Lincoln poets and biographers who ask, "Whence came this man?" and answer: "As if on the wings of the winds of God that blew!" On the other hand, it comported more with American notions of respectability that the hero should have at least some family connections. The Lincolns have, therefore, been traced in elaborate monographs back to the early Massachusetts settlers and even to the English family of that name. The Hankses have been "proved" to derive their name from an Egyptian dynasty, or, as an alternative explanation, they were relatives of the Lees of Virginia.

Regardless of origins, the biographers were sure of one thing. Lincoln loved his angel-mother. It is perhaps characteristic of the American attitude toward family life and of the extreme veneration for the maternal principle that the utterly unknown Nancy Hanks should be described as "a wholehearted Christian," "a woman of marked natural abilities," of strong mental powers and deep-toned piety," whose rigid observance of the Sabbath became a byword in frontier Kentucky—in short, "a remarkable woman." "A great man," asserted J. G. Holland in his widely circulated *Life of Abraham Lincoln*, "never drew his infant life from a purer or more womanly bosom than her own; and Mr. Lincoln always looked back to her with an unspeakable affection."

Lincoln's early life became, to this school of biography, an illustration of how determination and energy could triumph over circumstances; this Lincoln was the transcendant railsplitter. It was a carefully manipulated symbolism that had begun at the Illinois state Republican convention of 1860 when rails which Lincoln might have split were introduced to elicit applause. The theme was drummed and piped and bugled all through the campaigns of 1860 and 1864, and, regardless of its truth, the tale of Lincoln's "life of labor" which "brought forth his kingly qualities of soul" has become a part of the American tradition. Lincoln was never to escape; his Civil War administration would be appraised in terms of his early struggles:

> Out yonder splitting rails his mind had fed
> On Freedom—now he put her foes to rout.[2]

From these origins he rose to become president of the United States, and, surprisingly enough, a successful president. There must have been, a great many people believed, some supernatural force, some divine guidance behind his rise. "Out of the unknown, and by ways that even he knew not," orated one centennial speaker, becoming more mystical with each phrase, "came to this place of power, Abraham Lincoln. He came mysteriously chosen . . . by the instinctive voice of a predestined people. Called because he was chosen; chosen, because he was already choice."

There were elements in Lincoln's personality and career which did not blend well in this portrait of a demigod. He was indubitably homely—not a major difficulty, to be sure, yet if a hero is not handsome he should at least be impressive. Rhymesters went to great length to explain the truth. Was Lincoln "ungainly, plain?" Not at all. "Grave was his visage," it was admitted, "but no cloud could dull the radiance from within that made it beautiful." A more serious obstacle was Lincoln's levity. He told jokes—a thing unprecedented in the record of mythology. Writers were more familiar with the idea of "one who knew not play, nor ever tasted rest." How could a man of sadness and tears laugh at Artemus Ward? The solution finally achieved was either that Lincoln's laughter was designed to conceal his plans from his enemies or—more frequently—that it was called in as a sort of anodyne "to cease his ceaseless dole." Thus Lincoln became the laughing man of sorrows.

Another difficulty was Lincoln's religion. It was embarrassing that this "soldier of his Captain Christ" belonged to no Christian

---

[2] Dallas Williams, "The Rail-Splitter."

church. Shortly after Lincoln's death there began to appear a veritable flood of affidavits and statements to prove, as Holland put it, that "Lincoln's power" had been the "power of a true-hearted Christian man." Reminiscences on this point probably include more nonsense than can be found anywhere else in the whole tiresome mass of spurious Lincoln recollections. To him are attributed the most improbable statements. Lincoln was supposed to have had a secret conference with Newton Bateman, Illinois superintendent of public instruction, during which he pulled a Testament from his bosom and pointed to it as *this rock* on which I stand." "I know," he is alleged to have confided, "that liberty is right, for Christ teaches it and Christ is God."

Countless similar statements were given wide newspaper circulation. Lincoln reportedly ran upon one Benjamin B. Smith, a minister of Canton, Missouri, in a railway station, corralled him into his office, and begged from the willing pastor a private, hourlong discourse upon "foreordination, election and predestination." During the darkest hours of the war Lincoln was supposed to have left his post in Washington in order to pray with Henry Ward Beecher in New York City. So it went. There were those who could demonstrate that Lincoln was a Catholic, a Congregationalist, a Methodist, a Presbyterian, a Universalist, or a Spiritualist. Conflicting claims became so amusing that the editor of the Springfield *Illinois State Register* rejected them as "all wrong." "We are . . ." he remarked whimsically, "prepared to prove by indisputable documentary evidence that he was a Mormon, and the boon companion of Joe Smith."

For these minor defects Lincoln amply compensated by the manner of his passing. His assassination at once brought to mind the tender, familiar outlines of the Christ story. Lincoln as "Savior of his country" was by his death expiating the sins of the nation. The idea had universal appeal. One has only to leaf through the pages of Lloyd Lewis's *Myths after Lincoln* to discover how frequently the idea of vicarious sacrifice recurred to Northern preachers on that dread Black Easter of 1865. Some pointed to the significance of Lincoln's martyrdom on Good Friday. "It is no blasphemy against the Son of God," asserted a Connecticut parson, ". . . that we declare the fitness of the slaying of the second Father of our Republic on the anniversary of the day on which He was slain. Jesus Christ died for the world, Abraham Lincoln died for his country."

Even so early the pattern of apotheosis was complete. America had a martyr hero, a perfect man, born to do great things, pure in heart, noble in action, and constant in principle. This was Lincoln, "President, savior of the republic, emancipator of a race, true Christian, true man."

IV

Lincoln was saved from this kind of deification by a different stream of tradition, frequently Western in origin and more truly folkloristic in quality. The grotesque hero—the Gargantua or the Till Eulenspiegel—is one of the oldest and most familiar patterns in folk literature. In America the type had already been exemplified by such favorites as Davy Crockett, Mike Fink, and Paul Bunyan. Of a like cut was the myth of Lincoln as frontier hero. This Lincoln of "folk say" was not a perfect man, but he had divinely human imperfections. He was the practical joker, the teller of tall and lusty tales. Stupendously strong, he was also marvelously lazy. A true romantic, he pined over the grave of Ann Rutledge, but he also lampooned one woman who refused him and jilted another who accepted. He was shrewd, a manipulator of men, whose art concealed his artfulness. He was Old Abe, a Westerner, and his long flapping arms were not the wings of an angel.

This folk pattern of Lincoln as frontier hero had been sketched in outline before his death. After his assassination the details were filled in. Many of the stories in this strong Western tradition can be traced to Herndon, Lincoln's law partner, who has been called the "master myth-maker" of Lincoln folklore. Herndon did not invent the legends, but his singular personality made him peculiarly receptive to this type of Western mythology. Herndon was born in Kentucky, and, as an early German traveler put it, "the Kentuckian is a peculiar man." Moody, erratic, loquacious, addicted to high flown "philosophical" language, but with a penchant for barnyard stories, Herndon had shortly after his partner's death decided to write a biography of Lincoln. From the very outset he had in mind showing Lincoln as a Western character, shaped by the "power of mud, flowers, & mind" which he had encountered in the pioneer Northwest. Deliberately he sought to emphasize those factors which would distinguish Lincoln as a "Westerner" from his Eastern contemporaries. He proposed to exhibit "the type" of the "original

western and southwestern pioneer— . . . at times . . . somewhat
open, candid, sincere, energetic, spontaneous, trusting, tolerant,
brave and generous."

Seeking information about Lincoln, Herndon interviewed older
settlers in central Illinois and southern Indiana at just the time
when the outlines of the folk portrait were becoming firmly established. From his notes emerged the essentially fictitious picture of a
semilegendary frontier hero. The stories Herndon collected fall into
patterns familiar to the student of American folklore. Some remembered Lincoln as a ring-tailed roarer of the Davy Crockett type,
who would wave a whiskey bottle over his head to drive back his
foes, shouting that "he was the big buck at the lick." [3] There were
tales of the Paul Bunyan variety, describing how Lincoln would
"frequently take a barrel of whiskey by the chimes and lift it up to
his face as if to drink out of the bung-hole," a feat which "he could
accomplish with greatest ease." [4]

This was the Lincoln who chastely wooed Ann Rutledge, and
when she died pined sadly over her grave. "My heart," he was
supposed to have said, "lies buried there." More in the frontier
tradition was his courtship of Mary Owens, a well educated Kentucky lady who refused his hand. Afterwards Lincoln described her
as "weather-beaten," "oversize," and lacking teeth. Of a like pattern
were the tales Herndon accumulated of Lincoln's domestic unhap-
piness with Mary Todd, for the henpecked husband is one of the
oldest comic types in the history of humor and was a favorite in the
Western joke books of the day. Herndon also collected irreligious
or, as he called them, "infidel" statements attributed to Lincoln; the
folk hero is frequently anti-clerical.

Many of these tales probably had a grain of historical truth, and
their evolution exhibits the familiar developments of folk literature. "If a man has been well known for special powers," Robert
Price has pointed out in his examination of the Johnny Appleseed
traditions, "folk fancies soon seize upon particular instances of
these powers, begin to enhance them into facts of remarkable
quality, and then proceed, as the desire for greater color grows, to
invent still others that will markedly emphasize the quality ad-

[3] Herndon's interview with Green B. Taylor, Sept. 16, 1865 (Herndon-Weik
Collection, Library of Congress).

[4] R. B. Rutledge to Herndon, attested Oct. 22, 1866 (Herndon-Weik Collection).

mired." As the historical personage becomes absorbed in the myth, "the whole cycle of his birth, youth, education, loves, mating, maturity, and death becomes significant and grows increasingly in color and particular detail." On a rather sophisticated plane, the Lincoln of Western legend represented a true folk hero type.

The folkloristic quality of these stories is sometimes overlooked. When Herndon visited in Indiana, he was told of verses which Lincoln had written to celebrate the wedding of his sister:

> When Adam was created
> He dwelt in Eden's shade,
> As Moses has recorded,
> And soon a bride was made.

(The poem continues for seven additional stanzas.) Dr. Milo M. Quaife has traced this ballad back to early English folk verse and has shown that it was introduced into America before the Revolutionary War. In the process of being handed down, it somehow became identified in the minds of backwoods Hoosiers with Lincoln; it was related to Herndon as such; he published the verses in his Lincoln biography; and the poem is not infrequently cited as Lincoln's own original composition. Of the making of myths there is no end!

The process of evolving Western legends about Lincoln neither began nor ended with Herndon. Gossip, imagination, delayed recollection, and hearsay have all continued to multiply "Lincoln" stories. Sometimes the results of this accumulation of folk tales are very amusing. One can take, for example, a less familiar episode in Lincoln's early career—his projected duel with James Shields. The critical biographer admits that in 1842, Mary Todd and Julia Jayne published anonymously in the *Sangamo Journal* some satirical verses about Shields, then Illinois state auditor. That hot-tempered Irishman demanded of the editor the names of the writers, and Lincoln, to protect the ladies, offered to take the blame. After some stilted correspondence and much dashing back and forth of seconds, a duel with broadswords was arranged. Ultimately, however, explanations and apologies were made, and actual combat was averted. The affair remained a sore memory to Lincoln, and he disliked hearing the episode referred to. The actual facts of the case are easy to learn, and the whole matter is summarized in any good Lincoln biography.

As this same tale comes down in folklore, the whole emphasis is altered. It becomes an illustration of Lincoln the humorist and the practical joker. The duel had an amusing origin, according to one old settler, who had heard another old-timer tell the story:

> Lawyer Shields and Julia Jayne were seated together at the supper table. Across the table from them sat Abe and Mary Todd. By and by the lawyer squeezed Julia's hand. In those days, you know, a pin was a woman's weapon. Julia used it when Shields squeezed her hand. And that made him scream. . . . Lincoln, who was a laughing fellow, hawhawed right out loud, much to the embarrassment of Shields. Well to make a long story short, Shield[s] issued a duel challenge to Abe.[5]

Another version gives a play-by-play account of the duel that never happened. "Shields fired and missed," says this "eye-witness" reporter, speaking of an encounter which was to have been fought with broadswords. "Lincoln then took steady aim and fired. A blotch of read [sic] appeared on the breast of Shields who fell to the ground thinking he was mortally wounded, but in fact was unhurt. Lincoln's gun was loaded with poke-berries."

To treat such statements simply as exaggerated reminiscences is to miss their significance. They are really folk stories. Seldom do they have an identifiable author, for the narrator is recounting what "they said." The very pattern of the statements is significant; "to make a long story short" is a frequent formula to conclude the folk tale. The Shields episode is only one less widely known incident about which a surprisingly large amount of folklore has accumulated. The body of tradition concerning Lincoln's courtship, his marriage, or his law practice is much more voluminous. And there is an extensive cycle of ribald and Rabelaisian stories attributed to Lincoln, for the most part unprintable and unfortunately gradually becoming lost.

V

Few Negroes have written books about their great emancipator, and the viciously anti-Lincoln publications are nearly forgotten, but the other two major currents of tradition have produced a mountainous pile of Lincoln literature. Writers who fitted Lincoln

---

[5] Statement of William A. Clark, unidentified newspaper clipping from Blakeslee Scrapbook (Lincoln National Life Foundation, Fort Wayne, Ind.).

into the pattern of a mythological demigod had the early start at
the printing presses. A series of widely read and often quoted
biographies began to appear shortly after Lincoln's death, starting
with the Arnold and Holland lives and running without interrup-
tion through the work of Nicolay and Hay and that of Ida M.
Tarbell. All were characterized by a highly laudatory tone and all
presented Lincoln in an aura of great respectability.

Those who thought of Lincoln as the archetype of the frontiersman were outraged. Herndon was especially bitter at the "Finical
fools," the "nice sweet smelling gentlemen" who tried to "handle
things with silken gloves & 'a cammel [sic] hair pencil,'" but for
personal reasons his own book about Lincoln was delayed for many
years. The publication in 1872 of Ward Hill Lamon's biography,
ghost-written from Herndonian sources, marked the first widespread circulation in print of the Western version of Lincoln's
career; it was greeted as "a national misfortune." When *Herndon's
Lincoln* appeared seventeen years later, it, too, met with shrill
disapproval, and some shocked souls appealed to Anthony Com-
stock to suppress this indecent book. This food was too coarse for
sensitive stomachs.

It is a mistake to consider these two opposing currents of Lincoln tradition as representing respectively the "ideal" and the "real"
Lincoln. Each was legendary in character. The conflict in Lincoln
biography between the Holland-Hay-Tarbell faction and the Hern-
don-Lamon-Weik contingent was not essentially a battle over factual differences; it was more like a religious war. One school por-
trayed a mythological patron saint; the other, an equally
mythological frontier hero. Not all the Lincoln stories related by
either school were entirely false, but the facts were at the most a
secondary consideration. Acceptance or rejection of any Lincoln
episode depended on what was fundamentally a religious conviction. Even today this attitude is sometimes found. A recent writer
has attacked certain legends which he asserts "libel" Lincoln on
two grounds—first, because they "do not create a truer or finer
image of him" and, second, because the myths are "unsupported by
trustworthy evidence." The order of the reasons deserves notice.

It is widely recognized that the biographies of the Holland school
are remote from reality; they present a conventionalized hero who
is discussed from a "frankly eulogistic point of view." Naturally the
temptation has been to treat their opponents—such as Herndon,

Lamon, and Weik—as realists, intent on giving a "true" picture of Lincoln. If there is any meaning left in the word realism, which is rapidly becoming semantically obsolescent, *Herndon's Lincoln* (which is typical of the writings of this latter school) is "realistic" neither in literary style nor in biographical approach.[6] Herndon's book was dedicated to proving a thesis—that Lincoln had his origin in a "stagnant, putrid pool" and rose through adversity to "the topmost round of the ladder." All of its contents Herndon deliberately arranged to support this contention and to enlist readers' sympathies in behalf of his protagonist.[7] Rough and coarse elements were introduced into the biography, not primarily from conviction that these were vital aspects of human existence, but principally to serve the same function as the villain in the contemporary melodrama. Unlike the true realist, Herndon was concerned with the unusual and the sensational. It is difficult to understand how one can see in Herndon's emotionalized treatment of the Ann Rutledge legend the work of a biographical or literary realist. Actually the biographies of the Herndon school are stylized presentations of Western folklore. Herndon's own book recounts the epic of the frontier hero, transmogrified into the pattern of the sentimental novel.

Toward the end of the century the two conceptions of Lincoln— as mythological demigod and as legendary frontier hero—began to blend, sometimes with amusing results. John T. Morse's *Abraham Lincoln,* one of the better early biographies, made no effort to reconcile the two concepts but accepted them both. For Lincoln's early years Morse followed Herndon, and for the period of the presidency, Nicolay and Hay. The result, he frankly admitted, tended to show that Lincoln was "physically one creature, morally and mentally two beings." In the huge file of newspaper reminiscences preserved in the Lincoln National Life Foundation one can trace the process by which demigod and hero became inextricably scrambled. By the centennial year of Lincoln's birth the frontier

---

[6] Though the term has many meanings and more connotations, realism may be defined as "the method of literary composition that aims at an honest interpretation of the actualities . . . of life, free from subjective prejudice, idealism, or romantic color." It is "opposed to the concern with the unusual, which forms the basis of romance. . . ." James D. Hart, *The Oxford Companion to American Literature* (London, 1941), 625–26.

[7] "The reason why we wanted Nancy's character and acts was to show by contrast how a great man can rise out of the ashes. That's all." Herndon to Weik, Dec. 1, 1888 (Herndon-Weik Collection).

stories which had been considered gamy and rough by an earlier generation had been accepted as typical Lincolnisms; and on the other side, the harshness of the Herndonian outlines was smoothed by an acceptance of many traits from the idealized Lincoln.[8] The result was a "composite American ideal," whose "appeal is stronger than that of other heroes because on him converge so many dear traditions." The current popular conception of Lincoln is "a folk-hero who to the common folk-virtues of shrewdness and kindness adds essential wit and eloquence and loftiness of soul."

VI

One may question the value of studying these legendary accounts of Lincoln. A more conventional procedure is to assault these air castles of contemporary mythology, to use the sharp tools of historical criticism to raze the imaginary structures, to purify the ground by a liberal sprinkling of holy water in the form of footnotes, and to erect a new and "authentic" edifice. Such an approach has its merits. One cannot overestimate the importance of thoroughgoing historical investigation of Lincoln's career; despite the huge bibliography of Lincolniana, there has been far too little scholarly, scientific research into the realities of Lincoln's life. It should be remembered that the first comprehensive Lincoln biography by a professional historian appeared as recently as 1945.

But there is also room for investigation of another sort. Referring to the "debunking" of historical myths and legends, W. A. Dunning, in his presidential address before the American Historical Association, reminded his hearers that in many cases "influence on the sequence of human affairs has been exercised, not by what really happened, but by what men erroneously believed to have happened." In turning to history for guidance, he observed, men have acted upon "the error that passes as history at the time, not from the truth that becomes known long after." He concluded by pointing out that "for very, very much history there is more importance in the ancient error than in the new-found truth."

---

[8] It should be noted, for example, how greatly Lamon altered his point of view between the time of the publication of his first Lincoln book (1872) and the appearance of his *Recollections of Abraham Lincoln* in 1895. Similarly, Jesse W. Weik, Herndon's literary assistant, smoothed away many of the rough edges of the Herndonian tradition before publishing his *The Real Lincoln: A Portrait,* in 1922.

His warning applies in the field of Lincoln biography. As J. Frank Dobie has put it: "The history of any public character involves not only the facts about him but what the public has taken to be facts." It is important to examine the Lincoln legends as they have existed, for they express a collective wish fulfillment of the American people. This is no metaphysical abstraction; it is simply that "heroes embody the qualities that we most admire or desire in ourselves." Fully realizing their general inaccuracy and almost universal distortion, the student can use these myths for an understanding of what plain Americans have wished their leaders to be. "If the folk aspiration is worthy, its dreams of great men will be worthy too."

Unless one conceives of time as ending with 1865, the Lincoln of folklore is of more significance than the Lincoln of actuality. The historian may prove that the Emancipation Proclamation had negligible effect on the actual freeing of slaves, yet Lincoln continues to live in men's minds as the emancipator of the Negroes. It is the folklore Lincoln who has become the central symbol in American democratic thought; he embodies what ordinary, non-verbal Americans have cherished as ideals; he is "first among the folk heroes of the American people." From a study of the Lincoln legends the historian can gain a more balanced insight into the workings of the American mind. As it is now written, intellectual history is too often based on printed sources—sermons, speeches, commencement addresses, books, and newspapers. The result is inevitably a distortion. The men who write books or edit papers are not average citizens. It is much as though the Gallup poll were to interrogate only college presidents. To understand the thinking of ordinary men and women, the historian must delve into their beliefs, their superstitions, their gossip, and their folklore.

whose work appears twice in this volume, is now Senior Research Associate at the Huntington Library in San Marino, California. Born at Camp Point, Illinois, Mr. Nevins received his A. B. and A.M. at the University of Illinois; he was an English instructor at Urbana before going to New York where he became an editorial writer for the *New York Evening Post* in 1913. He was literary editor of the *New York Sun,* and editorial writer for the *Nation,* and then on the editorial staff of the *New York World.* His journalistic career was followed by academic service when he became a professor of American history at Columbia University in 1931. He won the Pulitzer prize for biography first in 1932 and again in 1937. Among his more recent books are *The Emergence of Lincoln; The War for the Union;* and, with Frank E. Hill, *Ford, The Times, The Man, The Company.* It is interesting that his first book was a history of the University of Illinois.

This article was first published in the *Journal of the Illinois State Historical Society,* volume 42 (December 1949), pages 385 to 410. "Not Without Thy Wondrous Story, Illinois" on page 3 is also written by Allan Nevins.

STEPHEN A. DOUGLAS: HIS WEAKNESSES AND HIS GREATNESS

ALLAN NEVINS

The fame of Stephen A. Douglas has passed through vicissitudes as curious as that of any American leader. For decades after the Civil War his career was used by most writers as a foil to that of Lincoln. The easiest way to illusrate Lincoln's statesmanship was to contrast it with Douglas' alleged demogogy, and the most effective way of illustrating Lincoln's moral elevation was to place it beside Douglas' supposed moral flatness. So late as 1915 William Roscoe Thayer, in his life of John Hay, scornfully dismissed Douglas as a man whose influence was negligible. But, wrote Thayer:

> History will not forget him, however much he might pray to be forgotten; because he is as indissolubly bound up with Lincoln's immortality as Brutus is with Caesar's. He remains as a warning to men of good intentions, much vanity, and no

solid morality, who, in a national crisis, when the difference
between conflicting principles stands out as uncompromis-
ingly as life and death, insist that it is only a matter of
shading.

The historian Rhodes, while praising Douglas' powers of leadership, declared that posterity must condemn him just as it condemned Taney. Charnwood, in his life of Lincoln, but expressed
the old conventional view when he wrote of Douglas as a powerful
parliamentarian who gained his effects by "the blustering, declam-
atory, shamelessly fallacious and evasive oratory of a common
demagogue."

It is a great misfortune, as Aaron Burr found out in Jefferson's
time, and Calhoun in Jackson's, to be the opponent of a president
who becomes a national hero. Impartial justice was not done to
Douglas until in 1907 a New Englander who had taught for a time
in Iowa College and imbibed the spirit of the West, Allen Johnson,
published the first good life of the man. He laid his finger upon two
of Douglas' chief claims to grateful remembrance, his comprehen-
sion of the value of the public domain, and his belief in territorial
expansion. He wrote:

> The ends which this strenuous Westerner had in view were
> not wholly gross and materialistic. To create the body of a
> great American Commonwealth by removing barriers to its
> continental expansion, so that the soul of Liberty might dwell
> within it, was no vulgar ambition. The conquest of the conti-
> nent must be accounted one of the really great achievements
> of the century. In this dramatic exploit Douglas was at times
> an irresponsible, but never a weak nor a false actor.

When Beveridge's life of Lincoln was published in 1928, he gave
Douglas a different type of credit. Accepting the validity of the
popular sovereignty principle, and flatly contradicting the Schou-
ler-Rhodes school of historians, he declared that Douglas had offered the most constructive of all proposals for ending the sectional
conflict. In some parts of this biography we see, not Douglas the
politician made a foil for Lincoln the statesman, but Lincoln the
politician made a foil for Douglas the statesman—or something
near this. And in George Fort Milton's *Eve of Conflict* the case for
Douglas the statesman is argued with a wealth of detail.

Behind these conflicting interpretations lies a personality which
was itself full of conflict. Douglas the man had aspects which

appear in stark contrast with one another. At one hour he could be
the heroically disciplined chieftain of a great party; in the next he
could exhibit the loose, boisterous manners of the frontier tavern.
Two scenes drawn from the last year of his life will illustrate the
gamut run by his traits and conduct.

Take the discreditable picture first. Charles Francis Adams, Jr.,
just out of Harvard, in 1860 accompanied William H. Seward on a
campaign tour into the Middle West. On their return they took a
sleeping car from Chicago to Cleveland. At Toledo they were roused
by loud cheering. Some man rushed into the car, loudly demanding: "Where's Seward?" It was Stephen A. Douglas. Seward's berth
was pointed out. Douglas threw back the curtains, exclaiming:
"Come, Governor, they want to see you. Come out and speak to the
boys!" Seward drowsily protested: "How are you, judge? No, I can't
go out. I'm sleepy." To which Douglas replied: "Well, what of that?
They *get* me out when I'm sleepy." "No, I won't go," persisted
Seward, and Douglas withdrew. He carried a bottle of whisky and
as he left paused for a swig. Men in the car said that he was half
drunk. He had been addressing the Democrats of Toledo; he knew
that they would credit him with a smart stroke if he dragged
Seward out as an exhibit; and so, bottle in hand, he had burst into
the car. At the time he was running for president.

It is pleasant to turn to the creditable scene. The date was a few
months later, April 25, 1861; the place was Springfield. The legislature was in session, while the city was alive with volunteers training at Camp Yates. Never had news that Senator Douglas was to
speak failed to bring a crowd into Springfield. It was announced
that he had left Washington to arouse the Northwest to battle, and
at eight o'clock that night would address a joint session of the two
houses. Evening found the capitol packed. When he rose the applause was deafening. He lifted his sonorous voice with a fiery
energy worthy of his cause.

Half a century later men recalled that speech with emotion. The
Republican editor, Horace White, was in the audience; and White
declared that he did not think it possible for a human being to
produce a more electric effect with the spoken word. Said Douglas:

> Hostile armies are now marching upon the Federal capitol
> with the view of planting a revolutionary flag upon its dome;
> seizing the national archives; taking captive the President.
> . . . The boast has gone forth by the Secretary of War of this

revolutionary government that on the 1st of May the revolutionary flag shall float from the wall of the capitol in Washington, and that on July 4th the revolutionary army shall hold possession of the Hall of Independence in Philadelphia. The simple question presented to us is whether we shall wait for the enemy to carry out his boast of making war upon our soil, or whether we shall rush as one man to the defense of our government and its capital.

Men left the building with their blood on fire.

Such contrasts run through the Senator's mature career. We have the Douglas of prodigious energy, toiling on legislation until his health sank; we have the Douglas who threw his arms about low cronies in Washington barrooms. We have the Douglas who bore one of Washington's most fashionable belles, Adele Cutts, to the altar; we have the other Douglas who offended guests at a Hartford reception by spitting tobacco on a floor swept by ladies' gowns. We have the Douglas who telegraphed his friend Lanphier when, early in 1859, the Illinois legislature re-elected him to the Senate: "Let the voice of the people rule." We have also the Douglas who, in that very moment, profited from a bad apportionment which defeated the voice of the people. We have the Douglas who demanded that popular sovereignty control every step in settling the affairs of empty Kansas; we also have the Douglas who was for annexing populous Cuba without consulting the will of her people at all. We have the Douglas who played into the hands of proslavery extremists in his Kansas-Nebraska bill of 1854, and who defied the proslavery extremists in his battle against Lecompton in 1858.

Is it true that, save in love for the Union and interest in western expansion, we look in vain for a unifying principle in Douglas' public career? Is it true that, save in ambition, we seek in vain for a binding cord in his personal life?

He is the harder to understand because he never took pains to reveal himself. If ever a man was an extrovert, a believer in action, it was Douglas; if ever a man was a practised, fluent speaker, it was Douglas. He was not secretive like Polk, who did not confide even in his Cabinet members; he was not speechless like Buchanan, who spent ten years in the Senate without saying anything worth hearing; he was not empty like Ben Wade. But he signally lacked the trait of self-revelation. Students of his life become exasperated by the paucity of letters from his pen. We might suppose that from

Washington the senator would write frequently to his close friend
James W. Sheahan, editor of the *Chicago Times,* and to Charles H.
Lanphier, editor of the *Illinois State Register.* Actually his epistles
to them are few, hurried, and full of poiltical directions to the
exclusion of news, ideas, or personal feeling. Sheahan, indeed, has
placed on record his sense of frustration because Douglas wrote to
him so rarely. Even when, in 1860, the impoverished Irish-Ameri-
can lost his newspaper to Cyrus H. McCormick and walked out into
the world penniless, he received no sympathetic letter from the
captain he had served so devotedly. To be sure, Douglas then had
his own financial difficulties; but Sheahan expressed a bitter sense
of grievance.

Douglas was eminently a son of the frontier. Brandon, Vermont,
was a frontier town when he was born there in 1813; Canandaigua,
New York, had scarcely emerged from its frontier character when
he went there in 1830; and western Illinois was a fringe of civilization when he first reached it. Like so many self-made sons of the
frontier, Douglas was always strenuously busy; and this might
seem the key to his silence upon his personal life, his ideas and
emotions. A man incessantly active in politics, business, Congressional work, and masculine society, he never found time to express
his inner self in letters or diary. Hurry, however, is an insufficient
explanation. Other hurried men, like Theodore Roosevelt, have
revealed themselves in thousands of frank letters. Something was
lacking in Douglas' nature, some element of inner richness. Essentially uncultivated in everything except politics, he was also essentially an unreflective, unphilosophical man, who thought only of
propulsive forces.

It is impossible to study his career in detail without a sense that
the animating principle of his character was a fierce practicality.
He wished to get things done, and get them done in the most direct
fashion, leaving ultimate consequences alone; trusting to fortune
that, as Banquo said of Macbeth's murder, the act would "trammel
up the consequence and catch success." No man was ever quicker
to take practical advantage of any situation, and few leaders have
been more careless of the long look ahead.

A year ago I paid a visit to the village of Winchester, near the
Illinois River, where he began his career. In the pleasant village
square is a well-executed statue of Douglas, showing not the stri-
pling who came to Winchester, but a mature man, seated in his

senatorial chair, the posture making the most of his great head and massive chest, and minimizing his short limbs. In that village were lawyers who loved to recall how the youth, with long curling hair, glowing blue eyes, and combative chin, all energy and ambition, had arrived in 1833, with just three bits in his pocket; how after earning $2.50 as auction clerk he had opened a school with forty pupils at $3.00 apiece; how he had boldly debated with a Jacksonville attorney on the merits of Jackson's administration; and how, when he did not know "enough law to write out a declaration," he had persuaded an indulgent judge to give him a license, and hung up his shingle in the Morgan County courthouse. Six weeks short of twenty-one, he was embarked in life. And, seeing that Jacksonville could give him few cases, he immediately took politics as his main profession.

Seldom has a man more quickly mastered his profession. He shook off his Eastern dress, manners, and speech for blue jeans, rough ways, and frontier vocabulary. He cultivated stump oratory with such effect that at twenty-one he had gained his name of the Little Giant. He made the most of Jacksonian control of the legislature by hurrying to Vandalia, helping put through a bill which displaced the Whig then serving as state's attorney in the Jacksonville district, and getting himself named to the place. The very judge who had given him his license declared: "He is no lawyer and has no lawbooks." But with a borrowed horse, a borrowed volume on criminal law, and unlimited self-confidence, he set out to prosecute the cases in his district.

Plainly, he was a youngster who knew how to improvise; and a brilliant improviser he remained all his life. A youth of different temperament would have tarried in Canandaigua, where he had attended an academy and first looked into lawbooks; would have perfected his education, as Douglas' mother begged him to do, before going out to conquer fortune. But Douglas had a headlong ambition. On leaving Canandaigua, he told his mother: "In ten years I shall stop by and see you on my way to Congress." He was almost better than his word. In 1837, running for Congress against that John T. Stuart who was Lincoln's first law partner, he came within thirty-five votes of winning. In 1841 he came within five legislative votes of gaining the senatorship, though a year short of the required age. In 1843, ten years after reaching Winchester, he was elected to Congress.

He had given these ten years to politics, not to law, to reading, or to any other more intellectual pursuit. He had worked in caucuses and conventions. He had spoken from the stump. He had treated voters at the liquor-counter of country stores. If he ever looked into any books, an old-time friend testified later, it was into legal commentaries, the *Congressional Globe,* and political handbooks, of which he became such a master that soon after entering the House he startled everybody by correcting the omniscient John Quincy Adams on a point of fact. His lack of general cultivation was to come out painfully in such episodes as his debate with Senator Butler of South Carolina in March, 1853. Butler, an old-school gentleman who was fond of his well-stocked library, pronounced a eulogy upon British literature and British statesmanship, explaining how much America owed to both. Douglas swept all this away with contemptuous impatience. European literature to him was mere useless lumber; European statesmanship he summed up in the single word "tyranny."

He did gain one titular distinction in these ten years of political training. He helped to push a bill through the Democratic legislature for a partisan reorganization of the State Supreme Court—a fact which the Republicans remembered when in 1857, after the Dred Scott decision, they talked of reorganizing the federal Supreme Court, and he was appointed to one of the five judgeships. "Judge" Douglas he was called all his life, though he quickly left the uncongenial bench. Later he spoke of his brief term as one of "my youthful indiscretions." The "Judge" had only a hedge-lawyer's knowledge of the statutes and no real grasp of jurisprudence. What matter? His brilliant improvisation had been successful. It continued to succeed, for in 1847 he entered the Senate.

Forward, forward! Hurry, hurry! Improvise, improvise! These were Douglas' mottoes. Such watchwords suited the crude, fast-growing West, the young Illinois. He had imbibed the pushing, inventive spirit of the restless Mississippi Valley. When he went back to Middlebury College to take an honorary degree, he first thanked the donors and then took them aback with the frank statement: "My friends, Vermont is the most glorious spot on the face of this earth for a man to be born in, provided he emigrates when he is very young." To the crowd at Jonesboro, Illinois, in his debate with Lincoln, he declared with a touch of self-complacency:

> I came out here when I was a boy, and found my mind
> liberalized and my opinions enlarged when I got on these
> broad prairies, with only the heavens to bound my vision,
> instead of having them circumscribed by the little narrow
> ridges that surrounded the valley where I was born.

What he meant was that in coming west he had dropped caution, precision, and a painful effort at foresight; he had exchanged them for a rough self-reliance, a heedless optimism, a faith in his star, and a trust that the future would catch up with any bold, forward step. It was natural for him to become a Democrat of the Jackson-Polk school. The Whig Party, the organization of Clay and his balanced American System, was the party of conservatism, moderation, and planning; the Democrats were the party of energy, confidence in the popular impulse, and spirited action.

It was part of the headlong practicality of the man, born of a union between his brilliant precocity and his rude western environment, that he was as deficient in general ideas of an abstract kind as he was fertile in working devices. He had little of the power of subjective thought exhibited by Hamilton, Madison, or Calhoun. I have read scores of his speeches without finding a single statement or idea (apart from the very practical idea of popular sovereignty) that could be torn from its context and set up as a principle. He was irresistible in debate; but he was totally incapable of writing a true state paper. When once in his life, in 1859, he undertook to prepare an essay of scholarly character presenting some generalized arguments to the country—his famous exposition of popular sovereignty in *Harper's Magazine*—all life departed from his pen, and he became incredibly labored, pedantic, and dull. His deficiency in this respect becomes most evident when we compare him for a moment with Lincoln.

Douglas was a great democrat, a natural man of the people; but he was not a democrat in the reflective sense in which Lincoln was one. Why can we never conceive of Douglas as making such a remark as Lincoln's famous epigram: "God must have loved the common people, because he made so many of them"? For two reasons, I think. The first is that to make such a remark requires a certain detachment. Lincoln, when he uttered it, was standing apart from the plain people, surveying them, and musing upon their relation to Providence. Douglas, however, never stood apart from the crowd; he was always in the thick of it, sharing its emotions, calculating on its movements. Lincoln's remark carried an implication that he was not quite one of the plain people, but was studying them from an outer, though sympathetic, vantage point. Douglas never for a moment thought of himself except as one of the democratic mass. The second reason is that Lincoln's remark states a rebuke to the aristocrats of this world with a philosophic kindliness of which Douglas was incapable. Lincoln's epigram must seem biting to all those who despise the masses—to H. L. Mencken, for example, talking contemptuously of *booboisie*. In fact, it is devastating. Yet it is humorous, inoffensive, even ingratiating. Douglas would have found this philosophic good humor impossible. His approach to the aristocrats would have been combative: "Think yourself better than us common folk, do you? Well, you silk-stocking scoundrels, you're not"—and then a stream of invective.

Douglas' lack of reflective and philosophical qualities come out in other relationships. It is shown, for example, in the almost complete lack of wit and humor in the man; for humor is impossible without a philosophical sense of the bizarre relationships of life. Lincoln saw humor in everything. But Douglas told few stories, coined no epigrams, and never delivered a Will Rogers thrust. His only form of humor was the belligerent form—sarcasm. I have found just one pun in his speeches. In his attack on Jefferson Davis in the Senate after the Charleston Convention in 1860, he harked back to the old battle of 1850 in Mississippi, when Davis and Henry S. Foote ran for senator with acceptance or rejection of Clay's Compromise as the issue between them, and Davis was defeated. Mississippi, said Douglas, put her Foote on Davis. He could poke fun at Lincoln for his clerkship in a country store. He could put Senator Bayard in his place by a jest at the tiny size of Delaware. But of the broad fun and humor of the West, so delightful in Tom Corwin, so lambent at times in the speeches even of Thomas Hart Benton, he had very little.

His idea of national union, too, was less philosophical than Lincoln's or Lyman Trumbull's. His concept of the Union was Jacksonian, while Lincoln's concept was Websterian. That is, Douglas saw the Union in a practical light; it was the Union which developed the country, guarded the frontiers, kept the Mississippi open to the mouth, and used its strong arm to annex new territory

for the swarming American millions. Lincoln's idea of the Union
embraced this and a good deal more. He, like Webster, thrilled to
the Union with an intense spirit of nationality, a passionate attachment to the republic as a whole, and a conviction that the people
must stand as a unit in defense of freedom. If the Union died,
liberty died with it. They were "one and inseparable."

The fact was that Douglas supplied the place of abstract ideas,
of such carefully pondered principles as had been laid down by
Hamilton and Jefferson, Calhoun and Clay, with three or four
broad emotional beliefs. One was his unreflecting, undiscrimina-
ting, ill-defined faith in the popular will. One was his belief in
national growth: the growth, he said, which having burst through
the Indian country, crossed the Rockies and Sierras, and come to a
halt on the Pacific, must then turn either north to Canada or south
to Mexico. A third emotional belief grew out of his optimism respecting America. He thought the future of the republic unbounded. Europe, he once declaimed, is "one vast graveyard," and
her legislation must suit that condition. "*Here* everything is fresh,
blooming, expanding, and advancing. We wish a wise, practical
policy adapted to our condition and position."

We have said that a headlong practicality, a gift for brilliant
improvisation, was the chief animating force of his career. It was
united with another ruling trait, his belligerence. He was born with
a love of battle. He reminds us of Dr. John Brown's story of the
Scottish farmer and his dour mastiff. "Why is your dog so sad and
grim?" they asked the farmer. "Eh, sir!" he said, "life is full of
sairiousness to him; he can just never get enough of fightin!"
Douglas had none of the urbane diplomacy of an Easterner like
Seward; he was as fond of attack as a stallion of the Western
prairies. We have noted that his first important act after opening
his school in Winchester was to plunge into battle with a neighboring attorney, and his first important act after getting admitted to
the bar was to wage a contest in the Vandalia legislature to unseat
the district attorney. He kept on fighting. In his joint debate with
Stuart for Congress, Douglas used such offensive language that
Stuart picked him up, tucked his head under his arm, and dragged
him around the Springfield square; Douglas meanwhile biting
Stuart's thumb almost in two. When John Quincy Adams first
heard the Little Giant speak in Congress, he thought the Westerner's ferocity against the Whigs almost insane. "His face was con-

vulsed," wrote Adams in his diary, "his gesticulation frantic, and he lashed himself into such a heat that if his body had been made of combustible matter it would have burnt out." Precisely similar was Carl Schurz's impression of him in the Senate—the impression of a grimly formidable parliamentary pugilist. He looked the incarnation of forceful combativeness, and his speech accorded with his looks. Wrote Schurz:

> His sentences were clear-cut, direct, positive. They went straight to the mark like bullets and sometimes like cannonballs, tearing and crashing. . . . He was utterly unsparing of the feelings of his opponents. . . . He would, with utter unscrupulousness, malign his opponents' motives, distort their sayings, and attribute to them all sorts of iniquitous deeds and purposes.

Quite so; even the patient Lincoln was nettled by his unfair tactics.

For an example of his combative skill in blackening the character of an opponent we may take a passage from his assault on Salmon P. Chase and Charles Sumner in March, 1854. The Ohio and Massachusetts senators had played their political game very much as Douglas had played his. Both had been elected to the Senate by coalitions. Yet they were assuming a tone of lofty moral superiority. Douglas used the gladiator's short sword on them, the *argumentum ad hominem.* "Mr. President," he rasped:

> The Senators from Ohio and Massachusetts have taken the liberty to impeach my motives. . . . I desire to know by what right they arraign me. . . . I must be permitted to tell the Senator from Ohio that *I* did not obtain my seat in this body, either by a corrupt bargain or a dishonorable coalition! I must be permitted to remind the Senator from Massachusetts, that *I* did not enter into any combinations or arrangements by which my character, my principles, and my honor were set up at public auction or private sale in order to procure a seat in the Senate of the United States!

This was quite unfair. His imputations of dishonor and corruption had no basis. But they were signally effective in turning Chase and Sumner from the offensive to the defensive.

This belligerent temper had its good and its bad sides. It was shown at its best in his indomitable pluck. The stouthearted Douglas never quailed against any odds. Horace Greeley wrote a letter to Congressman William Kellogg of the Canton, Illinois, district early in 1860. He wrote that Douglas and he had never agreed but upon one subject: Lecompton. They were political enemies. "I detest his doctrines," stated Greeley, "but I like his pluck." And with a sly dig at the Republicans who had endorsed Helper's *Impending Crisis* and then under attack had repudiated that book, Greeley added: "Had *he* [Douglas] signed, ever so heedlessly, a circular recommending Tom Paine's *Age of Reason,* you would never have found him prevaricating nor apologizing . . . ; he would simply and coolly have told his adversaries to make the most of it." Everyone admired the Little Giant's pluck. At times in his stormy career he faced a whole cohort of angry opponents, and worsted them all. Who can forget the great scene on the night of March 3, 1854, when he carried his Kansas-Nebraska bill through the Senate by an irresistible onslaught, extorting from his opponent, Seward, the tribute: "I have never had so much respect for the Senator as I have tonight"?

Another creditable aspect of his combative temper, which only those who have read scores of his speeches can appreciate, lay in his use of oratory as a businesslike, argumentative, factual weapon. America was afflicted in this period with a spread-eagle school of speech. Emerson remarked: "The curse of this country is eloquent men." In debate Douglas was like Charles James Fox: he was intent on convincing, and poured forth his arguments and facts as a general in battle throws successive waves of shock troops against a position. He was never flowery, never flatulent, never weak; he mastered all political subjects thoroughly, for they were the sole object of his interest—and woe betide the man who challenged his knowledge. He could tell precisely what had happened in a Congressional debate of 1846, or 1852, or 1856. He could state the precise provisions of the enabling act for Wisconsin or Arkansas. He could recite offhand the number of states which had levied tonnage-taxes. Like Al Smith, he was a walking encyclopedia of government, and like Governor Smith, he used this lore in a manly, downright elucidation of public issues.

One illustration of his irresistible businesslike readiness in debate will suffice. After the Charleston Convention in 1860, when the Democratic Party split between those who accepted Douglas' popular sovereignty platform and those who demanded a slave-code platform, Jefferson Davis taunted Douglas on the Senate floor. The seventeen certainly Democratic states were for the slave-code platform, he said; but the sixteen states which voted for the Douglas platform did not include one that was certainly Democratic. In a few crisp sentences Douglas turned on Davis and crushed him. Maryland had opposed the Douglas platform at Charleston; was Maryland surely Democratic? She had voted against Buchanan in 1856. Tennessee had opposed the Douglas platform; was Tennessee always Democratic? She had voted against Pierce in 1852, and of her ten Congressmen only three were now Democrats. Kentucky had opposed the Douglas platform; was Kentucky surely Democratic? She had voted against Pierce in 1852. Illinois had never once failed the Democratic Party in a presidential election. Could Jefferson Davis say as much for Mississippi? He could not, for the Whigs had once carried his state. Behind Douglas' combativeness lay an arsenal of exact knowledge.

His belligerent temper displayed its worst side in his frequent readiness to use any quarrel to gain an unfair advantage. He could be unscrupulous in domestic affairs. He could be still more unscrupulous in international matters, for he was always a chauvinist, an expansionist, and a narrow-minded assailant of foreign peoples. Here again a single illustration will suffice for many. In the spring of 1858 the British Navy was accused of aggressions against vessels bearing the American flag. Douglas was foremost in fanning the flame of national resentment. He proposed to give President Buchanan power to punish such outrages instantly and effectively, and declaimed:

> While I am opposed to war, while I have no idea of any breach of the peace with England, yet I confess to you, sirs, that if war should come by her act I would administer to every citizen and every child Hannibal's oath of eternal hostility as long as the English flag waved or their government claimed a foot of land upon the American continent or the adjacent islands. Sir, I would make it a war that would settle our disputes forever, not only of the right of search upon the seas, but the right to tread with hostile foot upon the soil of the American continent.

This is in the best vein of Jefferson Brick. We might dismiss it as rodomontade, but its offense lies deeper. What was the outrage committed by the British Navy? The boarding, off Africa or Cuba, of vessels flying the American flag but looking much like slave ships—which they sometimes were. Douglas was willing to use this minor controversy for seizing Canada, the British West Indies, and

Belize; just as he was ready to use any chance quarrel with Spain to seize Cuba.

The great danger incurred by the practical politician who rushes headlong into improvisation is this, that he oversimplifies the problems he faces. The great danger in habitual bellicosity is that it soon builds up an iron wall of enemies. Douglas had many engaging traits. His personal magnetism was almost irresistible. His loyalty to his friends, including the erratic James Shields and the wily Robert J. Walker, was admirable. He remembered everyone around him by name, and gave the humblest follower the feeling that he had in Douglas a personal champion. He delighted in every opportunity of mingling with human beings; in campaign trips, speeches, and caucuses, in dinners, receptions, and parties. He could stay up all night with good fellows in a railroad car, as George B. McClellan relates, and yet be ready in debate and punctual in business the next day. While always anxious to make money by speculation, he could be prodigally generous of funds for an associate or a cause. On great occasions he could be magnanimous. His telegram in 1856 urging his followers in the Cincinnati Convention to turn to Buchanan was written the moment he heard that Buchanan had a majority vote, and was a bright episode in the history of a party repeatedly divided by the two-thirds rule.

But his twin traits of impetuous improvisation and reckless belligerency were destined in the end to blot his claim to the rank of statesman, and to place him in a position where he had to make a mighty effort to recover his prestige. That he did make this effort and did re-establish his fame, there can happily be no doubt.

We find these traits exhibited in four critical events of his career. The first was his rash attempt for the presidential nomination in 1852, which ended in bitterness and humiliation. The second was the Kansas-Nebraska struggle of 1854, the unhappiest Pandora's box in our history. The third was the battle over the Lecompton Constitution, which would have brought Kansas into the Union as slave soil. The fourth was the renewed struggle for the presidency in 1860, with his final implacable contest against the Southern wing of the party. Three of these four contests shook the country and affected its destiny. The first two wore a dubious look. In the latter two he fought for principle and for personal ambition at the same time, and while his critics have laid stress on his ambition, his admirers have more justly emphasized his principles. In all four contests his essential characteristics were dramatically exhibited.

The attempt to vault into the White House was a serio-comic episode significant only in the humiliation it visited upon Douglas and the foundation it laid for Southern hostility. Had he been elected that year, he would have been President at thirty-nine, much the youngest man who has ever held the office. Thoughts of youth and inexperience never troubled him. Was he not the leader of Young America? Francis J. Grund wrote, "Douglas is going it with a rush"; and "rush" was just the word for his pre-convention campaign. For some months he believed that what he called "The Ticket," consisting of himself and R. M. T. Hunter of Virginia, would win the day. Actually the circumstances foreordained defeat, which any political veteran could have predicted. What hurt Douglas' feelings, in the end, was not that the Democratic Convention swiftly passed him over in favor of Franklin Pierce; it was the contempt and dislike which many Southern leaders expressed for him. Aristocratic, conservative Southerners of the old school, men like William R. King, Howell Cobb, and A. P. Butler, were scornful of Douglas' brash impetuosity. If he were nominated, wrote John Slidell of Louisiana, "I should despair of the republic." His election, said Senator King, would be an invitation to "every vulture that would prey upon the public carcass." "If we had named him," wrote Cave Johnson when all was over, "we would have been dishonored and disgraced."

When we turn to the Kansas-Nebraska Act, we turn to one of the most complicated and controversial chapters in American history. We turn also to the supreme illustration of Douglas' tendency to gain an immediate practical end by impulsive improvisation. No error in historical interpretation is more frequent than the attempt to rationalize every great public act, attributing it to reason and design. In his classic book, *Human Nature in Politics*, Graham Wallas points out that perhaps the greater part of political conduct is irrational; that it springs not from cool calculation of means and ends, but from impulses and instincts representing temporary emotion, environmental determinism, and other factors. To say that Douglas in 1854 carefully planned the Kansas-Nebraska Act is to do injustice both to the complexity of the situation and to his headlong impulsiveness.

Insofar as he acted on rational, well-considered grounds, he doubtless acted from a multiplicity of motives. He was aware that his friend Senator Atchison of Missouri had to be rescued from a sad political plight. He was aware that Chicago would never forgive him if New Orleans or Memphis gained a Pacific railroad and the lake city did not. He wished to push himself boldly forward as a national leader. He recalled that he had solved the difficult problem of organizing New Mexico Territory by using the popular sovereignty formula. He wished to add to his proud record as the principal leader of Congress in opening the West to settlement. He was keenly conscious that Pierce's administration was tottering and discredited, and that a strong policy was needed to rescue the party from disastrous squabbles. A mind so alert and sinewy as Douglas' would appreciate not merely one or two but all of these factors. It is difficult to believe that the railroad situation explained his bill. He was pressing for three transcontinental railroads, which would satisfy all sections; as chairman of the railroad committee he was in a position to block undesired legislation; and his bill actually delayed a Pacific railroad. The need for some strong new policy to unite the country was probably uppermost in his mind.

So much for the rational element in his action. It seems likely, however, that a semi-irrational impulse was more potent. A practical situation confronted him. His instinct was to improvise. To deal with the Kansas-Nebraska country in a way satisfying to both Northerners and Southerners was difficult; he saw what looked like a feasible solution, and without second thought leaped forward to apply it. His brilliant improvisations had always worked in the past. The mere force of western growth would make this one work. That he acted on heedless impulse is indicated by the fact that his momentous bill passed through three stages before taking final form. As first introduced, it merely stated that new Nebraska Territory should ultimately be admitted as a state with or without slavery as its constitution might prescribe. Then it was amended to declare that, pending statehood, all questions pertaining to slavery should be left to the people. Finally it was again amended to include an explicit repeal of the Missouri Compromise restriction against slavery. Plainly, Douglas had leaped into the situation without real forethought about his ultimate goal. He had taken a first hurried step. Then a group of Southerners pushed him to a second, more drastic step. Then still another Southerner, Dixon of

Kentucky, pushed him to the third step. His first leap had seemed safe enough, but its momentum carried him forward to ground that quaked with danger.

In all American history no more fateful piece of headlong improvisation can be found than this Kansas-Nebraska bill. Before he introduced it the slavery question had been settled for every inch of American territory. Under the compromises of 1820 and 1850 not a rod of ground was in dispute. This impetuous measure opened up two mighty quarrels. One, between Northern free-soilers and Southern proslavery men, was bad enough. The other, between Northern Democrats who held that popular sovereignty applied at once, and Southern Democrats who held that it applied only when a state asked for admission, was much worse. Both quarrels were latent in the time. Douglas had called them to life.

Douglas had meant to unify his party and lead it triumphantly against its foes. Instead, he spent the rest of his life leading the Northwestern faction of the party against the Southern faction. He could not accept the Southern interpretation of his law, that slavery must be allowed free access to a territory even *against* the will of its people until it became a state. He could not accept the Dred Scott decision which wrote that interpretation into the Constitution. He could not accept the policies of President Buchanan when that executive, controlled by Slidell, Howell Cobb, and other Southerners, lent himself to the Southern interpretation. In a sense, Douglas spent his final years battling for his one broad, hazy principle—the principle that the people who go to dwell in a given area should determine its institutions. It was not so sound a principle as Lincoln's doctrine that national morality and national health called for the containment of slavery within its existing bounds, but it might nevertheless be termed a principle. In another sense, Douglas spent his last years expiating his rashness in overthrowing an honest, workable compromise in favor of one that proved ambiguous and unworkable; and expiating the bellicosity which had raised up a host of personal enemies.

If we think of the battle for principle, Douglas in 1858 appears in a heroic role. A group of Southern leaders, incited by an angry Southern press, were determined to bring in Kansas as the sixteenth slave state. They seized upon the most dishonestly written state constitution in American annals, the so-called Lecompton Consitution, a child of fraud and violence. They browbeat President Buchanan into assenting to this constitution. Instantly, as the session of 1857–1858 opened, Douglas was in arms. His struggle against Lecompton was an exhibition of iron determination. The drama of that battle has given it an almost unique place in the record of American party controversies.

"By God, sir!" he exclaimed, "I made James Buchanan, and by God, sir, I will unmake him!" Friends told him that the Southern Democrats meant to ruin him. "I have taken a through ticket," rejoined Douglas, "and checked my baggage." His retort to Buchanan when the president reminded him how Jackson had crushed two party rebels is famous. Douglas was not to be overawed by a man whom he regarded as a pygmy. "Mr. President," he snorted, "I wish you to remember that General Jackson is dead." Less well known is his sarcastic rejoinder to that doughface member of Buchanan's cabinet, Isaac Toucey. When Toucey said that a battle between Douglas and the administration might cripple the party for a generation, the Senator declared this true. "Why, my dear sir," cried Toucey, delightedly, "you agree with me in everything—I don't see how we can disagree at all." "Certainly not," said Douglas with ironic tartness. "We *can't* disagree, Mr. Toucey; it's impossible; for you are always right on a constitutional question, and while the Constitution declares that *Congress* may admit new states, it hasn't a word in it about the *Cabinet* admitting them."

As for the Southern leaders, Douglas' scorn of the extremists was unbounded. He told the Washington correspondent of the *Chicago Journal* that he had begun his fight as a contest against a single measure. But a blow at Lecompton was a blow against slavery, and he at once had the whole "slave power" down on him like a pack of wolves. He added:

> In making the fight against this power, I was enabled to stand off and view the men with whom I had been acting; that I was ashamed I had ever been caught in such company; they were a set of unprincipled demagogues, bent upon perpetuating slavery, and by the exercise of that unequal and unfair power, to control the Government or break up the Union; and I intend to prevent their doing either.

It was a heroic battle; a battle, too, which Douglas gallantly won, for Lecompton was defeated. And yet did not the whole Kansas struggle have a deeper significance? As the country looked back on it, did it not teach a painful lesson of the gross miscalculation involved in the Kansas-Nebraska Act? That measure, which Douglas had said would quiet sectional antagonisms, had increased them. That enactment, which he had declared would furnish a relatively quick, automatic, and natural solution of the slavery issue, had produced delays, artificial interventions, and endless broils. That bill, presented as an embodiment of justice, had fostered fraud, dishonesty, and outrage. The shining role of Douglas in the final act could not conceal the fact that it would have been far better for Kansas, for the Democratic Party, for the South, and for the nation, had he insisted in 1854 on respecting the Missouri Compromise. For much that had occurred he could not be blamed. But he could be blamed for not foreseeing that false hopes of a new slave state would be aroused in the South, that the North would be filled with a sense of betrayal, that angry conflicts would ensue on the western plains, and that governors and presidents would be subjected to pressures under which they would bend.

All conventional treatments of Douglas describe as the final glorious phase of his career the months in which, as secession and civil war came, he threw himself with impetuous ardor into the cause of the Union. He pledged Lincoln the support of the Union Democrats; he would have made the first call for troops 150,000 men instead of 75,000. But it is not his position in the spring of 1861, fine as it was, which most deserves praise. After all, every truehearted Northerner after Fort Sumter was fired with patriotic ardor. I find the most splendid chapter of his life elsewhere.

It lies in the course he pursued in the last months of the presidential campaign of 1860. Douglas began that campaign with some hope of being elected. By midsummer he knew that these hopes were vain; that the four-cornered election could not even be thrown into the House; that Lincoln's victory was certain. His health was precarious, and his personal fortunes were at low ebb—he was almost bankrupt. Any less determined fighter would have given up and retired to his home. Douglas could have done so without criticism, for not one of the other candidates, Lincoln, Breckinridge, and Bell, undertook a vigorous canvass. But he believed that the Union was in danger. Meeting Senator Henry Wilson in Boston early in August, he predicted Lincoln's election, and declared that he was resolved to go South to urge the people to submit to the result and sustain the government. He was as good as his word. Traveling into slaveholding territory, he exhibited moral courage of the rarest kind by denouncing secession and warning Southerners that if it came it would be met with force.

At Norfolk he told a crowd of seven thousand that no Southern state would be justified in seceding if Lincoln were elected. He also told the crowd that it was the duty of the government to enforce the laws and preserve the Constitution. He himself would do everything in his power to maintain both; and he believed that the next president, whoever he might be, "should treat all attempts to break up the Union . . . as Old Hickory treated the Nullifiers in 1832." At Raleigh, he used even stronger language. "I would hang every man higher than Haman," he said, "who would attempt to resist by force the execution of any provision of the Constitution which our fathers made and bequeathed to us." At Raleigh he also told the South that the men of the Northwest would never let the lower Mississippi pass into the hands of a foreign country; before they did that, they would follow the waters of the Illinois with the bayonet down to the Gulf. Returning North to New York, he declared that all true Democrats must join in enforcing the laws against seceders. "I wish to God," he vociferated, "that we had an Old Hickory now alive that he might hang Northern and Southern traitors on the same gallows."

This was a brave stand, for most Democratic politicians were silent on the issue of secession. It was more—it was a farsighted stand, for most Republican leaders, including Lincoln, were scoffing at the idea that secession would come, while many leaders in all parties were denying that secession would be followed by war. While such Republicans as Greeley would let the Southern states go in peace, ex-President Franklin Pierce was writing Jefferson Davis that any Northern army which tried to march against the South would have to fight its first desperate battle at home in the North.

Douglas' greatest single service to his country was this gallant effort to recall the South, as Lincoln's election became certain, to its duty in the Union; this bold attempt to warn Southerners that any secession would mean Northern coercion and war. In that late summer of 1860 he loomed up as incomparably the bravest, wisest, and most candid statesman in the land.

The full meaning of this effort is not expressed in any of his surviving letters and speeches, and may easily be missed. It is stated in but one place: in Henry Adams' article "The Secession Winter, 1860–61," in the forty-third volume of the *Proceedings of the Massachusetts Historical Society.* Through his father, Charles Francis Adams, then a Massachusetts Representative who saw a good deal of Douglas, Henry Adams had learned the deeper significance of Douglas' tour.

The leaders of the cotton states had resolved to form a great new slave confederacy encircling the Gulf of Mexico. A widespread, intricate, and well-matured conspiracy had been formed. After the breakup of the Baltimore Convention in the spring of 1860 had made it clear that the Democratic Party was doomed to defeat, the most active guides of the Deep South had framed an astute plan. They nominated Breckinridge; they resolved to try to give him the votes of all the slave states; in particular they meant to carry Virginia and Maryland for him. If the election was thrown into the House, or if the Republicans carried it, the leaders of the cotton states then intended to execute a *coup d'état.* They would declare Breckinridge the properly-elected President, use Howell Cobb, Jacob Thompson, and John B. Floyd, three Southern cabinet members, to take control of Washington, and call on the Southern states to support their *de facto* government.

This was the conspiracy as Douglas described it to Charles Francis Adams. It was to defeat this conspiracy that Douglas invaded Maryland, Virginia, and North Carolina, speaking with militant force. And he gained his main object. In Virginia he broke the Southern line—he and the Bell-Everett ticket. He gained little for himself; but he believed later, and so told Charles Francis Adams, that he made it impossible for the fire-eaters to carry out the conspiracy. They could secede; but they could not seize Washington.

It would be difficult to find a contrast more striking than that between the scenes in which Lincoln and Douglas spent election night in 1860. Lincoln, surrounded by elated, cheering crowds, went from the old Statehouse to the telegraph office in Springfield. The little capital had never heard such a roar as went up when the news came: "New York fifty thousand for Lincoln!" Cannon boomed; men and women joined in songs of victory. Douglas spent the evening in Mobile, at the office of the *Mobile Register.* To the last he had pointed to the danger of disunion and the certainty that disunion would inaugurate a bloody war. As dispatches came in pointing to Lincoln's victory, Douglas sat in growing gloom; not because his friend Honest Abe had been elected, but because he

had become convinced, as he toured the South, that a great seces-
sionist conspiracy was approaching its climax. The editor of the
Register, Forsyth, tried to cheer him. He showed Douglas an editorial calling for a state convention to discuss Alabama's policy in
the crisis. The best course for Union men here, he said, would be to
accept the general demand for a state convention, elect as many
delegates as possible, and divert the proceedings into safe channels. Douglas roused himself like a lion. You are wrong, he said. If
you Union men cannot prevent a convention, then you can't control
the convention once it meets. But Forsyth insisted on printing the
editorial. And as Douglas walked back to his hotel through the
desolate streets, his secretary noticed that he was "more hopeless
than I had ever before seen him."

He was hopeless because he saw into the future; saw disunion
and battle just ahead. Hard experience had at last taught him
prevision. If we ask which of that night's figures seems the more
heroic, Lincoln or Douglas, we must answer Douglas.

It is not true that a great deal of the spirit of Illinois history in its
long formative period is concentrated in the career of Stephen A.
Douglas? Here is the hurry, the strenuosity, which were necessities
in the pioneer era. Here is the headlong improvisation which was
natural when men had to conquer great difficulties with little more
than their bare hands. Hurry, hurry!—Improvise, improvise!—
these were natural watchwords in a young state. Here, too, is the
reliance upon rapid material growth to atone for all the defects of
rash improvisation. Our American democracy, East as well as
West, has trusted much to improvisation, from the time when the
Fathers improvised the Articles of Confederation to the day when
Franklin D. Roosevelt improvised the NRA; in both instances with
somewhat unhappy results.

Today, Illinois, like other parts of the Union, must lay more
emphasis on planning. We must depend more on scientific calcula-
tions and the long look ahead. But in an age of planning, we can
still preserve some of Douglas' great virtues—his unfailing pluck,
his combativeness in great causes, his willingness to spend all his
strength in the public service, his scorn of sectional as distinguished from national objects, and his unquenchable patriotism.

PART IV

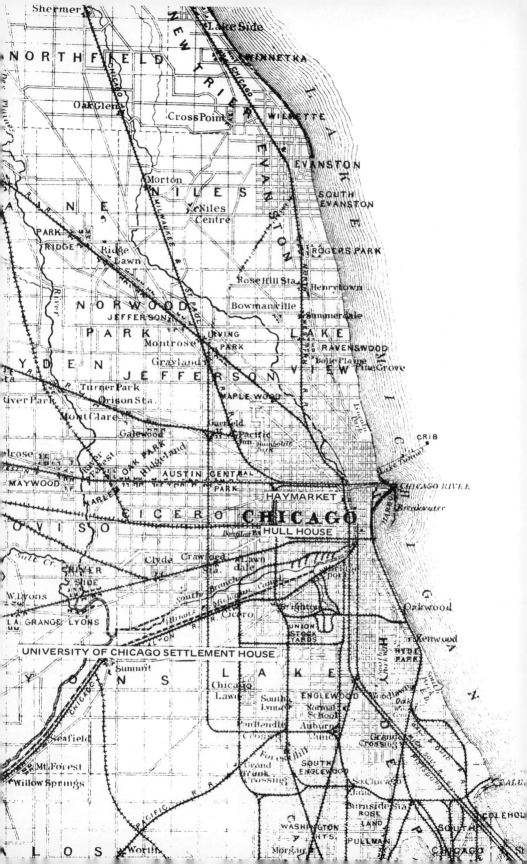

PART IV

The Maturing State

1886–1903

THE YEARS OF THE NINETEENTH CENTURY remaining after the Civil War saw Illinois develop into a mature member of the Union. As a microcosm, Illinois reflected national trends, conditions, and problems associated with industrial democracy. Few conditions and events in Illinois were unique or isolated from the national scene—except for the Chicago Fire of 1871 which destroyed $200 million worth of property and took the lives of approximately three hundred people.

The constitution ratified by the people of Illinois in 1870 was more suited to an agrarian state than it was to the needs of an expanding industrial commonwealth; as time passed, this constitution would prove to be an increasing handicap to flexible and responsive state government. In 1871, a state Department of Agriculture and a Railroad and Warehouse Commission were created to prevent charging of inequitable and excessive rates and to provide a specific department of the state government to which farmers could turn for advice and assistance. Labor legislation was enacted throughout the seventies that, among other things, protected miners and established what would become the Departments of Labor and Public Health. Illinois gained more than 500,000 new residents in this ten-year period, and now had a foreign-born population of more than 500,000. Throughout the remaining years of the century there was a steady shift from rural to urban areas, reflecting the growth of industrialization. As the number of Illinoisans who were involved in industry surpassed the number of those who worked on farms, the decade 1880–90 was marked by growing social unrest. Labor became plentiful, and as a result, during the middle years of the decade, wages declined. Workingmen found it necessary to band together in trade unions. The Knights of Labor appeared in Illinois to crusade for better working conditions and were soon joined by organizations of laboring men. In 1886 there were more than a thousand strikes in Illinois.

A notorious moment in Illinois history occurred on May 4, 1886, when a bomb exploded as the police attempted to break up a labor demonstration in Haymarket Square in Chicago. In the ensuing riot, more than a hundred police and demonstrators were injured; seven policemen were killed by the bomb. The outbreak followed a clash between strikers, strike-breakers, and police at the gates of the McCormick Harvester plant the day before in which six men were killed. For some time Chicago anarchists had been distributing inflammatory literature and advocating violence as a means of redressing grievances, and they had sponsored the mass meeting in Haymarket Square in protest to the six killed; seven of the anarchists involved in the riot were convicted and sentenced to death, and an eighth was given a fifteen-year sentence. Appeals to higher courts were unavailing but Governor Richard J. Oglesby commuted the sentences of two of the condemned to life imprisonment; four men were eventually hanged, and one committed suicide in jail. In 1893, Governor Altgeld pardoned the remaining three. The entire episode attracted national attention and stimulated protracted debate (similar to the Sacco-Vanzetti case in 1921) whether the accused had received a fair trial—whether they had in fact been proved guilty of the charge or had been convicted because they were foreign-born radicals who held unpopular opinions. The passions aroused by this tragedy would be important factors in Illinois politics for more than a generation.

Mass production techniques, the use of electricity, and the output of many and varied products enabled many Illinoisans to live easier, more comfortable lives. Although the state's vast railroad network made traveling much simpler than ever before, excessive railroad and warehouse rates forced legislative regulation. In Chicago, William L. Jenney designed the first modern skyscraper, the Home Insurance Building, which was completed in 1886 and was razed in 1931 to make way for the Field Building. Also, the nation's first compulsory school attendance law was passed in the 1880s. In 1889 Jane Addams founded Hull House in Chicago, one of the first social settlement houses in the United States, where she sought to improve the condition of immigrants by preparing them for useful, dignified, and more satisfying roles in life.

The Gay Nineties was a decade of prosperity and pleasure only for the lucky few. All too often the immigrant—and the laboring class in general—lived in substandard housing and paid high rents. If the workday, often as long as sixteen hours, did not destroy the worker's health, the poorly lighted, inadequately heated, and generally squalid workrooms did. Sanitary provisions were mimimal and machinery was designed for efficiency rather than safety. Wages were low while company profits remained high. Women toiled in sweatships at demanding, monotonous piecework, at rates so low that only by sustained effort could they earn a subsistence wage. The children of the lower classes often went to work at age ten; unprotected by child labor laws, they were all too often exploited by their employers. In 1893, a measure of relief was provided by legislation which set up some regulations against child labor and for factory inspection, but for the many who were victims of the industrial age, the "Gay Nineties" were not gay at all.

In 1890, the population of Illinois was 3,825,000, of which more than 840,000 were foreign-born—and among them was one of Illinois's most remarkable governors, John P. Altgeld. When Altgeld pardoned the three surviving Haymarket anarchists, he was aware that this action would end his political career; the poet Vachel Lindsay called him "The Eagle Forgotten." And 1893, of course, was the year of Chicago's World Columbian Exposition, perhaps the greatest international fair ever held. The Exposition attracted 27,500,000 visitors, many from abroad, gave them exciting demonstrations of industrial and scientific progress, and an enduring vision of beauty expressed by classic architecture.

The state's industrial turmoil reached a climax with the Pullman Strike of May-June 1894 against the Pullman Palace Car Company. The head of the sleeping-car company, George M. Pullman, had built a model—but wholly company-owned—town for his workers, and when a general depression brought wage cuts, his workers asked that either their rents be reduced or the wage cuts rescinded. When the company did not accede to either request, the men walked out and the company closed its shops. The American Railway Union, led by Eugene V. Debs, supported the strikers and refused to handle Pullman's sleeping cars unless the company would agree to negotiate the dispute. George M. Pullman, supported by the General Managers' Association, refused to talk with the strikers and, as a result of the A.R.U.'s support, a nationwide railroad strike was called. President Cleveland sent federal troops to Chicago to maintain order and move the mail—an action bitterly protested by Governor Altgeld as unconstitutional. When federal troops and the strikers clashed, the state militia was called out; the strike leaders were arrested and the strike collapsed. Some historians view this strike as a major episode in United States labor history for it indicated conclusivly that major economic changes had occurred and that major social changes were necessary.

In 1896, the Democratic party nominated a former Illinoisan, William Jennings Bryan, for the first of his three unsuccessful attempts at the presidency. As the century closed, the state sent 12,000 men to the Spanish-American War.

FRANCIS X. BUSCH

received his LL.B. from the Illinois College of Law in 1901 and after being admitted to the bar, began to practice in Chicago. He was Corporation Counsel of Chicago, 1923–1927 and president of the Chicago Bar Association, 1929–1930. Among his writings are *In and Out of Court; They Escaped the Hangman;* and *Enemies of the State.*

Mr. Busch delivered this address before a meeting of the Illinois State Historical Society held in May, 1955. This article was published in the *Journal of the Illinois State Historical Society,* volume 48, number 3 (autumn 1955), pages 247–270.

THE HAYMARKET RIOT
AND THE TRIAL OF THE ANARCHISTS

FRANCIS X. BUSCH

May first has long been a day on which to anticipate trouble. As for many years past, thousands of discontented workers and unemployed still parade the streets of European and American cities on that day, either to show their strength or to protest against real or fancied grievances.

On Saturday, May 1, 1886, in Chicago the grievances of labor were not imaginary. Times were none too good. Labor, skilled and unskilled, was overworked and underpaid. Workers in the stockyards, the industrial plants, and the smaller sweatshops labored from ten to sixteen hours daily. The wages of these unfortunates were far from sufficient to provide a sanitary place in which to live and decent food and clothing. There was no added pay for overtime, no paid holidays, nor any of the modern "fringe benefits."

This May Day found thousands on strike and many more thousands, discontented and sullen, threatening walkouts. The workers' cry for an eight-hour day—with ten hours' pay for the eight hours —had been taken up by the radical newspapers: the *Alarm,* the national organ of the American anarchists, the Communist *Arbeiter-Zeitung* and the *Anarchist* published in Chicago. The *Alarm* (published fortnightly and monthly) was printed in English; the *Anarchist* (monthly) and the *Arbeiter-Zeitung* (daily), in German.

Their combined circulation in Chicago was less than ten thousand.

This is a fair sample of the fuel which the *Alarm* kept pouring on the smoldering fire:

> Dynamite! Of all the good stuff, this is the stuff. Stuff several pounds of this sublime stuff into an inch pipe, . . . plug up both ends, insert a cap with a fuse attached, place this in the immediate neighborhood of a lot of rich loafers who live by the sweat of other people's brows, and light the fuse. A most cheerful and gratifying result will follow. . . . Dynamite is like Banquo's ghost, it keeps on fooling around somewhere or other in spite of his satanic majesty. A pound of this good stuff beats a bushel of ballots all hollow, and don't you forget it. Our law makers might as well try to sit down on a crater of a volcano or a bayonet as to endeavor to stop the manufacture and use of dynamite. It takes more justice and right than is contained in laws to quiet the spirit of unrest. If workingmen would be truly free, they must learn to know why they are slaves. They must rise above petty prejudice and learn to think. From thought to action is not far, and when the worker has seen the chains, he need but look a little closer to find near at hand, the sledge with which to shatter every link. The sledge is dynamite.

For six months before the Haymarket Riot such articles us this were pouring forth from the presses of the *Arbeiter-Zeitung:*

> The eight-hour question is not, or at least should not be, the final end of the present organization, but, in comparison to the present state of things, a progress not to be overrated. But now let us consider the question in itself. How is the eight-hour day to be brought about? Why, the thinking workingman must see for himself, under the present power of capital in comparison to labor, it is impossible to enforce the eight-hour day in all branches of business, otherwise than with armed force. With empty hands the workingmen will hardly be able to cope with the representatives of the club, in case, after the 1st of May of this year, there should be a general strike. Then the bosses will simply employ other men,—so-called "scabs." Such will always be found. The whole movement then would be nothing but filling the places with new men; but if the workingmen are prepared to eventually stop the working of the factories, to defend himself, with the aid of dynamite and bombs, against the militia, which will, of course, be employed, then, and only then, can you expect a thorough success of the eight-hour movement. THEREFORE, WORKINGMEN, I CALL UPON YOU, ARM YOURSELVES!

The incessant prodding of the workers to enforce their demands by violent means was not confined to the outpourings of these newspapers. For months a group of openly-professed anarchists had harangued and preached anarchy to the crowds of loafers in Union Square, Newberry Park, and other open spots in Chicago. Chief among these rabble-rousers were August Spies, Michael Schwab, Albert R. Parsons, Samuel Fielden, George Engel, and Adoph Fischer. None of these were members of the striking unions. All but Parsons were foreign-born; none had become naturalized. Spies was managing editor of the *Arbeiter-Zeitung*, Schwab its coeditor and editorial writer, and Fischer a contributor and stockholder. Parsons was editor-in-chief of the *Alarm;* Fielding was a stockholder in the company which controlled it and a frequent contributor to its columns. Engel was the moving spirit of the *Anarchist*.

May 1 witnessed the largest labor parade ever seen in Chicago up to that time; there were inflammatory placards, mutterings and threats a-plenty, but no open violence. Sunday passed peaceably, but on Monday, May 3, violence broke out at the struck McCormick Harvester plant when strikers gathered at the gates attacked strike breakers who had been hired to take their places. A riot call brought police to the scene. Clubs were freely used and several shots fired; one striker was killed and several wounded.

Before the riot both Spies and Parsons had harangued the strikers, inciting them to direct action against the "scabs" who were taking the bread out of the mouths of their wives and children. Neither was present when the rioting took place. That evening an article (later proved to have been written by Spies) appeared in the *Arbeiter-Zeitung:*

REVENGE! WORKINGMEN! TO ARMS!
Your masters sent out their blood-hounds—the police—
they killed six of your brothers at McCormick's this afternoon.
They killed the poor wretches because they, like you, had
courage to disobey the supreme will of your bosses. They
killed them because they dared ask for the shortening of the
hours of toil. They killed them to show you "free American
citizens" that you must be satisfied and contented with whatever your bosses condescend to allow you, or you will get
killed! . . . If you are men, if you are the sons of your
grandsires, who have shed their blood to free you, then you
will rise in your might Hercules, and destroy the hideous

monster that seeks to destroy you. To arms, we call you, to arms!

YOUR BROTHERS.

Twenty-five hundred copies of the article were printed in English and German and distributed in various parts of the city.

The following afternoon, Tuesday, May 4, handbills, later traced to Spies and his associates, advertised a giant mass meeting at the old Haymarket, Desplaines, and Randolph streets. These were distributed by thousands at the gates of the McCormick and other struck plants. Of these two or three hundred carried in bold, black type: "WORKINGMEN ARM YOURSELVES AND APPEAR IN FULL FORCE!" At Spies's insistence Fischer had deleted this caption from the remainder.

At 8:30 Spies, Parsons, Fielden, and Rudolph Schnaubelt mounted an empty truck wagon which stood next to the sidewalk on the east side of Desplaines Street about a hundred feet north of Randolph. There had been a more or less continuous drizzle, and the crowd was disappointingly small—probably not more than 1,200. Spies called the meeting to order and harangued the crowd in German for some twenty minutes, bitterly assailing McCormick "for the murder of our brothers." There were cries of "Hang McCormick!" from some of the more excitable members of the audience. Parsons followed, speaking in English. His language was even stronger than that of Spies: "It behooves you . . . if you don't want to see [your wives and children] perish with hunger, killed or cut down like dogs in the street, Americans, in the interest of your liberty and your independence, to arm, to arm yourselves."

When Parsons left off, Fielden took over. It was nearing 10:30 P.M. and about three-fourths of the crowd had left. "The law is your enemy," cried Fielden. "We are rebels against it. The law is only framed for those who are your enslavers." (Cries of "That is true" from the crowd.) Fielden continued:

> Men in their blind rage attacked the McCormick factory and were shot down in cold blood. . . . the law came to his defense; and [McCormick] was a large property owner, therefore when McCormick undertook to do some injury to the interest of those who had no property the law also came to his . . . and not to the workingman's defense when McCormick attacked him and his living. [Cries of "No."] There is the difference. The law makes no distinctions. A million men own all the property in this country. The law has no use for the

other fifty-four million. [Chorus of cries: "That's right enough, that's right enough."]. . . . Any animal, however loathsome, will resist when stepped upon. Are men less than snails and worms? I have some resistance in me; I know that you have too; you have been robbed, and you will be starved into a worse condition.

It was at this juncture that a small army of police—180, according to the later evidence—burst upon the scene, led by Captains Bonfield and Ward. The latter ordered the crowd to disperse. Fielden attempted to argue. The captain's demands grew sterner and louder. Fielden, Spies, Parsons, and some others unidentified started to climb down from the wagon. At this moment a dynamite bomb, thrown from the crowd, landed and exploded among the crowded police cordon. A fusillade of revolver shots followed—the number estimated later by witnesses as between seventy-five and a hundred. They came both from the crowd and from the police. The police closed ranks and charged and scattered the now screaming mob. When order was restored and accounting had of the casualties, one policeman had been killed, six others fatally wounded, and seventy injured. One of the crowd—a harmless spectator— was hit and fatally wounded by a police bullet; fifty others received bullet wounds or club injuries, none of which, however, proved fatal.

Such was the Haymarket Riot.

The excitement caused by this mass murder of seven policemen can be better imagined than told. With the aid of Pinkerton detectives, supplied and paid for by the Harvester Company, Spies, Schwab, Engel, Fischer, and Fielden were promptly arrested. Parsons could not be located. Investigation led to the subsequent arrest of Louis Lingg, William Seliger, and Oscar Neebe. All these, together with the absent Parsons and Schnaubelt, were promptly indicted on May 27 by a grand jury as accessories before the fact to the murder of Patrolman Mathias Joseph Degan, and for general conspiracy to murder. A number of others were arrested and indicted for inciting to riot.

Lingg had come to America from Germany about ten months before the Haymarket murders. He was a member of an anarchist organization—the International Arbeiter [Workingmen's] Association—in which he was closely associated with Spies, Schwab, Parsons, Fielden, Engel, and Fischer. He had no regular employment,

but spent his time manufacturing and experimenting with dynamite bombs. Seliger was Lingg's landlord and assisted him in his
sinister occupation.

Neebe was a member of the International Arbeiter Association, a
small stockholder in the *Arbeiter-Zeitung,* and next to Schwab and
Spies the most active man in its management.

Schnaubelt was also a member of the International Arbeiter
Association and participated actively in the arrangements for the
Haymarket meeting. Some witnesses (contradicted by others) tes-
tified that he threw the bomb.

Seliger and a number of other members of the International
Arbeiter Association, who were to a greater or less extent involved
in the conspiracy, testified for the State and thereby procured
immunity. Schnaubelt was never apprehended.

Spies, Schwab, Fielden, Engel, Fischer, Lingg, and Neebe were
brought to trial on June 21 before Judge Joseph E. Gary of the
Superior Court of Cook County, sitting as a judge of the Criminal
Court. Judge Gary was a highly regarded trial judge. He had been
on the bench for more than twenty years, had presided in many
important civil and criminal cases, and had acquired a nation-wide
reputation as a learned, wise, and upright judge.

At the prosecutor's table sat State's Attorney Julius S. Grinnell,
an able and experienced trial lawyer, and his assistants, Francis W.
Walker, Edmund Furthman, and George C. Ingham. Captain William P. Black, a first-rate trial lawyer, and William A. Foster, an
equally competent Iowa attorney, led for the defense. They were
assisted by two young members of the Illinois bar—Sigismund
Zeisler and Moses Salomon.

The first hundred veniremen had been summoned and the empaneling of the jury just begun when the trial was interrupted by an
event as dramatic as ever took place in an American courtroom.
Parsons, as has been noted, had not been apprehended. After the
dynamiting he had managed to disappear in the crowd, make his
way to a railroad station and board a train for Waukesha, Wisconsin, on his way to Canada. From his secret and safe haven he had
been kept informed of the course of events, and on the advice of
Captain Black, who assured him that his acquittal was certain, had
planned to appear in the courtroom when the case was called and
dramatically present himself for trial with his comrades. But when
he entered the courtroom, before he had a chance to make his

grandstand play, Grinnell was on his feet. Pointing at the erstwhile fugitive, he shouted: "I see in the courtroom Albert R. Parsons, indicted for murder, and demand his immediate arrest." Quietly Parsons replied: "I present myself for trial with my comrades, your Honor." Just as quietly Judge Gary followed with: "You will take your seat with the prisoners, Mr. Parsons."

With Parsons in his place inside the rail, the trial proceeded. Nine hundred eighty-one talesmen were subjected to examination; 757 were excused for cause—either they had formed a fixed and ineradicable opinion of the guilt or innocence of the defendants, or were opposed to capital punishment, or would not convict on circumstantial evidence. Of the remaining 224, the defendants eliminated 160 by exhausting their peremptory challenges. The State, which also had 160 peremptories, used 52 of them. The defense protested the swearing of two of the final twelve, but were compelled to accept them, since their challenges for cause were overruled and their peremptories exhausted. This was the first of the alleged errors of which more was to be heard in the courts of appeal.

The keynote of the trial was sounded by Mr. Grinnell in his opening statement:

> Gentlemen, for the first time in the history of our country are people on trial for endeavoring to make anarchy the rule, and in that attempt for ruthlessly and awfully destroying human life. I hope that while the youngest of us lives this in memory will be the last and only time in our country when such a trial shall take place. It will or will not take place as this case is determined. . . . In the light of the 4th of May we now know that the preachings of Anarchy [by] . . . these defendants hourly and daily for years, have been sapping our institutions, and that where they have cried murder, bloodshed, Anarchy and dynamite, they have meant what they said, and proposed to do what they threatened. . . . The firing upon Fort Sumter was a terrible thing to our country, but it was open warfare. I think it was nothing compared with this insidious, infamous plot to ruin our laws and our country secretly and in this cowardly way. . . .
>
> Everything was ripe with the Anarchists for ruining the town. . . . There was going to be one bomb thrown there [Haymarket Square] at least, and perhaps more, and that would call the police down; but the police. . . . were to be destroyed, absolutely wiped off the earth by bombs in other parts of the city.

The defense reserved its opening statement until the close of the prosecution's case, and the hearing of the evidence commenced.

The State's principal witnesses were Seliger and a number of the prisoners' other associates in the International Arbeiter Association and the *Arbeiter-Zeitung,* police officers, and two men, not in any way connected with the alleged conspiracy, who had been in the neighborhood and joined the crowd out of mere curiosity. One of these—Harry L. Gilmer—was badly discredited on cross-examination, and nine persons took the stand to swear they would not believe him under oath.

The evidence against all the defendants, with the possible exception of Neebe, was overwhelming. Dozens of inflammatory articles advising the manufacture and stocking of dynamite bombs for possible use against the police and the militia were shown to have been written by Spies, Schwab, and Parsons. A dozen or more witnesses—some co-conspirators, some police and some disinterested persons—testified to their attendance at meetings held shortly before the riot at which Spies, Schwab, Parsons, Fielden, Engel, and Fischer made inflammatory speeches in which they preached anarchy and counseled the free use of dynamite to bring it about.

There was a wealth of evidence as to the purposes and activities of the International Arbeiter Association. Its platform or declaration of principles was featured regularly in the *Alarm* and the *Arbeiter-Zeitung.* It urged the destruction of the present social order; that all property owned by individuals and all capital be transformed into common property. All past attempts at social and economic reform through the ballot had failed, it declared; there was only one remedy left—revolution and force. The association was divided into groups, of which there were eighty in the United States, located principally in the large industrial centers. There were at least seven of these groups in Chicago, which held meetings regularly in the various sections of the city. Schwab, Neebe, Lingg, and Seliger belonged to the North Side group; Engel and Fischer to the Northwest Side group; Spies, Parsons, and Fielden to a so-called "American" group. The members were known by numbers rather than by names.

Certain chosen members of the group were armed with rifles and drilled regularly under the direction of a former German army sergeant once a week at their meeting places. These men were known as the "armed sections" of the groups. The elite corps in these different international groups, known as the "Lehr und Wehr Verein," were armed with Springfield rifles of the latest pattern and drilled once a week. There were four of these elite companies in Chicago. In the spring of 1886 there were altogether in the city 3,000 armed anarchists, of whom Parsons wrote: "They were well-armed with rifles and revolvers and would have dynamite and bombs when they got ready to use them." These groups were directed by an Executive Committee, of which Spies, Schwab, and Parsons were members, which met every two weeks in the *Arbeiter-Zeitung* building. Meetings of the armed sections were called by code signals published in the *Arbeiter-Zeitung.*

A mass of evidence was introduced to show the particular contribution of each of the defendants to effectuate the avowed purposes of the International Arbeiter Association. It was proved that Engel and Parsons had been active for more than a year in the procurement of rifles and pistols; that Spies, Schwab, Fielden, Parsons, Fischer, and Lingg had been engaged in experimenting with dynamite and making bombs, and that a stock of bombs was kept in the offices of the *Arbeiter-Zeitung.* Parsons and Fielden were shown to have personally participated in the military drills of the armed section of the "American" group of the Arbeiter Association.

There was testimony that on the preceding Thanksgiving Day, before a meeting in Haymarket Square, Fischer gave to one Gottfried Waller, a member of the Lehr und Wehr Verein, a gas-pipe bomb 7 or 8 inches long, saying that it was to be used in the event of an attack by the police. Waller as one of the prosecution's witnesses testified that he kept the bomb in his house for two weeks, and then gave it to a fellowmember of the Verein who took it out to some woods on the outskirts of Chicago and exploded it. This was frequent practice on the part of the defendants and other members of the International, so that they might gain experience in the handling, lighting, and throwing of bombs.

Lingg had, as previously stated, recently arrived from Germany. Though only twenty-two years old, he had been active as a Socialist leader in Europe. The evidence established that he had been selected by the International to buy dynamite and experiment with it in the manufacture and detonation of various types of bombs. Seliger was his principal assistant. They produced several types of bombs. One type was designated as a "Czar" bomb—a crude affair made of two semi-globular shells, fastened together with a bolt and nut. Some of these were found in Lingg's possession when he was arrested, and one was traced to Spies. Fragments of the bomb exploded at the Haymarket and removed from the bodies of some of the victims were identified and offered in evidence. The parts corresponded exactly with parts of the Czar bombs in Lingg's and Spies's possession. A chemical analysis of the Lingg and Spies bombs showed the same composite of materials—tin, with traces of antimony and zinc—as did the parts of the bombshell taken from the victims of the riot.

The State's evidence further showed that on the afternoon of May 4 Lingg and Seliger carried a small hand trunk containing a number of bombs from Seliger's house, intending to take it to the headquarters of the North Side group of the International—a saloon at 58 Clybourn Avenue. On the way they were met by a fellow-member named Nunsenberg, who carried it to the headquarters. It was there placed upon the floor and left open. A number of persons called during the day, helped themselves to bombs and departed. No one was able to tell who these people were. Nunsenberg disappeared. The anonymous features of this incident highlight a quotation from the *Arbeiter-Zeitung*:

> In the commission of a deed, a comrade who does not live at the place of the action, that is a comrade of some other place, should, if possibility admits, participate in the action, or, formulated differently, a revolutionary deed ought to be enacted where one is not known.

The Lehr und Wehr Verein—the elite guard of the International —met in a hall near Haymarket Square the night before the riot. Copies of Spies's "Revenge" circular were distributed and discussed. Engel was the leading spirit at this meeting; his resolution for a plan of specific action was adopted. The central feature of this plan was that members of the armed sections should come to the aid of the striking workingmen if a collision with the police was threatened. A rallying word and signal was agreed on—"*Ruhe*," which in German means "rest" or "peace." The featured publication of that word in the "letter-box" column of the *Arbeiter-Zeitung* was to be the signal for members of the armed section to repair to specified meeting places described by code in the notice. If the police attacked the strikers, some of the armed sections were to respond with shots from their revolvers; other members were simultaneously to throw a dynamite bomb in each of the Chicago police stations. The resulting confusion was counted upon to disorganize the police, make further violence easier, and permit the revolutionists to escape. The word *"Ruhe"* did appear in the Tuesday morning edition of the *Arbeiter-Zeitung* in heavily leaded, emphasized type. Arrangements were made at these meetings of the armed sections for the distribution of thousands of handbills for the giant mass meeting the next evening in Haymarket Square. It was confidently predicted and expected that at least 25,000 would be present. The designated meeting place was less than a block and a half from the Desplaines Street police station.

There was cumulative evidence as to the gathering of the crowd, the calling to order of the mass meeting, the speeches of Spies, Parsons, and Fielden, and the throwing of the bomb. It was shown that the police captain addressed the crowd in the exact language prescribed by Section 253 of Division I of the Criminal Code to be used in dispersing an armed or riotous gathering of thirty or more persons: "I command you in the name of the People of the State of Illinois to immediately and peaceably disperse." According to some of the witnesses, Fielden replied to this command in clear and emphatic tones, "We are peaceable." Immediately the bomb was thrown. The State contended that the word "peaceable" was the equivalent of "Ruhe" and the signal for throwing the bomb.

The prosecution claimed that following the explosion of the bomb members of the crowd discharged revolvers into the crowded ranks of the police. The defense vigorously denied this, claiming that all the shots came from police revolvers. The testimony of disinterested surgeons who had removed bullets from the dead and wounded policemen proved that they were of definitely different types and calibers from those supplied for the guns of the police. That Spies, Parsons, and Fielden participated in and addressed the Haymarket meeting was not disputed. The testimony of several policemen that immediately after the bomb was thrown Fielden had a revolver in his hand and fired at the police, however, was vigorously disputed by him and other defense witnesses.

It was proved that during the meeting Schwab, Engel, Fischer, and twenty-five or thirty men were in the immediate neighborhood of the Desplaines Street police station, acting in a strangely excited manner; and that Seliger and Lingg in the early part of the evening were close by the North Avenue police station, and were later seen in company with members of the Lehr und Wehr Verein near the police station at Webster and Lincoln avenues.

Neebe was proved to be not only a stockholder of the *Arbeiter-Zeitung* and active in its management, but also a member of the North Side group of the International and a participant in the meetings of that group who frequently acted as presiding officer. He was shown to have been present at one of the group's meetings in April at which it was resolved "not to meet the enemy unarmed on May 1st." On Monday night, May 3, he was seen distributing the "Revenge" circulars which had been printed on the *Arbeiter-Zeitung* presses. In the distribution he was said to have made angry utterances such as "It is a shame the police act that way, but maybe the time comes when it goes the other way—that they [the strikers] get a chance, too." He said the dynamite found in the offices of the *Arbeiter-Zeitung* after the riot was used to clean type. When his house was searched on May 7 the police found a red flag, a sword, a breech-loading gun, and a .38 Colt revolver, of which four chambers had been fired and one was loaded. It was not shown that Neebe was at Haymarket Square or any of the police stations on the night of May 4.

All the defendants disclaimed any connection with the throwing of the bomb, any previous knowledge of an intent to throw it, or any idea as to who had thrown it. Schwab, Engel, Lingg, and Fischer claimed they were not at or near the meeting in Haymarket Square, and were supported by the testimony of their comrades.

Critics of the trial have laid great stress on the State's failure to prove who actually hurled the bomb, or that it was thrown by one of the conspirators or their agent. The indictment consisted of a number of counts, some of which charged that the bomb was thrown by Schnaubelt, indicted as a co-conspirator; others charged that it was thrown in pursuance of the plan of the conspirators by a person unknown. Several witnesses placed Schnaubelt in the neighborhood of Haymarket Square during the meeting, and a number of others present, when shown a photograph of Schnaubelt, identified him as the man who threw the bomb. Others called by the State, who saw some man hurl the bomb, were unable to identify Schnaubelt or anyone else as the thrower. All the evidence introduced by the defense tended to show that Schnaubelt was not in the Haymarket crowd at the time of the riot, and therefore the bomb was not thrown by him, but by an unidentified and unknown person with whom none of the indicted men had any connection. The State's theory of the law was that the bomb thrower was sufficiently identified when it was shown by either direct or circumstantial evidence that he was a member of the conspiracy, and threw the bomb to carry out the conspiracy or further its designs; that his identification by name or description was unnecessary. The jury was instructed on this theory, and this became one of the principal claims of error to the Supreme Court of Illinois.

The arguments of contending counsel were passionate and at times vitriolic. Captain Black's principal argument for the defense was a flamboyant piece of rhetoric, but whether judicious or not is seriously open to question. As one newspaper commented, it was "a defense of terrorism, directed more to appeasing his clients than persuading the jury." He thundered:

> Jesus, the great socialist of Judea, has preached the socialism taught by Spies and his other apostles. John Brown and his attack on Harper's Ferry may be compared to the Socialists' attack on modern evils. Gentlemen, the last word for these eight lives. They are in your hands, with no power to which you are answerable but God and history, and I say to you in closing only the words of that Divine Socialist: "As ye would that others should do to you, do you even so to them."

Grinnell's and Ingham's closing arguments for the State were inflammatory and exceeded the bounds of judicial propriety. Here is part of Ingham's summation:

> Fielden and Parsons have said that they would like to take a black flag and march up and down the avenues of the city and strike terror to the hearts of the capitalists. Why did they choose the black flag? The flag which represents their principles is the flag of the pirate, which now and always has meant, "No quarter"; a flag that means for men, death; for childhood, mutilation; for women, rape. That was the flag under which the defendants marched.

Grinnell went even further:

> The proof has been submitted; everything has been done for the defense that could be done. Gentlemen, it is time in all conscience that you did have a judgment; and if you have now prejudice against the defendants under the law as the Court will give it to you, you have a right to have it. Prejudice! Men, organized assassins, can preach murder in our city for years; you deliberately hear the proof and then say that you

have no prejudice! . . . Gentlemen, you stand between the
living and the dead. You stand between law and violated law.
Do your duty courageously, even if that duty is an unpleasant
and severe one.

There has been much criticism of Judge Gary's instructions to
the jury. Practically all the instructions on behalf of the State were
literal copies of instructions that had previously been given over
and over again in murder prosecutions and had been expressly
approved by the Supreme Court. The special instructions relating
to the law of conspiracy were clear and accurate expressions of the
law of Illinois. The Court refused to instruct in accordance with the
defense theory that the State was obliged to prove the identity of
the bomb thrower, holding that since several counts of the indictment charged that the bomb had been thrown by a person unknown, the jury were at liberty to find from the evidence either that
Schnaubelt threw it or that it was thrown by some unidentified
person acting in concert with the defendant conspirators.

The jury retired to consider their verdict on August 19—nearly
two months after the trial started. After three hours' deliberation
they reached a unanimous verdict finding all the defendants before
the Court guilty of murder as charged. On August 20 the penalties
of Spies, Schwab, Parsons, Fielden, Engel, Fischer, and Lingg were
fixed at death; Neebe was sentenced to fifteen years' imprisonment
in the penitentiary.

A motion for a new trial was made in due course and overruled.
The defendants were sentenced in accordance with the verdict of
the jury. An appeal was promptly taken to the Supreme Court of
Illinois. In the Supreme Court there was an addition to the list of
defense counsel—Leonard Swett, one of the ablest and most re-
sourceful lawyers at the Illinois bar. Captain Black and Messrs.
Zeisler and Salomon also appeared and argued for the defendants.
The State was represented by the same counsel as in the lower
court, with the addition of Attorney General George Hunt.

The opinion of the Supreme Court, rendered September 14,
1887, after elaborate written briefs and oral arguments, takes up
the first 267 pages of Volume 122 of *Illinois Reports*. After a
meticulous and exhaustive review of all the evidence, it held:

(1) That all the defendants were associated together, and were
dominating members of the International Arbeiter Association.

(2) That that association was unlawful, its avowed purposes

being to destroy the constitutional right of individual property ownership, to overthrow the government and to establish communism.

(3) That the means to accomplish the association's purposes, proposed to be used and used by members of the associaion, contemplated and involved the use of violence to destroy private property and kill those who wanted to protect it.

(4) That the riot at the Haymarket on May 4, 1886, occurred as a planned incident in the general conspiracy of the members of the International Arbeiter Association to overthrow the government, abolish private property and establish a communal state without law.

(5) That each of the defendants had an assigned part, which he carried out; and the death of Patrolman Degan was the direct consequence of their concurrent acts.

The opinion carefully reviewed and assembled the evidence as to each defendant, and concluded it was sufficient to establish, beyond a reasonable doubt, that each defendant was guilty of a conspiracy to murder, and guilty of the specifically charged murder of Patrolman Degan.

Answering the heavily stressed point that it was not shown that any of the defendants had any connection with the throwing of the bomb which had killed the seven policemen, the Court found:

(1) That Lingg had been selected by his fellow-conspirators to manufacture dynamite bombs.

(2) That bombs traced to the possession of Lingg and Spies were identical with the bomb which had been thrown and exploded in the Haymarket on May 4.

(3) That there was evidence from which the jury could properly conclude either that Schnaubelt or some unknown agent of the conspirators threw the bomb.

(4) That under the law as to the admissibility of evidence under the particular form of the indictment (in the alternative) the jury could find a verdict of guilty based upon either finding.

All the specific points raised by the defendants were dealt with; the Court, with ample citations of supporting authority, held there had been no prejudicial error in (a) overruling the motions of certain defendants for separate trials; (b) the disposition of challenges for cause in the empaneling of the jury; (c) the admission of incompetent evidence; or (d) the giving or refusing instructions.

The seven justices unanimously concurred in the opinion, written by Justice Benjamin D. Magruder, that the judgment of the Criminal Court of Cook County should be affirmed.

The decision of the high court was hailed far and wide as a victory for law and order and as a just disposition of the case. There were, however, dissenting voices. Few if any disputed the evidence that the defendants were anarchists, bent on destroying private property and overthrowing the government by violent means; but there was criticism of the verdict and judgment on the grounds that the defendants had not had a fair trial. Some held that in the absence of positive proof as to who threw the bomb, and that the thrower was an agent of the defendants, the defendants were entitled to an acquittal on the charge of murder. The best answer to this, it seems to me, is found in the bench statement of Justice John H. Mulkey at the time the opinion was delivered. This is his statement, quoted at the conclusion of the formal opinion:

> Not intending to file a separate opinion, as I should have done had health permitted, I desire to avail myself of this occasion to say from the bench, that while I concur in the conclusion reached, and also in the general view presented in the opinion filed, I do not wish to be understood as holding that the record is free from error, for I do not think it is. I am nevertheless of the opinion that none of the errors complained of are of so serious a character as to require a reversal of the judgment. In view of the number of defendants on trial, the great length of time it was in progress, the vast amount of testimony offered and passed upon by the court, and the almost numberless rulings the court was required to make, the wonder with me is that the errors were not more numerous and more serious than they are. In short, after having carefully examined the record, and having given all the questions arising upon it my very best thought, with an earnest and conscientious desire to faithfully discharge my whole duty, I am fully satisfied that the conclusion reached vindicates the law, does complete justice between the prisoners and the State, and that it is fully warranted by the law and the evidence.

There remained one last legal recourse—an application to the Supreme Court of the United States for a writ of error to review the decision of the Illinois Supreme Court. The lawyers, recruited to aid Salomon and Black for this task, though all able men, were a strange collection: John Randolph Tucker, who had served as

Attorney General of Virginia during the Confederacy; Roger A. Pryor, ex-Confederate brigadier general; and General Benjamin F. Butler, the Yankee firebrand who had won the undying hatred of the South by his tyrannical administration of the conquered city of New Orleans. State's Attorney Grinnell and Attorney General Hunt appeared for the State of Illinois. The petition was promptly heard by the full court. The arguments lasted three days. The issue before the Supreme Court was a narrow one: Was there a federal constitutional question involved?

The defense, handicapped by a trial court record made by other lawyers who clearly had not apprehended a possible appeal to the United States Supreme Court, made the most of a weak situation. They contended there had been a violation of four amendments: the Fourth, in that some of the evidence against some of the defendants had been obtained by an illegal search without warrant; the Fifth, in that Spies had been compelled to give evidence against himself; the Sixth, in that because of a failure by the trial court to recognize proper challenges of jurors for cause the defendants had been deprived of a trial by an impartial jury; and the Fourteenth, in that because of the foregoing, the defendants were about to be deprived of their lives and liberties without due process of law.

The Supreme Court made short work of the claims that the Fourth, Fifth, and Sixth Amendments had been violated. Adhering to a long line of established precedents, it held that those amendments were limitations upon the federal government and applied only to prosecutions in the federal and not in the state courts. In connection with the claim that the Fourteenth Amendment (violation of due process) had been infringed, the Court considered a number of specific points. The first of these was the contention that the trial court had improperly overruled the defense's challenge of a large number of jurors for cause. The Court examined the record as to only two jurors, because all the others challenged for cause had been eliminated from the jury by peremptory challenges; but when the challenges for cause as to these last two were denied, the defense, having exhausted its 160 peremptories, was obliged to accept them, and they served on the jury. Each of them —T. E. Denker and H. T. Sanford—had said in his *voir dire* examination under oath that he had formed an opinion of the guilt of the defendants from what he had read in the newspapers, that he still held that opinion and would carry it with him into the jury box; however, in response to subsequent questions by the state's attorney and the judge, both said they believed they could set aside that opinion and decide the case solely on the evidence as it came from the witnesses, and the instructions on the law as they came to them from the Court. These answers brought the jurors strictly within the Illinois statute, and for that reason the challenges for cause were overruled by the trial court. The defendants' lawyers contended before the Supreme Court that the examination of these jurors, taken in its entirety, showed that the defendants had been compelled to accept jurors who had already prejudged the case, and a jury which included such men constituted a lack of the "due process of law" guaranteed by the Fourteenth Amendment, which, it was conceded, was an express limitation upon the states. The Supreme Court, however, ruled that on the whole record it was "unhesitatingly of the opinion" that the defendants had not been deprived of a trial by a fair and impartial jury, and had not been denied due process of law.

The claim that Spies had been compelled to give evidence against himself was based on the allegation that he had been subjected to improper and prejudicial cross-examination. He had testified in his own defense. Under the law he was not required to take the stand, and had he not done so it would have been gross error for the prosecution to have referred to the fact that he had not. Having taken the stand, however, he was legally subject to cross-examination, the same as any other witness. The cross-examination was searching and exhaustive, but the Supreme Court held that the determination of the local courts as to what was and what was not proper cross-examination was a matter of local law, not subject to review by a federal court.

The point that a letter incriminating one of the defendants had been obtained by illegal search without warrant was shortly disposed of on the ground that such a contention, to have validity, must first have been raised in the trial court. No such point was there made. Similarly the final and rather diaphanous point that Spies, a German citizen, and Fielden, a British subject, were entitled to special procedural treatment by virtue of the United States' treaties with Germany and Great Britain, not having been raised in the trial court, could not be considered by the Supreme Court on appeal.

None of the points presenting a federal constitutional question, the petition for writ of error was denied by a unanimous Court. This decision of the Supreme Court on every question was supported by a long line of unquestioned precedents. The core of the whole matter was the maintenance of the fundamental theory of the supremacy of state law in matters of local concern, and that the decision of the highest court of a sovereign state could not be overridden by a federal court unless it clearly appeared that the result of such decision had been to deprive a person of his life, liberty, or property without due process of law. Even the sharpest critics of the ultimate consequences of the Spies trial have never questioned the soundness of the decision of the Supreme Court of the United States in refusing to review the case.

Now only one hope was left—a petition for executive clemency. Governor Richard J. Oglesby was literally deluged with petitions that the sentences be commuted to terms of imprisonment; few suggested pardons. The petitions came from all sorts of people in all walks of life—from leaders in commerce, labor, literature, and the arts. There were also many voices loud in protest against any interference with the sentences, with letters by the thousands from men and women of equal prominence.

On November 10, while an excited public was awaiting the governor's decision, a bomb similar to the one which had been thrown in Haymarket Square was smuggled into Lingg's cell. He exploded it and blew his head off. A few hours later Oglesby commuted the sentences of Fielden and Schwab to life imprisonment, but rejected the pleas on behalf of Spies, Parsons, Fischer, and Engel, who were executed in the early morning of November 11, 1887.

Fielden, Schwab, and Neebe served five years. In November, 1892, John P. Altgeld, a former judge of the Circuit Court of Cook County, was elected governor. One of his first official acts was to announce his intention of reviewing the record of their trial. "If I decide they were innocent," declared Altgeld, "I will pardon them, . . . no matter what happens to my career." His eighteen-thousand-word message was a thorough review of the evidence, couched in language of unrestrained passion. He declared the eight defendants had been "railroaded"; the jury which tried them had been "packed"; their constitutional rights had been violated, improper evidence admitted, erroneous instructions given and proper ones refused, and that Judge Gary had conducted the trial "with a

malicious ferocity . . . unparalleled in history." Altgeld granted all
three prisoners an immediate and unconditional pardon. His fear
of the effect of his act on his career was justified. He was beaten
when he ran for re-election, never again sought public office, and
died a frustrated and broken man.

The trial of the anarchists has continued a subject of active
dispute up to the present. There are those who see in the execution
of Spies and his companions a trial by alleged judicial process
which was in fact a lynching of innocent men under the forms of
law, but controlled by a whipped-up, hysterical public opinion. On
the other hand, there are those who feel that even if Spies or some
one of his co-defendants did not actually hurl the murderous mis-
sile that took seven lives, the act was directly incited by their
inflammatory writings and speeches, and that their prompt conviction and punishment forestalled a reign of anarchy and terror in
Illinois.

There is a geographical rallying point for each group. At the
north end of Union Park in Chicago one can see a weather-beaten
monument commemorating the seven policemen who lost their
lives in line of duty. Farther west, in Waldheim Cemetery in Forest
Park, is a monument as large and as costly as that in Union
Park—a bronze figure of Justice crowning a dying worker with a
wreath of laurel, dedicated to Spies, Parsons, Engel, and Fischer.
Every year on May 4, the anniversary of the Haymarket Riot, the
various police organizations, with appropriate ceremonies, place a
wreath at the foot of the monument in Union Park. Every year just
after November 11, the anniversary of the execution of Spies and
his three associates, a wreath is found on the monument at Waldheim—but who places it there has never been determined, or at
least, if known, has never been published.

HARVEY WISH

was born in Chicago and received his Ph.D. in history from
Northwestern in 1936. He taught at DePaul University, Smith
College and was the Elbert J. Benton Distinguished Professor
at Western Reserve University. He was a Fulbright professor
at the University of Munich, and he had also lectured in Eu-
rope, England, and Hawaii. He has written *George Fitzhugh,
Propagandist of the Old South; Slavery in the South; Con-
temporary America; Readings in Society and Thought; The
American Historian.* He was editor of *Diary of Samuel Sewall.*
Two articles by Dr. Wish appear in this volume. The second,
"The Pullman Strike: A Study in Industrial Warfare," appears
on page 352.

This article first appeared in the *Journal of the Illinois
State Historical Society,* volume 31, number 4 (December
1938), pages 424–448.

GOVERNOR ALTGELD PARDONS THE ANARCHISTS

HARVEY WISH

The Haymarket Affair, America's *cause célèbre* of the eighties,
requires no extensive introduction. It is no longer considered as an
instance of alien violence momentarily transplanted to an American
environment but rather as a chapter of the indigenous eight-hour
movement and the resultant class warfare. During the panic of
1873, particularly in the great railroad strikes of 1877, the labor
issue attained unusual national prominence. With the depression
of 1885–1886, the agitation for shorter hours again reached a
critical stage. The choice of May Day, with its radical European
connotations, for the inauguration of widespread strikes alarmed
employers everywhere. Pinkerton detectives, the industrial hirelings
of that period, found ready employment at this time in investigating alleged "anarchist" plots and in breaking strikes. During
1885–1886, the state militia were repeatedly invoked to deal with
labor disputes in various sections of Illinois. On May 1, 1886, a
general strike of organized workers began in Chicago and other
industrial centers of the country in behalf of the eight-hour day. In
Chicago, where some forty thousand workmen left their tasks,

public attention was directed particularly to the large McCormick Harvester organization on the far west side. When the McCormick officials began to import outside workmen, rioting followed. Patrol wagons, filled with strikers, were sometimes attacked by angry mobs of men and women. Every railroad in the city was crippled, all the freight houses were closed and barred, and most of the industries of Chicago were paralyzed. The situation was tense.

On Monday afternoon, May 3, August Spies, editor of the semi-anarchist labor paper, *Die Arbeiter-Zeitung*, addressed a large meeting of strikers about a quarter of a mile north of McCormick's plant. While he was speaking, about two hundred men left the crowd and ran towards the factory; in about three minutes several shots were heard and detachments of police arrived and opened fire on the fleeing crowd which had remained behind to hear Spies. Five or six of the people were mortally wounded and several times that number hurt. Spies, aroused by the attack, issued circulars calling for "Revenge!" and announcing a meeting for the evening of May 4 at the Haymarket Square. The mayor, Carter H. Harrison, decided to be present but after listening to several innocuous speeches became bored. He noted that the crowd was small and unarmed and finally left after suggesting to Captain Bonfield at the Desplaines Street station that the police reserves be released. Shortly thereafter, a force of 180 policemen under Captains Bonfield and Ward marched upon the meeting demanding its immediate dispersal. At this point something like a miniature rocket rose out of the crowd from the east sidewalk in a line with the police and exploded among the officers. Uniformed men fell on all sides. A bell tolled the riot alarm.

Immediately the press gave vent to a determined lynching sentiment. The police began its anarchist hunt under the terrific pressure of newspaper attacks. Homes were invaded without warrant and ransacked for evidence; suspects were beaten and subjected to the "third degree;" individuals, ignorant of the meaning of socialism and anarchism, were tortured by the police, sometimes bribed as well, to act as witnesses for the state. Eventually the suspects were reduced to eight individuals, Albert Parsons, Samuel Fielden, August Spies, Michael Schwab, Louis Lingg, Oscar Neebe, George Engel, and Adolph Fischer. Only Fielden had been present at the time of the explosion; Parsons and Spies had left some time before; the others were either at home or speaking elsewhere. They were tried jointly for conspiracy, despite the failure to find a chief conspirator or agent. The ensuing trial under Judge Joseph E. Gary, conducted with singular disregard for civil guarantees, merely enacted the judgment rendered by the leading newspapers. All were sentenced to death except Neebe, who, although declared guilty of murder by the jury, was sentenced by Gary to fifteen years' imprisonment. Upon appeal, the Illinois Supreme Court defined socialistic principles as advocating a theft of property; hence the juror was entitled to a prejudice against socialists. Subsequently the United States Supreme Court refused jurisdiction, ruling that no federal question was involved. The strong protest of distinguished liberals of Europe and America to Governor Richard J. Oglesby failed to turn the tide of public hysteria. The Governor's offer to commute the sentences of life imprisonment was spurned by the prisoners, save for Schwab and Fielden; Lingg, soon thereafter, committed suicide. On November 11, 1887, the four condemned men, Parsons, Engel, Fischer, and Spies calmly met their death.

During the years following the execution, the cause of the surviving Haymarket prisoners, Neebe, Schwab, and Fielden, became closely identified with the struggle of labor everywhere for better conditions. Early in the case an Amnesty Association had been organized by George Schilling, later secretary of labor statistics under Governor Altgeld. In Chicago alone, the association gathered 100,000 members, chiefly from trade unionist bodies; by June 1893, there were 375 branch lodges of the organization. Although the intervening administration of Governor Joseph Fifer had proved devoid of results for the prisoners, there were ample grounds for the widespread belief that the new governor, John Peter Altgeld, would act. Schilling initiated an appeal for a monster petition to the governor. Preparations were made for a new descent upon Springfield by an Amnesty Committee consisting of prominent Chicagoans of all classes. Many conservatives now feared the worst.

This movement gained momentum with the adhesion of a large business and professional class element who felt that the prisoners should be pardoned on the ground that they had been sufficiently punished. There was little, if any, desire to gain exoneration for the three men by casting any doubt upon the fairness of the Gary trial itself. Lyman J. Gage, president of the First National Bank of Chicago and later secretary of the treasury in McKinley's cabinet, took a prominent part. He declared to Schilling that the hanging had created a dangerous rift between classes and it was necessary to remove the resentment of the working men who placed the responsibility for the collapse of the eight-hour movement upon the shoulders of the middle class. Another banker, E. S. Dreyer, who admittedly had shared in the hysteria of 1886–1887, proved of great service in the struggle for an executive pardon. The publisher and proprietor of the *Chicago Inter-Ocean,* William Penn Nixon, who was a prominent Republican, became the chairman of the Amnesty Committee. Among other amnesty leaders who acted persistently in behalf of the prisoners were Judge Samuel P. McConnell, Edward Osgood Brown, Clarence Darrow, Judge Murray F. Tuley, Lyman Trumbull, Edward F. Dunne, and William C. Goudy.

At the time of the famous trial of the anarchists, Altgeld, who was then a judge, refrained from comment upon the case, though he sent money and clothing to the distressed families of the defendants. During his election campaign and almost up to the moment of his message, he refused to commit himself as to what he would do regarding the anarchists. A labor delegation which came to see him while he was a candidate for governor was given no definite answer on this matter and when one member proved unpleasantly aggressive he was shown the door. The Republican newspapers, however, pretended to be better informed. The editor of the *Illinois State Journal* declared: "Every vote for John P. Altgeld will be a vote for the pardon of the anarchists in Joliet Penitentiary." Altgeld's remark during the campaign that he could see no harm in anarchists and socialists carrying red flags was bitterly attacked as an indication of the lawless character of the Democratic candidate.

Altgeld's humanitarian ideals were the sole basis for the belief that he would pardon the anarchists. During the late fall of 1891, he had protested against police brutality in the perennial raids to discover anarchist plots. In a letter to the chief of police, Major R. W. McClaughry, Altgeld expressed himself strongly:

> The American people are not prepared to substitute government by police ruffians for government by law. . . . We can not for a moment admit that by simply applying an unpopular or obloquious name to men, whether that name be anarchist or socialist . . . an officer can be justified in depriving men of rights guaranteed by the fundamental law. . . . I will say to you that it will be an evil day for our country when the poor

and the ignorant, misguided though they may be, shall feel that a bullet is the only minister of justice which can right their wrongs, and the conduct of your officers now, like the conduct of certain officers in the spring of '86, will certainly tend to create that feeling and to accelerate its growth.

This protest reveals clearly Altgeld's understanding of the conditions underlying democratic government. Rule by ballot can exist only so long as it is effective in operation; otherwise there remains an undisguised tyranny. Police brutality, fostered in the interests of a united minority, is a preliminary to popular revolt. Altgeld's belief in the possibility of redressing the balance of social inequality by parliamentary methods is the key to much of his life.

Shortly after Altgeld's inauguration, an event occurred which caused a number of thoughtful men to reconsider the entire anarchist trial. On January 19, 1893, the Illinois Supreme Court, in the case of *The People* v. *Coughlin*, a trial for murder, ruled that a juror who had read about a case and formed an opinion that the defendant was guilty, was ineligible to act. In the anarchist case, that same court had decided otherwise. Justice Magruder, who delivered the majority opinion in the case of *Spies* v. *Illinois*, now declared that if the court was right in the Coughlin case, it was wrong in the anarchist case. To a good lawyer like Altgeld, the inference was plain: a sound legal argument on irrefutable grounds could be built up for the three men in Joliet Penitentiary.

Meanwhile the amnesty group began to feel impatient and wondered whether they had been deceived in Altgeld. Clarence Darrow went to see the Governor and told him that his friends were growing restless and disappointed; something should be done at once. Darrow further assured him that the pardon "had been generally asked for by all the people, that it would not even create hostility toward him," and that no one could see any excuse for waiting. Darrow wrote that Altgeld deliberately and calmly replied:

> Go tell your friends that when I am ready I will act. I don't know how I will act, but I will do what I think is right. . . . But don't deceive yourself: If I conclude to pardon those men it will not meet with the approval that you expect; let me tell you that from that day I will be a dead man.

When the secretary of the Amnesty Association wrote to Altgeld concerning the pardon after his first month in office, the governor replied that he had been unable to give it any attention.

The activity of the pardon-seekers had impelled Judge Joseph E. Gary to review the case for the *Century Magazine*. In this he added nothing new beyond what had already been said by the state's attorney, Julius S. Grinnell. The anarchists, he declared, were guilty of conspiracy to murder, not because they had specially instructed the bomb-thrower, but for the reason that they had advocated this course by a general address to readers and hearers. This article occasioned considerable comment and was considered by some to be in poor taste, if not deficient in logic. It influenced to some extent the bitter note sounded by Altgeld in the pardon message.

The task of reviewing the monumental records of the Gary trial was a stupendous one. A greater lawyer than Altgeld would have hesitated to undertake it. The governor himself was keenly aware of his limitations and looked about for some prominent lawyer to prepare the arguments for the prisoners. He sent his secretary of labor statistics, George Schilling, who acted as the governor's personal representative, to Chicago in order to sound out Lyman Trumbull on the matter. Trumbull, who had once been Lincoln's close associate and had since enjoyed a brilliant national career, had signed Judge McConnell's petition in 1887 requesting a commutation of sentence for the condemned men. He had declared to McConnell that the accused did not have a fair trial. Schilling was received hospitably and when the discussion came around to the trial, Trumbull compared it with a New England witch hunt. Following such an encouraging response, Schilling asked if he would go to Springfield to present the case for a pardon before the governor, but Trumbull refused to undertake the task.

When the emissary returned to report his failure, Altgeld asked him what he surmised to be the real reason for Trumbull's rejection. To this Schilling suggested the fact that such lawyers owed their livelihood to corporations. Altgeld paused, and began pacing the floor thoughtfully, gazing intently at the portraits of early Illinois statesmen which covered the walls of the Executive Mansion. He stopped before a picture of Lincoln, staring at it with his hands burrowed in his pockets. Schilling watched the scene quietly and then remarked: "I would like to help you, but the corporations have intimidated the great lawyers. We ought to drop this case if you can't handle it yourself." This spurred Altgeld into a determined reply, "We don't need them, Schilling! We don't need them!"

The heavy research work on the anarchist case began at once. Affidavits were collected, newspapers were carefully scanned, hearsay statements were cautiously validated by other proofs, individuals concerned in the trial were interviewed. McConnell and Schilling worked hard to check upon this material. During a conversation with McConnell held in the governor's library, Altgeld, pointing to a stack of great volumes, remarked: "There is the record of the anarchist case. I have read every word of it and I have decided to pardon all three of the men and I want to read you my message." The judge criticized it as "too much Altgeld and not enough governor in it." He objected to the criticism of Judge Gary as entirely too personal. Altgeld agreed and promised to change it, but the pressure of subsequent affairs prevented his alteration of the message.[1]

When the governor's course became evident to the secretary of state, William H. Hinrichsen, the latter asked, "Do you think it good policy to pardon them? I do not." To this Altgeld replied, "It is right!" and struck his desk emphatically with his fist. Later, after the message had been delivered, he remarked to Hinrichsen, "You are younger than I and will live to see my pardon of the anarchists justified."

Shortly before the pardon message was delivered, the press learned of Altgeld's intention. There prevailed a tense atmosphere of expectation in many quarters since it was understood that the subject would be dealt with in no orthodox fashion. On June 26, 1893, Altgeld's message was given to the press where it was in many instances reproduced in full.

As the case has already been discussed, it will be sufficient to note Altgeld's specific contributions and his basic reasons for pardoning Fielden, Neebe, and Schwab. After a primary statement of the events of May 4, 1886, he outlined five aspects of the trial which deserved particular attention:

1. Was the jury packed?
2. Were the jurors legally competent?
3. Does the proof show guilt as charged in the indictment?

---

[1] Waldo R. Browne, Altgeld's biographer, states that McConnell was in error regarding the Gary criticism because—so he claims—Gary's article had not appeared at the time of McConnell's interview with Altgeld. This is a curious correction since Browne himself gives the date of the interview as "a few weeks before the pardons were issued" and the *Century* article, as he must have been aware, had already appeared in April, 1893.

4. Is there any case against the defendant, Neebe?

5. Did the judge grant a fair trial?

He refused to consider the argument that the defendants had been sufficiently punished. If the men were guilty then this was no case for executive interference. "Government must defend itself," he declared.

Proceeding to the jurors in the case, he showed that their names had not been drawn from a box containing many hundreds of them as the law contemplated. Instead an exceptional procedure of allowing the bailiff absolute power to select a jury had been followed. Such a course had been sustained only in cases in which it did not appear that either side suffered thereby. In support of his assertion that the bailiff wilfully selected a large number of prejudiced jurors in order to exhaust the defense attorney's challenges, Altgeld cited the affidavit of Otis S. Favor, a Chicago merchant. The governor then pointed out certain evidence that showed collusion between the state's attorney, if not the judge himself, and Otis Favor, the affiant. When the charge was made in court that the bailiff, Henry L. Ryce, had packed the jury, Grinnell obtained Favor's refusal to make an affidavit which the defendants could use upon this point, and Judge Gary refused to intervene despite the fact that it was known Favor would testify if compelled to do so by subpoena. As a result, Favor's affidavit was not before the Illinois Supreme Court at the time it reviewed the case.

Regarding the competency of the jurors, Altgeld quoted the recent decision of the Illinois high court in *The People* v. *Coughlin,* known as the Cronin case. The judge, delivering the opinion of the majority, had made the following declaration:

> It is difficult to see how, after a juror has avowed a fixed and settled opinion as to the prisoner's guilt, a court can be legally satisfied of the truth of his answer that he can render a fair and impartial verdict. . . . Under such circumstances it is idle to inquire of the jurors whether they can return just and impartial verdicts. . . . Nor can it be said that instructions from the court would correct the bias of the jurors who swear they incline in favor of one of the litigants.

Altgeld showed that the bias in the testimony of the anarchist case was more extreme than in the Cronin case.

When he dealt with the nature of the proof itself, he could not refrain from several caustic remarks concerning the failure of the prosecution to show any connection between the defendants and the bomb-thrower. He attributed the apparently seditious utterances of the accused to the excitement of men who felt they had been wronged. According to his theory the bomb had been thrown by someone seeking personal revenge, particularly against Captain Bonfield and his police. This was supported by letters, affidavits, and newspaper quotations showing the extreme brutality of Bonfield against laboring men and his indiscriminate clubbing of strikers and spectators.[2] Even Michael J. Schaack, a police captain, who was far from tender in his relations to strikers, wrote that Bonfield's course was brutal and unnecessary. If the theory of the prosecution was correct that the bomb had been the outcome of a conspiracy, reasoned Altgeld, then several bombs, not one, should have been thrown.

Regarding the alleged prevalence of anarchist plots, the governor introduced some highly important evidence to the contrary. With the cooperation of Captain Frederick Ebersold, who had been chief of police at the time of the Haymarket Affair, Altgeld was able to validate a significant interview of the former published in the *Chicago Daily News* on May 10, 1889:

> It was my policy to quiet matters down as soon as possible after the 4th of May. The general unsettled state of things was an injury to Chicago.
> On the other hand, Captain Schaack wanted to keep things stirring. He wanted bombs to be found here, there, all around, everywhere. I thought people would lie down and sleep better if they were not afraid that their homes would be blown to pieces any minute. But this man Schaack, this little boy who must have glory or his heart would be broken, wanted none of that policy. Now here is something that the public does not know. After we got the anarchist societies broken up, Schaack wanted to send out men to again organize new societies right away. You see what this would do. He wanted to keep the thing boiling—keep himself prominent before the public. . . .

---

[2] At the trial Barton Simonson, a traveling salesman, testified concerning Captain Bonfield: "I spoke to Captain Bonfield about the trouble at McCormick's [May 3, 1886] and he said that the greatest trouble the police had in dealing with the socialists was that they had their women and children with them at the meeting, so that the police could not get them. He said he wished he could get a crowd of about 3,000 of them together without their women and children and he would make short work of them."

> After I heard all that, I began to think there was, perhaps,
> not so much to all this anarchist business as they
> claimed. . . .[3]

This amazing evidence clears up a number of points in connection with the case. Though Altgeld did not include another matter closely related to this in his message, he knew that Schaack and others like him were being paid by worried citizens to watch the alleged anarchists of Chicago.[4] The opportunity for a police officer to obtain promotion in this manner is obvious.[5]

The case against Fielden, as Altgeld demonstrated, was based on the weakest of legal grounds. Police witnesses had stated that Fielden had urged his hearers to attack the police and had drawn a revolver, firing at them. These witnesses were mutually contradictory on these points. Newspaper reporters, who were closer to the scene, denied the truth of these allegations. Judge Gary had written to Governor Oglesby that Fielden "was more a misguided enthusiast than a criminal conscious of the horrible nature and the effect of his teachings and of his responsibility therefore;" he added that Fielden had a natural love of justice and in his private life was honest, industrious, and peaceable. The state's attorney, Grinnell, during a conference at the home of Lyman Gage in the fall of 1887, declared that he had serious doubts whether Fielden ever had a revolver. As for Schwab, the evidence against him was even less and his conduct during the trial had created a favorable impression upon the state's attorney, who regarded him as a pliant tool of more designing people.

If the matter were not so tragic, the case against Neebe would be laughable indeed. His two dollars' worth of stock in the *Arbeiter-*

---

[3] Captain Ebersold, though a German himself, seems to have taken a bitter dislike to the anarchists of his nationality. When Spies was brought before him, he not only insulted the prisoner coarsely but beat him up until Bonfield (!) intervened. Ebersold was finally induced to write out an account exposing the anarchist scares as fakes. This was achieved through the efforts of Judge McConnell.

[4] Two months later Altgeld declared: "I have been informed at different times during the last seven or eight years, that some wealthy business men of Chicago were kept in such a state of uneasiness by this anarchist talk, that they were induced, from time to time, to pay money to these fellows [the police] for the ostensible purpose of watching the maneuvers of a class of people who in reality had no existence."

[5] Captain Schaack had played a leading part in obtaining the evidence for the prosecution. He claimed the chief credit for the final conviction. For a short time he even posed as an authority upon anarchists whom he describes in his amazing book, *Anarchy and Anarchists* (Chicago, 1889).

Zeitung and his connection with its management on the day *after* the Haymarket Affair were the only bits of evidence against him. According to the letters of Mayor Harrison and Frederick S. Winston, the corporation counsel at the time, Grinnell had declared to them in the courtroom that he did not think he had a case against Neebe and that he wished to dismiss him, but was discouraged by his associates who feared that this step might influence the jury in favor of the other defendants. While the others had been accused of using seditious language this could not be said of Neebe.

In his conclusion, Altgeld paid his respects to Gary and referred to the recent article written by the latter as "full of venom." He spoke of the judge's "ferocity of subserviency" and compared him with Lord Jeffries. Altgeld admitted the personal nature of these charges but asserted they were borne out by the record of the trial and the papers before him. He concluded with an absolute pardon for Samuel Fielden, Oscar Neebe, and Michael Schwab.

Brand Whitlock, who was then employed by the secretary of state, was asked to prepare three pardons with the official seal of the state. They were turned over to E. S. Dreyer, who had been active in the amnesty movement. At 11:20 P.M. that day, the prison gates opened for the newly freed men.[6] Whitlock remarked to the governor, "Well, the storm will break now." Altgeld replied with an apparent pretense of indifference, "Oh, yes, I was prepared for that. It was merely doing right."

It would have been hard enough for the newspapers to accept a pardon on the grounds that the men had suffered enough. But for the Governor to override judge, jury, and public opinion, and to declare that the men had been unjustly tried—that was too much. Even some of the amnesty people were appalled. The *Chicago Inter-Ocean*, whose editor-publisher was a chairman of the Amnesty Committee, wrote that Altgeld's attack on Gary and Bonfield was without excuse and "positively outrageous." The *Chicago Times*, a Democratic journal which had been sympathetic to the

---

[6] At this time Voltairine DeCleyre wrote a poem commemorating Altgeld's message:

> A grating of the doors, and three poor men,
> Helpless and hated, having naught to give,
> Come from their long-sealed tombs, look up and live,
> And thank this Man that they are free again!
> And he—to all the world this man dares say,
> "Curse as you will! I have been just this day."

pardoning of the anarchists, scolded the governor for going beyond an act of executive clemency, and declared that it was not his prerogative "to pry into the motives" of judge, jurymen, prosecutors, and witnesses. The editor charitably concluded that Altgeld had erred on the side of mercy. Scarcely a journal, outside of the ranks of labor, was willing to go beyond an icy condonation of the pardon message. The majority regarded the arguments used as an attack upon the sanctity of judicial processes. Americans have been loath to apply everyday standards of conduct to those sheltered by the judicial ermine.

If the friends of executive clemency were dissatisfied, the opponents, who objected to any form of pardon, were virulently hostile. The *Chicago Tribune,* characteristically a pioneer in such matters, led the outcry. "Never," said its editor, "did the governor of an American state—with the exception of those southern governors who issued secession proclamations—put his name to so revolutionary and infamous a document." On the next day, the editor, noting the widespread denunciation of Altgeld with satisfaction, remarked that "the political remains" of Altgeld would draw the salary of governor for forty-two months longer. The *Chicago Herald,* the organ of the Walsh Democratic machine, published a severe condemnation of the pardon message. The editor of the *New York Tribune* professed to believe that Altgeld's pardon was evidence of a plot to deliver the criminal and anarchist elements over to the Illinois Democrats; the approval of several New York anarchists was cited as proof. In Milwaukee, where labor difficulties closely paralleled those of Chicago, the *Sentinel* feared that Altgeld's message would breed more anarchists "than all the speeches and writings of the men he had released." The *Washington Evening Star* put up a mock political ballot for 1896 with Altgeld for president on the platform, "We are 'agin' the Government." The *Chicago Tribune* collected a page of masterpieces of vituperation drawn from sixteen Illinois newspapers and fifty-three papers outside the state. In these editorials, the vocabulary of opprobrium attained new levels.

Powerful individuals and organizations joined in the hue and cry. Justice David J. Brewer of the United States Supreme Court attacked Altgeld in an address delivered at Woodstock, Connecticut. Choosing as his text, "Economic Individualism," he pointed to Altgeld as its arch-enemy in a struggle comparable to the Civil

War. "Is Governor Altgeld," he asked, "waiting to be the Jefferson Davis of tomorrow?" Later, in the campaign of 1896, Theodore Roosevelt was to declare that "Altgeld's hands were dyed in blood and [he] had condoned murder." One Illinois club rejected Altgeld's application for membership. Another attempted to expel him. Many were certain that Altgeld had committed political suicide.

A small band of liberals drawn from Europe and America wrote letters of heartfelt gratitude to Altgeld, congratulating him on his courageous action. Labor bodies passed highly eulogistic resolutions, commending the support of the governor to their cause. These were the saving remnant, for the majority stood aloof, inarticulate or frankly hostile. One friend of Altgeld wrote to him:

> It is a sad commentary upon the so-called liberalism and intelligence of the American people that millions still deliberately shut their eyes and stop their ears to keep from being convinced. The prejudices of the ignorant, aroused and steadfastly nourished by a corrupt press, are not easily overcome.

Once again the *Chicago Tribune* lent fuel to the denunciations of the message by printing an alleged exposé of the personal motives which influenced Altgeld in pardoning the anarchists and in his attacks upon Judge Gary. This tale, widely repeated, was evidently believed by many and therefore deserves some notice. It appeared under the caption, "Altgeld Displays His Venom." During April, 1889, the appellate court of which Judge Gary was a member, had set aside a judgment of the circuit court of Cook County which awarded Altgeld, then judge of the superior court, the sum of $26,494. The appellate judges, Garnett, Gary, and Moran, had attempted to sweeten their decision by declaring that the course pursued by Altgeld "was fair, open, and free from any grounds for censure."

This attempt to give him a "certificate of character" was added insult. Altgeld had then replied to the judges in a long letter protesting against the decision as a "moral outrage" and that it was an example of their setting aside settled questions on technical grounds. At no time did Altgeld regard judges as a class apart whom it was censurable taste, if not unpatriotic, to criticize.

The *Tribune* declared that since Judge Gary was the only one of the three judges now on the bench, Altgeld had sought to "get even with him" by pardoning the anarchists and attacking him personally. The editor remarked that any judge "even a poor judge like Altgeld" should have had a greater sense of propriety than he showed in addressing a letter such as he did to brother-judges.

Altgeld, in keeping with his policy of silence beneath attack, refused to comment upon these charges except to say that they were ridiculous. While it is possible that Altgeld's attack upon Gary in the message was partly due to some incident such as the *Tribune* letter indicated, the pardon of the anarchists cannot be attributed to such narrow motivation. Altgeld's career and philosophy of justice cannot be reconciled with any theory that he acted here on any save the highest motives. His remarks concerning Gary seem justified by an examination of the court record.[7]

To the newspapermen of Chicago and New York who asked him for his reaction to this abuse, Altgeld was defiant. He declared to a *Tribune* reporter: "I have done what I thought was right, and if my action was right, it will stand in the judgment of the people. . . . It is a noticeable fact that my critics employ abuse and in no case reason." When a New York reporter asked him how he was enduring the criticism of the papers, he laughed and said: "Let them pitch in and give me the devil if they want to; they could not cut through my hide in three weeks with an axe." He derided the talk of anarchist plots in Illinois and insisted that there never had been fifty anarchists in the whole state. The stories were the products of pseudo-detectives who were financed by wealthy business men.[8] Later in life, when asked whether he had ever regretted his pardon of the anarchists, he replied emphatically:

> Never! Never! If I had the matter to act upon again to-morrow, I'd do it over again. . . . I knew that in every civilized land, and especially in the United States, would ring out curses loud and bitter against me for what I did. I saw my duty and I did it. There was no evidence to convict those men. . . . The trial was a farce.

---

[7] Such individuals as Jane Addams and Brand Whitlock have stated in their writings that they felt that the attack on Gary marred the pardon message. Even Clarence Darrow, who previously referred to Gary as "the Lord High Executioner," held a brief for the trial judge, stating that the latter labored under unusually difficult circumstances and that he was a "pretty good fellow."

[8] The *Chicago Herald* of Jan. 4, 1892, printed an account of a meeting of 300 prominent citizens who met shortly after the Haymarket Affair and subscribed $115,000 to the police to stamp out anarchist plots and pledged $100,000 annually for the continuation of such work. This was paid until 1891. The cessation of payment inspired new anarchist raids on the part of the police.

It is perhaps unnecessary to add that Altgeld suffered severely from the journalistic abuse and general malignment of his motives. To Mrs. Altgeld he remarked that it might not be long before the Altgelds took up their abode by the wayside. He had no illusions as to the effect of the message upon his career; nevertheless, he attempted to put his case before the public by the circulation of his famous message. With Schilling and Henry D. Lloyd, he arranged to distribute some fifty thousand copies to help the reform Democratic element. Trade unionist and populist support came readily. Biographies of the governor, together with the message, were printed in friendly newspapers. Schilling prepared to organize a bureau for the systematic distribution of the pardon message. Altgeld's correspondence shows how this publicity made many converts to his cause.

That the governor's popularity had not been wholly dissipated was indicated on "Illinois Day," August 24, 1893, at the Chicago World's Fair. His arrival aroused general enthusiasm. During the afternoon, when he prepared to receive the citizens of the state in the main court under the dome, crowds poured in to shake hands with him. At the doors people fought to gain admission; a solid mass pressed about the square "as strong as the rock of Gibraltar." There was no place to move.

In the fall elections, the local Republican machine decided to capitalize on the Gary issue. Judge Joseph E. Gary was persuaded to run as a Republican candidate for a sixth term as judge of the superior court in a campaign that was obviously intended to undermine Altgeld. The editor of the *Chicago Tribune* declared, "A vote for Gary is a repudiation of Altgeld and the pardon message." The issue, as stated by this journal, was whether the judiciary was dependent upon the executive power. During a Gary meeting held on October 25, a former governor, Richard Oglesby, took up the cudgels in behalf of the judge and described him as above partiality or prejudice. He gave an enthusiastic description of the city's fight against anarchy. One judge at this meeting referred to Altgeld as a man who had "disgraced our government." A special verse for this occasion was sung, "Pardon Altgeld has got to hide away."

This challenge was accepted by the governor, who took charge of the opposition at his office in the Unity Building. Copies of his message were distributed among workmen. Henry D. Lloyd published an open letter to Gary, which was enthusiastically received by the liberal elements but appeared too late for adequate circulation. Clarence Darrow assisted Altgeld in reprinting this letter in various Chicago newspapers. Samuel Fielden, one of the pardoned men, spoke at the Sunset Club to assist the reform Democrats. The local machine of his party saw no profit in following Altgeld's leadership by putting up good candidates, but preferred to support personal choices. Thus John Barton Payne, the able Democratic candidate, failed to receive support from this element. On election day, Gary won by a vote of 78,912 to 73,777. It was not a clear-cut victory, but the Republican newspapers interpreted it as a rebuke for Altgeld.

After the anarchist pardon, partisan newspapers attacked Altgeld's policy in the granting of pardons under any circumstances; they referred to him as John "Pardon" Altgeld. Immediately after the June pardon, Brand Whitlock approached the governor with the papers concerning a young man in the Joliet Penitentiary who was dying of tuberculosis. His mother petitioned that he might die at home. Without looking at the papers, Altgeld shook his head: "No, no, I will not pardon any more. The people are opposed to it; they do not believe in mercy; they love revenge; they want the prisoners punished to the bitterest extremity." Later, he apologized for his remarks and asked for the papers. He was told that the boy had just died. The effect of such an incident upon the sensitive mind of Altgeld can easily be imagined.

The famous pardon message of 1893 was but one of a series of decisive blows that Altgeld struck in behalf of the common man. Despite the overwhelming indictment of the governor in the national press, a large inarticulate group of humbler citizens intuitively recognized their champion. It would be a mistake to conclude that Altgeld became a political cipher after 1893. In the councils of his party he became increasingly dominant and, despite bipartisan opposition, succeeded in enacting a program of state reform that attracted national attention. His party leadership enabled him to write the notable Democratic platform of 1896 and only the constitutional technicality of his German birth prevented his nomination for president. In that election, although defeated, he secured a gubernatorial vote considerably in excess of Bryan's in Illinois. It had been necessary for his opponents to employ wholesale corruption at the polls in order to insure the defeat of the Springfield "Anarchist." For labor and its allies the deed of 1893 went far to obliterate the defeat of 1886.

JANE ADDAMS

was born in Cedarville, Illinois, and received the A.B. degree
from Rockford College in 1881. In 1888, with Ellen Gates
Starr, she opened Hull House on the west side of Chicago.
Her progressive activity in the field of social work as head
resident of Hull House and her never-ending interest in peace
and individual freedom brought her international fame. In
1931 she shared the Nobel Peace Prize with Nicolas Murray
Butler. Perhaps her best known books were *Twenty Years at
Hull House* and *The Second Twenty Years at Hull House*.

This article appeared first in the *Transactions of the Illinois State Historical Society* for 1906, pages 162–171.

SOCIAL SETTLEMENTS IN ILLINOIS

JANE ADDAMS

As I understand it, I was asked to speak of the rise and growth of
the social settlement movement in the state of Illinois. It makes
one feel very old, to be considered an historic document, as it were!
We have been accustomed so long to think of the social settlements
as one of the pioneer forces, at least in the matter of their organization and social advancement, that it comes to me with something
of a shock to realize that we are sixteen years old, and have for
better or worse, made our history in the state.

Albert Shaw, who perhaps more than any other man in America
has studied the historic growth and development of cities, said last
year, at the St. Louis Exposition, that in a very real sense the
European cities were as "new" as the American cities, that London
and Paris, the cities on the Rhine, even St. Petersburg and Moscow,
were new in that they had little to do with the mediæval cities
which lay back of them, and that they were faced by problems
which were the result of the present industrial organization of
cities. These new cities began with the industrial revolution at the
end of the eighteenth century. People are coming in from the
country in all directions and living in great masses because they
are being brought together in response to the newer methods of
business, and newer methods of manufacturing. There is the same
social problem all over the world, to be found in these cities of

industrial origin. The social life of these cities was made more difficult from the fact that no one was looking out for their social organization. The politicians who were responsible for the charters, and for the administration of the laws, were of course more or less alert for changes in governmental machinery, but no one was doing the same thing for those institutions upon which the social life of the cities might develop. We know, of course, that Moscow has grown more rapidly during the last twenty-five years than New York, that Berlin has grown more rapidly than Chicago. We like to say that one reason affairs are so bad in American cities, as we have to admit they are, is because of their rapid growth, until we consider that other cities, all over the world, have grown quite as rapidly, and more rapidly, than American cities; and what is needed is groups of people who shall make it their effort to find out wherein the cities lack, publish the facts and make clear the situation in the more crowded quarters, where the lack of social organization is most keenly felt, that the citizens as a whole may see to it that needed changes are brought about.

Now, something of this sort, I take it, a settlement group undertakes to do. A group of people move into a quarter of the city which lacks many things, because the people are newly emigrated to this country, because they are bound down with the necessity of earning their daily bread during the long hours of work, and have very little leisure or intelligence to give to the larger social needs, because they do not intend to live long in that part of the city, and are trying to save money in order to pull out and move somewhere else, and so take little interest in it—for a dozen of reasons perhaps, certain quarters of the city fail to keep up with the rest, and they tend to pull back in the general progress. Now settlements move into such a quarter consciously, meaning to give to it their very best efforts in the way of investigation, and in the way of healing, and more than anything else perhaps hoping to uncover resources of civic power and ability in the neighborhood itself.

When I speak of the first settlement in Illinois, I am obliged to speak of Hull House first because it was founded first, and, though it sounds somewhat conceited, I suppose chronology is very important with an historical association.

Hull House was opened in the fall of 1889. My friend, Miss Starr and myself discovered this old house on the corner of Polk and

Halsted streets, in the Nineteenth Ward of Chicago, just about a mile from the post office building.

In every large city, right back of the business quarter, there is a tendency for people to gather who do casual work. The men who have intermittent work, in unloading cars, or on the docks, the men who do janitor service in the large downtown buildings, the men who carry packages, and the teamsters and deliverymen, all naturally wish to live near their business, simply because it is irregular, and therefore get right back of the business quarter. So that every city, so far as I know, London, and the European cities, and the American cities, all have this quarter of poorer people adjacent to the business districts. In such a district property is held provisionally because people are sure business is coming in there, and so there is no need of making improvements, and as a result of this, paving, lighting, and sewerage do not advance, because it is considered a mere matter of a few years until the business interests occupy it. The whole situation from the civic standpoint is low. Such conditions prevail in a general way in the eastern half of the Nineteenth Ward, and the three other river wards which lie back of the business quarter of Chicago. There were only two of us to begin with. Gradually other people came, and now the settlement numbers thirty-four residents, with perhaps one hundred people who come once a week for evening clubs or classes. The average attendance in a winter week is seven thousand people, counting those who belong to something, in the way of clubs, classes or social organizations. We have a group of buildings which have developed year after year, so that we now have a litle group of ten buildings, one containing the gymnasium and shops, another being the children's house, a third the woman's club building, and so forth.

I hardly know where we can attach ourselves to the history of the state, save perhaps in one or two investigations which may have aided legislation. After we had lived there a very little while we became much impressed with the evils of the sweatshop system. In 1889 there were no laws regulating the sweatshop industries, and practically no factory law at that time in the state of Illinois, although Illinois stood third among the states of the union in the point of its manufactured products. We still had a fiction that Illinois was solely an agricultural state. There was no child labor law, except one pertaining to children in mines, and another which had no method of enforcing a penalty, and no officers to administer it. We found children of all ages going to work whenever it suited the convenience of their parents, and many of them coming to grief from premature labor. We found many newly imported Italians and others working in sweatshops for phenomenally low wages, with no regulations as to the sanitary conditions under which they were working. We took up the agitation naturally along this line of the most glaring evils. Mrs. Kelley, who at that time lived in the house, received a commission from the State Bureau of Labor to make an investigation into the sweatshops. It ended in a committee being appointed from the Illinois Legislature in the winter of 1891–92, to go into the subject more thoroughly, and their report finally resulted in the first real factory law of the state of Illinois, which went into operation July 1, 1893, and Mrs. Kelley was appointed the first factory inspector. Mrs. Stevens was her deputy and there were twelve inspectors. We can, I think, claim some credit for Hull House, though of course many other forces joined the agitation, for the passage of this first law which attempted to regulate the sweating system. The law has since been simplified into a full-grown factory law, which compares favorably with that of older states.

We can also claim a little credit for bringing to light, from time to time, some of the facts connected with child labor. It seems so easy, when one does not know the children, to assume it is a good thing for a child to go to work early. In the country it is a good thing for the child perhaps, with a variety of employment and under healthy conditions. But in a city, with long hours and monotonous work, it is a very different matter. We have been able to trace the lives of children, year after year, and to follow out little histories which have proved very convincing, in the matter of child labor agitation. One year, in connection with the municipal lodging house in Chicago, we found many tramps who were worn out at the age of seventeen or eighteen, because they had gone to work too early. I remember one boy, dying of tuberculosis, who seemed to have worked very steadily from the time he was nine. He had worked in Pittsburgh, I am happy to say, not in Illinois, until he was thirteen. He then contracted typhoid fever and made a poor recovery, after which he "laid off steady work" and began to go around with shows, trying to get some of the pleasure denied him in young boyhood. He could not endure this sort of life long, and he died with tuberculosis at the age of seventeen. That sort of history can be duplicated over and over again if one follows the children who take the strength which should go into growth and put it into premature labor. I instance these things to show the service a settlement may perform in the way of getting accurate information in regard to its neighbors.

John Morly says that social progress must always depend upon the initiative of groups of people who are touched with the unimproved condition of things and who make it their business to appeal to public sentiment as a whole, concerning that unimproved condition. When the public is aroused and understands the situation that it is a mere matter of time until conditions will improve.

We have done some investigation for the United States Labor Bureau, and for the United States Department of Agriculture. One such investigation was concerning the food of the Italians. We discovered Italians were eating foods not at all adapted to a cold climate, and were paying very high prices for imported foods; because no one had initiated them into the foods they could buy more cheaply, and which would suit their changed conditions better. I could name several other investigations, but this is but one side of settlement activity.

I have said little of the philanthropic, the educational or of the more strictly social side of the settlement for perhaps in a state meeting these broader issues are more germane.

Hull House was followed by a settlement established by the Northwestern University in 1891. Mr. Charles Zeublin, whom many of you know as a university extension lecturer, was a resident there, and hoped to provide a center from which the students of Northwestern might test their moral enthusiasms and sociological theories. It has grown rapidly, and although it lived for ten years in rented buildings, it is now housed in a very charming building of its own, built in 1901.

The Maxwell Street Settlement was established by a group of Jewish young men, largely graduates of Harvard, who had been interested in the settlements in the East. In 1903, the year in which there was a great influx of immigrants among the Russian Jews, they went into the midst of the Russian Jewish quarter. The Baron de Hirsch fund, part of which was spent in Chicago, seemed utterly inadequate to keep the immigrants from actual distress through their first months of experience in their adopted country. The settlement tried to assist them after that first period of adjustment, and to induct them into the civic and industrial side of American life. It has had a very vigorous life and is about to finish a new house.

The Forward Movement is a settlement opened in 1903 in the ward next to Hull House. It grew out of the efforts of Dr. Gray and his brother. The former had a very large dispensary practice among the casual-labor men, who are now cared for largely in the municipal lodging house, but at that time they had no free lodging place except the police stations. I well recall the impressive funeral service on the death of Dr. Gray, which was attended by hundreds of these men, who are not quite tramps, but are so unskilled they are only drawn into the industrial system at the times of the year when there is plenty of work to do, and they are sure to encounter a precarious living for some weeks at least out of every year. His brother, who is a Methodist minister, has developed the nucleus of Dr. Gray's work into the settlement called The Forward Movement. Among other activities they conduct large fresh air work every summer at Saugatuck Park on the other side of Lake Michigan. They are very hospitable and all the settlements send people there. It has developed into something between a summer school and a fresh air camp. The crippled children from the public schools are sent there every year.

The Chicago Commons was opened in 1894. I am sure many of you know of Dr. Graham Taylor, and of the fine work that is being carried on at Chicago Commons. He came to Chicago from the East, as a professor of sociology in the Chicago Theological Seminary. He insisted from the first that the young men under his charge must know the city, and become familiar with the poorer quarters, maintaining that it was more or less a disgrace to the Protestant ministry that while many churches were established in the comfortable quarters, but little religious provision was made by the Protestant churches for the poorest quarters of the city. He finally established a settlement where he could carry on more thoroughly his careful study of the industrial quarters and their needs. The Commons has been no mean factor, I think you will all agree with me, in the civic life of Chicago. Dr. Taylor himself has been a very active member of the Municipal Voters' League. One election at least they were able to turn in favor of a good alderman, as against a man with a reputation for corruption; and they have had a definite effect not only upon the civic and political life of their neighborhood but of the city.

They have also for many years held "free floor discussions." As you know, in Chicago there are people of various social beliefs. To my mind nothing is better than to get a very radical socialist up against a very radical individualist or a very radical single taxer. The only way you can modify a man who is radical in his social opinions is to bring him in contact with some one who is very radical in another direction. The ordinary person who is not convinced of anything very much can never modify the radical, and real modification comes only through clash of opinion. Dr. Taylor, I think, would agree that his free floor discussions, and at one time we had something of the same sort at Hull House, are very valuable factors in the development and modification of social thought. Workingmen are accustomed to a sharp give and take. While their discussions are quite animated, they seldom have any real animosity, although the listening public is often misled by the active discussions.

I am giving these social settlements, as you will note, in their chronological order. The University of Chicago established a settlement the same year as The Commons, in 1894, in the southwest corner of the Stock Yards District, at what they call "The back door of the stock yards." Their fortunes have been identified very largely with the large group of people who work in the stock yards, who are composed at different times of varying immigrants. The Irish and German are being pushed out by the Italians and they in turn by the Lithuanians at present, and numbers of people from the southeastern part of Europe, with a large sprinkling of Greeks and Syrians. A group of people with Miss McDowell as head resident have lived there during ten years and have been closely identified with the fortunes of their neighbors. The Sociological Department of the University of Chicago has made some studies there. The settlement has seen at least two groups of labor organizations rise and fall in the stock yards. They were able to give some very substantial service to the situation during the stock yards strike a year ago. A settlement does not take sides in a labor difficulty, neither does it desert its friends when they are in the midst of a labor trouble; and I think Miss McDowell had the respect and the good will of both sides in the very bitter controversy in the stock yards, from the fact that she was able to stand somewhat as a third party during that long and trying contest. As you will note, I am speaking of these settlements in a most superficial way, as there is not time to talk of them in detail, and I must assume that you know that all of them have a certain round of educational and social activities which I do not mention in each case.

The Eli Bates House was opened in 1895. It was a settlement on Goose Island in the northern part of the city. It was started years ago as an industrial school, by Mr. Eli Bates, and was known as the Elm Street Industrial School, but was re-organized as a settlement in 1895. They found, among other things, that the Irish boys of the neighborhood formed themselves into street gangs, through sheer lack of anything to interest them. By giving them industrial work and by making another side of life dramatic and interesting, they were performing a real civic service to that part of the city. They have lately received a gift of a beautiful boys' club building and the settlement is developing in many directions. When I touch on the boys' side of the work more than on another, it is not because the other activities are lacking.

Fellowship House was started by All Souls' Church the same year, gathering around a visiting nurse work, although it is now doing a general settlement work.

Neighborhood House was started by Mrs. Van Der Vaart in 1896, and has been from the start largely managed and financed by the immediate neighborhood. They are cooperating now in a very interesting way with the adjacent small parks. The South Side Park Commissioners have opened twelve small parks which are equipped with park houses. These are supplied with baths, gymnasiums, lecture halls, and rooms for general social purposes. The settlements are most happy to turn their energies into cooperating with such an undertaking and to be identified with these larger public measures. No settlement wants to build up a big institution of its own, but is glad to turn over as much as possible to public bodies. At Hull House, for instance, we used to have public baths. When the Health Department opened a bath within a block of the house, we were only too happy to turn all our bathers over there. We used to have a reading room in the house, until the public library authorities became convinced it was beneficial to have one in that neighborhood, when they opened a permanent one within two blocks of the house. For ten years we have managed a playground in connection with Hull House.

We have it still, but we hope next year the West Park Commissioners will open a play-ground, so we may turn the children over to them, and they will be able to do much more for them. This is an illustration of what the settlements try to do. We initiate such things as seem needful, but we hold our activities in the hollow of our hands, ready to give them up at a proper opportunity. It is quite the reverse of the old story about the superintendent of the orphan asylum, who prayed the Lord to send him many orphans the next year so he could build a new wing to his asylum. We want to keep ourselves adaptable and ready to turn over to someone else what they can do better than we. In the same spirit all of the settlements are doing more or less work with the evening schools, and hope to make them more social in spirit. It is better that a public building, like a school, become a center of a neighborhood, than a quasi-private building like a settlement.

Gad's Hill Center, near the McCormick works, was opened in 1898. It is interesting because it scatters its activities through different points in the vicinity, and in some instances is able to cooperate with social organizations established by the manufacturing interests there. Gad's Hill has a beautiful country place on the north shore which was partly responsible, at least, for developing the tuberculosis camp in connection with the Visiting Nurse's Association. They too hold their activities ready to give them up, as you see.

Henry Booth House was established in 1898, and Association House of the Young Men's Christian Association in 1899. They have each had a fine new building recently erected. Armitage Avenue, a little settlement opened in 1900, although small, has accomplished some very interesting work.

The newest settlement in Chicago is the Frederick Douglass Center, which is in the colored quarter. It is believed that a house will be useful where people interested in the social and ethical development of our colored brethren may meet with the leaders of the colored race, and discuss matters which pertain to both races, instead of emphasizing the things which divide one race from another, to unite upon those which are common to both. It is rational and careful and has the confidence of the colored people, as well as some of the most intelligent people of our own race. It was opened in 1904, but Mrs. Wooley, who is living there, has always been interested in the problem of the colored people. They have, on their walls, a statement from Booker Washington: "I will permit no man to degrade me by making me to hate him," which might be called the keynote of their effort.

There are six other establishments in Chicago which call themselves settlements, although some of them might better be classed as missions. I put in this classification, the Central Settlement, under the auspices of the Paulist Fathers, the Frances Willard Settlement, which has a large day nursery and kindergarten, the Frances Clark Settlement, established by the Christian Endeavor Societies, the Marcy Home and Olivet House, both of which grew out of missions started some years ago, although at present they have incorporated many settlement activities.

There is a distinction I should like to make between a settlement and a mission, for we find that they are often confused. They are really two distinct things, and harm is done to both movements, from this mental confusion. The first settlement in London was started by Canon Barnett, who is a canon in the Church of England, and at that time was vicar of St. Jude's, and although he founded Toynbee Hall, he has always kept the settlement distinct from the church. He says a mission is a group of people who are committed to one point of view, a religious point of view it commonly is, although a mission might be established for single tax, for temperance, or any other one thing upon which people are deeply convinced. They go into a neighborhood, and try to persuade the people who live there to believe as they believe, and to this end, in order to increase their acquaintance, they have classes, clubs, and many of the things a settlement has, but it is all secondary as it were, for they hope in the end that they may promote their propaganda. I am ready to say a mission is a much finer thing than the settlement. It has back of it the stirring history of the Christian church for 2,000 years, and some of the most wonderful names in religious history have been identified with missions. It is therefore a distinct thing with a history and purpose of its own.

A settlement on the other hand is a group of people who go into an industrial neighborhood, not in order to convert the people living there to given religious or social beliefs but to find out, so nearly as they may, what the social and civic needs of that neighborhood are, to awaken in a neighborhood a sense of responsibility that they may demand and work for better civic, educational and industrial conditions. They do not try to disturb the people in their religious beliefs. We have coming to Hull House people who belong to the Roman Catholic Church, the Greek Catholic Church, Jews both liberal and orthodox, and a sprinkling of Protestants. We would not try to change their religious beliefs any more than we would try to make them all single tax advocates. Difference of belief may divide us but there are things we can unite on, such as the manifest needs of the community. We unite so far as we can. The things that make people alike are much stronger and finer than the things which make them different. This attitude is quite unlike the mission attitude of propaganda, although the activities are much the same. The mission people and the settlement people are glad to have the distinction made. To reproach a settlement because it does not give religious instruction as a mission does, or to reproach a mission for not being a settlement, is equally absurd. I am very glad to make this distinction when it comes in my way, because a certain confusion has taken place in the public mind, very unfair to both movements. The social settlements in Chicago number about twenty. There are, I think, no settlements in the state outside of Chicago, although there are many centers which have very much the spirit and very much the effect in the community, of settlements.

We have not as many settlements in Chicago, naturally, as they have in New York, where they are growing very rapidly. A settlement is of course in its essence a democratic movement. Whatever one may think when one first goes to live in a foreign neighborhood, of crossing a social gulf, drops away very quickly in the general comradeship which develops there, so that one looks back to the time when it seemed unnatural to live in one part of the city, rather than in another, as a thing very much of the past.

At the present moment I do not know of any place more interesting than South Halsted Street. There one can meet young men recently come from Russia, as I saw some a few months ago, who had broken their fingers and forearms, in order that they may escape service in their army. These men started months ago. If a Russian Jew deserts when he is of military age his family is fined 300 rubles; but if he goes to the recruiting station and joins the army his family is freed and the sergeant is responsible. If he joins the army and escapes and then takes the precaution to break his arm or fingers, so that he cannot pull a trigger, his escape is doubly sure. These men are only now coming to Chicago, having come through Portugal and all sorts of ways to escape detection. They are now beginning to report of the first difficulties in Odessa and Kieff and other places in south Russia. It is very exciting, interesting and genuine, this thing. We have formed a little organization in Hull House, to which various people are encouraged to bring in their letters from abroad, so that we may discern something of the actual condition of things in Russia, not as they are put in the newspapers by correspondents, but written in a friendly letter by actual friends of people here.

I wish very much we had some of the ability this historical association has, to sift this evidence, for, in a sense, it is first-hand historical information. It is the event recorded as it happens, as it is being seen and felt—the sort of thing which may later be gathered into historical libraries, if indeed any of it survives. There is much work of that sort to do, for the scholar who can see life from the historical point of view, the linguist who can make some distinction between the various patois the Italians use, the anthropologist, who can trace something of life as it survives in quaint customs. For instance, the south Italian women bake their bread round, because the south of Italy was settled by the Greeks who baked bread in that form; while the north Italians bake it with a hole in the middle. There are all sorts of interesting customs which only the scholar can trace. The point of view of the man who looks at life, not from the immediate, but from the historical standpoint, is what is constantly needed in a settlement. Sometimes we feel that we ought to have more help from associations such as these. The great foreign colonies coming in ought to be recognized more by the scholars who are able to understand something of their pasts and their inherited capacities.

The Greeks are always clamoring for this recognition. I recall a striking instance of a Greek who sold fruit near the Polk Street railway station. For three years, in Greece, while he was saving money to come to America, he used to make drawings of ancient Athens, of which he was very fond. He was a graduate of the Institute of Technology, and drew very well. He had collected a large book of drawings and photographs. He thought that when he came to America, where we had no ruins, that we would be interested to hear about them and would enjoy his description of the great beauty of the white columns of the Propylea against the blue sky. He said he had sold fruit to Americans for years in Chicago, and that although he often had tried to lead the conversation to his beloved Acropolis, no one had ever seemed interested. He came to the conclusion no one in Chicago had heard of ancient Greece, nor knew that it had a wonderful history. He talked to me about Greece because he happened to see a small picture of Athens at Hull House, and he thought that here at least was someone who had heard that such a place as Athens existed. That man was disappointed and Chicago was losing something he could have given to it. I did not like to tell him we had become so snobbish in America that it did not occur to a man that a shabby-looking foreigner selling apples could have his mind and heart full of the deathless beauties of ancient Greece, although that was really the matter. I said that we were always in a hurry in Chicago, and the people with whom he came in contact were probably going to trains, so that no one had time to talk about Greece; but I assured him that there were people who were really interested.

One who has not come into social contact with these foreign citizens of ours can not appreciate how absorbing are the things they can tell, or the interest attaching to some of the correspondence they receive. All these things are possibilities to people who have historical taste and education. You know they used to tell us, in our school days, that Europe was waked up by the crusades, because people were brought in contact with the eastern civilization. We have a chance today in America, the other way 'round. The crusaders are coming to us, and we have this old civilization all around us, in the large groups of foreign colonies at our very doors, and we could receive the mental awakening if we saw them from the larger point of view. It is a great chance to bring us to an appreciation of the great resources of historical material which are available here, but it requires moral enterprise and a spirit of intellectual adventure, if you please. The settlements are perhaps pioneers in a movement which in time will become much more general and so large that the settlements will drop away as having been a mere formal expression of what all people will care to do later.

MARY E. MCDOWELL

was a member of the faculty of the University of Chicago,
and director and head of the University of Chicago settlement in the stockyards district in 1893. A world famous
settlement and social worker, she was untiring in her efforts
to better the lives of immigrants and members of minority
groups generally. She was the Commissioner of Public Welfare for Chicago in 1923, and the recipient of many honors,
including awards from the governments of Lithuania and
Czechoslovakia.

This article was published in the *Transactions of the Illinois State Historical Society* for 1920, pages 72–83.

A QUARTER OF A CENTURY
IN THE STOCKYARDS DISTRICT

MARY E. MCDOWELL

I am taking for granted that twenty-seven years in an industrial
community must be of value today because the struggle of the
wage earners the world round is full of significance, and, if one
could know the meaning of their struggle in the stockyards district,
then one might get at the meaning of the universal unrest of the
workers. To understand that struggle, to get at the point of view of
the wage earners was my own reason for coming to this community, as it has been that of so many who have thrown in their lot
with the struggling mass the existence of whose members depends
upon whether they have a job or do not have a job. That very word
"job" came into my vocabulary in 1894 and has since become a
sacred word, for I have learned that it means to my neighbors,
food, clothing, shelter, and a chance to be human. It is the word
first learned by the immigrant, the children lisp it and the aged
cling to it to the end. "A steady job," "no job," or "please get me a
job" is ever at the front of their minds and on the tips of all
tongues.

It was in September of the eventful year of 1894 just after
Chicago's World's Fair, after the Pullman strike, when the stockyards workers went out on a strike in sympathy with the railroad

men. The stockyards at that time was unorganized and therefore undisciplined, and the strike futile and disastrous. Disorder reigned back of the yards that autumn that I came to live on Gross Avenue, between "Whiskey Point" and Ashland Avenue. Cars had been burned a few blocks from this point, blood had been shed near the corner of Gross and Ashland Avenues where the regular army had been encamped. The people were left cowed and helpless.

The old citizens—property owners whom I learned to know— were conservative and critical of a sympathetic strike, but were also bitter in their denunciation of the attitude of the public towards the railroad union men, who, these conservative citizens said, put out the fires that the hoodlums and the mob set going. This was my first touch with the real struggle of labor for industrial democracy—an experience that made me question the practicality of the sympathetic strike, for the community was disheartened and the packing house workers possessed with fear and left unorganized. In my home life I had been used to men with courage—men who had gone into battle for a conviction, and now for the first time I was meeting men who "for fear of losing a job" went and came from work with a silent protest against conditions, and a sense of justice that they were afraid to express. When in my ignorance I would inquire about organization, there would be sudden, awful stillness and the man questioned would afterwards avoid me for fear I might again touch on this forbidden topic.

For the first two years I slept in a front room so close to the sidewalk that all hours of the night I could hear the tramp of men going to or coming from work. The impressions are vivid of these first autumn mornings when I would look out on the great army of men, women, and children, as they tramped to their work through the fog and smoke. That tramp, tramp, tramp of the "mighty army of the poor" and the significance of it will be with me always as a symbol of the tread of those who shall never cease marching onward and upward through suffering, through mistakes and blunders, until some day the machine will become the servant and the brutish will become humanized.

In those days, we read often for comfort and hope, Thomas Wentworth Higginson's poem,

I hear the tread of marching men, the patient armies of the poor.
Not ermine clad or clothed in state, their Title deeds not yet made plain;
But waking early, toiling late, the peers of all the earth remain—

The peasant brain shall yet be wise, the untrained pulse grow calm and
   still,
The blind shall see, the lowly rise, and work in peace Time's wondrous
   will.

In these early days the Settlement home was upstairs over a day
nursery; every morning when it was barely light in the winter, I
would be wakened by the cry of the little children who wanted the
mother to stay at home and not go to work. Here again for the first
time in my life I saw the meaning of the job and how wage-earning
women had to carry two burdens—that of the home and that of the
wage-earning world. In that day there was no child-labor law and
the packing industry found useful the boys and girls of eleven
years of age, and men and women and children had no limit to
their day's work. When I would ask why the people came from
work at all hours of the day and in the evening, I was told that the
killing had to go on until there were no cattle left to be cared for
over night; and when in my greenness I would ask why a packing
industry could not keep cattle over night when farmers did it very
well, I was surprised to learn that because it cost something to feed
and water them, men must butcher often sixteen hours at a stretch.
It was then I learned for the first time how it happened that when
in the morning these men, women, and children went out to work,
large numbers could not tell whether they would return home for
supper, or work from one to sixteen hours.

My social education—so slow in the beginning—was quickened
by personal contact and neighborly relationship with all kinds of
workers. One of my best friends was a German cattle butcher who
began work at eleven years of age on the "killing floor," where he
worked for twenty-five years until his right arm began to shake
from the constant wielding of a huge cleaver, more like a battle
axe.

This sober, intelligent and loyal worker was most unsocial—he
much preferred to work by himself and to go home to his family,
put on his slippers, light his pipe, and read his church and foreign
papers. He was not by nature "a joiner" but was happy in studying
history at the settlement with a young university student, who is
now a president of note in a Western university.

Another pleasure the settlement offered this intelligent cattle
butcher was that of meeting the university student in a genial
social atmosphere and giving the workingman's point of view with

regard to the organization of labor. The student on purely theoretical grounds argued for the organization of labor—while the conservative cattle butcher who had gone through the eight-hour strike and the sympathetic railroad strike and had seen both fail, took the opposite view. The university student needed this opportunity to meet the workingman face to face and with "feet under the same table," and to give and take ideas with perfect freedom. It was the unsocial cattle butcher who held to the opinion that if men were out of work it must be their own fault. He had seen the eight-hour movement fail in the yards and had gone through the disastrous railroad strike, but had kept a steady job all the way, which gave him a sense of security.

But at thirty-five years of age this loyal worker had a new experience which he could not understand. Why after going twenty-five years on a "killing bed," where he had been one of the few skilled workers, receiving forty-five cents an hour, he should be suddenly dismissed without any reason given by the boss, except that his right arm was shaking and that he was unable to keep up with the "pace maker," who was a giant. The day he was turned off, he stopped in to tell me that he had been "thrown out on the industrial scrap heap at thirty-five years of age," and with a face white with emotion he said that he could not understand that his long and loyal workmanship had not been considered by those whom he had served for twenty-five years. "I understand now," he said, "why men are not sure of a job always, and why they organize, for at thirty-five I have reached my old age limit. I shall never again receive forty-five cents an hour." And he never did, though for a quarter of a century he had been working and had given his best strength to this trade that demanded so little skill and such physical endurance. After many odd jobs he again, for a short time, got back into the packing house in another department, at less pay.

In 1900 when I arrived at Cologne, Germany, on a summer's vacation, I found a letter from my German neighbor welcoming me to his Fatherland and announcing the news which he said he wanted to be the first to tell me: "The cattle butchers of the yards are organized and I am a member, and so strong are we that we have won without a fight a limit to our day's work." No more would they butcher until no cattle were left in the pens, for a cattle butcher's life was the first consideration of a Cattle Butchers' Union.

The "pace maker" was still in their midst but the speed was stopped at the end of a ten-hour day. From that time on, the organizing by Michael Donnelly, a former sheep and cattle butcher, of all the departments of the packing industry, from the "squeegee man" to the floorsman on the killing floor, proceeded until in every packing district in the country there was an Amalgamated Meat Cutters' Union with a reported membership of fifty thousand. It was the first time that the yards had been organized by a butcher workman and the first time that the unskilled, 60 per cent of all the workers, were recognized. All of the different trades working in the yards were then federated into a Packing Trades Council presided over by a member of the Amalgamated Meat Cutters and Butcher workmen. Michael Donnelly began this work of organizing by a house to house canvass, having the first little gathering on the prairie where no one could discover it and cause the members to "lose their jobs," for this was the constant fear before them.

At first, the women workers were not recognized as ready for organization. It was difficult to learn just how many worked in that square mile, where it was said thirty to forty thousand people were employed. Then, too, they had come into new departments so quickly that the men were not aroused by their inroads until they were given a knife as a tool. Only then did these "petticoat butchers" become a factor to be dealt with. The women had in the early days of this comparatively new packing industry been working in the canning department, painting and labeling the cans. When men went on a petty strike in the stuffing room, women—mostly girls—were given the men's places at much lower wages. In this way the girls entered the sausage room where they linked the sausages with their hands as tools; but it was in the trimming room that they were given a "man's tool," a knife to cut the fat from the lean, though women had used this tool in their home longer than men. In one packing house the room is kept to the freezing point and considered scientific. I visited a room colder than your ice box —a veritable cold storage box, where pork was prepared for shipping long distances. "Here nothing is wasted," the superintendent told the visitor. But the immigrant girls worked in mid-winter wrappings—while cold sweat ran down the walls of the enclosed room. As soon as they became Americanized they found a better job if they lived through the experience.

Piece-work as a method of modern industry was revealed to me for the first time by my friendship with Maggie, her sisters, and Hannah, who worked in the labeling room of one of the principal packing plants. Maggie and Hannah were born in Ireland, but came with their parents to the "Town of Lake" when they were infants. There was no child labor law when these girls were eleven years of age. The old country parents had the old country notions and were in need of money; so these young Irish girls began their industrial life in this rather new industry of packing meat. In the early days of the industry the girls painted and labeled by hand the cans filled by men and boys. There was no ten-hour law to limit the day, and no child labor law; and there was no public opinion demanding light, fresh air, sunshine and fire escapes. The steam from the canning room permeated the labeling room, making the turpentine all the more pungent. This room had one row of windows and high stacks of cans obscuring the light from the middle of the room where the girls worked much of the time by artificial light. The half-hour for lunch was in this same atmosphere. If they chose they could go into a dressing room, partly partitioned off from the work room and filled with the same turpentine odor. Maggie told me that while she was at work she could not eat or even drink for it all tasted of turpentine.

The fathers and brothers of these Irish girls were working in the packing houses as butchers of cattle, sheep or hogs, while the Germans and after a time the Bohemians manned the sausage departments. It was when the men and boys struck and lost their places that the girls of the new incoming immigrants, Bohemians, Poles, and at the last, Lithuanians, took the places of the young men, and the boys, at one-third to one-half the wages, and did the work quite as well and with much less "fooling." For boys liked to play with knives at the risk of injury to themselves and others, while the girls took their work seriously and patiently, especially if it were piece work. Maggie represented the serious idealistic Irish type while Hannah was the social solvent of the shop, loved by all the girls, friendly with the boss and the forelady, until her sense of injustice was aroused; then she was the one inspiring to action and became for the moment a leader. Maggie had fine ambitions; Hannah had few, except to aid Maggie with her loyal admiration. Maggie wanted some things in her home that only her wages could procure. The old country father and mother could not understand Maggie's untiring, unresting ambition for a parlor with a piano,

where she and her beautiful young sisters could have company.
She wanted privacy—a room for herself—and comforts for the
father and mother who had worked hard all their lives. Maggie had
long, tapering fingers and a nervous temperament that could be
keyed to a speed that was marvelous while it lasted. She could paint
cans by the many thousands a week and often made $22 a week.
Just when Maggie, the unconscious "pace maker" of the shop would
reach the goal of $22 a week and begin to feel that she could secure
the necessities of her fine nature, a cut would come, and again she
would urge herself and all her co-workers to renewed and more
difficult speed, and once more she would reach the $22 a week
mark, and again would come the cut in wages by adding a greater
number of cans to be painted for a stipulated amount. It was after
the third cut that the Irish girls began to see the method of the
"boss," and Maggie and Hannah called a strike in the shop. All the
girls laid down their tools, and when the boss was obdurate, Hannah tied a red handkerchief to her umbrella and the girls marched
up and down the streets of Packing-Town, having no one to turn to
in this time of distress, for they were without organization. The
men had no union at that time. They had heard of some Knights of
Labor and they were determined to appeal to these knights. But
they received no response from the men.

At last they organized a Maud Gonne Club, in honor of the only
patriot they knew. This organization took place about the sick bed
of Maggie, who was found to have tuberculosis, and who pleaded
with them to be as courageous and unselfish as the Irish heroine
who suffered for Home Rule; for, said Maggie, "You know we must
work for those who come after us." The Maud Gonne Club had a
short life but the memory of it held this small group together until
Michael Donnelly organized the men and the appeal for help from
the girls to the Settlement brought them and Mr. Donnelly together
resulting in the local which was organized with ten girls from
several packing houses as charter members. This was the first
Packing House Woman's Union in the Meat Cutters' organization.
Maggie lived just long enough to serve as their first vice-president.

I shall never forget that meeting very early in the organization
when two of the young women who had worked for fifteen years in
one packing house were discharged because they were discovered
to be officers of the union. But this experience, disheartening as it
was to me, only inspired the Irish girls to renewed and eager

efforts. The girls of the red flag demonstration had not been able to get back to work. They formed a group of so-called "black listed girls," who now began to work in earnest for the union which they hoped would protect them from the injustice of "speeding up" followed by "cuts."

The next significant experience of this union of "petticoat butchers" was the night of a thunderstorm when we sat, a frightened group, in the settlement gymnasium and discussed whether it would be harmful or helpful to march with the men on Labor Day of 1903; for the timid ones felt that all who marched would lose their jobs, as the officers had a few weeks before. The lightning and the thunder filled all with present and future fear, but at last the Irish spirit rose above the storm and it was decided that they would not march but would ride in busses, sing labor songs, wear white dresses, and carry the flag of the red, white, and blue.

It was a pretty sight on Labor Day when the two busses, filled with packing house girls in white—young, attractive, full of courage, singing of Labor, rode out of Gross Avenue to meet a procession of men who were also running a great risk that day. Perhaps they too would never go back to the job so necessary to their existence. The effect of that act on Labor Day—of the thousands marching together for collective bargaining—was magical.

At the next meeting of the Woman's Union, a crowd of girls and women stood waiting at the door for membership, and the following meeting brought in immigrant girls who needed interpreters to aid in their initiation. It was a dramatic scene, the night when the first colored girl asked for admission. The president, an Irish girl whose father before union days had left his job because a colored man had been put to work with him, was naturally expected to be prejudiced against the reception of Negro women. Hannah as doorkeeper called out in her own social way, "A colored sister is at the door. What'll I do with her?" "Admit her," called back the president, "and let all of ye's give her a hearty welcome." The tall, dignified, good-looking, well-dressed colored girl, much frightened, walked down the center aisle of the hall while the room rang with cheers and the clapping of hands. Soon after at a meeting, when the question in the ritual, "Have you any grievances?" was put to the house full of girls, black and white, Polish, Bohemian, Lithuanian, German, Irish, Croatian, and Hungarian, a shy, sensitive, colored girl arose and said she had a grievance against a Polish girl in the shop who was always teasing her. The president called them both up before the union and made each tell what the other had done. "She called me a Polock first, before I called her a nigger." Then the president arose and said, "Ain't you ashamed of yourselves? You promised in the union to be sisters and here you are fighting. Now shake hands and don't you bring any more of your personal grievances here. Tell it to your shop steward, and remember this is where only shop grievances are to be brought."

The Women's Union was represented by delegates at the Packing Trades Council and at the annual conventions on an equal footing with the men. The Women's Local had their own paid business agent, a clever German girl who learned in a few days to use a typewriter, though she had never practiced on one before, and found, as she said, "your spelling does jump and hit you straight in the eyes."

This agent was the go-between the women and the bosses. Any shop grievance was reported to her and then it was her business to confer with the employers, and thus prevent the petty, hysterical strikes of former days when the girls would protest against a grievance by stopping work without warning.

Soon after an experience that Hannah and I had at the Cattle Butchers' Union was quite as suggestive of the broadening influence of organization. A colored man was the officer who brought in for initiation the men of so many different nationalities that it took four interpreters to make clear the obligations of the organization. As we left the meeting, Hannah said: "Well, that's brotherhood of man all right, isn't it?" It was in such union meetings that the Slavic immigrant for the first time had the experience of belonging freely to a self-governing organization, holding office and working on committees if they could understand English at all.

The real test of brotherhood came in the summer of 1904 when after weeks of conference between the packers and the union over the wage scale for both skilled and unskilled a strike was called, and 22,000 workers came out. The struggle centered about the wages of the unskilled. The employers agreed not to touch the skilled workers, cattle, sheep, and hog butchers, but they were determined to reduce the unskilled back to the rate before the union had raised them 2½ cents an hour. The skilled workers, feeling that this would disrupt the union if the unskilled were discriminated against, determined to stand with them.

Michael Donnelly and his executive committee for weeks were conferring with the packers, but without avail. After much discussion within the locals a referendum vote was taken on whether to strike or not. The vote was to strike, and then began the first organized strike in the yards. It came as a great surprise to employers and employees when the thousands of workers obeyed the order to leave work quietly and "everything in order," as if returning to their tasks the next day. "Do not stop until all your butchering is done," was the order, "then walk out." This was done so faithfully that the strike was on for several days before the community became conscious that 22,000 people were on strike in the yards. After twelve days a settlement was made with the packers.

Mr. Donnelly did not approve of the method employed in taking the men back to work after the strike. He pleaded for a different method, but he was unable to gain his point, and what he feared happened. Some of the men who were officers of the union were not taken back and very early in the day telegrams came from other places demanding that the strike continue on the ground of "discrimination and suspicion of trickiness." The demand was so persistent from certain quarters that he did what his own best judgment afterwards decided against. He issued the order for the strike to continue before consulting with the packers. This action lost him and his union the sympathy and backing of the strongest labor leaders in America; for they believed that Mr. Donnelly had made a very good agreement and had won a victory. The strike was on again and for over two months after this apparent victory for the union, the neighborhood of the yards was the scene of an unusually orderly strike of 22,000 people, equal to the population of many small cities. Thousands of cards were printed and distributed, large posters in different languages posted, pleading for law and order to prevail. The speeches even of the socialists were never inflammable. Indeed, most of the violence committed was done by certain newspapers. On one occasion a fight between two Polish brothers was turned into a serious disturbance because of the bad judgment or because of an ambition to make a record on the part of police officers who called out the whole force to quiet a group of Poles watching the fight. To be sure there were often physical arguments used. Such an argument one girl used with another who took her place in the packing house. When I protested against such methods by saying, "Why don't you try to persuade her to join your union instead of slapping her?" the girl replied. "Yes, that's all right for you. You know how to talk, but when a girl takes my job, when I'm out to raise my wages, and then sasses me, I slap her; that's my way." But not always was this method used. Another Irish girl found a drunken Irishman on his way to the yards with an axe in his hands to do some damage, and persuaded him to give her the axe and go home to his wife.

This strike was called by those who had known previous ones in the yards "a pink tea strike," because as the police captains put it, "the girls and boys were kept so busy at the Settlement afternoons that they were not disturbing as they always had been in former strikes," and because, by the police sergeant's records there were fewer arrests during this July and August than in previous summers.

The Woman's Union had always met at the Settlement gymnasium because "there was no saloon there," for the leaders of strikes generally agree that the saloon hall is the hotbed of trouble, and yet the Settlement gymnasium was positively the only hall that was available for a union meeting in the whole district that did not open into or was above a saloon.

If all the saloons in a strike zone could be closed as soon as trouble began, there would be less violence and a better and earlier understanding, and if church and school halls were at the disposal of labor unions it would raise the morale of the organizations. And if more of our American labor leaders would stand with their English union brothers for temperance, it would help toward a saner unionism.

The community's interest in the struggle for two and a half cents an hour is not easily understood by outsiders. Two and a half cents an hour meant a higher standard of living that the workers were unwilling to give up—we can't live "the decent American way" they said over and over. One wonders after hearing this so often if it is not this growing standard of living that the workers call "the decent American way," one of the strongest factors in the great unrest today, this, with the uncertainty of a steady job, and the demoralization of the casual or seasonal work.

The immigrant who is intelligent enough to send his children to the public school finds a constant tug upon his lean purse by demands that were not made upon his parents. The school nurse and the medical inspector report the children need glasses, that they may see clearly; their ears must be cared for that they may hear distinctly; the teeth must be cared for and the adenoids removed so that the children may be healthy and may keep up with their grades in school.

Rents advance, yet the parents with this growing standard of living are not willing to deprive their children of the privacy needed, and will not take in lodgers as some with lower standards do to help out the lack in income. The rent must be paid and food is high.

The children, therefore, must have less nourishing food. The employer and the economist tell us that wages cannot come up to the worker's standard, as long as the many wait for jobs at the doors of the industry. Industry is so specialized that perhaps a surplus of labor is a necessity to the business, but surely it should not be a menace to the higher standard of living of the working people.

After ten weeks of waiting and arguing, after priest and politician had failed to bring together the leading representatives of both sides in the struggle and the situation was getting tense and serious —for the union had no funds to feed the strikers, and hunger makes men desperate—a woman physician filled with the spirit of the "called of the Lord" secured audience with the packer who agreed to see the men's representative. While the 22,000 persons waited and talked of the decent American wage ideal, a cattle butcher who waited with me for the momentous word from these two representatives, said a significant thing that I shall never forget. "You know," he said, "I think the world has to learn that Michael Donnelly represents quite as important an interest as does the representative of the packers, Mr. J. Ogden Armour."

After hours of waiting the word at last reached the 22,000 outside that the skilled workers could return to work with the wages unchanged but the unskilled workers must be reduced two and one-half cents. When a plea was made for some recognition of this long struggle for higher wages for the 60 per cent of the workers, the answer was, "As long as there are thousands waiting for a job every morning we cannot pay a higher rate of wages." Then the plea was made for a more stable week's work in order that the casual work might be lessened, and it was urged that the industry might be so organized as to carry the needed surplus and make work steadier. Of course some recognition has to be made of the fact that this is in some sense a seasonal industry in that the supply of cattle, hogs and sheep is not a fixed or certain supply, but the packers promised to consider the proposition of steadying the work but would not consider the raising of wages. Michael Donnelly urged a labor commissioner such as the mine operators of Illinois had to deal with on matters brought up by the union, which commissioner would make it possible to do away with shop stewards. One superintendent who had to deal with over three hundred in a large packing plant, said he found the strike a rest cure from shop stewards.

The proposition to end the strike was brought at once before the members of the various unions with the argument that the strike benefit fund was gone and that if the men did not go back to work they would not be cared for. This compelled an affirmative vote. But at one mass meeting of the unskilled I heard a Polish worker speak in four languages urging the men to hold out for the two and one-half cents for the same reasons that I had heard over and over. He spoke quietly and with ease, and was listened to with dignified attention. When he said, "You know that you can't give your children an American living; you can't send them to school and give them what they ought to have; you can't have a decent American home on 15½ cents an hour and only forty hours a week the year around." And the men who listened were ready to vote against returning to work until the officers of the union explained the lack of funds. Then they agreed to give up, though most reluctantly, and some showed a lack of faith in those who had settled the strike.

It was Labor Day when these negotiations between packers and men were in progress. There was no procession and no picnic, but an ominous stillness lay back of the yards. Inside the one square mile of packing houses and stock yards, the imported workers, Negroes from the far South and immigrants from the East, were having a holiday, playing games and trying to feel at home in their temporary abiding place.

I walked through the yards hoping to find some one who would help to bring about some kind of a satisfactory solution of the tense situation. At one of the vacant spaces between the buildings I found two groups of Macedonians, having a holiday of a unique kind. One group was chanting their old country songs, while the other group was dancing the folk dance of their own Greek people to the music of a primitive goat skin pipe which their classic ancestors might have used. Near by and overseeing this Greek festival under the shadow of the slaughter house of one of the greatest of the packing houses was the padrone who brought from the seaport these newly arrived immigrants. He was talkative and interesting. He said these men received 25 cents a day in Macedonia. While in the role of "the Commodity of Labor," going from one point to another whenever there was a strike, they received $2.50 a day with board and lodging. Knowing that the strike was about ended I asked: "What will you do with these men when this strike is over?" He answered laughingly, "We will go to the next place when we are needed."

I had never before seen what was called "Labor as a commodity" but here it was. In my ignorance I wondered what was the relation between this artificially supplied "commodity" and that so-called natural demand of thousands every morning at the time-keepers' offices. I put my question to the economist who walked with me but I received no satisfactory answer. Outside were the immigrants who were paying $9.50 per month for the cottages they hoped to call their own. They were filling up every inch of space with lodgers and putting to work every pair of hands that were strong enough to be paid, and yet they were uncertain of a steady job themselves, and as unconscious of the reasons for their unrest as were the Macedonians of being an expensive commodity for the time being, or a pathetic spectacle or a baffling fact to the sympathetic onlookers.

The protest of the 50,000 seemed futile for without an adequate strike benefit fund these workers were powerless to hold out. The power to wait is what the workers did not have. The strike ended. Most of the men and women, except the leaders, were taken back. Many never got back their old places, and many of those who did were dismissed after a time. Some went away to better places. Some took to a different kind of work, while a few were demoralized; in the struggle for industrial democracy the strike, like a war, carries a long train of evils. On the whole it was an education by chastening to both employers and employees, and some results were permanently good. Light was let in which opened the eyes of those who live far away before they had known the stock yards only as a marvel among industries, now the hands that prepared the meat had made themselves felt. When the roast of beef or sweetbreads became an uncertain quantity then the hands that prepared the meat for a world's market were recognized—perhaps with scorn or impatience—but recognized as a human reality with power, and a new point of view was reached by a great public, the same public that had a chill of horror over sanitation a few years after, but forgot the worker in their fear that cleanliness would not save their stomachs.

But this year of 1904, the human product of the packing industry had been considered something more than a brutal force for turning out meat food, more than an integral part of the great machinery. From this date changes began in the plants for the bettering of sanitary conditions. Where Maggie worked is now a concrete building covered within by white tiles, a dust-proof building. The awakening after the Iroquois Theatre tragedy demanded fire escapes. The Child Labor Law was generally obeyed to such an extent that children under sixteen are rarely to be found in the large packing houses. The state law, limiting women's work to ten hours is obeyed.

A new social consciousness has awakened, and has expressed itself in many ways. Welfare nurses are employed, sick benefit, insurance schemes, and in some plants lunch and improved locker rooms, shower baths and other conveniences have been established since 1904. Before the war, smoke from the chimneys was consumed and streets in the yards have been paved and the best of modern structures replace old buildings that have been destroyed by fire. One firm has a minimum weekly wage and not less than forty hours work per week, one result of the strike.

At present the packers have offered the most advanced methods of industrial relationship that they have ever tried. This is the employees representative plan that has an assembly composed of representatives elected by secret ballot in each shop. In some plants the power of veto is left to the higher officials, while in a few there is no veto after a two-thirds vote decides the issue before the assembly. If the assembly decides on arbitration or a fight it is the last word. From the point of view of the packers this is democracy in industry, to the community it is only an experiment, while the average worker looks upon it as a method to down the unions, though some men elected are union men. It is at least the most constructive policy ever offered by the employers to their employees, and is well worth trying out. It may fail as such schemes have in many places, but it will be an educational experiment to both workers and officials.

The sanitary conditions and the humane slaughtering are perhaps as good if not better than that of any industry of its kind in the world; but the cause of industrial democracy is weaker than it was in 1900 and the problem of casual labor and its effect upon the family and community is still a social question that will be answered perhaps some day by the industry itself carrying the burden of that surplus of labor which is called a necessity of the business but demoralizing to the health and morals of the people. One wonders whether the unskilled workers, forgotten in this country by the skilled unions who are strongly organized on an aristocratic basis, and helpless before the powerful employers, and so often unable to organize—one wonders whether they will not have to be protected by a general state minimum wage, an out-of-work insurance, and by municipal housing as well as public clinics for their children. Shall the police power of the state be evoked to insure a strong and intelligent citizenship which is, of course, the business of a democracy to produce; for after all is it not the human output that must be the important interest of the public who want to preserve this Democracy that is not yet established.

THE PULLMAN STRIKE:
A STUDY IN INDUSTRIAL WARFARE

HARVEY WISH

With the descent of the panic of 1893 upon the country, the average American became more concerned with economic problems than with the old political and personal issues. Many of that generation had already experienced the general insecurity and industrial warfare associated with the depressions of the seventies and the middle eighties. The march of unemployed armies upon Washington, like those of Jacob Coxey, Lewis C. Fry, J. H. Randall, and Charles T. Kelly, though peaceful in intention, appeared as an ominous development in our industrial history. In the huge Illinois coal fields, perennial labor discontent broke out in aggravated form. During the spring of 1894, the United Mine Workers of America, under the leadership of John McBride, inaugurated a national strike covering the mineral area from Pennsylvania to Iowa and from Indian Territory and Tennessee to Michigan. In Illinois, as well as in other states, the militia was repeatedly invoked to deal with the situation. This was but the prelude to one of the greatest labor conflicts in American history—the Pullman Strike of 1894. As the center of industry gravitated westward, Chicago frequently became the battlefield of industrial conflict. The Haymarket Affair had already established the city's reputation for militancy; now the Pullman Strike was to overshadow it in extent and significance.[1]

The Pullman Car Company, which enjoyed a monopoly of railway sleeping-car manufacture by virtue of its patents, was established in 1867 with a capital of $1,000,000. In 1880, it bought 500 acres of land for its "model town" and plant. Under the paternalistic regime of George M. Pullman, the company town was modern in design, well-kept, and had its own church and library. The employee-residents, however, were indifferent to the aesthetic benefits de-

---

[1] The history of the Pullman Strike can be drawn from unusually rich materials. Shortly after the strike, through the efforts of Dr. Carroll D. Wright, commissioner of labor, a federal investigation was held in Chicago which reviewed the testimony of principals on both sides. See *Report on the Chicago Strike of June-July, 1894* (*U.S. Sen. Exec. Doc. no. 7*, 53 Cong., 3 sess., Washington, 1895).

rived, and competent observers were skeptical of Pullman's philanthropy. Settlement authorities such as Jane Addams noted that rents, which were fixed by the company, soared from 20 to 25 per cent above rents for similar accommodations in Chicago. Nor did the depression bring any reduction in rents, though a number of salary reductions were put into effect. The federal commissioners later declared:

> The conditions created at Pullman enable the management at all times to assert with great vigor its assumed right to fix wages and rents absolutely, and to repress that sort of independence which leads to labor organizations and their attempts at mediation, arbitration, strikes, etc.

While wages had been drastically reduced upon the advent of the depression, the generous salaries paid to high officials remained untouched. During the fiscal year ending July 31, 1893, dividends of $2,520,000 had been distributed and wages of $7,233,719.51 paid; but for the year ending July 31, 1894, dividends rose to $2,880,000 while wages dropped to $4,471,701.39. The company enjoyed a paid-up capital of $36,000,000 and a lump surplus of $25,000,000 in undivided profits. The average daily wage, earned on a piece-work basis, in most departments was about 90 cents, while the rent approximated $11 to $12 per month. Union activities were strictly proscribed but seem to have been secretly developing for some time before the strike.

At length a workmen's committee approached Thomas H. Wickes, the second vice-president, on May 7 to ask for a return to the wage schedule of June, 1893. They were told that this was impossible since the company was losing money on contracts for the purpose of keeping the men employed. An alternate request for a reduction in rent was rejected on the ground that only 3 per cent was being earned on Pullman's rental investment. On May 10, when three of the commitee were discharged for alleged lack of work, the local unions voted to strike.[2]

---

[2] While Pullman's claim that he was then operating at a loss is demonstrably true, there is little reason to accept the contention that he was continuing operation as an act of charity to labor. The Strike Commission reported: "The commission thinks that the evidence shows that it [the Pullman Company] sought to keep running mainly for its own benefit as a manufacturer, that its plant might not rust . . . that it might be ready for resumption when business revived with a live plant and competent help, and that its revenue from its tenements might continue."

The next day, some two thousand men left their posts with the assurance of support from the powerful American Railway Union. The company then closed its shops and George Pullman left for the East. The Railway Union, under the militant leadership of Eugene V. Debs, had recently been victorious over James J. Hill of the Great Northern in an eighteen-day strike which had restored 75 per cent of current pay cuts. The union had been organized the previous summer and claimed a membership of 150,000 railway employees. Its arch-enemy was the General Managers' Association, organized in 1886 as a national organization and having as members the twenty-four railroads "centering or terminating in Chicago." It represented a mileage of 40,933 and a capitalization of $2,108,522,617. Each member paid an assessment for such services as that of furnishing strikebreakers, maintaining a national blacklist, upholding a common schedule of wages, and dealing with related problems of employment. Discontented employees were regularly met by a committee of the association rather than by the heads of their particular plant. A total of 221,097 employees were subject directly to its rulings. As the federal commissioners later wrote:

> The association is an illustration of the persistent and shrewdly devised plans of corporations to overreach their limitations and to usurp indirectly powers and rights not contemplated in their charters and not obtainable from the people or their legislators.

It was to meet this national combination that the A.R.U. had been formed.

On June 21, the Railway Union voted in convention to refrain from handling Pullman cars on and after June 26 unless Mr. Pullman would consent to arbitrate. All members would refuse to handle the sleeping cars; inspectors, switchmen, engineers, and brakemen would not perform their duties as far as these cars were concerned. If attempts were made to replace the boycotters, declared Debs, every union man would strike. The Pullman Company entrusted its cause to the General Managers' Association and refused to deal with the strikers. The A.R.U. was ignored. Thomas H. Wickes, second vice-president, announced to the press, "As the men are no longer in our employ we have nothing to arbitrate." [3]

---

[3] Wickes was later asked by the Federal Labor Commissioner: "Don't you think that the fact that you represent a vast concentration of capital, and

Eugene Debs, the strategist of the strike, was not as yet a Socialist in the Marxian sense. Like other trade unionists he was influenced by the teachings of Laurence Gronlund who advocated a cooperative commonwealth with several of the features of state socialism. He hoped that the successful issue of the strike would be a first step in the direction of governmental ownership of the means of transportation and communication. His instructions as to strategy were coupled with repeated injunctions against violence in any form since the latter would provide a basis for military intervention. Up to the moment of his arrest he was able to keep the situation under control.

The railway union began its work first upon the great national lines. Switchmen who were ordered on June 26 to attach Pullman cars to the Illinois Central trains refused and their subsequent discharge brought about the strike of the remaining union men. By the next day employees of the Northern Pacific and the Santa Fe lines had joined the sympathetic strike. On the twenty-ninth, the General Managers' Association accepted the gage of battle by announcing that no striker would ever be re-employed by the road whose services he left. Soon the association was importing private detectives into Chicago despite the Illinois law of 1893 forbidding their employment in industrial disputes. On July 3, just previous to President Cleveland's despatch of federal troops to Chicago, the *Times*, then under the supervision of Carter H. Harrison Jr. (later mayor) and Willis J. Abbot, declared significantly:

> There has been no rioting in or about Chicago; no blood has been shed; no one has been killed; and were it not for the clamorous utterances of a number of Chicago newspapers, which at this time seem anxious to foment trouble through distorted reports of the labor strike, the average citizen would affirm that the great city of Chicago was never in a more pacific mood than at present.

Bulletins were issued by the Chicago superintendent of railway mail and the General Managers' Association confirming the free passage of the mail and of passenger trains for July 2 and 3, although delays in freight occurred. Chief of Police Michael Bren-

are selected for that because of your ability to represent it, entitles him [the employee] . . . to unite with all of the men of his craft and select the ablest one they have got to represent the cause?" To this Wickes remarked: "They have the right; yes, sir. We have the right to say whether we will receive them or not."

nan, in his official report, declared that "until July 4 there was little or no trouble at any point within the limits of the city of Chicago."

The unusual expedient of Attorney-General Richard Olney in sending federal troops to Chicago, in spite of an apparently contrary constitutional provision, requires explanation. On June 28, Olney appointed Edwin Walker, who was affiliated with the General Managers' Association, as special attorney for the national government. Of this act, Clarence Darrow remarked: "The government might with as good grace have appointed the attorney for the American Railway Union to represent the United States." In a telegram to Walker, Olney clearly revealed his intention to break the strike:

> It has seemed to me that if the rights of the United States were vigorously asserted in Chicago, the origin and center of the demonstration, the result would be to make it a failure everywhere else and to prevent its spread over the entire country. . . . But I feel that the true way of dealing with the matter is by a force which is overwhelming and prevents any attempt at resistance.

Despite the fact that Governor John P. Altgeld of Illinois was sending troops to the various points requested by local authorities and that Olney had approved his course in the current coal strike, he was ignored this time by the United States Attorney-General. Instead, Olney prepared to obtain the issuance of blanket injunctions tending to paralyze the leadership of the American Railway Union. This was done largely on the strength of the federal commerce power and also, according to Olney's view, could be based on the Sherman Anti-trust Act of 1890—an act never intended to apply to labor organizations.[4] Instructions were issued to Edwin Walker on July 1 providing for the application of the injunction against Debs and his associates for the following day. Judge P. S. Grosscup of the federal district court, and Judge William A. Woods of the United States circuit court, issued the injunction preventing any person from "directing, inciting, encouraging, or instructing any persons whatsoever to interfere with the business or affairs, directly or indirectly" of the railway companies. Judge Grosscup remarked privately that he opposed such employment of the judiciary in labor disputes because it was partisan action.

---

[4] Olney pleaded before the Supreme Court that the Sherman Act should be liberally construed since labor organizations represented combinations of capital.

The American Railway Union had had experience with the injunction during the Great Northern strike a short time previously and had successfully ignored it. Its members prepared to repeat their performance now. Debs telegraphed to a western branch of the A.R.U.: "It will take more than injunctions to move trains. Get everybody out. We are gaining ground everywhere." The *Chicago Times,* alone of the Chicago metropolitan dailies, denounced the injunction as a menace to liberty and asserted that if it was good law then there was no sense in maintaining labor organizations. On the other hand, the railway operators all over the country recognized the magic which Olney had performed at Chicago and telegrams poured into the office of the attorney-general requesting an injunction "like the Chicago bill." Federal injunctions were issued frequently in anticipation of strikes in southern Illinois, Arkansas, California, Colorado, Idaho, Indiana, Iowa, Kentucky, Michigan, Minnesota, Mississippi, Missouri, New Mexico, Ohio, Oklahoma, Tennessee, Texas, Utah, and Wisconsin.

Olney now prepared the capstone of his legal structure—the sending of federal troops to Chicago. On July 2, Walker telegraphed Olney: "It is the opinion of all that the orders of court can not be enforced except by the aid of the regular army." [5] The "federal" representatives who cooperated in this move were then, according to the *Tribune,* meeting in an office adjacent to that of the General Managers' Association in the Rookery Building. Olney decided to permit Walker to judge of the exact time for the introduction of federal troops. The "overt act" could not be found in Chicago; hence alleged rioting in Blue Island, outside of the city limits, served as the basis for military intervention. John W. Arnold, the United States marshal, telegraphed to Washington that no force less than the regular troops could procure the passage of mail trains or enforce the orders of the federal court. This telegram was accompanied by another from Walker declaring that it was "of utmost importance that soldiers should be distributed at certain points within the city by evening."

In a conference with President Cleveland on the Pullman Strike, General Nelson A. Miles, who was in command of the troops ordered to Chicago, stated that "he was subject to orders, but that

---

[5] Several telegrams of importance appear to be omitted in Olney's Report to Congress, for on July 3, he wrote to Walker: "Legal situation could not be improved. . . . Understood you think time for use of United States troops has not yet arrived. . . . Rely upon you to advise me when the exigency necessitates use of troops."

in his opinion the United States troops ought not to be employed in the city of Chicago at that time." To this General Schofield objected, and he supported the Olney program of intervention. Arrangements were made for the transportation of the entire garrison at Fort Sheridan to the lake front in Chicago.

The Railway Association expressed its satisfaction with the action of President Cleveland. General Manager Egan of the association declared that the fight was now between the government and the A.R.U. The railroads were no longer concerned. The strikers were correspondingly depressed. Debs predicted that the first shots fired upon the mobs in Chicago would be the signal for civil war. Anticipating trouble, Chief of Police Brennan ordered the city policemen to guard the trains conveying the military to camp. During the night of July 3, the troops were brought into Chicago. Brennan later testified:

> On July 4th trouble began. The workingmen had heard of the federal troops and were incensed. . . . There was trouble at Halsted Street and Emerald Avenue and on the Lake Shore tracks.

General Miles reported on July 5 that a mob of several thousand was moving eastward along the Rock Island Railroad "overturning cars, burning station-houses and destroying property." He asked Schofield for permission to fire on mobs obstructing trains. By the sixth, matters became worse. Mobs threatened to hang the federal marshals and the policemen. Military reinforcements were deemed necessary.

To demonstrate the popular feeling in favor of the strikers, Debs asked all sympathizers to wear white ribbons on their coat lapels. This met with strong response. To one union leader he wired:

> Calling out the troops is an old method of intimidation. Commit no violence. Have every man stand pat. Troops cannot move trains. Not enough scabs in the world to fill places and more occurring hourly.

In another telegram he declared:

> Strong men and broad minds only can resist the plutocracy and arrogant monopoly. Do not be frightened at troops, injunctions, or a subsidized press. Quit and remain firm. Commit no violence. American Railway Union will protect all, whether member or not when strike is off.

A meeting of citizens on Boston Common passed a resolution endorsing the strike and declaring that Olney had delivered the federal government "to the railroad kings." The *Chicago Times* accused Cleveland of making the bayonet dominant in American affairs and asserted that the presence of the federal troops in Chicago had done more to inflame passion than to suppress violence. The strikers, however, had few such articulate supporters in the press of the country, and relied upon popular demonstrations of sympathy.

The situation in other parts of the country was not unlike that at Chicago. In California, particularly, public sentiment was against the Southern Pacific Railroad for monopolistic practices before the strike, and the introduction of federal troops stirred up a fresh antagonism to the railroads. When the militia of Stockton and Sacramento were called out to fire upon the crowds, the soldiers removed cartridges from their guns and refused to use bayonets. After the strike, which had resulted in considerable destruction of property, a federal district attorney, Joseph H. Call, stated that there was an overwhelming sentiment not only against the railroads but against the government as well, due to a conviction that the laws of the nation were being enforced with great severity against laboring people and not against the corporations. He added:

> I do not hesitate to speak plainly when I say, that in my opinion, if the United States Government can not protect the people of the Pacific states against these monopolies, it will require a larger standing army than the Government now possesses to uphold the power and dignity of the United States.

Nor were the situations in Illinois and California unique. In order to enforce the Walker-Olney type of injunction federal troops were sent to Colorado, Idaho, Indiana, Michigan, Montana, Nevada, New Mexico, Oklahoma, Utah, and Wyoming.

As the railroad strike spread over Illinois, Governor Altgeld, who had scarcely disposed of the urgent problems arising from the coal areas, now was compelled to devote much of his time to the employment of militia in the new industrial dispute. He conferred constantly with the adjutant-general of Illinois and other officers, preparing to put 100,000 men in the city of Chicago if it became necessary. His experience with the demands of the railroads for troops was similar to the situation in the coal strike. Attempts were made by the railroads to utilize the militia in order to run trains whose crews had struck. This was thwarted by Altgeld whenever possible. In one instance where troops were ordered to one point and found no riot but a line of trains without crews, several soldiers were compelled to act as engineers and brakemen to transport the militia home. At Danville crowds of strikers opposed the movement of all trains, except mail cars. Altgeld showed his willingness to prevent any cases of actual rioting but refused to become a convenient pawn for the General Managers' Association.

In the midst of these policing activities, Altgeld now learned that the Cleveland administration, ignoring the state and local authorities, had sent troops to Chicago. His indignation was immediately aroused for he suspected that a deliberate attempt was being made to set a precedent by which federal troops could be sent to any state long before any violence occurred in order to intimidate strikers. He therefore determined to request the immediate withdrawal of federal troops. On July 5, Altgeld addressed a long telegram to President Cleveland outlining the situation in Chicago and the rest of the state as an indication of the unjustifiability of sending troops there. He stated that the local officials had been able to control the situation and that nobody in Cook County, whether official or private citizen, had even intimated to him that the assistance of the state militia was desired. The application for federal troops, he charged, was made by men who had "political and selfish motives" for ignoring the state government. The federal marshal for the Northern District had but to ask for military assistance of Altgeld in order to get it. He concluded with a reference to the constitutional issues of the case:

> The question of federal supremacy is in no way involved. No one disputes it for a moment, but, under our Constitution, federal supremacy and local self-government must go hand in hand, and to ignore the latter is to do violence to the Constitution.
> As Governor of the State of Illinois, I protest against this, and ask the immediate withdrawal of the federal troops from active duty in this state. Should the situation at any time get so serious that we cannot control it with the state forces, we will promptly ask for federal assistance, but until such time, I protest, with all due deference, against this uncalled-for reflection upon our people.

President Cleveland, who later described this telegram as "frivolous," made a brief, formal reply. He stated that the troops were sent to Chicago in order that obstruction of the mails should be removed, that the processes of the federal courts might be served, and upon proof that conspiracies against interstate commerce existed. Cleveland was actually disturbed, however, and discussed the Altgeld telegram with his cabinet. Two cabinet members, Walter Q. Gresham and Richard Olney, later expressed their contempt for the governor, the former declaring that Altgeld's telegram was "state's rights gone mad."

But neither the authority of the president nor the criticisms of the press, which now easily recalled that Altgeld had pardoned the surviving Haymarket prisoners in 1893 and hence loved anarchy, were able to hush the outspoken governor. He replied at once to Cleveland with another long telegram, criticizing the president's stand and concluding:

> This assumption as to the power of the executive is certainly new, and I respectfully submit that it is not the law of the land. The jurists have told us that this is a government of law, and not a government by the caprice of an individual, and further, instead of being autocratic, it is a government of limited power. Yet the autocrat of Russia could certainly not possess, or claim to possess, greater power than is possessed by the executive of the United States, if your assumption is correct.

Cleveland, who was temperamentally the antithesis of Altgeld, later remarked that his "patience was somewhat strained" by the "rather dreary discussion" of state's rights and the dangers to constitutional government. His reply consisted of a sentence denying Altgeld's charge of executive usurpation and declaring that discussion might well give way to active cooperation on the part of all authorities. Cleveland remarked privately to Assistant Secretary of the Treasury Curtis that he proposed, regarding the strike, to "stand up and stamp this out if it takes the whole army and militia to do it."

Shortly after the cabinet meeting, Olney issued a public statement scathingly reviewing Altgeld's telegrams. The soil of Illinois, he declared, was the soil of the United States and for all national purposes, the federal government could be there with its courts, its marshals, and its troops, not by mere permission, but as a right.

Altgeld's idea of the sacredness of the territory of a state, according to Olney, had become extinct with the close of the Civil War. He hinted that if necessary the militia of other states might be brought into Chicago. Olney's conversion to the doctrines of centralization had been comparatively late. In 1875, as a Democrat, he had attacked the Grant administration for its intervention in Louisiana in words similar to those in Altgeld's telegram of 1894:

> Apparently, it [the administration] meant to assert that the President might enter a State with troops, to suppress disorder and violence at his own discretion, upon his own view of the exigency, and without waiting for the consent or request of the State itself. No more glaring attempt at usurpation can be imagined. If successful it would revolutionize our whole governmental system; if successful it would clearly annihilate the right of local self-government by a State, which could be exercised thereafter only by the sufferance and kind permission of the Federal Government.

Meanwhile other American governors were finding federal intervention in their states as objectionable as in Illinois. Governor William J. Stone of Missouri protested to Cleveland that the use of federal troops to protect the mails was a mere pretext to set aside local authorities. He declared that there was no disorder that could not be put down by state and local authorities. From Colorado, Governor Davis H. Waite wrote a bitter letter to Cleveland announcing that the federal troops were carrying on war in that state and would permit no interference by country or state officials. He demanded to know by what right the federal marshal had suspended the writ of habeas corpus in Colorado. Arbitrary arrests without any warrant were being made.[6] Governor James S. Hogg of Texas wired the president that he would not tolerate federal troops in his state unless he was first consulted, and attacked the "order to invade Illinois." Similar protests came from Governor Sylvester Pennoyer of Oregon and Governor Lorenzo D. Lewelling of Kansas.[7]

---

[6] In a letter to a federal judge, Governor Waite quoted the U.S. Marshal as expressing a willingness to use horse thieves, thugs, and hoboes, so long as they could fight.

[7] *New York Tribune*, July 7, 1894. This newspaper editorialized on Altgeld: "In a moment of general insanity the people of Illinois elected a Governor who is the faithful friend of the sworn enemies of society." In Congress a resolution was passed commending Cleveland for his vigorous policy in the strike. During the congressional debate, Pence of Colorado accused Olney of

Since both Mayor John P. Hopkins of Chicago and Sheriff Gilbert of Cook County had refrained so far from calling on the governor for aid, Altgeld sent an official representative, Assistant Adjutant General Bayle, to the city for an investigation of the reports concerning strike violence. As he received confirmation of rioting on the premises of the Illinois Central Railroad, he wired to the president of the railroad that he should ask the mayor and Sheriff Gilbert to request assistance from the state; if both refused, then Altgeld would furnish troops regardless. On the same day, July 6, the governor sent this telegram to his brother-in-law and partner, John W. Lanehart, who represented Altgeld's interests in Chicago:

> The federal troops having accomplished nothing in Chicago so far, I want Hopkins to relieve the situation before they can get their re-enforcements in, in order that the city officials and State troops may get the credit. It is very important for his administration that this should happen. . . . Hopkins being on the ground will be worth more than a regiment of soldiers. The two country regiments will begin to arrive tonight. See him at once . . . show him this telegram and insist on his acting along this line.

The governor hoped to obviate the presence of federal reinforcements by the immediate presence of sufficient militia at all threatening points. Mayor Hopkins found the assistance opportune. He professed a deep contempt for the regulars who, he declared, sat on top of box cars rather than do their duty as needed. Up to the morning of July 6, no railroad companies had called upon him for protection. By this time, however, the situation was steadily getting out of the control of his police. Many of the latter were in sympathy with the strikers and squads would disappear in the crowds without result. Hopkins ordered the discharge of all such policemen. To maintain order he had issued a general proclamation on July 5 asking all citizens to refrain from meeting in crowded places. The lawlessness was chiefly along the railroad lines, where more than one hundred box cars had been destroyed, many stations demolished, and even telegraph lines cut. The federal troops were kept

---

being a counsel for one of the railroad corporations, a stockholder in another, and a member of the board of directors of several railroads. The use of federal injunctions was denounced by Richard Bland of Missouri. Senator Palmer of Illinois, who severely arraigned Altgeld's telegram to Cleveland, had himself protested a similar intervention by President Ulysses S. Grant during the Chicago Fire of 1871 when Palmer was governor.

busy supporting the marshals in making arrests of injunction-violators. Of the twenty-three roads centering in Chicago only six were in complete operation. General Nelson Miles of the federal troops reported that trains moving in and out of the city had been stoned or fired upon by mobs; one engineer had been killed. At 11:30 A.M. on July 6, shortly after receiving the governor's instructions, Hopkins called for five regiments of militia.

The request for state troops was complied with immediately, Altgeld ordering the Chicago and Aurora brigades into action. To Brigadier-General Horace A. Wheeler, who was stationed in Chicago, he wrote an admonition that all unnecessary bloodshed was to be avoided. "There is no glory in shooting at a ragged and hungry man," he said.

The situation which the militia was called on to cope with was a difficult one. On July 5, the seven largest buildings of the World's Fair in Jackson Park had been set on fire, resulting in the death of one man and injuries to four others. The correspondent for the *New York Tribune* reported that on July 6, for the first time since the strike began, a feeling of alarm had permeated the community. The militia was compelled to patrol a wide area over the city and its suburbs. At the Union Stockyards, where, up to that time, federal troops had failed to move the meat, the militia succeeded in clearing the blockade, thus preventing a threatened food shortage. Reports from various parts of the state outside of Chicago indicated that the militia played a major part in overawing resistance.

On July 7 occurred the most serious affray of the strike. A crowd had gathered at 49th and Loomis streets to watch a wrecking crew raise an overturned box car. A regiment of state militia stood on guard. They were hooted and stoned; several shots were fired at them. When the commander's order that the crowd should disperse met with derision, the soldiers were directed to load. The crowd, emboldened by the forbearance of the militia, knocked down four soldiers and the lieutenant. Upon this, orders were given to fire at will. Four men were fatally wounded and twenty others seriously hurt. According to Lieutenant David J. Baker, a federal officer attached to the regiment, this incident virtually ended violence on any appreciable scale thereafter.

A study of the available evidence concerning the responsibility for violence during the strike corroborates Altgeld's theory that the rioters were not, in most instances, former railway employees. A reporter for the United Press, W. J. Guyon, who was a close observer of events in Illinois, later confirmed this analysis. He was even asked by the officials of the American Railway Union to help them in apprehending rioters. Lieutenant Baker reported that the burning of box cars was done by toughs but that "the tampering with switches and couplings, and the blockading of trains, was done by strikers." Chief of Police Brennan made this significant report:

> In some cases there were strong suspicions that the fires were set by Deputy United States Marshals who hoped to retain their positions by keeping up a semblance of disorder. . . . While there were some honest men among them a large number were toughs, thieves, and ex-convicts. . . . Several of these officials were arrested during the strike for stealing property from railroad cars. In one instance two of them were found under suspicious circumstances near a freight car which had just been set on fire. . . . They [the deputies] fired into a crowd of bystanders when there was no disturbance and no reason for shooting. . . . One of them shot and killed a companion by carelessly handling his gun and another shot himself.[8]

In Chicago, the amount of property damage totaled $355,612, of which $338,972 was a single item of July 6 when the fire department was unable to make adequate water connections at an outlying area. For the nation as a whole, the amount of property loss was estimated at $80,000,000.

During the second week of July, Olney was pressing for federal reinforcements, but Walker, who was working steadily on the case against Debs and his associates, objected, suggesting that the President should issue a proclamation ordering rioters to disperse as a preface to martial law in Chicago. Accordingly, Cleveland issued such a proclamation on July 8 affecting some nine states.

Despite an initial rebuff the American Railway Union continued to look for a possible basis for arbitration. Mayor H. S. Pingree of Detroit, Mayor Hopkins, and officials of the A.R.U. formed a com-

---

[8] A similar opinion appeared in the *Chicago Record*, July 10, 1894. The General Managers' Association was aware of the type of deputies being appointed. On July 9, for example, Walker wired to Olney, "At the risk of being thought meddlesome, I suggest that the marshal is appointing a mob of deputies that are worse than useless." Several deputies who were arrested for murder were defended on the advice of Olney. Another theory that the destruction was the work of *agents provocateurs* on the European model is supported by some important, if hearsay, evidence.

mittee to meet with the General Managers' Association but the latter refused to consider arbitration. From the East, George M. Pullman declared to the press that he opposed arbitration because it violated the principle of private property. The wage question was "settled by the law of supply and demand." Vice-President Wickes, in response to the committee's request for arbitration, threatened to move the Pullman factories to New Jersey. The General Managers' Association insisted that the sole issue was whether the A.R.U. should be permitted to dictate to the American people as to what sort of cars they might travel on and under what conditions.[9]

Organized labor, under the leadership of Debs, was not yet ready to yield. Plans for a general strike throughout the country beginning Wednesday, July 11, spread consternation. In Chicago, a wholesale exodus of union men occurred on the first day: teamsters, painters, cigar makers, bakers, carriage makers, wagon makers, workers in the building trades, and affiliates of the Knights of Labor.[10] Each of these trades claimed special grievances of its own. An unprecedented situation in American industrial history—an incipient general strike—was taking place.

Now came the great coup of Walker and Olney. On July 10 orders had been issued for the arrest of the leading A.R.U. officials —Eugene V. Debs, George W. Howard, L. W. Rogers, and Sylvester Keliher—for contempt of the court injunction. Walker had been unwilling to act until he had successfully subpoenaed Western Union Telegraph to produce all telegrams sent by Debs and other officials during the strike. The telegraph company had protested, and even Olney remonstrated: "The Government, in enforcing the law, can not afford to be itself lawless." Walker prevailed, however. The success of his course was admitted by Debs who later declared during his trial:

---

[9] Debs defended the strikers' position in an interview: "It has been asked: What sense is there in sympathetic strikes? Let the corporations answer. When one is assailed, all go to the rescue. They stand together, they supply each other with men, money, and equipments. Labor, in unifying its forces, simply follows their example. If the proceeding is vicious and indefensible, let them first abolish it."

[10] There are evidences of sympathetic strikes as far back as the history of organized labor extends. Most of them appear to have been failures as far as immediate objectives are concerned. In 1891, there were four instances of sympathetic strikes; in 1892, three; and in 1894, twelve, besides the great strike involving twenty-four railroad organizations.

> The strike was broken . . . not by the army and not by
> another power but simply and solely by the action of the
> United States Court in restraining us from discharging our
> duties as officers and representatives of our employees. . . .
> Our headquarters were temporarily demoralized and aban-
> doned and we could not answer any message.

The coup de grace to the Pullman Strike was given by Samuel
Gompers, president of the American Federation of Labor, upon
whom the strike leadership devolved. He had been opposed to the
militancy of the American Railway Union as too radical and now
declared that a general sympathetic strike would react unfavorably
upon the cause of labor. On July 12, Gompers prepared the report
of the federation stating that the unions affiliated with the American Federation of Labor could not join in any general strike and
recommended that all return to work. The General Managers' Association then proceeded to reap the fruits of its toil, and refused to
deal with any labor leaders. It marshalled its forces in such a way
as to insure to each road the maximum advantages in dealing with
the returning men. The subsequent rejection of active union men
by their former employers effectually crippled the Railway Union.
As for the Pullman workers, a large number of them were rejected
and compelled to appeal to Governor Altgeld for relief—a plea
which not only brought food but also moral support from the
"Anarchist" at Springfield, who took this occasion to publish a
bitter arraignment of George M. Pullman and his policies. Sentence
was pronounced by the Supreme Court of the United States against
Debs in a noted case of American constitutional history which
confirmed the new doctrines of centralization; and he remained in
jail to emerge as a determined Socialist, convinced that only a total
displacement of the prevailing economic system could right the
wrongs of his class.

The Pullman Strike has had notable repercussions in our history.
It was the occasion for Governor Altgeld's writing of the famous
planks in the Democratic platform of 1896 stigmatizing "government by injunction" and federal intervention in industrial disputes. For labor the Pullman defeat meant a definite shift in leadership to the less adventurous American Federation of Labor and the
consequent victory of craft unionism. State experiments in the
creation of arbitral and mediation boards received a new impetus,

laying an important foundation for subsequent labor legislation. For some of the thoughtful men of the nation the episode revealed sharply the incompatibility of many of the prevailing economic attitudes and the challenging problems of an increasingly complex industrial order.

This article appeared first in the *Journal of the Illinois State Historical Society,* volume 32 (September 1939), pages 288–312. See page 307 for biographical sketch. Ed.

PART V

U.S. GRANT HOME STATE MEMORIAL
OLD MARKET HOUSE STATE MEMORIAL

HAYMARKET
HULL HOUSE
DOUGLAS TOMB

CHICAGO PORTAGE NATIONAL HISTORIC SITE

ILLINOIS MICHIGAN CANAL TERMINUS

BISHOP HILL STATE MEMORIAL

NAUVOO STATE PARK

FORT CREVE COEUR STATE PARK

FORT EDWARDS MONUMENT

POSTVILLE COURT HOUSE STATE MEMORIAL

MT. PULASKI COURT HOUSE STATE MEMORIAL

LINCOLN'S NEW SALEM STATE PARK

LINCOLN HOME STATE MEMORIAL

MARQUETTE CROSS
PERE MARQUETTE STATE PARK

VANDALIA STATE HOUSE STATE MEMORIAL

CAHOKIA COURT HOUSE STATE MEMORIAL
CAHOKIA MOUNDS STATE PARK

ALBION

FORT CHARTRES STATE PARK

KASKASKIA STATE PARK
PIERRE MENARD HOME STATE MEMORIAL

SHAWNEE NATIONAL FOREST

CAVE IN THE ROCK STATE PARK

PART V

In Recent Times

1910–1959

ALTHOUGH LARGELY a product of her own history until the beginning of the twentieth century, Illinois's character has been increasingly shaped by national and world developments. At the time of the Revolutionary War, for example, events in Illinois were little more than far-distant symptoms of the conflict on the Eastern Seaboard and the rivalry between England, France, and Spain. More recently, Illinois has been more directly affected by international affairs. Within the United States, Illinois both acts and is acted upon; national political trends are effected and reflected by her internal affairs. Although Republican most of the time since 1856 (the state has elected only five Democratic governors), in twentieth-century presidential elections, Illinois has gone Democratic eight times—in overall conformity with the national pattern.

As the new century began, the population of Illinois exceeded 4,800,000 and by 1910 had increased to almost 5,640,000. The twentieth century also brought Illinois a multitude of social problems, associated with its increasing industrialization and urbanization and the inflation-recession cycle of the national economy. One such problem was employers' exploitation of women and children, but in 1903 Illinois established an eight-hour workday and a forty-eight-hour workweek for children, and additional child labor legislation since that time has so protected the health and welfare of children that exploitation is all but impossible. Similarly, the workday for women was limited to ten hours in 1909 and to eight hours in 1937; minimum-wage standards for women became effective in 1933. However, women achieved political equality somewhat earlier: they were able to vote in school board elections in 1891, and by 1913 woman's suffrage had been extended to all the state's nonconstitutional offices. On June 10, 1919, Illinois ratified the Nineteenth Amendment and women thereafter had the same voting rights as men.

Although women's citizenship rights have been vindicated in the twentieth century, the role and the rights of the workingman in modern industrial society require further definition. Generally, because the workingman has been listened to when he spoke in solidarity with other workingmen, there has been a steady growth of craft and industrial unions. Perhaps the best example of organized labor's triumph can be seen in the history of coal mining, where differences between labor and management had frequently resulted in violence. Indeed, labor's struggle for improved working conditions, job security, and higher wages has achieved considerable success in almost every area. Even during the Great Depression, when jobs were scarce and wages low, advances were made.

In Illinois, as in the rest of the nation, the good times of the 1920s were largely illusory; a thin veneer of prosperity concealed the approach of economic disaster. With the collapse of the stock market in 1929, coal mines shut down, farm mortgages were foreclosed, banks failed, and the number of unemployed soared. By 1930, the Great Depression had settled upon Illinois and brought suffering and extreme economic distress to many of the state's 7,630,000 residents. As unemployment lessened the demand for goods, more factories closed, creating more unemployment. More banks failed. Prices for farm products dropped so low that farmers could not make a living, and many, as a consequence, lost their farms. Thousands were jobless, homeless, hungry, and ill clothed.

The Illinois General Assembly, to alleviate distress, held five special sessions between 1930 and 1932, all for the purpose of passing relief measures. To raise money for those in need, it enacted the 2 per cent Retailer's Occupational Tax (the sales tax) in

1933 and increased the rate to 3 per cent in 1935. Illinois also was helped by national economic-relief measures and various federal aid programs directed by such agencies as the Works Progress Administration and the Public Works Administration, which operated throughout Illinois.

In southern Illinois the misery of the depression was compounded by a natural disaster, the Ohio River flood of February 1937. The homes of more than 73,000 persons in eight Illinois counties were destroyed; entire towns were evacuated; and the property damage came to $75 million. No other flood in Illinois history caused such widespread suffering and destruction.

It was not certain, as 1940 came to an end, whether the economic conditions that caused the Great Depression had been remedied; it seemed, rather, that national defense and the requirements of an expanding army and navy, together with increased industrial production as a result of the European war, accounted for the favorable change in the general economy. Indeed, war and preparation for war has exerted an ever greater effect upon people and the conditions of life in the twentieth century.

The citizens of Illinois have participated in all the great military events of their time—more than 350,000 of them in the First World War, some of whom formed the 33d Division, the all-Illinois National Guard organization. At home the State Council of Defense coordinated Illinois's war effort. Farmers produced record crops while factory workers forged the modern sinews of war and other citizens participated in Liberty Loan bond drives and otherwise supported the war.

In 1917, while the war still raged in Europe, Illinois National guardsmen were sent to East St. Louis to quell a major race riot. In 1919 the National Guard was called out in Chicago for the same regrettable reason. Both riots were caused, at least in part, by fear that the employment of large numbers of Southern Negroes in northern factories would deny employment to white workers.

In 1940, most of Illinois's 8,000,000 people, although aware of the new war in Europe and our deteriorating relations with Japan, were profoundly shocked by the Japanese attack on Pearl Harbor and our consequent declarations of war upon Japan and the other Axis powers. Elements of the Illinois National Guard had been federalized in early 1941 and sent to the Philippines, where they fought the invading Japanese in a heroic but futile holding action. Altogether, more than 950,000 Illinoisans, women as well as men, served in the armed forces in World War II.

In 1942, because of the secrecy imposed by wartime, an event of profound significance passed unnoticed by the people of Illinois. Enrico Fermi and his group of scientists, in a top-secret laboratory beneath the stands of Stagg Field at the University of Chicago, conducted man's first controlled nuclear chain reaction. Both the need and the justification for the atomic bombing of Hiroshima and Nagasaki, made possible by Fermi's achievement, have been argued pro and con; nevertheless, it was a factor in ending the final, Asian phase of World War II, in August 1945. Despite the portended dangers of nuclear capability, Americans rejoiced that the war was over and that the course of world history seemed to have been changed for the better. But war and the specter of war still intruded on the international scene. The invasion of South Korea again called forth Illinoisans to fight on foreign soil, as did later the national commitment to the government of South Vietnam.

The development of radio and then television has made possible not only the almost instantaneous transmission of news but has, perhaps, brought people closer together by making them more aware of the world in which they live. Illinois has produced distinguished leaders in the more traditional forms of communication, particularly journalism. Chicago, for instance, has had many powerful, colorful, and sometimes eccentric newspaper publishers, but none was more widely known or more influential than Robert R. McCormick of the *Chicago Tribune*. His death in 1955 seemed to signal the passing of a great period of personal journalism in Illinois.

Like all the Midwestern states before the twentieth century, Illinois lacked an integrated system of good, hard-surface roads. Then, in 1918, Illinois voters approved a $60 million bond issue "to get Illinois out of the mud" by constructing a statewide network of paved roads; a second bond issue of $100 million was approved for the same purpose in 1924. The Illinois Toll Road Commission, created in 1953, opened a high-speed highway from South Beloit and across northern Illinois to the Indiana line in 1958. In 1956 a non-toll, four-lane, divided highway was in operation between Chicago and St. Louis. More than a thousand miles of interstate highways were then built that crisscrossed the state to connect all cities with a population of 50,000 or more. In 1935 the first diesel streamliners crossed Illinois: the *Green Diamond,* the *Panama Limited,* the *Rocket,* and the *Zephyr.*

Commercial air service was inaugurated in Illinois in 1918 and Midway Airport (Chicago Municipal Airport), which opened in 1926, soon became the busiest air terminal in the world, to be succeeded in 1955 by Chicago's O'Hare International Airport. As more and more people traveled by air and Illinois's highway network was extended and improved, the airlines preempted long-distance railroad passenger service and the private automobile replaced the local-service passenger train.

In 1960, as the population figure passed the ten-million mark, fewer and fewer Illinoisans lived on farms and more and more resided in cities, until today more than 95 per cent of the population lives within an urban area. Decreased immigration from abroad, greatly increased migration of Negroes from the South into the cities, and an exodus of whites to the suburban areas seem to be the most recent demographic patterns in Illinois. Urban renewal, open-occupancy laws, and "Model Cities" programs—all designed to rehabilitate the cities—some of these may be able to reverse or stabilize population shifts. Primarily through her schools and universities and her political leaders, Illinois has committed herself to the quest for universal civil rights.

Today Illinois is subject to events that take place far from her borders and perhaps is less able than ever before to control her destiny through her own initiative. But insofar as she can be "master of her fate," all measurable trends and events suggest that Illinois, in the second half of the twentieth century, has accepted her responsibilities and faces the future with the same sturdy optimism that served her so well in the past.

DAVID R. WRONE

is a native of Clinton, Illinois. He received his doctorate in history from the University of Illinois, with a dissertation on "The Prairie Press in Transition." He has contributed to *Illinois Libraries* and to other periodicals. Presently he is teaching at Wisconsin State University, Stevens Point, Wisconsin.

This article appeared first in the *Journal of the Illinois State Historical Society*, volume 58, number 1 (spring 1965), pages 54–76.

ILLINOIS PULLS OUT OF THE MUD

DAVID R. WRONE

With rare exceptions, the roads of Illinois in 1910 differed only in the number of miles from the roads of 1818. They billowed clouds of dust in the summer, froze into ruts during the winter, and for two months each spring and fall became quagmires to trap the stoutest horse and the most powerful automobile. The railroads and the rivers thus maintained their unassailed position as the twin arteries of transportation.

The condition of the roads was of vital importance to the rural inhabitant. Social relationships were limited to the scope of horse-drawn vehicles. Social functions, shopping occasions, and mail delivery were equally dependent on the accessibility of the roads. Work life, too, was affected by the condition of the roads. Farm products were profitably marketable only if railroad or water shipping centers were nearby; drays and wagons could not stand the incessant stresses of the rough roads. Moreover, horses could not endure the constant strain of pulling through mud, nor could farmers spare the hours to negotiate distant trips. An Illinois farmer's diary containing daily entries for the year 1910 reveals the average rural resident's preoccupation with spring road conditions: "Severe thaw this morning—was married this afternoon—The roads froze tonight."

Urban residents suffered no less than the farmer from the handicaps imposed by this antiquated road system. Most of the downstate city streets in 1910 were still little improved from the original prairie sod. Attempts to repair the most traveled streets dissipated city funds, discouraged pedestrians, and left merchants frustrated. Double-teamed draft animals pulled through the spring mud or waded hock-deep in the summer dust. The automobile owner was beginning to have an impact upon the state, but his driving was restricted to the summer months, for mud, slush, and potholes during the spring and fall made motoring an exacting sport, and the roads rendered winter excursions an impossibility. Most drivers stored their vehicles in garages during the winter and left their batteries with a local mechanic, who had a "line" with a low electrical charge for them.

Road maintenance was a complex local affair, organized and operated on the township level. These 1,600 administrative units functioned independently and were hampered by an inadequate tax system that confused the township road commissioners, who were easily befuddled when anything beyond simple road dragging was required. A joint committee of the General Assembly investigating road maintenance in 1912 found that:

> In each of these districts there are three commissioners, making a total of forty-eight hundred road officials to be paid from the road tax. As the office is constantly changing hands, no systematic plan can be followed from year to year. Each farmer wishes to have the road opposite his property improved and the result is a thin veneer of attempted improvements spread over the 95,000 miles of roads in the State.

Late in the nineteenth century, the bicycle clubs of America, vigorously supported by the bicycle manufacturer, A. A. Pope of Hartford, Connecticut, initiated a movement for good roads upon which to ride. This movement was squelched by the hostility of the rural voters, who believed that city idlers were scheming to utilize farm taxes to subsidize work-avoiding play. In sum, the good roads idea lay dormant before 1900, despite the promptings of an occasional editor or energetic public servant.

As the twentieth century unfolded, the idea began to gain more prominence among small, circumscribed groups in Illinois. In 1905, a temporary groundswell of public interest prompted the legislature to pass a law providing for investigation of the road problem by a state engineer and three newly-appointed state highway commissioners. This legislative gesture had little consequence, as enthusiasm again abated, though the commissioners lingered on in their posts until removed by the Tice Law of 1913.

The good roads movement in Illinois passed through three distinct phases. In the first it was a vigorously growing movement concerned with and operating under the Tice Law. This phase developed into the second, the $60 million road bond issue of 1918. The movement culminated in the 1920s with the completion of the statewide system under the $100 million road bond issue of 1924. During the earliest stage the particular and unique case of Vermilion County revealed the inadequacies of the Tice Law. Promotion and then construction problems highlighted the second phase, while the last phase was more concerned with legal and political details. Throughout the first two phases of the movement the Illinois Highway Improvement Association, with William G. Edens of Chicago as president, played an important role.

Prior to 1911, the townships and municipalities had endeavored to solve the road problem by levying special taxes on motor cars. The confusion created by these arbitrary taxes led to action by the legislature. Under the sponsorship of Homer J. Tice of Greenview, the Forty-seventh General Assembly established a uniform licensing process, stipulating that the fees were to be used as a fund for road construction.

Spurred by the belief that the means had been provided for renovating the roads, many organizations formed good roads committees. The Chicago Motor Club's committee on good roads thoroughly examined the laws of Illinois to determine what could be done to improve the roads in Cook County. This able committee declared that mitigation of the road problem was not possible under existing laws. The group further stated that the Chicago organization was too localized to accomplish any significant changes, and that a statewide organization of individuals and clubs should be formed to promote highway improvement.

The Chicago Motor Club adopted the committee's suggestion and issued an invitation to state organizations to convene in Chicago on March 12, 1912, to discuss the road laws. At this meeting the committee's findings, a report from the Illinois Bankers Association, and a summation of a study by a special investigative committee of the state legislature were read. Out of the exchange of opinion which ensued, the delegates decided to constitute themselves into the Illinois Highway Improvement Association, with the object of harmonizing and correlating "all efforts for the improvement of the public wagon roads of Illinois, to the end that an adequate and efficient system of road construction, administration and maintenance will be adopted."

Modification of the legal structure to facilitate practical action was the first task of this group. A statewide convention was scheduled to be held in Peoria on September 27, 1912, to decide the strategy for obtaining the requisite legislation and to broaden the base of better roads support. An invitation was extended to all members of the legislature and to various agricultural, commercial, and labor organizations. The 150 delegates were a fair representation of state organizations and interests, including bankers, editors, farmers, realtors, merchants, and others. Out of this meeting came the resolution to demand a bill in the next session of the General Assembly.

The climate of opinion was markedly in favor of good roads during the early months of the legislative session. Governor Edward F. Dunne was enthusiastic for the idea, and held a series of conferences with officers of the Illinois Highway Improvement Association and representatives of banker, farmer, labor, and other groups. The governor's inaugural address compared the system of permanent roads in Illinois to those in other states and, in general, restated the Highway Improvement Association's platform. Ambitious politicians introduced many road bills that spring, but the association withheld endorsement of any measure while waiting for the opposition to appear.

Resistance did arise from two sources. Some members of the State Association of Highway Commissioners and Town Clerks appointed committees to halt endorsement of the Improvement Association's program. James F. Donovan, president of the township commissioners and chairman of their legislative committee, used his executive skill to obtain amendments to the proposed legislation and then procured endorsement by the recalcitrant commissioners. Supporters of good roads were relieved when this obstacle was cleared, because seventeen years before this same group had opposed the first good roads movement.

The second source of opposition sprang from the farmers, who objected to the abolition of the three-man highway commissioner system. However, progressive rural leaders arranged a compromise which would permit a popular vote in any township to designate the number of commissioners for the community. With these two articulate groups successfully silenced, there was no serious resistance to the good roads movement when the association convened in Springfield on May 13, 1913, to ascertain which bill was to be supported.

Representatives of ninety-one organizations attended the day-long session. They called *en masse* upon the governor. Dunne spoke to them on the necessity of good roads and stressed the employment of convicts on road work. The governor commented, "It will be good for the prisoners and good for the roads." The delegation thereupon reasserted a plank of its Peoria platform which sanctioned the use of convicts and endorsed the main provisions of the Tice bill.

With the governor's approval secured and organized dissent eliminated, the association concentrated its full attention on the members of the legislature who, despite personal sympathy for the bill, were apprehensive lest their constituents somehow be antagonized. Thousands of letters, resolutions, and telegrams poured in upon these legislators as a result of the association's agitation. The final vote—110 to 34 in the house, and 43 to 3 in the senate—was a tribute to the association's tactics. The governor signed the bill without delay.

The Tice Law of 1913 provided for a bi-partisan state highway commission of three members and a state highway engineer, who were responsible for the general supervision of the highways constructed by the state. Each county was to have a superintendent of highways, appointed on the basis of selective tests. The state was to advance half the money for highways built according to standardized specifications and would assume the maintenance of such roads. The law permitted the issuance of county bonds for state-aid roads, so individual counties could hasten construction. In essence, responsibility for the roads was taken away from the townships and placed under the counties, with the consultation and assistance of the state.

Leaders of the good roads movement realized that the Tice Law was merely a temporary measure, which they hoped would suffice until a more comprehensive program could be hammered out. The state-aid provision of the law was a failure, while the section enabling counties to issue bonds for local construction resulted in only a few hundred miles of roads scattered about the state. Vermilion County passed a bond issue under the law and constructed a fairly complete road system. The deficiencies of the Tice Law are focused most clearly by the experience of this east-central Illinois county.

In the late nineteenth century, the downstate good roads movement was centered in Vermilion County. Such dedicated public servants as James W. "Phocion" Howard, a political writer for the *Chicago Inter-Ocean*, and devotees of cycling led by A. G. "Grady" Woodbury, pioneered this worthy cause. They soon found that educating the farmers, who were steeped in individualistic traditions, to the multiple benefits of good roads was frequently a futile undertaking. The crusaders did, nevertheless, gradually build experience in the methods of approaching the problem. The remnants of this organization became the nucleus of a new organization which brought good roads to Vermilion County.

In 1913, after the new road law was passed, the Vermilion good roads movement was formally instituted during a meeting of the Danville Industrial Club. A few members mulled over the potentialities of the Tice Law, while the legatees of the early movement proffered their hard-gleaned insights. From this preliminary discussion, a demand for permanent hard roads germinated, which sprouted within a few days into an organization known as the Vermilion County Good Roads Association. Republican and Democratic businessmen, farmers, railroaders, laborers, and attorneys pooled their time and ability to work for the organization. A few were dreamers; many thought it would increase business and elevate property prices; all were tired of mud.

The plan sought to build a 174-mile network of hard roads. It was bolstered by a plethora of facts to convince the board of supervisors that the entire proposition was a sound business investment. In the ten years preceding 1914, the supervisors were told, Vermilion County had spent almost $1,750,000 on roads. The county had, in return, fifteen miles of pavement, a few miles of rock and gravel roads, and 1,558 miles of dirt highways, which were impassable three or four months a year. During the preceding decade, these unsatisfactory highways had cost the county $1,108.89 per mile for maintenance. The proposed bond issue of $1,500,000 would call for yearly payments of $103,500 compared to $236,698.17 allocated under the prevailing road system in 1914, and, in addition, the new roads would be permanent. This barrage of persuasive figures eliminated the board's reservations with regard to the bond issue, and it heartily embraced the plan in June, 1914, by passing a resolution to submit the proposition to the voters. The Vermilion County Good Roads Association promptly awarded honorary membership to each supervisor.

To launch the movement, O. N. Jones, president of the association, summoned a general meeting on July 16 in Danville to appraise the program. Jones appointed a twenty-five-member publicity committee to organize a drive which took them to hamlets and agricultural halls for speeches and queries. Full-page advertisements in the local newspapers and strenuous exertions at the precinct level showered a barrage of data on the voters. On November 3, 1914, the electorate rewarded the toil of the Good Roads Association by ratifying the bond issue. There was, however, a deceptive aspect in the vote, because the people had accepted only the bond issue, not a road plan. The bonds were legalized without stipulations as to how the board of supervisors was to apportion the $1,500,000. The voters had evidently simply signed a *carte blanche* to the road authorities.

The movement was further diverted by the intrusion of another factor. Between the June resolution and the November vote, the sentiments of the board of supervisors had shifted. The June resolution stated that approximately 17 miles of the project were to be brick, as depicted in red on a map drawn by the Association. About 160 miles were tentatively assigned as concrete, shown in green on the map. On September 17, the supervisors quietly changed the resolution to allow bids on a complete system of either brick or concrete roads. There is not enough evidence to indicate whether this was motivated by a local brick manufacturer, but the incident did direct the attention of Good Roads Association members to facets of the plan which had escaped their notice.

Inasmuch as the state designed and ratified the road plans, the distress of the association stemmed chiefly from doubts of the competency of the state engineers. The road design of P. C. McArdle, the resident state engineer, placed bricks on a concrete base 3 inches thick in the center, tapering to 2 inches at the edge. The concrete base was a mixture of one part cement, three and one-half parts sand, and six parts gravel. Gravel was pressed into the surface of the partially hardened mixture. A compound of equal parts of cement and sand was poured into the brick interstices. The bricks were then smoothed with a hand roller. The adhesion of cement to brick formed a road type known as monolithic.

The Good Roads Association judged the state design to be faulty on two counts. It considered the 2-inch concrete base too thin, insisting that a minimum thickness of 4 inches was indispensable for lasting quality. The state favored a diminutive, or "light," supplement of cement in the mix, whereas the association, drawing upon the diverse knowledge of its members, was aware of the undesirable consequences of the use of this base. The state engineers claimed that the taxpayers' money should be spent on more highly processed brick materials, because the brunt of wear fell upon the surface. This argument, when subjected to scientific analysis, is entirely fallacious and could be attributed to ignorance, if it had not been put forward at a time when the Danville Brick Company was vehemently urging the use of its new-type brick on the roads. The apparent, though by no means substantiated, collusion between the engineers and the brick interests aroused the suspicions of the Good Roads Association.

The association petitioned the state highway commission for a frank reassessment of the road design, but met with a passive refusal. The group then collected material which corroborated its grounds for dispute, but again received no hearing. The organization, finally took a third avenue of protest and pleaded for a close surveillance of the board of supervisors.

While the Vermilion County Good Roads Association was still investigating, the state design was submitted, complete in 119 sections, for certification by the board of supervisors. Although the board granted the association an opportunity to examine the plans, the recommendations of the association were ignored. The board authorized simultaneous bids on 2-, 3-, and 4-inch bases, but the number of miles of brick and concrete remained undesignated.

The association was irate, and redoubled its efforts. The state's chief highway engineer, William Marr, was asked to re-evaluate the Vermilion County system. His vague answer was devoid of real content, and his dubious reasoning appeared to be based on meager contacts with other Illinois roads. The adhesion principle was not fundamental to good design, he said; adequate drainage was the governing precept and had little relevance to the depth of the base. With this response, the association dispatched dozens of letters to individuals and institutions throughout America for information germane to the Vermilion County specifications.

The replies were characterized by a massive support for a 4-inch base and repudiation of the one-to-nine-and-one-half mixture ratio. With this backing, the association again asked state officials to reconsider the design. A. D. Gash of the state highway commission answered:

> Permit me to say that I do not do anything with reference to road work that I do not give utmost careful consideration. When I designed the profile for the roads at Danville I knew what I was doing. (The Vermilion County roads are excellently designed.) I have the advice of Mr. Marr and all of the state engineers upon the question as well as my own judgment, and I have the greatest confidence in the ability of the engineers in your county who drew the plans.

Although the Good Roads Association had proved the inferiority of the state design, the supervisors persisted in receiving bids. The only recourse for the association was to try to convince enough supervisors to let the contracts on the 4-inch base of the original specifications. Despite dilatory maneuvers by the brick interests, which snarled the committee meeting for several hours, the association won. The public was on its side. Bids were opened on 28 miles of brick paving with a 4-inch base and on 146 miles of concrete with a one-to-six mix ratio.

The contracts were let on April 7, 1916, and construction began by the middle of May. On July 20, 1916, the county celebrated the completion of the first small strip of the highway. Congressmen, legislators, automobile club officials, brass bands, 500 decorated automobiles, and a bevy of attractive girls proudly made the 10-mile grand tour. On this occasion, Governor Dunne said wistfully:

> But it is not alone in Vermilion county that this meeting is significant. The whole state should have its eyes upon what you are doing here, because what one county has done another can do. . . . It means . . . that we are learning as a people to conduct our public affairs as intelligently, as economically, as honestly, as scientifically, as we do our private affairs.

The failure of other counties to imitate the Vermilion scheme made revision of the Tice Law necessary. Even Vermilion County was beset by difficulties, as it struggled to finish the road work.

Rising prices of labor and material, a manpower shortage, high freight rates, low priority ratings, and other aggravating complications hindered construction. By local efforts alone were the highways completed. Farmers voluntarily contributed their teams to aid the contractors. Although the state engineers worked long and hard at their task, certain of their idiosyncrasies might bring a chuckle from later generations—for example, when they built the highway on both sides of a farmer's shade tree rather than remove it or alter the route.

Under the Tice Law, Vermilion County labored three long, disconcerting years to construct 174 miles of roads. Just prior to the statewide drive for a $60,000,000 road bond issue in 1917, only three other counties (Cook, Jackson, and St. Clair) had approved bond issues. Numerous counties had merely managed to take tentative steps. Clearly, the Tice Law was inoperable, unless a strong civic movement, as had existed in Vermilion County, pushed for road improvement.

Moreover, rapid progress could not be achieved under the law, and if the growing desire of an ever increasing number of motorists for good roads was to be met, an alternative solution was imperative. The advantages of a more centrally controlled system had also been demonstrated in the money saved in maintenance costs.

Widespread dissatisfaction with the haphazard, unfruitful results of the Tice Law combined with a multitude of fresh events to provide the impetus behind the second phase of the Illinois good roads movement. In 1916, a Federal law was passed which offered to match state appropriations for the construction of highways having interstate importance. The $12 million which Illinois could receive stood as a powerful incentive for the formation of a general plan extending the highway network. However, the most politically captivating factor was a "phenomenal growth of sentiment" for good roads among the voters of 1918. Automobile registrations had mushroomed from 131,000 in 1914 to over 375,000 in 1918, with the number swelling daily.

Toward the end of 1916, the state highway commission developed a plan for a statewide, 4,000-mile network of hard roads. The plan was unique in its financing, which involved a state road bond issue estimated as high as $50 million. The money was to be collected from motor license fees and general taxation. The architect of the plan was Samuel Ellsworth Bradt, one of the three state highway commissioners, chairman of the Illinois Bankers Association good roads committee, and first vice-president of the Illinois Highway Improvement Association. He pressured the Association to engage in a second campaign. The organization's directors gave unanimous approval to the plan, which ultimately entailed private financing, the cooperation of the governor, a statewide organization, and competition with the war effort.

Bearing in mind the attitude of former Governor Dunne, the Highway Improvement Association knew the indispensability of forceful executive leadership. The governor-elect, Frank O. Lowden, proved to be an invaluable ally. When the plan was first presented to him after the election, he objected to the proposed financing. His reaction was to be expected, inasmuch as he had pledged to trim government expenditures. He did, however, propose an amendment, which he thought would make the plan more palatable to the public. If the entire bond issue could be financed through automobile-license fees, he would be willing to defend the association's drive and to insert a better roads plank in his program. The association resolved to devote its resources to the passage of a $60 million bond issue for the construction of 4,800 miles of roads, and Governor Lowden backed legislation calling for a statewide referendum on November 5, 1918.

When the Illinois Highway Improvement Association assumed the responsibility for promoting the good roads issue, it realized that the program faced three handicaps. First, unless the rural areas received adequate information about the proposed means of financing the roads, the farmers would undoubtedly vote against the plan. Second, the bond issue had to obtain a majority of the total vote cast for members of the legislature. Third, the priority demands of World War I might hurt the issue.

Shortly after the passage of the referendum bill, public sympathy swung sharply away from the good roads movement. Internal improvements were vastly overshadowed by sympathy of the boys "over there." Governor Lowden assuaged the anxieties of good roads men with public statements priming the public response to the roads plan. After all, cautioned the governor, a depression might follow the war. No roads would be constructed, he said, until international amity had been restored, and once road-building projects were underway, there would be few better sources of continuing employment opportunities for veterans. This logic silenced even the most outspoken critics.

The association organized committees in every county. Over 6,000,000 maps, folders, posters, and pamphlets were distributed. Lecturers, motion-picture theaters, and newspapers also played their part. When the issue carried—661,815 to 154,396—it was the result of this prodigious campaign, guided by some of the most agile minds in the state. The proposal carried in every county except two.[1]

Members of the Illinois Good Roads Association saw this resounding victory as the cherished goal of their weary years of labor. How wrong they were! Two years elapsed before major construction commenced. Not until 1925 were the 4,800 miles of the road system completed—and then only with funds supplied by the second bond issue.

Despite an ever-growing public demand, Governor Lowden refused to sell bonds during his term. As a sop to the public, he allowed 550 miles of roads to be built, including a few federal-aid highways. A gamut of obstacles retarded construction during the Lowden administration: railroad car shortages, an unfavorable bond market, a raft of strikes, lack of competitive bidding, and a depleted labor force. Beneath these impediments lay a more persuasive factor—the price of cement. As soon as the bond issue was passed, the retail cost of cement rose 80 per cent. Governor Lowden suspected that the portland cement manufacturers were conspiring to boost prices. Before a closed session of a legislative committee probing the "cement combine," he divulged the findings of a confidential investigation. During these committee proceedings, cement prices dropped 20 cents a barrel. Because the governor would not inaugurate full-scale construction until cement prices were lowered another 20 cents, only a small number of roads were built in Illinois during his tenure in office.

However, his contribution cannot be appraised on this count alone, for it was under his executive command that the department of public works surveyed, graded, and erected bridges for many of the proposed routes. The state had acquired 3,000 miles of right-of-way by the end of 1920. When Len Small took over the governor's office, it was evident that construction work had been ad-

---

[1] Hamilton County in southern Illinois, one of the dissenting counties, received only a small part of the proposed mileage; and the other, DeWitt County, possessed an eccentric political leader with enough strength to defeat the issue. Byron F. Staymates was opposed as a matter of principle to issues which other people supported and desired.

vanced at least one year by Lowden's preparations. Furthermore, Lowden had 2 miles of experimental highway for research purposes started at Bates, just west of Springfield.

Good roads men grew impatient waiting for the realization of their cherished dream. In the autumn of 1920, the Illinois State Automobile Association called for greater highway-building activity. Governor Small recognized this spirit of unrest when he announced in his inaugural address: "The greatest economic good that can be accomplished for the country districts of our state is to push this road system to completion." Push he did. The eight years of his administration produced one of the finest road systems in the world. Superb construction was guaranteed by superior engineering skill, while a diplomatic path was tactfully trod between various interest groups—railroads, village officials aspiring to place their towns on the "hard" road, and businessmen. With a heavy political hand, Small replenished the exhausted larder of the highway department, when it became clear that the $60 million bond issue would not stretch far enough to cover the public desire for more roads.

Large-scale construction began as soon as the new administration was able to let the contracts. Wheels set in motion by economic forces in the early 1920s abetted the administration's zeal for road development. The price of cement had slipped slightly from its peak in 1919, and the nation was shaken by the impact of a recession. Road laborers' wages, for example, dropped from 50 to 28 cents an hour within a few months, while railroad deliveries were becoming more dependable. In addition, most of the right-of-way for the highways has been obtained. Where local squabbles flared up, the state merely paved the roads in other sections of the county.[2]

The public clamor for good roads goaded the administration into heightened activity, as the number of automobile purchases increased. From 1918 to 1925, the total of motor vehicle licenses increased by over 850,000. Although the Small administration was increasing road construction with more efficient crews and improved techniques, it soon became apparent that all funds for

---

[2] "Clinton Gap" was a six-mile stretch of unpaved road in DeWitt County that isolated Clinton from the paved roads. Uninformed citizens, vested interests, and misunderstanding kept the community bickering and wallowing for six years.

highway construction would be utterly consumed in 1924, leaving a little more than 1,300 miles unfinished. Small recommended a $100 million bond issue, which would satisfy the immediate needs of the $60 million system and would allow the construction of another 5,100 miles of hard-surfaced roads, bringing the state's primary system up to 9,900 miles. The politically astute governor, however, endeavored to use this measure, the third phase of the good roads movement, as a means of assuring his continuance in office.

In thus attempting to further his own political ends, the governor followed a rather set pattern. He would nominate a local candidate, promise to build roads if his protégé were elected, and then back up his promise. In the case of La Salle County, he picked a candidate for the state senate who danced to the governor's tune. He accompanied the puppet to a local rally, where he pledged that election of his man would ensure roads for the country. If the individual should be defeated, on the other hand, the county would be denied a highway system. Such bluntness may seem overbearing —and, indeed, this La Salle County protégé overstepped propriety by pursuing the same tack in his campaign, picking out the routes for a road system, and guaranteeing construction upon his election to office. The candidate was defeated; and the governor kept his word. Only four contracts were let, and La Salle County got less than half a mile of new roads.

La Salle County editors decried this vindictiveness:

> In various counties over the state where the residents are extremely anxious to get paved roads, they are kowtowing to the Governor's demands of endorsement of the hundred million dollar bond issue scheme. They seem to be more interested in securing the roads than the future of road building in the state. . . . Politics may be politics and roads are roads, but you can't mix politics with the cement and gravel that goes into the highways.

And State Senator Thurlow G. Essington of La Salle County was at once a sage and a prophet when he deduced from the governor's attitude that highway development in Illinois "never will be free from political considerations as long as we are building roads."

Many of the state's business and civic organizations were persuaded that the new bond issue proposed by Governor Small was superfluous. Thirty-two state groups, including the Illinois Highway Improvement Association, condemned the measure. These organizations were dominated by conservative businessmen to whom the multi-million-dollar bond issue was repugnant as an extravagance, particularly when the state treasury was already encumbered by the previous highway bond issue. Basically, the opponents could find no justification for the allocation of more money, and argued that the income from license fees and anticipated federal aid would provide all the funds needed to complete the original plan in six years. Frank T. Sheets, state superintendent of highways, calculated that the road crews would soon be able to build 1,000 miles of road each year. If given the money, the state could manage to satisfy the impatient demand for more roads; if denied added income, the state highway department predicted that the 1918 bond issue roads would not be completed before 1929, relying on the "pay-as-you-go" policy. To the chagrin of his detractors, Governor Small's engineers succeeded in constructing 1,085 miles of paved roads in 1923, and 1,230 miles in 1924. This record drew the full might of public sanction for his program.

The people wanted roads. Not even the desire of the opposition for a pay-as-you-go program to avert any future manipulations— real or fancied—of public money could stave off the mounting craving for an adequate highway system. The opponents of the new bond issue had no confidence in the financial reliability of future governors, nor did they trust Governor Small completely, but politicians recognized that a negative vote on the bill was tantamount to political suicide. The General Assembly, therefore, agreed to the referendum by a large majority, and the public approved the bond issue overwhelmingly.

To finish building the state's primary road system, it was necessary not only for Illinois to use all the money provided by the 1924 bond issue, but also, in a few years, to allocate more funds through a tax on gasoline. The building program was incessantly beset by difficulties during the last half of the 1920s. The state sought to obtain land for right-of-way, sometimes without adequately reimbursing property owners, and understandably met with resistance. A myriad of complications was ushered in by the Great Depression. Even so, by the end of 1930, Illinois could boast the finest system of permanent roads in America. From its northern border to Cairo, between the Wabash and the Mississippi, 76 per cent of the 10,098 miles comprising the basic highway system was surfaced with concrete. The secondary, or state-aid county roads, amounting to 17,369 miles, were one-quarter surfaced, mostly with gravel, while 84 per cent of the remaining 69,767 miles of Illinois roads under the jurisdiction of local township or road district authorities were dirt.

of Chicago and Oak Park, was widely known as a lecturer. She was active in a wide variety of women's clubs and organizations, but was perhaps best known for work on behalf of women's suffrage. She was president of the Illinois Equal Suffrage Association in 1912, and led the fight in Springfield for that cause in 1913.

This article was published in the *Journal of the Illinois State Historical Society*, volume 13, number 2 (July 1920), pages 145–179.

SIDE LIGHTS ON ILLINOIS SUFFRAGE HISTORY

GRACE WILBUR TROUT

When we look back to the early fifties of the last century and contemplate the beginning of equal suffrage work in Illinois, we realize the marvelous change in public sentiment that has taken place since that time. A married woman in those days had no jurisdiction over her own children, she could not lay claim to her own wardrobe—about all that she could call her own in those days was her soul, and some man usually had a claim on that, although it had been solemnly declared during a previous century by a learned council of men that women really did possess souls.

The first local suffrage club in Illinois was organized over a half century ago in Earlville in the early sixties, and a few years later the Illinois Equal Suffrage Association was founded in Chicago (in 1869). It was founded the same year that the National American Woman Suffrage Association was organized, and with which it has always been affiliated.

The Illinois Equal Suffrage Association was organized by men as well as women. One of the early founders of the association was Judge Charles B. Waite, who was appointed associate justice of Utah Territory by Abraham Lincoln. His wife, Mrs. Catherine Van Valkenberg-Waite, was also one of that first group that started the state suffrage movement in Illinois, and associated with them were a number of other eminent men and women. The work during those early years was slow, educational work, the association patiently and persistently plodding forward toward its ultimate goal—full political freedom for the women of Illinois.

My first active participation in suffrage work was as president of the Chicago Political Equality League, to which office I was elected in May, 1910.

The first active work undertaken under my administration as league president was to secure permission to have a suffrage float in the Sane Fourth Parade to be held in Chicago. There was some hesitation on the part of the men's committee having this in charge as to whether an innovation of this kind would be proper. Finally however, permission was granted, with the understanding that we were to pay the committee $250 for the construction of the float. We had no funds in the treasury for this purpose, so money had to be raised—mostly by soliciting contributions from our friends and neighbors in Oak Park. It was difficult also to secure young ladies whose mothers would permit them to ride on a suffrage float. All obstacles were finally overcome and the suffrage float received more cheering in the procession than any other feature of the parade, with the single exception of the G. A. R. veterans, with whom it shared equal honors. The suffrage float aroused interest in suffrage among people who had never before considered the question seriously.

While planning for the suffrage float, preparations were also being made for the first organized Suffrage Automobile Tour ever undertaken in Illinois. As league president I was asked by the state board of the Illinois Equal Suffrage Association, to take charge of this experimental tour, which required about six weeks of preparatory work to insure its success.

I visited the newspaper offices and was fortunate in securing the co-operation of the press. The tour started on Monday, July 11, and the Sunday edition of the *Chicago Tribune* the day before contained a full colored page of the women in the autos, and nearly a half page more of reading material about the tour. The *Tribune* sent two reporters along on the trip, who rode with us in our auto, one to report for the daily paper and one to report for the Sunday edition. Other Chicago newspapers, the *Examiner, Record Herald, Post,* and *Journal,* sent reporters by railroad and trolley, who joined us at our various stopping places.

Through the kindness of one of our Oak Park neighbors, Charles W. Stiger, the Winton Motor Company donated the use of one of their finest seven passenger autos to carry us as far as Woodstock, furnishing also an expert chauffeur. There we were met by an equally fine Stoddard Dayton car which carried us to Naperville where Mr. Stiger's own car was waiting to take us back to Chicago. At the meetings during this week's tour, contributions were taken and enough money was raised to pay all expenses of the trip and a balance of over $100 was turned into the state treasury.

We usually spoke from the automobile, driving up into some square or stopping on a prominent street corner which had previously been advertised in the local papers and arranged for by the local committees in the various towns visited. It had been difficult, however, in many towns to secure women who were willing to serve on these local committees, the excuse usually given was that the people in their respective towns were not interested and did not care to hear about suffrage.

I selected as speakers for the tour, Mrs. Catharine Waugh McCulloch, who spoke on suffrage from the legal standpoint, Miss S. Grace Nicholes, a settlement worker, who spoke from the laboring woman's standpoint, and Ella S. Stewart, state president, who treated the subject from an international aspect. I made the opening address at each meeting, covering the subject in a general way, and introduced the speakers. I, in turn, was presented to the various crowds by some prominent local woman or man, and on several occasions by the mayor of the town.

The towns visited were: Evanston, Highland Park, Lake Forest, Waukegan, Grays Lake, McHenry, Woodstock, Marengo, Belvidere, Sycamore, DeKalb, Geneva, Elgin, Aurora, Naperville, and Wheaton. In every one of these towns the local newspapers gave front page stories about the Suffrage Automobile Tour, which helped greatly in arousing interest. The following comments of the *Chicago Tribune* show the success of the trip:

> Suffragists' tour ends in triumph . . . With mud-bespattered "Votes for Women" still flying, Mrs. Grace Wilbur Trout, leader of the Suffrage automobile crusade, and her party of orators, returned late yesterday afternoon. . . . Men and women cheered the suffragists all the way in from their last stop at Wheaton to the Fine Arts Building headquarters.

The success of this tour encouraged the Illinois Suffrage Association to go on with this new phase of suffrage work, and similar tours were conducted in other parts of the state.

The Chicago Political Equality League had been organized by the Chicago Woman's Club in 1894, and in May 1910, had only 143 members. We realized that for sixteen years work this was too slow a growth in membership to bring speedy success to the suffrage movement. As a consequence in the summer of 1910 a strenuous campaign for new members was instituted, and in the League Year Book published in the fall, we had added 245 new names, nearly trebling our membership.

The league had previously held its meetings in the rooms of the Chicago Woman's Club, but in 1911 it had grown to such proportions that more spacious quarters were needed, and the Music Hall of the Fine Arts Building was secured as a meeting place. On account of the league's increased activities it was voted at the annual meeting on May 6, 1911, to organize legislative, propaganda, and study sections for the purpose of carrying on different phases of the work, and it was decided also to hold meetings four times a month instead of once as heretofore.

My term of office as league president expired in May 1912, and through the splendid co-operation of the league members we had succeeded in raising our membership to over 1,000 members.

On October 2, 1912, at the state convention held at Galesburg, Illinois, I was elected state president of the Illinois Equal Suffrage Association. In addition to my league work I had been serving as a member of the state board of this association since October 1910. Thus having had several years of strenuous experience in suffrage work I desired above all things to retire to private life, and in spite of the urging of many suffragists, would not have accepted the state presidency had it not been for the arguments advanced by one of my sons. This son had been out in California during the 1911 suffrage campaign when the California women won their liberty. He had seen every vicious interest lined up against the women and had become convinced of the righteousness of the cause. He said to me: "Mother, you ought to be willing to do this work—to make any sacrifice if necessary. This is not a work simply for women, but for humanity," and he added, "you can do a work that no one else can do." He had that blind faith that sons always have in their mothers —and I listened to his advice.

This son, who had just reached his majority, had met with a severe accident some years before, from which we thought he had completely recovered, but just three weeks after my election an unexpected summons came to him and he passed on into that far country where the principles of equality and justice are forever established. So our work sometimes comes toward us out of the sunshine of life, sometimes it comes toward us out of life's shadows, and all that we do is not only for those who are here, and those who are coming after us, but is in memory of those who have gone on before.

Immediately after my election to the presidency we realized the necessity of strengthening the organization work, for in spite of all of the previous organization work, there were many senatorial districts in which there was no suffrage organization of any kind, and as the time was short, competent women were immediately appointed in such districts to see that their respective legislators were properly interviewed, and to be ready to have letters and telegrams sent to Springfield when called for.

All of this work was difficult to accomplish without funds. Our board found the association about $100 in debt, and immediate solicitation of the friends of suffrage was begun for the purpose of raising funds. After legislative work began, however, this work was of paramount importance and I had to call often upon Mr. Trout for funds with which to finance the Springfield campaign.

During the previous session of the legislature in Springfield (in 1911) I had accompanied Mrs. McCulloch, who had been in charge there of the suffrage legislative work for over twenty years. At that time I was indignant at the way the suffrage committee was treated. Some men who had always believed in suffrage, were exceedingly kind, but no one regarded the matter as a serious legislative question which had the slightest possibility of becoming a law. Mr. Homer Tice had charge of the suffrage bill in 1911 in the House, and he said that in consequence he became so unpopular that every other bill he introduced in the legislature during that session, was also killed. It certainly required moral courage for an Illinois legislator to be an active suffragist at that time.

Having had this experience, as soon as I was elected to the presidency of the Illinois Equal Suffrage Association I sent for Mrs. Elizabeth K. Booth of Glencoe, the newly elected legislative chairman, and we agreed upon a legislative policy. This included a campaign without special trains, special hearings, or spectacular activities of any kind at Springfield, as too much publicity during a legislative year is liable to arouse also the activity of every opponent. It was decided to initiate a quiet, educational campaign, and not to attack or criticise those opposed to suffrage, because the only possible way to succeed and secure sufficient votes to pass the measure was to convert some of these so-called opponents into friends. We agreed also that a card index, giving information about every member of the legislature, should be compiled. This plan of procedure was submitted to the state board at its regular meeting on November 8, 1912, and the plan of campaign as outlined was approved and adopted by the board. The following women served on the state board at this time:

OFFICERS:

President ....Grace Wilbur Trout
First Vice-President ....Miss Jane Addams
Second Vice-President ....Mrs. Joseph T. Bowen
Recording Secretary ....Miss Virginia Brooks
Corresponding Secretary ....Mrs. Bertram W. Sippy
Treasurer ....Miss Jennie F. W. Johnson
Auditor ....Mrs. J. W. McGraw

HEADS OF DEPARTMENTS:

Organization ....Mrs. Mary R. Plummer
Press ....Miss Margaret Dobyne
Literature ....Dr. Anna E. Blount
Publicity ....Mrs. George S. Welles
Legislative ....Mrs. Sherman M. Booth
Church ....Mrs. H. M. Brown
Lecture ....Miss S. Grace Nicholes
Industrial ....Miss Mary McDowell
Woman's Journal ....Mrs. Lillian N. Brown

DIRECTORS:

Officers, Heads of Departments

Mrs. Elvira Downey   Mrs. Charles A. Webster
                    Mrs. Ella S. Stewart

On December 19 a suffrage mass meeting was held in Orchestra Hall in honor of the Board of Managers of the National American Woman Suffrage Association which at that time was holding a board meeting in Chicago. The mass meeting was given especially in honor of Miss Jane Addams and Mrs. Joseph T. Bowen, who had both been elected to the national board at the national convention held in November. Miss Addams and Mrs. Bowen were also respectively first and second vice presidents of the Illinois Equal Suffrage Association. As state president I presided over this meeting, and

Dr. Anna Howard Shaw and other members of the national board addressed the audience.

As soon as the legislature convened in January 1913, an immediate struggle developed over the speakership in the House. There was a long and bitter deadlock before William McKinley, a young Democrat from Chicago, was finally elected speaker. Then another struggle ensued over who should represent Illinois in the United States Senate. During these weeks of turmoil little could be accomplished in the way of securing votes for the suffrage bill.

Before the legislature had convened the Progressive Party had made plans to introduce as a party measure a carefully drafted woman's suffrage bill. Hearing about this Mrs. Booth and I at once consulted with the Progressive leaders and suggested that it would be far better to let the Illinois Equal Suffrage Association introduce this measure than to have it presented by any political party. The Progressives realized the force of this suggestion and finally very kindly agreed to let the Illinois Equal Suffrage Association take their carefully drafted bill and have it introduced as an absolutely non-partisan measure.

In the meantime, on February 10, Mrs. Booth, as legislative chairman, was sent to Springfield to study the plats and learn to recognize and call by name each member of the legislature. Mrs. Catharine Waugh McCulloch—who had declined to serve as legislative chairman this year on account of family duties—volunteered on this occasion to accompany Mrs. Booth to Springfield. As this was Mrs. Booth's first trip no action had as yet been taken to introduce the Presidential and Municipal Suffrage Bill which had been drafted by the Progressives and which we were to introduce. Mrs. McCulloch, however, took with her a suffrage bill which she had drafted and which she insisted upon having introduced without one word being changed, which was done. It contained however, in its second section, no blanket clause, but specifically named the officers for whom women should be allowed to vote, instead of being worded like the Progressive draft which said: "Women shall be allowed to vote at such elections for *all offices* and upon *all questions and propositions* submitted to a vote of the electors, except where the Constitution provides as a qualification that the elector shall be a male citizen of the United States." Mrs. Booth being inexperienced in legislative work, and as Mrs. McCulloch was a lawyer, she believed this bill to be regular in form and to cover the subject fully. When Mrs. Booth returned and reported what had been done we were all very much distressed that the plan agreed upon with the Progressives had not been carried out and their bill introduced. In the interests of harmony, and out of deference to Mrs. McCulloch's long years of service as legislative chairman, and some of us not being so well versed in constitutional law then as we became later, the matter was allowed to stand.

Because we failed to introduce the form of bill agreed upon with the Progressives, they proceeded to introduce their bill in both the House and Senate. This complicated matters and made confusion, but finally the Progressives, in order to help the suffrage cause, very graciously withdrew their bill. Medill McCormick, one of the leading Progressives in the legislature, helped greatly in straightening out this tangle. He was our faithful ally and rendered invaluable service during the entire session. Other Progressives in the House who also rendered important services were: John M. Curran and Emil N. Zolla, both of Chicago, J. H. Jayne of Monmouth, Charles H. Carmon of Forrest and Fayette S. Munro of Highland Park.

While the state legislative work was being taken care of at Springfield we did everything possible to co-operate with the National American Woman Suffrage Association in its national work. On March 3, the day preceding President Wilson's first inauguration at Washington, suffragists of the various states were called to come to the national capital and take part in a suffrage parade. I was very proud to conduct eighty-three Illinois women in Washington. We left Chicago by special train on March 1, 1913, and were extended every courtesy by the Baltimore & Ohio Railroad. An elaborate banquet was served on the train including fresh strawberries, and every other delicacy, at only $1.00 a plate, and special maids were provided to wait upon the suffragists.

This Washington parade and the brutal treatment accorded the women along the line of march aroused the indignation of the whole nation and converted many men to the suffrage cause. It was openly asserted that if law-abiding women, who had been given an official permit to have the parade, could be so ill treated on the streets of the national capital, it was time that the legal status of women was changed and women accorded the respect to which every loyal American citizen is entitled. The police claimed they could not control the jeering mob, who spat upon the women and

roughly handled many of them, but the next day the inauguration
parade down the same streets was a manifestation of perfect law
and order and was in marked contrast to the disgraceful procedure
of the day before. The Illinois women wore a uniform regalia of cap
and baldric and were headed by a large band led by Mrs. George S.
Welles as drum major. We had a woman outrider, a young Mrs.
Stewart recently converted to the cause, who on a spirited horse
helped keep back the mob from our group. I led, carrying an
American flag, and our Illinois banner, too heavy for a woman, was
carried by Mr. Royal N. Allen, an ardent suffragist and one of the
railroad officials, who had our special suffrage train in charge. Our
women had been drilled to march and keep time, and the discipline
manifested seemed to affect the hoodlums and our women were
treated with more respect than the majority of the marchers. In
fact, the newspapers particularly commended the order and system
manifested by the Illinois division.

On March 10 I went to Springfield to consult with Governor
Edward F. Dunne, and secure, if possible, his support of the Presidential and Municipal Suffrage Bill. He agreed to support this
statutory suffrage bill if we would promise not to introduce a
suffrage measure which provided for a constitutional amendment,
as but one constitutional amendment (according to Illinois law)
could be introduced during a legislative session, and this, if introduced, would interfere with the Initiative and Referendum Constitutional Amendment upon which the administration was concen-
trating its efforts. We assured the governor that we would not
introduce a resolution for a constitutional suffrage amendment
because we knew we had no chance to pass such a resolution and
we also wished not to interfere with the administration's legislative
plans. I remained in Springfield during the rest of the week to size
up the legislative situation.

The next week I went again to Springfield to attend the meeting
of the Senate committee to which our suffrage bill had been referred. Senator W. Duff Piercy was chairman and had offered to
arrange a suffrage hearing if we wished it. As we ascertained that a
majority of this committee were friendly it seemed wiser not to
arouse antagonism by having public discussion on the suffrage
question at this time, so there was no hearing.

During the next two weeks I spent my time in visiting the
districts having legislators not as yet converted to the suffrage

cause. Mass meetings were held in some towns and arranged for in many others.

The first week of April the Mississippi Valley Conference of Suffragists was held at St. Louis and it seemed imperative for me to attend. This large gathering of suffragists would have been helpful to our legislative work in Springfield if a prominent Illinois suffragist in her speech at the conference, had not attacked the lawyers in the Illinois legislature, saying they were either crooks or failures in their profession, or words to that effect. As there were many lawyers in both the House and Senate whose votes we had to secure in order to pass the suffrage measure, such attacks were most unfortunate and made the work exceedingly difficult.

Another shock was in store for us, for on April 2, at the request of a well known suffragist, a resolution providing for a constitutional amendment was introduced. It had been thoroughly explained to her that this was against the wishes of the governor and would be construed as a breach of faith on our part, especially as she had been identified for so many years with the suffrage legislative work. It was hard for the legislators and for the governor to realize that any suffragist, not a member of the lobby, nor a member of the state board, would proceed entirely on her own judgment. At our state board meeting held on April 8 Mrs. Joseph T. Bowen, our first vice president, introduced a resolution which was afterwards sent to Mrs. Catharine Waugh McCulloch, asking her, in the interest of the equal suffrage movement in Illinois, to have this resolution withdrawn. It was not withdrawn, however, but was afterwards killed in committee.

The work at Springfield became more and more difficult and at times it seemed hopeless. No politician believed that we had the slightest chance to pass the suffrage measure. On April 7 I began attending the sessions of the legislature regularly.

During all of our work at Springfield we had splendid co-operation from the press. Nearly every week end when we returned to Chicago I made it a point to see one or more managers of the newspapers and explain to them the difficulties we were encountering, and asked them to publish an editorial that would be helpful to the situation. By not appealing too often to any one newspaper helpful articles were kept coming along in some newspaper nearly every week. We had these various newspapers containing suffrage propaganda folded so that the editorial (blue penciled) came on the outside. They were then placed on each legislator's desk by a boy engaged for that purpose. These editorials were a surprise to the representatives of these various Chicago newspapers who were at Springfield, for it seemed best to make it appear that these editorials were spontaneous expressions of sentiment. I remember one of the legislators, unfriendly to suffrage, who had tried a little parliamentary trick which was indirectly referred to in an editorial, growling about those Chicago newspapers that attend to everybody's business but their own. He even complained to the Springfield representative of the newspaper, who of course declared his innocence, because he knew nothing about it.

The Springfield papers also became exceedingly friendly and published suffrage articles and editorials when we asked for them.

Among the Chicago newspaper men whom I remember with special gratitude at this time were: Mr. Keeley and Mr. Beck of the *Tribune,* Mr. Chamberlain of the *Record Herald,* Mr. Eastman and Mr. Finnegan of the *Journal,* Mr. Andrew Lawrence and Mr. Victor Polachek of the *Examiner,* Mr. Curley of the *American,* Mr. Shafer and Mr. Mason of the *Post* and Mr. Frank Armstrong of the *Daily News.*

We were deeply indebted at this time for the help given us by Mr. Andrew J. Redmond, a Chicago lawyer and grand commander of the Knights Templar. I remember one instance in particular when much pressure was being brought to bear on Governor Dunne to prejudice him against the suffrage bill—I wished Mr. Redmond, who was a personal friend of the governor, to go down to Springfield and help counteract this harmful influence. Mr. Redmond was a next door neighbor of ours in Oak Park, and he had an important law suit on that week, and in talking the matter over with Mr. Trout we both decided it would be imposing upon the kindness of a friend to ask him to leave his business and go at that time. Mrs. Redmond, however, called me up by phone to ask how things were going. She and her husband were both deeply interested in having us win the fight. I told her the facts but told her I was not going to ask Mr. Redmond, much as we needed him, to go down the coming week on account of his business. When Mr. Trout took me to the Springfield train, where I met Mrs. Booth, there on the platform with his grip in hand, stood Mr. Redmond. My husband said at once "Why, I thought you were not going to ask him to go this week." I explained that I hadn't, but told about my conversa-

tion with Mrs. Redmond, and of course if his wife wished to interfere with his business and send him to Springfield, I was not
responsible. Mr. Redmond not only called upon the governor, but
saw several downstate legislators whom he knew well, and through
his influence several very important votes were secured.

I discovered at Springfield that we had just four classes of
legislators—"wets" and "drys" and "dry-wets" and "wet-drys." The
"dry-wets" were men who voted for the wet measures but never
drank, themselves. The "wet-drys" were those who voted for dry
measures but imbided freely themselves. The "drys" warned us not
to trust a single "wet" and the "wets" on the other hand counseled
us to take no stock in those hypocritical "drys." As the measure
could not be passed without "wet" votes, our scheme of education
necessarily had to include "wets" as well as "drys."

I well remember of asking a certain "wet" legislator from a
foreign section in Chicago if he would vote for the suffrage bill. He
looked surprised and said, "Don't you think the women would vote
out all of the saloons?" I answered that I hoped so. He seemed
dumfounded by such frankness and sort of gasped, "Yet you ask
me, a 'wet,' to vote for the bill?" I then explained as best I could,
that I supposed all honest "wets" as well as "drys" felt the same way
about the saloons, that while we might differ on how to settle the
temperance question, still we all really hoped that those places
where men wasted their money and where boys and girls were
frequently lured to destruction, were done away with. He looked a
little dazed and said nothing. I of course thought we had lost his
vote, and was happily surprised the next morning when this same
man came to me with a very sober face and said: "I thought and
thought about what you said all night, and I guess you are right—
you can count my vote," and he kept his word.

The Presidential and Municipal Suffrage Bill was introduced in
the House by Representative Charles L. Scott (Dem.) and in the
Senate by Senator Hugh S. Magill (Rep.). It was decided however,
to let the suffrage bill lie quiescent in the House and secure its
passage first through the Senate.

After nearly three months of strenuous effort the bill finally
passed the Senate on May 7 by a vote of twenty-nine yeas (three
more than the required majority) to fifteen nays.

It is doubtful whether we could have secured this favorable
action had it not been for the good judgment and diplomacy of

Senator Hugh S. Magill, who had charge of the bill in the Senate. We also had the assistance on each and every occasion of the Democratic Lieutenant Governor, Barratt O'Hara, and among other senators who helped and who deserve mention were: Martin B. Bailey, Albert C. Clark, Michael H. Cleary, William A. Compton, Edward C. Curtis, Samuel A. Ettelson, Logan Hay, George W. Harris, Walter Clyde Jones, Kent E. Keller, Walter I. Manny, and W. Duff Piercy.

The day the bill passed the Senate I left Springfield immediately to address a suffrage meeting to be held in Galesburg that evening, and the next day went to Monmouth where another meeting was held. In both of these towns there was a member of the House who was marked on the card index as "doubtful." Both of these legislators however, afterwards through the influence of their respective constituents voted for the suffrage measure. We soon discovered that there was no class of people for whom a politician had so tender and respectful a regard as for his voting constituents.

After I left Springfield that week Mrs. Booth remained to see that the suffrage measure got safely over to the House. In the meantime there was a mix-up and the suffrage bill was taken by mistake directly to the committee on elections without first being recommended to that committee by the Speaker of the House. There was an immediate outcry on the part of the opponents of the measure at such irregular procedure. It was very amusing to find that other Senate bills had been put through in this way and no objections had been raised, but it aroused fierce indignation with the suffrage bill, for the men at Springfield said there had never been such opposition to any other bill.

When I returned to Springfield the following week after this mistake had been made, I learned a lesson about the inadvisability of talking on elevators. I was on an elevator at the capitol when some of our legislative opponents, who were in a facetious mood, got on, and one of them remarked, with a sidelong glance at me, "How surprised some folks will be later on," and laughed so jubilantly as I got off the elevator that it made me thoughtful. After some meditation I decided that there was an intention to put the suffrage bill into the wrong committee, and this surmise was afterwards proved correct. We wished it to go into the elections committee, where we had already ascertained we had sufficient votes to get it out with a favorable recommendation, however, if it was ordered into the judiciary committee, it would fall into the hands of the enemy and be killed forever. We worked into the small hours of the night carefully making our plans for the next day. In the meantime James A. Watson, one of our faithful friends and chairman of the elections committee, had returned the suffrage bill to Speaker McKinley, and arrangements were made that the speaker could properly turn it over to the elections committee. When the morning session opened the bill was ordered to the elections committee before our opponents realized their little plot had been frustrated. We were not surprised, but they were.

It is doubtful whether we could have secured this favorable action without the powerful assistance of David E. Shanahan. The latter on account of being from a foreign district in Chicago, felt he could not vote for the suffrage bill, but he gave us the benefit of his wise counsel. In fact to overcome the pitfalls, which surround the passage of every bill upon which there is a violent difference of opinion, I appealed to the enemies of the measure to give the women of Illinois a square deal. On account of his great influence with other members I especially appealed to Mr. Lee O'Neil Browne, a powerful Democratic leader and one of the best parliamentarians in the House. Mr. Browne had always opposed suffrage legislation but he finally consented to let the bill, so far as he was concerned, come up to third reading, so that it could come out in the open and be voted up or down on its merits, stating frankly that he would try to defeat the bill on the floor of the House. It was this spirit of fair play among the opponents of the measure as well as the loyalty of its friends, that afterwards made possible the great victory of 1913.

During this time Mrs. Booth and I worked alone at Springfield, but now we sent for Mrs. Antoinette Funk of Chicago, who had been an active worker in the Progressive Party, to come to Springfield and she arrived on May 13. Mrs. Funk was a lawyer, and her legal experience made her services at this time very valuable. A week later, on May 20, Mrs. Medill McCormick, with her new baby girl, moved from Chicago to Springfield and we immediately enlisted her services. Mrs. McCormick, as the daughter of the late Mark Hanna, had inherited much of her father's keen interest in politics and she was a welcome and most valuable addition to our forces.

The suffrage bill was called up for second reading on June 3. There was a most desperate attempt at this time to amend, and if possible kill the measure, but it finally passed on to third reading without any changes—just as it had come over from the Senate. During this period we found that we were being shadowed by detectives, and we were on our guard constantly and never talked over any plans when we were in any public place.

The hope of the opposition now was to influence Speaker McKinley and prevent the bill from coming up, and let it die, as so many bills do die, on third reading. Sometimes bills come up that many legislators do not favor but to preserve their good records they feel obliged to vote for, then afterwards these legislators appeal to the Speaker of the House and ask him to save them by preventing it from ever coming to a final vote. If he is adroit, this can be done without the people as a whole knowing what has happened to some of their favorite measures. Mr. Edward D. Shurtleff said this was done session after session when he was Speaker of the House by the men who had promised to vote for the suffrage bill but never wanted it under any circumstances to pass. The young Speaker of the House looked worn and haggard during these trying days—he told me he had not been allowed to sleep for many nights—that hundreds of men from Chicago and from other parts of Illinois had come down and begged him to never let the suffrage bill come up for the final vote, and threatened him with political oblivion if he did. He implored me to let him know if there was any suffrage sentiment in Illinois.

I immediately telephoned to Chicago to Margaret Dobyne, our faithful press chairman, to send the call out for help all over the state, asking for telegrams and letters to be sent at once to Speaker McKinley asking him to bring up the suffrage measure and have it voted upon. She called in Jennie F. W. Johnson, the state treasurer, Mrs. J. W. McGraw, and other members of the board and secured the assistance of Mrs. Judith W. Loewenthal, Mrs. Charles L. Nagely, Mrs. L. Brackett Bishop and other active suffragists to help in this work, and wherever possible they reached nearby towns by telephone.

In the meantime I also phoned Mrs. Harriette Taylor Treadwell, president of the Chicago Political Equality League, to have Speaker McKinley called up by phone and interviewed when he returned to Chicago that week, and to also have letters and telegrams waiting for him when he returned to Springfield. She organized the novel, and now famous, telephone brigade, by means of which Speaker

McKinley was called up every fifteen minutes by leading men as well as women, both at his home and at his office from early Saturday morning until Monday evening, the days he spent in Chicago. His mother, whom we entertained at a luncheon after the bill had passed, said that it was simply one continuous ring at their house and that someone had to sit right by the phone to answer the calls. Mrs. Treadwell was ably assisted in this work by Mrs. James W. Morrison, president of the Chicago Equal Suffrage Association, Mrs. Jeane Wallace Butler, a well known manufacturer and exporter, who appealed to business women, Mrs. Edward L. Stillman, an active suffragist in the Rogers Park Woman's Club, Miss Florence King, president of the Woman's Association of Commerce, Miss Mary Miller, president of Chicago Human Rights Association, Mrs. Charlotte Rhodus, president of the Woman's Party of Cook County, Miss Belle Squire, president of the No-Vote No-Tax League, and others.

When the speaker reached Springfield Tuesday morning there were thousands of letters and telegrams waiting for him from every section of Illinois. He needed no further proof that there was suffrage sentiment in Illinois, and acted accordingly. He announced that the suffrage bill would be brought up for the final vote on June 11. We immediately got busy. We divided up our friends among the legislators and each man was personally interviewed by either Mrs. Booth, Mrs. Funk, Mrs. McCormick, or myself.

As soon as the bill had passed the Senate we had realized that with 153 members in the house, we would need help in rounding up the votes, so we immediately selected sixteen House members whom we appointed as captains, each captain was given so many men to look after and see that these men were in their seats whenever the suffrage bill come up for consideration. The following representatives served as captains, and rendered efficient service: William F. Burres, John P. Devine, Norman C. Flagg, Frank Gillespie, William A. Hubbard, Roy D. Hunt, J. H. Jayne, W. C. Kane, Medill McCormick, Charles E. Scott, Edward D. Shurtleff, Seymour Stedman, Homer J. Tice, Francis E. Williamson, George H. Wilson, and Emil N. Zolla.

The latter part of the week before the bill was to be voted upon I sent telegrams to every man who had promised to vote for the bill in the House, asking him to be present if possible on Tuesday morning as the suffrage bill was to be voted upon Wednesday, June 11, and we would feel safer to have our friends on hand early.

When the morning of June 11 came there was suppressed excitement at the capitol. The captains previously requested to be on hand were there rounding up their men and reporting if any were missing. We immediately called up those who were not there, and if necessary, sent a cab after them, which we had engaged for the day to be ready for any emergency. There was one young man who was especially efficient in the telephone booth so we engaged him to stay at his post all day, so that we could secure quick telephone service when needed.

We all wanted to be in the gallery where we could see that last dramatic struggle, but it seemed to me wiser to have the entrance of the House guarded to prevent any friendly legislators from leaving during roll call, and to prevent any of our opponents from violating the law and entering the House during the session. The husky door-keeper, who was opposed to suffrage, could not be counted upon to keep out anti-suffrage lobbyists if they desired to enter, consequently I took up my post near the House door, which was the only entrance left open that day, and was furnished a chair by the man who conducted a cigar stand near the entrance. Mrs. Booth and Mrs. McCormick sat in the gallery and checked off the votes, and Mrs. Funk carried messages and instructions and kept me advised of the developments in the House. Shortly after the session opened the before mentioned door-keeper came and very brusquely ordered me to go the gallery. Around the rotunda rail lounged a number of our opponents, so I said I preferred to remain where I was. He scowled his disapproval, and presently returned and said that one of the House members who was an active opponent of our measure, said if I did not go to the gallery at once he would introduce and pass a resolution forcing me to do so. I answered politely saying that of course the member was privileged to introduce any resolution he desired, but in the meantime I would remain where I was. The men around the rotunda rail were watching the whole procedure and when I still remained in spite of this warning they regarded me with unfriendly eyes. There was a lawyer among them who longed to get inside that day, but he did not like, even with the backing of a friendly door-keeper, to violate the law—that forbade any lobbyist to enter the House after the session had convened—in my presence. The door-keeper in reporting the incident afterwards said "I did not dare touch her and march her up into the gallery where she belonged." As a matter of fact any citizen of Illinois had a legal right to be where I was, if he so desired. In the meantime several friends becoming tired with the long discussions and frequent roll calls, started to leave, but I persuaded them in the interest of a great cause, to return. So while I could only hear the sound of voices and from Mrs. Funk's reports get some idea of the fight that was raging inside, I was glad that I had remained as guardian of the door, for the main all-important object after all was to pass the bill.

During this time a House member came rushing out and said "We have lost." I immediately sent the boy, whom we had engaged for this purpose, for Mrs. Funk and told her I knew there was a mistake for we had the votes and no men had left the House. Shortly afterwards there was a deafening roar and several men rushed out and exclaimed "We have won. The bill has passed." I remember of turning my face to the wall and shedding a few quiet tears and when I looked around there were about ten men who were all surreptitiously wiping their eyes. The Presidential and Municipal Suffrage Bill passed the House by the following vote: Yeas eighty-three (six more than the required majority) to Nays fifty-eight.

It was a great victory. It was claimed there was plenty of money at Springfield—a million dollars or more—ready to be used to defeat the law, but not one Illinois legislator could be influenced to break his word. The bill was passed through the co-operation and voting together of men from all political parties, men of different religious faiths, and it was dramatic on the floor of the House to have the fight for our bill led by Edward D. Shurtleff, at that time leader of the "wets" and George H. Wilson, leader of the "drys." It was clearly demonstrated that we may as a people, differ on questions of creed, and honestly differ on questions of policy—these differences of opinion are after all, purely matters of birth and environment—but there are great fundamental principles of right which touch human happiness and human life upon which we all stand together.

In fact the men who voted for the suffrage bill at Springfield had become convinced that the suffrage bill was basic in its nature and stood back of, and took precedence over all other measures for philanthropy and reform. They realized also that no state would

even be approaching permanent better conditions with a fundamental wrong at the core of its government, and that "in a government of the people, by the people, and for the people"—"people"
could be interpreted only as meaning women as well as men.

The Illinois legislators in voting for the suffrage measure made
themselves forever great—they gave Illinois a place in history no
other state can ever fill, for Illinois was the first state east of the
Mississippi and the first state even bordering the great father of
waters, to break down the conservatism of the great Middle West
and give suffrage to its women. It was claimed that there had been
no event since the Civil War of such far reaching national significance as the passage of the suffrage bill in Illinois. This seemed
like a prophecy, for since that time Mrs. Carrie Chapman Catt,
president of the National American Woman Suffrage Association,
said that New York women never could have won their great
suffrage victory in 1917 if Illinois had not first opened the door in
1913, and the winning of suffrage in New York so added to the
political strength of the suffrage movement in Congress that it
made possible the passage of the Federal Suffrage Amendment in
1919, so the work in Illinois was fundamental and as vitally important to the women of the whole nation as it was to the women of
Illinois.

We were especially grateful when we had secured the vote of Mr.
Edward D. Shurtleff, always before opposed to suffrage. He had
been for years speaker of the House, and was acknowledged to be
one of the most astute and able men in Springfield. We went to him
frequently for counsel, and his practical knowledge of legislative
procedure tided us over many difficulties.

Charles L. Scott, who introduced the bill in the House, deserves
especial mention. Mr. Scott was liked by all of the legislators and
he refused to introduce any other bills during this session so that
he could be free to devote all of his time and energy in working for
the passage of the suffrage bill. Other men who helped, and some
of whom stood out against strong pressure of our opponents, were:
John A. Atwood, Joseph C. Blaha, Randolph Boyd, Lucas I. Butts,
Thomas Campbell, Franklin S. Catlin, John M. Curran, Israel
Dudgeon, Thomas H. Hollister, John Houston, F. E. J. Lloyd,
Thomas E. Lyon, William R. McCabe, Frank J. Ryan, James A.
Watson, and others.

Immediately after the passage of the suffrage bill terrific pressure was brought to bear on Governor Dunne to get him if possible to veto the measure. Our opponents tried to get Attorney General Patrick J. Lucey, to declare the law unconstitutional. We were given great assistance at this time by Hiram Gilbert, a constitutional lawyer—a prominent Democrat and powerful with the administration, who declared the suffrage law was constitutional.

We gave a banquet in the name of the Illinois Equal Suffrage Association, to the Illinois legislators and their wives, at the Leland Hotel on June 13, and I remember at that time some of the lobby objected to inviting those who had voted against the measure, but this would have been bad policy and it was finally decided that all must be invited, opponents as well as friends, and telegrams were sent to suffragists throughout the state, urging them to be present, and many came. I asked Mrs. McCormick to take charge of this banquet, which was a brilliant success. She had printed a roll of honor which we asked all of the men who had voted for the suffrage bill to sign. Governor Dunne was given an ovation when he entered the banquet hall and he also signed the roll of honor.

Immediately after the banquet Mrs. McCormick was sent to Chicago to secure favorable opinions from able lawyers on the constitutionality of the suffrage bill. These opinions she forwarded to me and I delivered them personally to the governor. Mr. William L. O'Connell, a personal friend of Governor Dunne, and a prominent Chicago Democrat was in Springfield at this time and helped to counteract the work being done by the enemies of suffrage. Margaret Haley was also in Springfield and made many calls upon the governor at this time, urging him to sign the suffrage bill. The governor stood out against all opposition and signed the suffrage bill on June 26, and by so doing earned the everlasting gratitude of every man and woman in Illinois who stands for human liberty. After the bill was signed the good news was telegraphed all over the state and by previous arrangement flags were raised simultaneously all over Illinois.

As there had been no time during this strenuous period to raise funds, when we returned to Chicago we found the state treasury empty although the entire cost of the Springfield campaign, which lasted for over six months and included railroad fare for the lobbyists to and from Springfield, innumerable telegrams, and long distance telephone calls, postage, stationery, printing, stenographic help, hotel bills and incidentals, was only $1,567.26. We therefore very gratefully accepted the offer of the Chicago *Examiner* to publish a suffrage edition of that paper, and netted as a result, about $15,000, for the suffrage cause, which included over $4,000 which we paid out to local organizations that had secured advertisements for the paper on a commission basis, as well as several thousand dollars worth of furniture with which we beautifully furnished the new suffrage headquarters which were rented that fall in the Tower Building, Chicago.

I was again elected president of the Illinois Equal Suffrage Association at the convention held in Peoria in October 1913.

The enemies of suffrage were beginning to attack the constitutionality of the bill simultaneously in different towns throughout the state, and finally suit was brought against the election commissioners of Chicago which involved the constitutionality of the suffrage law. We secured as our counsel John J. Herrick, a recognized authority on constitutional law, and Judge Charles S. Cutting. These two men by agreement with the election commissioners took charge of the fight. They consulted, however, with Charles H. Mitchell, their regular counsel as well as with Judge Willard McEwen whom the commissioners engaged as special counsel on the case. They also entered into counsel with Judge Isaiah T. Greenacre, regular counsel for the Teachers' Federation and Joel F. Longnecker, a young lawyer active in the Progressive Party, both of whom donated their services. There was a hot fight in the Supreme Court which lasted for many months, the case being carried over from one term of the Supreme Court to the next without being decided.

During this time it was vitally necessary to demonstrate public sentiment by getting as many women as possible to vote at the municipal elections in April, so Civic Leagues were organized in every city ward. Splendid work was done by Mrs. Ida Darling Engelke, ward chairman for the Chicago Political Equality League, and all of the city work was directed by Mrs. Edward L. Stewart, chairman of organization work for the Illinois Equal Suffrage Association. They called upon all other organizations to help, and as a result over 200,000 women registered in Chicago alone, and thousands more down state.

On May 2, 1914, we held the first large suffrage parade ever given in Chicago. Governor Edward F. Dunne with Carter H. Harrison, mayor of Chicago, reviewed the procession and over 15,000 women marched down Michigan Boulevard with hundreds of thousands of people lining both sides of the way for over a mile and a half.

The General Federation was also going to hold its bienial convention in Chicago in June and we realized, with our suffrage bill hanging in the balance in the Supreme Court, that it was most important to secure the passage of a suffrage resolution by the federation.

I was appointed by the state board to look after this work, and through the help of local suffragists as well as through the co-operation of the General Federation board we succeeded in securing the adoption of a suffrage resolution on June 13, and by an extraordinary coincidence on this same day the Supreme Court of Illinois pronounced the suffrage law constitutional. A banquet had already been planned by the Illinois Equal Suffrage Association for that evening to be held in the Gold Room of the Congress Hotel in honor of the General Federation. All of these events came at an opportune moment and this great banquet became historic in its significance and was transformed into a banquet of thanksgiving where over a thousand women gave expression to their joy over these two great victories. This banquet was ably managed by Mrs. George A. Soden, assisted by Mrs. Edward L. Stewart, Mrs. J. W. McGraw, Mrs. Charles A. Nagely, Mrs. Judith W. Loewenthal, Mrs. Albert H. Schweizer, as well as many others.

It was demonstrated that all of these events had changed public sentiment in regard to the suffrage question. Congress was in session this summer and congressmen were unable to fill their Chautauqua dates and I was asked to make suffrage speeches at fifty Chautauquas covering nine states, filling dates for a Democrat, the Honorable Champ Clark, and for a Republican, Senator Robert LaFollette, and afterwards filled dates for William Jennings Bryan.

The State Equal Suffrage Convention was held in Chicago in 1914 and I was again re-elected president.

When the legislature convened in January, Mrs. J. W. McGraw, the newly elected legislative chairman, and I went to Springfield and attended every session of the legislature from January until it closed in June. A resolution was introduced to repeal the suffrage law and several measures were introduced to amend the law to give the women the right to vote for some minor offices. We were advised by our lawyers never to amend the law, because to do so would involve the whole question and bring on a fresh fight in the Supreme Court in regard to the constitutionality of the law. We employed all the tactics used in 1913 and finally succeeded in killing the repeal resolution in committee and the other bills during various stages of their progress. The Illinois suffragists fully realized the importance of preserving intact the Presidential and Municipal Suffrage Bill passed by the Illinois Legislature in 1913, because it was the first bill of the kind ever passed in the United States, and established the precedent which enabled many other states afterwards to pass similar bills and the Presidential and Municipal Suffrage Bill is called in other states "The Illinois Law." We were assisted greatly during this session by Mr. Randolph Boyd in the House and Senators Richard Barr and Edward Curtis in the Senate, and by Harriet Stokes Thompson, president of the Chicago Political Equality League, who rendered invaluable assistance by helping to counteract the wrong kind of propaganda that was being carried on at this time and which was most detrimental to our work at Springfield. It was hard for some women, even suffragists, who did not understand the political situation and the dangers that threatened the suffrage law, to comprehend why the suffrage law could not be amended any time, if by so doing, they could secure the right to vote for even one more minor office. They did not realize that in grasping for more we would be imperiling all.

In the fall of 1915 I positively declined the presidency and Mrs. Harrison Monroe Brown of Peoria was elected president of the Illinois Equal Suffrage Association, and I went to our home in Florida for a much needed rest.

I returned the following spring in time to raise some money for the depleted treasury of the Illinois Equal Suffrage Association, and to help a little in what is now known as the famous "rainy day suffrage parade" which was held while the National Republican Convention was in session in Chicago in June 1916. On this memorable occasion 5,000 women marched through the pouring rain over a mile down Michigan Boulevard and from there to the Coliseum where the National Republican Convention was being held. I was one of a committee of four representing every section of the country whom Mrs. Catt selected to address the platform committee of which Senator Henry Cabot Lodge of Massachusetts was chairman, and request that an equal suffrage plank be incorporated into the national platform of the Republican Party. Just as we finished our plea the rain-drenched marchers made a dramatic climax by marching into the Coliseum where the hearing was being held, and in spite of the opposition of Senator Lodge, a full suffrage plank was put in the national platform of the Republican Party. Among the women who assisted in organizing this parade were: Mrs. James Morrison, Mrs. Kellogg Fairbank, Mrs. Harriette Taylor Treadwell, Miss Dora Earle, Mrs. J. W. McGraw, Mrs. Edward L. Stewart, Mrs. Charles E. Nagely, Mrs. Judith Weil Loewenthal, Mrs. George A. Soden and other members of the state board.

As there was much important legislative work to be done at the next session of the legislature I was persuaded to again accept the presidency of the Illinois Equal Suffrage Association. There were delegates present at this convention from every section of Illinois, and after a thorough discussion the suffrage policy of the Illinois Equal Suffrage Association for the ensuing year was adopted. The consensus of opinion was that owing to the iron bound constitution of Illinois next to impossible to amend, the only practical way to secure full suffrage for Illinois women by state action was through the medium of a new constitution.

The Citizens' Association, composed of some of the leading men of Chicago and of the state, had been working to secure a new constitution for more than thirty years. They sent Shelby M. Singleton, secretary of the association, to consult with us about the work to be done at Springfield, and asked us to take charge of the legislative work, as they said our association was the only association in the state powerful enough and which all men trusted, to secure its adoption.

Mrs. McGraw and I went to Springfield at the beginning of the 1916 session, and after a struggle that lasted over ten weeks the Constitutional Convention Resolution was finally passed. It would have been impossible to have passed the resolution without the powerful support of Governor Lowden, Lieutenant Governor Oglesby, Attorney General Brundage, and other state officers as well as Senator Edward Curtis in the Senate and Randolph Boyd in the House who rendered especially efficient service, and at the last moment Roger Sullivan of Chicago threw his powerful influence in favor of the resolution.

While this work was going on Mrs. Catharine Waugh McCulloch, who disagreed with the policy of the Illinois Equal Suffrage Association, organized what she called the "Suffrage Amendment Alliance" and sent lobbyists to Springfield to work for a direct suffrage amendment to the constitution. She had such an amendment introduced and it was defeated in the Senate where it received only six votes and in the House it was defeated by a vote of one hundred Nays to eighteen Yeas. This action showed moral courage on the part of the legislators because many of those who voted against the measure had been the loyal, valiant friends of suffrage for years. They believed as we all believed—that a suffrage amendment, under the difficult-to-be-amended constitution of Illinois, would be doomed to certain defeat if submitted to the men voters of the state, and furthermore that a resolution calling for a Constitutional Convention had already passed and would adequately take care of the suffrage question. In urging Mrs. McCulloch to withdraw this amendment, Governor Lowden and other prominent suffragists pointed out to her that the defeat of the suffrage amendment at the polls would mean that a suffrage article would not be incorporated in a new constitution, for the members of the Constitutional Convention would feel dubious about incorporating an article in a new constitution that had just been defeated at the polls.

After the close of the legislature the Illinois Equal Suffrage Association realized that a state wide campaign of education would have to be instituted at once to insure a favorable vote at the polls, so the Woman's Emergency League was formed to raise a fund sufficient to establish educational centers in every one of the 102 counties in Illinois. Just as all plans were laid for this campaign the United States entered the great World War, and immediately we women were thrust into the rush of war work. I was appointed a member of the executive committee of the Woman's Committee of the State Council of National Defense, and every member of our board was immediately busy with Liberty Loan, Red Cross, and other war work.

While doing our war work we went on with the work of the Woman's Emergency League. We held over a thousand meetings that summer, arousing the people to a realization that they must manifest not only national patriotism but state patriotism by voting for a new constitution in Illinois. On account of the numerous Liberty Loan and Red Cross drives we raised only about $15,000 but the educational work carried on this summer was an important factor in later on winning success at the polls. The money raised helped us to publish large quantities of literature and to send many speakers out into the state.

Among the women who rendered valuable service in the Woman's Emergency League were: Mrs. George A. Soden, first vice president of the Illinois Equal Suffrage Association, who rendered most efficient service as its treasurer; Mrs. Stella S. Jannotta, president of the Chicago Political Equality League; Mrs. Albert Schweizer, Mrs. George S. Haskell, Mrs. Julius Loeb, Mrs. Lyman A. Walton, Mrs. J. W. McGraw, Mrs. Charles E. Nagely, Mrs. Judith W. Loewenthal, Mrs. Mable Gilmore Reinecke, Mrs. Harriet Stokes Thompson, Mrs. Anna Wallace Hunt, Mrs. Jeane Wallace Butler, Miss Nellie Carlin, Mrs. Thomas McClelland, Mrs. Edward L. Stewart, Mrs. Samuel Slade of Highland Park, Mrs. Charles Wilmot and Mrs. Louis E. Yager, both of Oak Park, Miss Catherine K. Porter of Freeport, Mrs. Blanche B. West of Bushnell, Mrs. Mary E. Sykes of Monmouth, Mrs. E. B. Coolley of Danville, Mrs. O. P. Bourland of Pontiac, Mrs. William Aleshire of Plymouth, Dr. Lucy Waite of Parkridge, Mrs. Mary B. Busey of Urbana, Mrs. E. B. Griffin of Grant Park, Dr. M. D. Brown of DeKalb, Mrs. George Thomas Palmer of Springfield, and Mrs. Elizabeth Murray Shepherd of Elgin.

During this period of strenuous activity another attack was made by the liquor interests on the constitutionality of the suffrage law, and the case brought before the Supreme Court. We engaged Mr. James G. Skinner, an able lawyer who had acted as Assistant Corporation Counsel under a previous city administration. He prepared an elaborate brief covering all disputed points and won the case, and the woman's suffrage law was again pronounced constitutional in December 1917.

At the state convention held in Danville I was again re-elected president. The Illinois Equal Suffrage Association now had organizations in every senatorial and congressional district with an affiliated membership of over 200,000 women.

After this election I was soon called to Washington by Mrs. Catt to work for the passage of the Federal Suffrage Amendment, and spent many months in Washington during this year. I was very fortunate while there to have a personal interview with President Wilson which lasted for fifty-five minutes and added my plea to all

of the other pleas that had been made, urging him to personally
address the Senate on the question of the Federal Suffrage
Amendment.

In the meantime Mrs. J. W. McGraw ably directed the educational and organization work of the association. We were working
to secure the adoption of the Constitutional Convention Resolution
at the polls and Mrs. McGraw secured the co-operation of Mrs.
Reed, legislative chairman of the Illinois Federation of Women's
Clubs, and they together appointed two women in each congressional district to organize the educational work in their respective
districts.

During this time Mrs. McGraw and I prepared and published a
leaflet entitled "Why Illinois Needs a New Constitution" which was
widely circulated among men's as well as women's organizations.

In the spring of 1918 Governor Lowden appointed Judge Orrin
N. Carter of the Supreme Court as chairman of a statewide committee that worked in co-operation with the statewide committee of
women we had already appointed.

In 1918 the State Equal Suffrage Convention was held in the
latter part of October in Chicago and I was re-elected president.
This convention was planned as a climax to the ten day whirlwind
campaign for the Constitutional Convention Resolution that was being held throughout the state. A feature of this campaign was the
Constitutional Convention Tag Day. This tag day did not include
the payment of any money for the privilege of being tagged, and
consequently was a pleasant surprise to the people. Each man was
given a tag who promised to vote for the Constitutional Convention
Resolution. Mrs. Albert H. Schweizer was in charge of the Tag Day
in Chicago, as well as the rest of the city campaign.

As a result of all of this labor the Constitutional Convention
Resolution was passed at the general election on November 4. The
total vote cast was 975,545; those in favor of the constitution 562,-
012, majority of all votes cast at the election for a new constitution
was 74,239.

In 1919, the delegates to the Constitutional Convention were
elected and it convened at Springfield in January 1920. One of its
first acts was to adopt an article giving full suffrage to Illinois
women to be incorporated in the new constitution.

I was again called to Washington in the early part of 1919 to help
round up votes for the Federal Suffrage Amendment. When it

finally passed the Senate in June 1919, word was telegraphed to me while I was in Peoria where I had gone to address the state convention of the Illinois Federation of Women's Clubs. Wild enthusiasm prevailed among the women when they learned the news. I was literally showered with peonies from the banquet tables and the women acted as though it was a suffrage jubilee convention.

Mrs. McGraw and I now immediately hurried to Springfield where we had already made arrangements for the ratification of the Federal Suffrage Amendment, and the Illinois legislature ratified the Federal Suffrage Amendment on June 10. The vote in the Senate was as follows: ayes 46, and no votes against the measure. The vote in the House was ayes 135, nays 3.

A minor mistake was made in the first certified resolution sent from the secretary of state's office at Washington to the governor of Illinois. To prevent the possibility of any legal quibbling, Governor Lowden telegraphed the secretary of state at Washington to send on at once a corrected certified copy of the resolution. This was done and the ratification was reaffirmed by the Illinois legislature on June 17, the vote in the Senate then being ayes 49, nays none, and the vote in the House was ayes 134, nays 4.

Owing to a misunderstanding of the facts in the case for a short time there was some controversy as to whether Illinois was entitled to first place as being the first state to ratify the federal amendment. An exhaustive study of the case was made by Attorney General Brundage and a brief prepared showing that the mistake in the first certified papers did not affect the legality of the ratification on June 10, as the mistake was made in copying the introductory resolution, and not in the law itself. The opinion of the attorney general was afterwards accepted by the secretary of state's office at Washington. So Illinois, the first state east of the Mississippi to grant suffrage to its women, was also the first state to ratify the Federal Suffrage Amendment.

In celebration of this great Illinois victory a jubilee banquet was held on June 24 at the Hotel LaSalle. I presided over the banquet and the guests of honor were Governor and Mrs. Lowden. Among the speakers were the leading suffragists of the state as well as the Governor, Lieutenant Governor Oglesby, and prominent members of the state legislature.

In October 1919, the State Equal Suffrage Convention was held in Chicago and I was re-elected president for the seventh time.

Women were present from every section of Illinois. It was voted at this convention to continue the work for the speedy ratification of the Federal Suffrage Amendment, and if this failed to succeed in 1920, to work for a full suffrage article in the new Illinois constitution when it was submitted to the men voters of the state.

At the national convention held in St. Louis the early part of 1919 I had invited, in the name of the Illinois Equal Suffrage Association, the National American Woman Suffrage Association to hold its next annual convention in Chicago. This invitation was accepted and the national convention was to convene in February 1920. Immediately after the state convention, plans were formulated by our state board to take care of this convention. We called together representatives of the Chicago Political Equality League, Chicago Equal Suffrage Association, Seventh Ward Auxiliary of the State Association, The Evanston Political Equality League, The Federation of Chicago Women's Clubs, The North End Woman's Club, Chicago Woman's Club, The Oak Park Suffrage Club, and other local organizations. I was elected chairman and Mrs. McGraw vice chairman of the committee having this convention in charge. Different organizations were appointed to take charge of different days of the convention and different phases of the work. In addition to the work necessary for the preparation of the convention proper, there were also five conferences to be held of the different departments of the League of Woman Voters which had been tentatively organized at St. Louis the year before. We engaged the Gold Room of the Congress Hotel for the general convention hall and the Elizabethan Room was engaged also for the entire convention, as well as many other rooms to be used for committee meetings, press and conference rooms. Mrs. McGraw watched every detail and rendered especially valuable service. The chairman of the finance committee, Mrs. Samuel Slade, also deserves especial mention, for she, with the help of her committee raised the funds with which to defray all expenses of the convention.

The ratification by the states of the Federal Suffrage Amendment was progressing so rapidly that this convention was called "Jubilee Convention" and the National American Woman Suffrage Association having practically completed its work—the full enfranchisement of the women of the United States—disbanded, and its members united with the League of Woman Voters formally organized at this convention. In the meantime it was voted that the board of directors of the National American Woman Suffrage Association remain intact until the thirty-sixth state should ratify.

The convention was said to be the most brilliant convention ever held in the history of the national association. Prominent women from every section of the United States were present and I was gratified to have the hotel management of the Congress Hotel, which is made the headquarters for so many conventions, tell me it was the best managed and most orderly convention ever held in their hotel.

The convention was held in February, and Mrs. Catt hoped we would secure the thirty-sixth state within a month, but anti-suffrage forces were active and the ratification was delayed. In April she telegraphed me that a campaign was to be launched in Connecticut where every state was to be represented, and she wished me to represent Illinois; the object of this campaign being to persuade if possible, the Connecticut governor to call a special session for the purpose of ratifying the suffrage amendment, which in spite of this demonstration of national sentiment, he refused to do.

As it was being used as an anti-suffrage argument that the women in many suffrage states failed to exercise their full franchise rights it seemed best on my return from Connecticut to call a board meeting at once and make preparations for a state wide campaign among Illinois women and get as many of them as possible to go to the polls in November and participate in the presidential election. An "Every-woman-at-the-polls Committee" was organized for the purpose and women were appointed in the downstate towns and cities to take care of the work in their various localities and a large committee was organized in Chicago. I was elected chairman of the state wide committee, Mrs. J. W. McGraw, state vice-chairman, and Mrs. Albert H. Schweizer, a member of the state board was appointed Chicago chairman. The Chicago Political Equality League and the Woman's City Club took an active part in this campaign and the club rooms of the latter were selected as the headquarters of the Chicago committee and the state headquarters of the Illinois Equal Suffrage Association for the executive committee rooms. This work was all preparatory to a final drive which was to immediately precede the fall election.

In the midst of the summer, on August 18, the joyful news came that Tennessee was the thirty-sixth state to ratify the Federal

Suffrage Amendment. The Illinois Equal Suffrage Association immediately sent out a call for its state convention to be held in
September in Chicago. At this convention the Illinois Equal Suffrage Association, its work finished and Illinois women now free,
disbanded, and its members formed the Illinois League of Women
Voters, affiliated with the National League of Women Voters and
prepared to go on with the great patriotic work of arousing women
to a realization that it is as vitally important to vote for one's
country as it is to fight for one's country.

RICHARD L. BEYER

received his Ph.D. in history from the University of Iowa in
1929 and was interested in Illinois history and active in
the work of the Illinois State Historical Society. He was chairman of the department of history at Southern Illinois University and helped to organize the Southern Illinois Historical
Society. In addition to contributing to the *Journal of the Illinois State Historical Society,* Dr. Beyer wrote for the *Illinois
Blue Book* and (with Paul M. Angle) wrote *A Handbook of
Illinois History.*

This article appeared first in the *Journal of the Illinois
State Historical Society,* volume 31 (March 1938), pages
5–21.

HELL AND HIGH WATER

RICHARD L. BEYER

"It is the Ohio only which has ever given the city of Cairo any
trouble of consequence," wrote John M. Lansden in 1910. "Even
when both rivers are high at one and the same time, little or no
notice is taken of the matter unless the Ohio reaches one of its very
highest stages. It is the Ohio that claims for itself the right to rise
and fall through a perpendicular distance of fifty feet." The observations of the learned southern Illinois judge were sound in so far
as he evaluated the devastating qualities of the Ohio and Mississippi
rivers, respectively, but the floods of 1937 revealed that he had
missed the swelling possibilities of the Ohio by nearly ten feet.

The rampage of the Ohio River in late January and early February 1937, constituted one of the major catastrophies in the history
of this state. Results of the tragedy are frightfully plain, and even
at the risk of sacrificing some of the mellowness that time and
perspective afford the historian, the author believes that the outlines of this disaster should be preserved before records are erased
and the memories of victims and relief workers are tinctured with
too many dashes of imagination and illusion.

In trying to estimate the materialistic consequences of the disaster, one learns the proportions of the Ohio River flood. Thousands
of residents of the state were rendered homeless and property

423

damages estimated at $75,000,000 resulted. In one community of less than two thousand inhabitants, Shawneetown in Gallatin County, the losses are calculated at nearly $500,000. Damage to the state highways has been placed as high as $200,000 and injury to county and township roads is estimated by some to be even greater. The effects of death (from both drowning and disease), sickness, privation, disruption of industry, shattering of home life, and rupture of morale can scarcely be measured in this, southern Illinois's greatest trial.

Floods are not new in Egypt and accounts of them date back into the pre-state history of the region. Their frequent threats to life and property and the refusal of the people to move from areas threatened by inundation amazed and irritated visitors in the Illinois country years ago. For example, in August 1817, Morris Birkbeck, an English traveler in the Middlewest, was astounded at that which he found at Shawneetown. In his heavy polysyllables, he wrote:

> Shawneetown. This place I account as a phenomenon evincing the pertinacious adhesion of the human animal to the spot where it has once fixed itself. As the lava of Mount Etna cannot dislodge this strange being from the cities which have been repeatedly ravaged by its eruptions, so the Ohio, with its annual overflowings, is unable to wash away the inhabitants of Shawnee Town.—Once a year, for a series of successive springs, it has carried away the fences from their cleared lands, till at length they have surrendered, and ceased to cultivate them. Once a year the inhabitants either make their escape to higher lands, or take refuge in their upper stories until the waters subside, when they recover their position on this desolate sand-bank.[1]

Granting the ravages of these nineteenth-century floods, it must be indicated again that none ever reached the proportions of the swell of the Ohio in January and February 1937.

Omens suggesting floods for southern Illinois began to appear by the middle of January. The weather had been mild, but heavy rains had fallen in the entire Ohio Valley. Rivers were rising rapidly, and

---

[1] The "pertinacious adhesion" as Birkbeck puts it, apparently still prevails in Shawneetown. About two months after the flood, when the question of moving the town to higher ground was being discussed, a St. Louis paper printed a letter from an irate Shawneetown resident who wrote: "We were harder hit than most cities, yet the real business people want to keep Shawneetown at the present site. . . . Shawneetown is the Alpha and Omega to me. . . . If I could choose a heaven, it would be Shawneetown."

in many places highways were already covered. Predictions on January 20 were to the effect that within a week the Ohio would reach a 52-foot stage at Cairo, but this occasioned no alarm since that figure was almost a foot lower than the crest in the flood of the previous year. "Protected by 60-foot sea walls, neither Cairo nor Shawneetown is in danger," an Associated Press correspondent wrote at this time.

However, by Friday, January 22, it was apparent that southern Illinois was on the verge of disaster. Thirty hours of rain in the upper Ohio Valley, coupled with sleet and a 6½-inch snowfall in Egypt, contributed to the uneasiness of those who watched the river rise. At Shawneetown it had already reached the 55-foot mark. Disquieting, too, were the reports of the rampage of the Ohio in the eastern part of the valley. Even this early, the river had climbed to 70 feet at Cincinnati and shattered the 69.9-foot mark, which had previously been the all-time high for that city. Observers now predicted that the greatest flood on record was imminent. Illinois read of these happenings and of the exodus of 50,000 people from their homes in the river towns in Ohio and Indiana. To battle the impending flood in Illinois, forces of WPA workers, engineers, and boatmen were mobilized. Residents in threatened towns began to pack, while some had already left for higher ground.

With the passing of the hours, the Ohio, a churning yellow fury, continued to rise to new record heights, and danger grew as the river mounted inch by inch. The lower part of Shawneetown was filling with seepage water from the sea wall and levee, and doubts were expressed as to whether the flood could be resisted. Elizabethtown, Golconda, and Rosiclare were isolated. Rescue work was started in earnest as pleas for help came from the valley towns. Naval militia boats were sent into the flood area. National Guard planes soared over Egypt to help establish communication with the isolated region and make necessary observations. The rescue work itself was hampered by wind, snow, sleet, and cold weather. Telephone and telegraph lines were injured by storm, and communication was largely confined to amateur radio stations. Waves two feet high and a powerful current made it impossible to use small boats for rescue work on the Ohio. It seemed that all nature was in a conspiracy against man on Saturday, January 23. But in the face of terrific obstacles, relief work went ahead, and in the towns on the lower river, men patrolled the levees and piled row after row of sandbags on top of sea walls.

The evacuation of the Ohio Valley began in earnest with the advent of the new week. Flood waters had climbed beyond the 57-foot mark at Shawneetown and future safety for the inhabitants became increasingly dubious. About five hundred refugees were taken up the river by the steamer, *Patricia Barrett,* pushing a barge. Some people fled to the uplands. The Shawneetown High School, situated on a ridge outside the town, provided a haven for hundreds of people who remained jammed together there for days. By Sunday evening, apart from those engaged in rescue or defense work, only 150 persons remained in town, and they sought safety on the second and third stories of buildings. Red Cross and WPA workers were rushed in to help the people. This was merely part of a gigantic rescue-relief program that was started by state and nation. In Washington, President Roosevelt put five federal agencies on what was described as virtually a wartime basis to help suffers from the flood. The United States Coast Guard mobilized the greatest flood relief force in its history when it sent 800 men and 200 boats, representing practically every one of its units from Maine to Texas. Governor Henry Horner issued the statement, "I want everything necessary done to aid the flooded areas." In Illinois, the Emergency Relief Commission, the Health Department, the National Guard, and the Division of Highways swung into action to work with the regular Army and with the American Red Cross.

On Monday, January 25, the river at Cairo had risen to 58.3 feet at seven A.M., and the evacuation of that city began. Five thousand people left by automobile and train in the first exodus. The refugees were women and children. Men were allowed to escort their families northward on condition that they would return to help bolster the defense of the city. Meanwhile the flight of the inhabitants from the other river towns, with the exception of the flood fighters, was practically completed.

The story of caring for the thousands of refugees in towns outside of the flood area is a monument to the generosity and compassion of the people of Illinois. The chronicle, to be complete, would far outstrip the limits of this article, for it was a program that directly or indirectly involved the entire state. There was hardly a town in Egypt, outside of the stricken region, but what had refugees to care for, and some communities in central and northern Illinois were also havens for the needy. Just to illustrate the type of work that was done, let me select the city of Carbondale as an example.

Refugees poured into this town by the hundreds. Some of them came by automobile and truck, but more often they were brought by railroad. Four trains, with a total of more than one hundred cars, carried about a thousand refugees and their belongings to Carbondale in one day. The victims who were financially able took rooms in hotels or with private families. However, the majority were destitute and were completely dependent on the accommodations that charity could provide for them. Some of the sufferers left their homes with no possessions other than the clothes they wore. Others managed to gather together pieces of movable property, livestock, and their pets. And speaking of pets, the devotion of human beings to their dogs, cats, and birds never has had better illustration than it did in this flood. Refugees refused to leave their pets at home and even objected to being separated temporarily from them, when assigned to relief stations. The tenacity with which one aged woman clung to a square cage containing four canaries, during the trip north in a box car, is simply one case in point.

When trains bearing victims arrived, they were met by volunteers who assisted with the unloading, and escorted the refugees to registration depots and thence to their living quarters. College and high school students, as well as Boy Scouts, were prominent in this type of work. The sick were rushed to hospitals, while the able-bodied were quartered in churches, public buildings, and gymnasiums, and in Carbondale at the Teachers' College. Eventually 700 people were being cared for at the college. White refugees were placed in the gymnasium, while the Negroes were put in the old science building. For several weeks these victims were accommodated and so efficiently was the project managed that not one day of school time was lost.

Rows of cots were arranged in the two buildings used for relief purposes at the college. This equipment, together with pillows and blankets, was supplied by the Army. Refugees were given food that was prepared in a field kitchen built on the south end of the main building of the school. Under the supervision of the National Guard, groups of WPA workers, students, and refugees quickly built this kitchen and it was immediately put into use. Donations of food came from various parts of the state, while the remainder was purchased in the area. Heading the commissary was Leland P. Lingle, track coach of the college, who fed the refugees well and economically. Captain William McAndrew, athletic director, supervised the entire relief project at the school.

The problem of handling the refugees was rendered easy by the cooperation of many individuals and groups. The American Red Cross acted with its customary efficiency and was aided by groups of townspeople, faculty members at the college, and students. A health service was set up and refugees were given the best of medical attention. Vaccination against smallpox and inoculation against typhoid fever were provided. Refugees suffering from minor ailments were given attention in the gymnasiums, while those who developed serious symptoms were taken to the hospitals. It was this keen observation of, and ready attention for, the victims that did much to keep disease minimized among the worn, weakened people from the flood zone. As the relief work continued, the refugees aided in the management of affairs. Kitchen details were organized and these assisted in the serving of hundreds of people daily. At the college, special classes were organized so that refugee children would lose as little school work as possible. Entertainment in the form of concerts and motion pictures was furnished for adults and children.

The behavior of the refugees themselves provided an excellent opportunity for a psychologist interested in the conduct of fellow humans in distress. No generalizations are possible beyond the statement that so quickly had disaster come to Egypt that the majority of the victims were dazed, and that they were completely grateful for the accommodations afforded. In a few cases the people were hysterical. Others were dejected as they reviewed their losses. Many were resigned to the fact that they had lost all of their property, but were thankful that their lives and the lives of their associates had been spared. All of them were eager for information about their homes and were anxious to get in touch with relatives and friends from whom they had been separated. Some found consolation in prayer. They were an orderly group, anxious to help their benefactors in the relief program and resolved to cause no more trouble than was necessary. For the most part they spent their time in little huddles around their cots, talking in hushed tones. Here they were, friends and neighbors from the same town, suddenly bunched together in a queer environment. "We have our entire missionary society here," a Brookport woman said to me as she looked up from a group that was seated on and about her cot.

No thought of belittling other communities that did relief work is intended by the author in his mentioning the program in Carbondale. What was done in that place was repeated in a score of other towns. Indeed the towns of Egypt showed every disposition to share the work, and when one place became saturated with victims, it could answer a half-dozen invitations to share the burden with others. Ultimately tented cities were created, and they lightened the load that the towns had borne at the outset of the disaster.

While many refugees were pouring out of the Ohio Valley, the able-bodied men remained to fight the flood. Temporary recess from the attack was given Cairo with the dynamiting of the fuse plug levee on the Missouri side. This was the old levee that followed the course of the Mississippi from the Ohio confluence to New Madrid. The blasting of this levee allowed the floodway of 131,000 acres to admit the waters and relieve the pressure on Cairo. Instead of watching the steady rise of the river, Cairo now saw a drop of two-tenths of a foot in twenty-four hours. The defenders were heartened by the information that the stage of the river would not change appreciably for two or three days. Then, when the floodway basin would be full, the waters were expected to rise again. The truce, however, was welcome for it gave Cairo workers more time to extend the 3-foot sandbag and timber bulkhead they were building on top of the wall that protects the city.

"FLOOD RECEDES AT LOUISVILLE" screamed the headlines on Thursday, January 28, and the public that had been gripped by the disaster in the upper Ohio Valley, now turned to watch the western part of the river. Inevitably, attention was focused on Cairo which was waiting for its crisis. For the first time since the Civil War, Cairo had the eyes of all America riveted upon it. By the next day, Cairo's first line of defense was completed, and the *Cairo Evening Citizen* commented: "Residents of Cairo, Alexander, and Pulaski counties, WPA, CCC, and other workers by the thousands have done one of the fastest jobs of bulkheading ever accomplished anywhere. Thursday, the bulkhead was being extended with such rapidity that it seemed to be walking."

One of the surprising aspects of the Cairo situation, to those of us who were high and dry, was the attitude of the people from that city. During the course of the relief work among the refugees, many times did I hear the statement, "Cairo has never had, and will never have a flood." Some of the refugees felt that their departure from the town was unnecessary, and that all would be well at Cairo. The *Citizen* reflected this attitude. Here was Cairo waiting for the crest, the river was rising again, more rains were forecast, and the bulkhead was yet to be tested. One would think that, in view of the tense situation, streamer headlines would have been used to deal with the local conditions. Yet in picking up the issue of January 30, one finds, "QUAKE FRIGHTENS TIPTONVILLE" as the major headline. A minor tremor in Tennessee was played up— the vital Cairo situation subordinated. Even when the river was crawling close to the 59-foot mark, a headline writer facetiously composed the following: "OLD MAN RIVER SETS A NEW ALL-TIME HIGH RECORD FOR THIS CITY."

Towns near Cairo—Mound City, Mounds, Ullin, and others— were not to be spared. High water in the Cache River basin and backwater from the Ohio were responsible for this further disaster to Illinois. Mound City was completely deserted as the flood wrought damage that is not even yet fully repaired. The town of Mounds, earlier in the flood period, had been a refugee center; but, as the waters rose, its evacuation became necessary. Many of the victims made their escape before the road to the north was inundated and the town was completely cut off from the world. A few took refuge in a school building at the north of the town. The rapid rise of the flood waters was one of the remarkable aspects of the situation at Mounds. According to a school teacher who assisted with the rescue work there, the water rose from 2 to 3 feet in two hours' time. In the southern end of the town, my informant says it eventually attained a depth of 15 feet. He estimated the property damage at Mounds, a town of about two thousand inhabitants, at $200,000.

As January ended, eight counties in southern Illinois were either completely or partly inundated, and the Red Cross estimated that the homes of 73,876 people were flooded. Almost half that number were refugees. One of the astounding phases of the disaster was the flooding of Harrisburg, a city located more than 20 miles from the Ohio. The Saline River spilled over when the Ohio backed up and water rose in Harrisburg an inch an hour. From the county seat of Saline County to the Ohio River, there was practically a continuous sheet of water. All of Harrisburg was flooded except for a downtown orbit that encircled the courthouse. National Guard boats were the means of transportation in this community and several thousand people were hauled about in them every day. It was from Harrisburg that one of the most helpful services in the disaster came. This was the valuable work of radio station WEBQ, which devoted most of its broadcasting time to relief and rescue work, not only for Saline County, but for all of southern Illinois. Thousands of Egyptians kept their radio dials constantly tuned to this station and listened to its bulletins about the crisis.

Meanwhile, the Ohio was rising and the crest drew nearer to Cairo. By Sunday, January 31, the peak of the disaster was at Evansville, Indiana, and southern Illinois knew that it was to experience the full strength of the river's fury next. Cairo, never completely shaken in confidence in its defense, became wary. A double bulkhead was constructed at the levee near the waterworks, and elsewhere the wall of sandbags was tightened. August Bode, mayor of the city, issued the following proclamation, which was ostentatiously carried on the front page of Sunday's *Citizen:*

PROCLAMATION

The proclamation for the evacuation of the city of Cairo by all citizens except able-bodied men must be observed. All persons who have no means of transportation, other than able-bodied men, must report for transportation at once as follows:

White people at Safford School, Cross at Walnut.

Colored people at Sumner High School, 22nd and Poplar.

This must be done not later than 10 P. M., Sunday, January 31st.

The Red Cross has arranged for movement and care of all persons reporting at above places without expense. This order will be enforced by the Sheriff, police officers and the National Guard.

No persons will be permitted to enter the City of Cairo until further notice without a permit or on official business. No able-bodied men will be allowed to leave the city without a permit.

August Bode
Mayor.

The above document was issued because some fifteen hundred women and children, in addition to the aged, sick, and infirm, were still within the city limits, despite potential danger and previous opportunities for evacuation. Indeed, the population of the town was actually growing, due to the arrival of refugees who had returned, workers from the outside, the sight-seers who were panting with curiosity. Once again the Cairo confidence asserted itself. It was not so much danger from the roaring Ohio that warranted the evacuation, it was stated, but the possibility of a fuel shortage.

The early days of February, nonetheless, were tense ones in Cairo as the town awaited the predicted crest of the flood. The Ohio finally rose to the 59.62-foot mark. On Thursday, February 4, the first slight recession was noted after the waters had come within 6 inches of the top of the concrete sea wall. Observers rejoiced, but continued their vigil. By Friday, Cairo was positive it was victorious, for the Ohio continued to recede and the town began to resume its normal life. Refugees, however, were not allowed to return immediately, for engineers concluded that there would be no absolute assurance of safety until the river dropped to the 55-foot mark. On February 10, the return of some of the people was allowed; those who were financially able to come back, and were willing to do so at their own risk, were given this permission. Scores of men who had remained in town to fight the flood now took their automobiles and went after their families who had been removed from the threatened area.

With the passing of danger, southern Illinois began the grim task of reconstruction. Many agencies contributed to this task, and conspicuous in the work were the State Department of Public Health and the National Guard. Approximately one thousand officers and men of the latter, under the command of Lieutenant Colonel Robert W. Davis, assisted in the rehabilitation program. Colonel Davis has described the task in an article in *The Illinois Guardsman* for March, 1937. He wrote:

> The [flood] area was divided into four sub-areas with their headquarters at Norris City, Harrisburg, Vienna and Cairo. Each of the sub-area commanders was given the necessary troops, trucks and equipment to handle the operations within his sub-area. He was advised that it was his show and that it was up to him to handle it; that my headquarters would interfere only as was required to co-ordinate the whole tasks. Camps were established near the points of principal operations—buildings, tents and even box cars were used for these camps. Troops began the work of patrolling, sometimes in boats, the towns which had been affected in order to protect

life and property. Trucks were furnished for the hauling of food, water and other supplies and the moving of refugees from the scattered points to the central refugee camps. The Military Police Company was assigned the task of policing the refugee camps and the handling of traffic on the roads in the vicinity of the inundated towns and villages. Fire protection was established in the villages and towns. Only the necessary traffic was permitted to enter any particular area until such time as the roads and streets were cleared and ready for normal traffic. A railhead was established in West Frankfort and the 108th Quartermaster Regiment, in addition to the general hauling mentioned above, was given the task of distributing food and clothing to the units in the area. This railhead was efficiently operated by members of the State Detachment.

Also prominent in the cleanup program were the WPA and the Red Cross. The former supplied much of the labor, while the latter fed and clothed the refugees and handled the administration of the refugee camps until it was possible for the homeless to return. As late as February 19, over 2,700 refugees still had to be cared for, and four camps—located at Anna, Marion, Wolf Lake, and Pinckneyville—were still in operation. According to Walter Wesseulius, who directed the flood relief work in Egypt, the Red Cross spent $1,100,000 in relief and rehabilitation work in southern Illinois, and in addition distributed approximately a half-million dollars' worth of donated foodstuffs among the sufferers.

Even in late February, Shawneetown was still inundated, and observers on February 25 found that 8 to 10 feet of water remained in the town. The opening of the clogged sewers (two mattresses were found in one pipe) permitted a drop of an inch of water every two hours. So stricken was the community that investigators learned that only twenty houses in the entire place were fit for habitation when the waters receded.

Throughout the emergency period and during the weeks of reconstruction, another agency played an important part. It was the State Highway Department, the men of District Nine having the chief responsibility of fighting the floods that covered 1,000 miles of primary and secondary roads. Keeping some of the roads open, saving others and repairing still others constituted the job of the Highway Department, which operated efficiently throughout the crisis. Saline and Gallatin were the two counties that particularly required the work of the department.

Now that the waters have subsided and the work of rehabilitation is progressing, thoughtful people are raising the question, "What can Illinois do to prevent the recurrence of these floods?" As these disasters grow mightier with the years, the answer is one that should be evaded no longer. Indeed, it has already been postponed far too long. One thing is certain—the problem is not that of this state alone—it is a problem for all America. Illinois, at the receiving end of the Ohio Valley, cannot solve the flood question without cooperation from the upper valley and from the areas washed by the many streams that enter the Ohio.

The first step that can be taken is to make the people of Illinois and the rest of the nation highly conscious of the perennial danger of floods, and of the ruthless raping of our natural resources that has so largely contributed to creating them. Then the task will be to find remedies. To create an intelligent understanding of the subject, I suggest that volumes such as Stuart Chase's *Rich Land, Poor Land* be made required reading for our voters and taxpayers.

At least three types of artificial flood control should be studied. They are the development of immense storage reservoirs, improvements on river channels so that the capacity of flow may be increased, and finally, more levees and higher sea walls. Since the flood of 1937, a reaction has set in against the latter device. To many, the use of the levee-sea wall is a costly method that is becoming less and less satisfying. It is the opiate that lessens the pain and does not go to the origin of the malady. For two centuries, men have depended on the levee as a major protection against floods, but as Stuart Chase phrases it: "Every year it grows more preposterous. With river bottoms rising because of the piles of silt that are washed from fields, the use of the levee becomes increasingly impractical."

The only sound method of attacking the flood menace is a long-range program of planning in a cooperative manner by federal and state governments. It would have as a principal phase the introduction of a program of conservation on a scale never before attempted in this country. It would try to prevent (1) destruction of forests, (2) stripping of grass lands, and (3) improper cultivation of lands in the river valleys. An important cause of floods today is the rapid run-off of water from the watersheds. Geographers insist that our thoughtless use of natural resources has permitted water to run off the hills into the rivers at a rate three times faster than was the speed before our ruthless methods began. If mankind can be educated (or possibly legislated) into stopping its blundering tactics, if a system of reservoirs can be provided, if river channels can be deepened or widened, then it is possible that in some Utopian tomorrow, Illinois may be spared repetitions of the disaster of 1937.

received his A.B. degree from Notre Dame, worked as a reporter at the Chicago City News Bureau, and then joined the *Chicago Tribune* in 1929. He has been assigned to the Washington Bureau of that paper since 1934, and has been chief of that bureau since 1949. He has had a number of assignments abroad, was president of the White House Correspondents Association in 1937–1938, and has been heard regularly over radio station WGN. He has contributed to various periodicals and has written one book, *Jim Farley's Story: The Roosevelt Years.*

Mr. Trohan delivered this address before a meeting of the Illinois State Historical Society held at Wheaton College in October 1959. The article was published in the *Journal of the Illinois State Historical Society*, volume 52, number 4 (winter 1959), pages 477–502.

MY LIFE WITH THE COLONEL

WALTER TROHAN

On inauguration day, March 4, 1929, Arthur Sears Henning, Washington correspondent for the *Chicago Tribune,* braved the cold and rain to view the outdoor ceremony at the Capitol. He saw a deeply moved Herbert Hoover raise his right hand and repeat the oath of office after the bearded dignity that was Chief Justice Charles Evans Hughes, while Calvin Coolidge glumly contemplated his loss of power and prestige. As the drenched new president began outlining the measures of reconstruction and development, the reforms of the social and business life and the reorientation of foreign relations which he proposed as the course of the ship of state, Henning hurried to the *Tribune* bureau to begin writing the inaugural story. He had completed his lead when, at 12:20 P.M., a telegram was thrust before him which read, "THIS MAN WON'T DO."

The telegram was signed "McCormick," a signature I later came to know all too well. Herbert Hoover had lasted exactly twenty minutes with Robert Rutherford McCormick, editor and publisher of the *Tribune,* although the American people did not write him out until three and a half years later. Henning, ever the gentleman and always an intelligent bureau chief, tore out the paper on which he had written his first paragraph, inserted a fresh sheet and began a new lead. Curiously enough, Franklin D. Roosevelt lasted more than ten weeks. The *Tribune* had not endorsed either Hoover or Roosevelt in the 1932 campaign, but no president was more warmly applauded by the *Tribune* on taking office than FDR, but in those days the mellifluous Roosevelt was denouncing "government by oligarchy masquerading as democracy." It wasn't until seventy-four days after his "we have nothing to fear but fear itself" inaugural that FDR launched the Blue Eagle of the National Recovery Administration, which appalled McCormick for its revolutionary character and doubtful constitutionality, and the break came.

At the time McCormick wrote off Hoover, I was beginning my eighth day on the *Tribune,* covering the county building, a post of placidity such as I have never known since. By the time he broke with Roosevelt, whom I got to know before the 1932 nominating convention, I had graduated to the more exacting but still far from turbulent life of general assignments. It was not until I went to Washington in 1934 that telegrams signed "McCormick" and letters signed "McC" began to explode over my life like Roman candles. And it was not until I became executive director and later bureau chief that these explosive missiles set the tempo of an existence that makes James Thurber's *The Years with Ross* as uneventful as the meditation hour in a Trappist monastery. The fact that I survived is a tribute not only to human endurance and mental agility but also to abiding affection, deep respect, and stimulating astonishment. There was seldom a dull moment and few idle ones in the Gatling gun spray of messages, letters, and telephone calls. The pace quickened, although it was already furious, when McCormick began dividing his time between Chicago and Washington after the purchase of the *Times-Herald.*

To those who worked intimately with Robert R. McCormick, he was known affectionately as "the colonel." Like a benevolent Ebenezer Scrooge he was the author of our feasts, and mighty good eating it was, too. He figured so much in our daily lives that the late Edward Scott Beck, onetime managing editor, said he was going to write a book entitled "The Colonel Told Me." And with a characteristic twinkle in his eye Beck would cover the other side of the coin by noting that Louis Rose, onetime circulation manager, was going to write the sequel, which would be entitled "I Told the Colonel."

To those who saw him from a distance with something less than affection, he was also known as "the colonel" but with an accent that branded him as a pompous martinet or a satrap of Satan. Although he was a hard man to be indifferent to, he was actually shy. From what he told me I have always believed that the shyness came from the fact that his mother favored his brother, Medill McCormick, later a United States senator, and that his childhood in schools in England and the United States was lonely and unhappy. At times the colonel seemed to enjoy cultivating hate rather than affection, but above all he could not tolerate indifference and he seldom got it.

The colonel was a personage in his own right and, as such, was sought after from Buckingham Palace to the executive mansion at Monrovia. About ten years ago the governor of Jamaica was in a dither because, as he explained, "I've invited the colonel to lunch and can't move the picture." An aid, who thought the good governor had been touched by the island sun, asked, "What picture?" "The picture of George III," replied the governor. The aid suggested that the governor seat the colonel so the picture would be at his back. The governor said he could not do that because, "It's the governor's chair, you know." Finally, assured that the colonel was a gentleman and had gone to school in England, the governor went ahead with the luncheon. When the time came for toasts, he arose and proposed, "To the King." Slowly, because he was mindful that Harry Truman was in the White House, the colonel rose to respond. He looked at the portrait of the king, at the ceiling, back at the king, and said, "To the Father of my Country."

The colonel had another experience with British toasts. At a quiet and private dinner in the home of Winston Churchill, the Britisher said, "I assume you'll want to begin with one of those abominable American cocktails." The colonel said he would like an old fashioned. "Good," said Churchill, "the only drinkable cocktail." Dinner proceeded with white and red wine and champagne. At the end of dinner the butler produced port. The colonel said he couldn't take anything more. "But this port was laid down by father in the last century," Churchill protested. "You would insult any British host by not drinking his port." The colonel accepted port under the circumstances. "Now, how about a spot of brandy?" Churchill invited. "I don't care whether I insult the king, the queen and the whole British Empire," responded the colonel, "no, thank you."

"Good," exclaimed Churchill, "then we'll proceed to Scotch and soda."

As historians you know how difficult it is to chronicle all the events of a single day in the life of any man and to say which event was crucial and which was not. In the first place, it is difficult to recapture all the events, and then the testimony and credibility of witnesses must be weighed and considered. Even so, there is no way of knowing whether any of the recaptured events were the important factor in any great decision or whether the die was cast on the basis of some offhand remark in some casual exchange we know nothing about.

Over the years I spent many days and hours with the colonel in great intimacy. He was my boss but he became my friend. Some of these days he made quite eventful in facing the political and social problems of a turbulent era. In the space of time I have, I would hesitate to trace any crucial decision, even any I might think I influenced. I would not attempt to unfold a mind as complex as the colonel's any more than I would try to grasp a handful of quicksilver.

It is my considered judgment that the colonel was a great man. I might, out of reverence, conclude, as James Boswell did of Samuel Johnson, that his "talents, acquirements and virtues were so extraordinary that the more his character is considered, the more he will be regarded by the present age, and by posterity, with affection and reverence," but even one so admiring as myself would never conclude, as Plato did of Socrates, that he was "the man, we hold best, wisest, most just of his age."

I would prefer to say the colonel was the most interesting character I ever met. I was constantly amazed by his penetration. I wondered at his varied abilities and interests. There were times when his courage made me proud to know him. There were times when I loved him for the enemies he made and times when I loved him for his loyalty and generosity toward his friends and those close to his friends. There were times when I marveled at his understanding and knowledge of history, particularly of the War of the Revolution and the Civil War and of the stormy Stuart period in English history. I could admire him for having given up playing cards in college as a waste of time or for giving up smoking because he would not be chained to a habit.

I know that as a lawyer he founded one of Chicago's greatest law firms. I know that as a businessman he was the first to recognize the value of North Michigan Avenue by locating Tribune Tower across the river. I know that as a publisher he had the vision to conquer forests, establish towns, build his own TVA and create his own fleet so that trees might grow into *Tribunes*. I know also of his pioneering with color, his interest in type, his emphasis on mechanical equipment. I followed his experimentation in making rubber from wood, his experimental farm.

The vision he displayed built the *Tribune* into the largest full-sized newspaper in America. This vision led him to see the value of elevated highways for Chicago, although this improvement did not come until after his death. He also saw the necessity and value of a lakefront airport, which has not yet reached the dimensions needed by the people of a city he loved. He was proud of his career as a soldier, seeing service on the Mexican border and in France, where he also displayed vision and courage.

But the colonel's real place is as an editor, and it is in this field that his reputation will live or die. He was the last of the great personal journalists. He didn't found the *Tribune,* but he took control in a critical period and built it to its present eminence. He exercised a tremendous influence upon the thinking of an area and attracted attention far beyond the normal circulation field that the paper could be expected to command. His greatest quality as an editor was the courage of his convictions. He was a conservative, one who based his principles and his scale of values on an appreciation of the wisdom of the generations that have gone before, the understanding of history and the reconciliation of the altered circumstances of current life with the experience of the past.

The colonel was constantly seeking, reasonably and prudently, although, it must be confessed, with some impatience, to reconcile the best of the wisdom and the experiences of our ancestors with the changes which are perhaps essential to a vigorous social existence. He had no patience with throwing past wisdom and experience out of the window. He could not see that anything new was holy solely because it was new. In his way he was a religious man, although he did not employ God for profit or for argument. I never heard him mention God, in a reverential way, but at least he wasn't critical of Him. As with Yale, his interest was with his class, so with God his interest was in the Presbyterian Church.

Under the "great man" theory of history, with which you are all familiar, it was George Washington who spent the winter at Valley Forge, not the Continental Army. Under this theory it isn't the people in mass but the leaders who have wrought changes in war, economics, social life, and religion. As far as the *Tribune* is concerned, there is much to be said for the simplification that the *Tribune* was and is Colonel McCormick. Yet the *Tribune* goes on and the colonel is gone. That's what he expected and that's the way he wanted it to be. In this connection it has been written in sections of the so-called liberal press that the colonel feared death and tried to ban its mention in his presence. Nothing could be further from the truth, as is evidenced by the way he prepared for death. He left his personal fortune almost entirely to charity, a fact which does not measure well with the attempt to portray him as the stanchest defender of the robber barons and one of the biggest of them all. And he left control of the paper and his charities to trusted employees.

It can now be told, I believe for the first time, that one day, about a year before his death, the colonel came out of Tribune Tower with Major General Levin Campbell, former chief of ordnance. While they waited for traffic, the general looked up at the Tower, remarking that the colonel must be proud to have built so lasting a memorial to himself as the *Tribune*. The colonel pursed his lips, a characteristic gesture when he was mulling over a thought, and then observed: "I suppose it will last about the way I leave it for about ten years." He wanted the *Tribune* to continue strong and vibrant, but he wanted also to have those following him to be independent and free and not chained to his grave.

As I said before, I would as soon try to grasp a handful of quicksilver as to attempt to present a complete and lasting appraisal of so accomplished and so mercurial a man as the colonel. All I can do is present a few facets of life with him in his most important role as editor. Some of these, I must confess, drove me to exasperation, so that while I loved him I could cheerfully have strangled him many times. But I could never neglect him because in the midst of the most trivial and exasperating flow of suggestions, requests, and unrelated inquiries, he would come up with the most accurate information and the most penetrating observations. I can best sum up my feeling, in this respect, by recalling the words of the wife of one of my closest friends, who is more than a little difficult—I seem to attract characters—when she was asked if she had ever considered divorcing her husband. "Divorce," she mused, "never! Murder, many times."

I knew the general, and many of the intimate, circumstances of the colonel's life. What I did not see or know of myself, he told me a great deal about, and friends and enemies supplied considerable. He told me of his school days in England, where he studied history at first hand; his days at Groton, where he was a schoolmate of Franklin D. Roosevelt; of his days at Yale, where he was directed by the reading of Frank Merriwell; his service on the Mexican border, where he bought a machine gun for his national guard unit —the first machine gun in the American military establishment, General Willis Crittenberger told me; his service in World War I, where the First Division became one of his few shrines; his taking over the *Tribune* with his cousin Captain Joseph Patterson; his explorations in Canada, and much more. I knew a wide circle of his friends, associates, and enemies. I knew something of his economic circumstances and outlook; he was fond of remarking that he and I were of the middle class, but I couldn't help feeling that his view of that class was as broad as a Democratic Party which can include Senator Harry Flood Byrd along with Senator Hubert Horatio Humphrey.

In a burst of frankness the colonel once confided to me that all McCormicks, except himself, were crazy. Then with the fine sense of humor that was at constant war with his shyness, he added, "You wouldn't agree with that, would you, Walter?" In all honesty I had to answer that there were times when I would not. I knew he disliked divorce but was proud of the fact that two women had divorced their husbands to marry him. I have eaten his bread and drunk his wine and he has eaten and drunk mine. Once in a restaurant, when he reached for his pocketbook, I remarked that I was getting the check. He put the pocketbook away, declaring, "What do you think I brought you along for?"

On visits to New York the colonel would write a few days in advance for theater tickets. Once aboard the train he would meet someone or decide to invite someone along and wire for four tickets. This happened when Eugene Struhsacker, of the New York advertising office, had filled instructions after exhausting every friend and mortgaging advertising space to get four seats together for four shows on the hit level with "Oklahoma!" When we called on the colonel together, Gene asked me to ask the colonel how he liked the show and why he picked the four particular shows.

"Last night's show was the greatest I ever saw," said the colonel, and then after a moment he added, "How did it come out?"

Struhsacker swallowed and his mouth gaped, but he managed to ask in turn, "How did it come out?"

"Yes," said the colonel, "I left before the last act."

The explanation for the selection of the shows was more simple. The colonel said he had read in Claudia Cassidy's column that those were the four hardest shows to get into, so he concluded they must be the best.

The colonel was most impatient. Often we would set out for Bull Run, Gettysburg, or some other historic site only to have him order the car around as we got near. Once he went to see "Hamlet" with his chauffeur. They were late and had to stumble over feet to get to their seats. The stage was dark, as a doubting Horatio awaited the appearance of the ghost. When it came, instead of Horatio's astonishment, the audience heard McCormick's booming voice cry out, "Come on, Bill, let's go. I saw this play in college."

While I know much of the colonel, I would not attempt his biography, much less give even an outline in the time I have. I can only present facets which will shed some light on the manner of man he was, as I have been doing. He was, as I said, the last of the great practitioners of personal journalism, in the school of Joseph Medill, his grandfather, of Horace Greeley, who became a presidential candidate, and William Randolph Hearst, a contemporary but not an intimate. McCormick was ever mindful of his grandfather's role in the founding of the Republican Party and as kingmaker in the 1860 nomination of Abraham Lincoln, as is evidenced by his support of a wide variety of Republican white hopes, notably the late Senator Robert A. Taft. It always seemed to me he felt in some way that he had failed his heritage by not nominating his choice. I felt even more strongly that he, like Greeley until his nomination, felt that his party's nomination often went to men worse than himself. With this I could agree, although my nightmares often concerned running the *Tribune's* Washington bureau with McCormick in the White House.

He saw the Republican shift to the left, writing in 1946, after the Republican congressional victory, "I'm afraid the Republicans are going New Deal. Vandenberg went that way when it looked as though it were irresistible and his authority and White's [1] are apparently going to put them into positions of leadership." Now and then his thoughts would turn toward a third party. Once he wired in jubilation, "I have found my Frémont. It's Wedemeyer." The fact that General Albert C. Wedemeyer might not be interested didn't occur to him. He was a little miffed with the general and took it out on a *Tribune* editor, threatening to fire him, although he seldom— in fact, almost never—fired anyone.

That's what makes the colonel so difficult to pin down and classify. He was often as cryptic as the Delphic Oracle and as devious as a dictator. At other times he was as direct as a child and as blunt as a sledge hammer. And at all times he believed in stirring up the animals. He kept me busy, but at the same time he kept his various editors, reporters, and foreign correspondents busy. He kept his farflung chain of executives in advertising, maintenance, and operations equally busy. In this connection it must be noted that he was quick to forgive mistakes. At times it appeared as though he delighted to have a mistake made so that he could be forgiving and correcting.

In politics he was not one to cry over spilt milk, having had considerable experience in defeat. After the 1948 Republican convention he wrote, "Of course the news now is in the Democratic convention—the Republican convention is now history." The colonel had contributed to the problems of this convention by issuing anti-Dewey statements without giving them to his own paper, at a time when its publication was hampered by a printer's strike. He made life almost unbearable when he appeared to believe a defeated presidential candidate and a senator jealous of the role of Illinois's Governor Dwight Green, as convention keynoter, sought to implant the idea that a *Tribune* editor was working with Green to doublecross Taft and the colonel to nominate Thomas E. Dewey. Taft lost the nomination but survived the convention. For a time it was touch and go whether the editor would.

By 1949 we were back on the convention merry-go-round. The colonel called on General Eisenhower at Columbia, reporting, "He talked very reasonably, said there was a limit to the amount of money we could spend on defense, and that the three services

---

[1] Wallace Humphrey White, senator from Maine, who became majority leader when the Republicans gained control of the 80th Congress.

ought to be less pigheaded and work together." Ike was then not a candidate, but was shaping up, as a December 7, 1950, letter indicated. This read:

> You may have noted the very catchy song in Ethel Merman's play—"They Like Ike." It is obviously political propaganda.
>
> I don't know anything about Berlin's connections or whether he is mixed up in subversive activities.

About this time the colonel said, "Ike is now candidate for president although he wasn't some years ago. This is certainly not the time to campaign against him, but you might collect the arguments that could be used against him if he were nominated."

McCormick was again with Taft, but the Ohio senator wrote a book on foreign policy which did not please the editor. Shortly after the book appeared I got the following message:

> The continuous repetition of the Taft-Eisenhower story is getting monotonous. I find it hard reading myself. I think you will pick up readers if you discuss the possible candidates for vice-president.

At the same time a politician came to McCormick asking for his support for John Foster Dulles for vice-president. The colonel reported, "I told him I would just as soon support Judas Iscariot."

In March 1952 the colonel went abroad and called on Eisenhower at SHAPE headquarters. There he became more interested in a map on the wall of Brigadier General Charles T. (Buck) Lanham, showing a segment of the world running from England to the Caspian Sea and from North Africa up. He cabled me to get the map, while I wondered whether or not Ike got him.

The respite from the presidential race didn't last long. He was soon swinging his broadax in the editorial columns and in Washington dispatches. It was a constant source of irritation to me that he often ordered stories to follow editorials instead of the other way around. I was never able to change him, for all my pleading. Sometimes I had a feeling that he took as his guideline for the editorials he ordered the title of a book by a medieval scholar *De Omni Re Scibili et Quibusdam Aliis* (Of Everything Knowable and Certain Other Things).

When Taft's hopes faded, I got a message from the senator asking me to see him immediately. I was on deadline, but managed to tear away. The puzzled senator said he had just received a visit from Mrs. McCormick urging him to withdraw in favor of General Douglas MacArthur. Taft got the implication that such was the colonel's will, although he said the colonel had phoned him earlier to go down with his flags flying, which was Taft's own desire and thinking. My advice was to follow the colonel, noting that he was not given to being influenced by anyone, even one wearing petticoats.

The colonel's friendship with MacArthur went back to World War I days. He liked to tell of calling on MacArthur when the latter had been made a brigadier general and noting that MacArthur "commented smilingly I had gained on him but had not yet caught up, as I was a major when he was a colonel." At that time General John J. Pershing told the colonel he would have to go back to America and bring back a brigade in the spring, which would have meant a general's stars for the colonel. McCormick once confided that he was most disappointed when the war ended because he had missed the stars, but then he realized that he would have had men die so that he could be a general, a realization which he said awakened him to the terrors of military ambition.

During World War II the colonel had me send a personal message of congratulations to MacArthur through an officer I knew who was flying to join the general. In his complimentary and cordial reply MacArthur said he wished the colonel were with him. It took a bit of convincing to keep the colonel from getting his uniform out of moth balls and setting off to join what I am sure would have been a flabbergasted commander.

When MacArthur was abruptly removed from command in the Pacific, McCormick wired me that Dwight Young, president of the American Society of Newspaper Editors, had invited the general to address the society's convention. McCormick advised me he thought it would be better that MacArthur address a joint session of Congress. I could take a hint and went to work. I don't claim that the colonel and I got MacArthur invited, but we didn't stop the invitation. When the great day came, the colonel wanted seats for himself and Mrs. McCormick, no small problem, as you can imagine. I twisted the arms of Congresswoman Marguerite Stitt Church and the late Congressman Sid Simpson, who twisted mine right back by sending, along with the ticket, a copy of a speech he said he thought might interest me. For the address I occupied the

Tribune seat in the House Press Gallery. Over the years I had become used to the unexpected, but I must say I was more than surprised to see the colonel rise up in the hushed gallery across the way, stumble over the knees of sitters and make his way up an aisle to an exit just as MacArthur launched into his peroration about old soldiers fading away. There wasn't a dry eye in the house, nor an empty seat—except the colonel's.

The State Department was a favorite whipping boy. Assignments such as "What about the society boys in the State Department?" or "Have a story on the colleges of the diplomats" were frequent. He was given to answering State Department explanations of any situation by such messages as, "The State Department explanation would carry more weight if the department were not so full of reds." He was never tired of running the list of holders of foreign decorations of knighthood, ordering, "Send the full list of American knights," but he never turned any down himself, even taking one from Perón. Once when Syngman Rhee offered me the Order of Teigook, the oldest order in the world, I dodged the saintly fellow by suggesting he give it to the colonel. It did surprise me, but only mildly, when the colonel explained that Korea was a small country, so he would take it. He made a special trip to get the order and another when Korea presented him with the medal of the Republic of Korea some years later.

Diplomats were a frequent target, especially when they pleaded immunity after embassy cars killed pedestrians. He exhausted all avenues to bring such malefactors to justice, even to suggesting civil suits for damages, but was stymied by the code of diplomatic immunity, which he was convinced had been stretched beyond reason.

One never knew what the mail or wires or phone would bring. One letter read:

> My portrait has me in the uniform of a colonel of artillery with a cannon. After that was painted I was appointed to the general staff. I would not want to take the cannon off.
> Find out if it would be proper for me to have the braid around the cuff painted black, as it is in the general staff, or to put it another way, would it be objectionable to do that?

Once the colonel wired to ask the name of his London hatter. Knowing only one hatter in London, I said I didn't know but

presumed it was Locke. He didn't think so. A few days later I got a
letter reading:

> I thought you had the wrong man for my hatter. He was
> A. J. White. My haberdasher was Muhlenkamp; my shoemaker
> was John Lobb: my tailor was Hill Brothers, who since have
> joined with Peale. I may say they were my father's before me.

He would froth at the mouth at suggestions of Union Now,
asking, "What makes Kefauver so un-American?" Or, "What do
Kefauver and his Atlantic Union police propose to do with king and
nobility in the European countries?" He was concerned with the
possibility of overriding the constitution through treaty power.

Messages such as the following frequently enlivened the day:

> There must be enormous corruption in the Army or the Air
> Force. There is no way for you to investigate it, but someone
> may have noticed whether the wives are sporting clothes far
> beyond officers' salaries.
> Look out for Senator Butler's speech in the Senate, Tues-
> day, April 10.
> Is Saltonstall descended from the Saltonstall who left Bos-
> ton with Gage in the Revolutionary War?
> There were Confederate flags on sale in the Yale bowl last
> week, but I did not see anybody carrying one.
> From whom must I obtain permission to land at Fernando
> Noronha?
> Cannot understand O'Dwyer going to Mexico with his bad
> heart. Mexico City is 8,500 feet high.
> In view of the enormous expense, is the *Missouri* still being
> kept in commission?
> What does Acheson propose to do to get the British army of
> conquest out of Egypt?
> A couple of weeks ago I told you about seeing an army ship
> going up the Welland canal with a tank on its deck and the
> tank looked pretty big. Have not heard any comment from you
> about it. [He didn't hear for a very good reason. The move-
> ment was classified because the tank was being shipped back
> to Detroit for alteration after tests.]
> What do you know about the airport at Malta?
> I think you could have a special story on the women spies
> and their motives—romantic, financial or political.
> My file of correspondence with General Willoughby is miss-
> ing. Did we send it to you?
> I hear Vandenberg wants to run his son to succeed him.
> I wonder what it costs changing postage stamps all the
> time.

I see there was a double turreted *Monitor* at Fort Fisher. I think a double turreted *Monitor* went around the Horn and afterwards crossed the Pacific to Manila. Was it the same ship?

A long time ago Syngman Rhee was supposed to have sent me some weapons via a Korean who came to this country. They never showed up.

I have a straight cavalry sword. The saber I want is curved. It was used by the cavalry about 1916, and of course swords have become obsolete.

——————— insists secretary ——————— is a crook. What is your impression?

I don't like the expression "young turks." Stick to New Deal Republicans.

Ask the British Embassy for the exact language that was used to the effect that Belgium occupied by a first-class power is a pistol pointed at the heart of England. [The British Embassy knew nothing of the quote, but the Library of Congress found that Napoleon said, "Antwerp is a pistol pointed at the heart of England."]

Once the colonel phoned me to ask who licked James J. Corbett. I told him it was Robert Fitzsimmons.

"Your memory is better than mine," he wrote the next day. "I thought it was Joe Wolcott."

"At whatever time is most suitable send a list of all corruptions that have taken place in Truman's administration," he wired on April 2, 1951. Four days later he was prodding, "You have coming up . . . the scandals in the Truman administration." At other times he either wrote or wired:

Griffin [Eugene Griffin, *Tribune* correspondent in Canada] says there is no British statue on Boston Commons. Perhaps there is one somewhere else—can you locate it?

Does the Committee on Un-American Activities interest itself in anything but Communist activities?

For my information are the White House, the Washington Monument and the Jefferson Memorial in line with each other?

I don't hear anything of Representative Taber anymore. Is he in Congress still?

Who was third man at our luncheon with Wherry and Taft? [It was Senator Martin of Pennsylvania, with whom he spent much time in reminiscing about World War I.]

I noticed on a whiskey bottle that it was not to be sold or refilled. I cannot imagine any reason for that other than a racket. Some whiskey bottles are very decorative and can be used as decanters.

In 1951 I wrote the colonel I was going to the twenty-fifth reunion of my college class. It was usually advisable to get his OK for any travels, because he might have something in mind. The colonel wrote back an OK and said he had just come back from one of his Yale reunions, noting, "Almost everybody has had a prostate operation."

During the Korean War a message came in declaring, "If we don't get some of those Korean bulls into this country they will become extinct. Is anything being done about it?" The only answer was that if we didn't get men and guns in, the Koreans would be extinct.

Another time an Arabian stallion became a bureau problem. The colonel was offered a stallion by Ibn Saud during one of his plane trips. He turned it down. When his niece, who raises Arabians, heard of it, she called attention to her interest in the steeds. The colonel instructed me to get the horse. This necessitated negotiations with the embassy, the king, steamship lines, railroads, the Department of Agriculture, and customs. Things got critical when the horse refused to eat at sea or aboard train. He arrived more dead than alive, and it soon developed he should have stood in his Saudi Arabian stall because he was more goat than horse.

The colonel at one time launched me on an extensive campaign to have the State Department translate and send overseas various great American documents on independence. When he found this was being done, he kept expanding the list until he found documents the State Department was not sending out, like the Otis Writs of Assistance.

After one of his trips he got interested in having monuments erected at Tripoli to commemorate the daring exploit of Stephen Decatur in the Tripolitan harbors, another off Spithead, England, marking the exploits of the daring Admiral John Paul Jones, and one off France, marking the battle between the *Alabama* and the *Kearsarge*. He noted, "I forget the name of the captain of the *Kearsarge* [John A. Winslow], but Farragut's admiration of him was so enormous as to warrant a monument to him."

The British weren't anxious for a monument to Jones, the French were uninterested in the duel between the *Alabama* and the *Kearsarge*, and the Tripolitans saw nothing in raking up an unfavorable episode in the careers of their Barbary pirate ancestors. Only the colonel was enthusiastic, and he insisted the State Department put up the money. The State Department was less than enthusiastic. He then said, "I am sure we can negotiate the money by private subscriptions to pay for them." They have still to be erected.

Frequently I got such messages as, "There seem to be delusions of grandeur all over the place in Washington." And, "Wake up those Washingtonians, dead from the neck up, as to the peril they are in."

Many of you are familiar with the colonel's broadcasts on the Chicago Theater of the Air. All too often they began with some such exciting opening as, "In 1858 the army was armed with the muzzle-loading rifle developed. . . ." But quite often they hit on more pertinent topics. This would bring such messages as, "Response to MacArthur, United Nations and Hope for the Future broadcasts shows that Congress is way behind public opinion. Tip off anybody you can to get out in the lead." Or he would instruct, "Please have someone put my broadcast appearing in last Sunday's *Times-Herald* in the *Congressional Record*." This would be followed up by, "Be sure to get the text from two-star edition Sunday as I made a little change between editions."

I became something of an expert on decodifying the colonel's cryptic and ambiguous messages. This task was complicated by the fact that his battery of secretaries had no knowledge of current events, so that Syngman Rhee would, likely as not, come out as Seaman Reed or Chief Justice Fred Vinson as Red Vincent. J. Loy Maloney, former managing editor, often consulted me on the meaning of cryptic messages. Once I received a wire from the colonel himself, which read, "This is a paragraph from my radio broadcast. What do I mean?"

The colonel was engagingly frank about his radio talks. Now and then he would have someone write these for him, but he never passed them off as his own. When anyone complimented him on these, he was quick to identify the real author. His reason for these broadcasts can best be explained in his own words. During a pretrial examination in a suit involving the *Times-Herald* a lawyer pressed the colonel on the broadcasts, finally leading up to the question, "Colonel, why do you make these broadcasts?" The colonel looked at the ceiling and then turned his eyes directly on those of the lawyer and said, "Vanity, I guess." This blew the point the examiner was trying to make right out of the hearing.

"Please attend Drum funeral as my representative." Such assignments brought me to more funerals in Arlington than most military men. I can't go by the place without hearing the echoes of taps from countless services which I attended as civilian aid. Need I remind you that, in meeting trains and planes, arranging to see the grave of the unknown stranger, the grave of Abigail Adams, various museums, battlefields, and points of historic interest, I qualify as the highest-priced civilian aid in Washington.

One of the most dreaded messages came regularly about once every six months. These always started innocently like, "How about having you and the gang for lunch on Monday, February 4." The first of these ended with the suggestion that two or four men be cut from the bureau. It took weeks to change that decision. When later suggestions came, I was prepared for him. Members of the staff and myself rehearsed the luncheon conversation, spicing it up with inside information from Congress, the departments and the international scene. We kept the conversational ball bouncing on a wide variety of McCormick interests so that he would return to Chicago reporting that the bureau had done a fine job and that he hoped it would continue to do so.

And here are some more of those messages:

> When the conspiracy case is finally out of the way, look into the people who have been convicted in other cases and see if they were framed or if they were guilty.
>
> In connection with our many stories on attempts of the Communists to interfere in American activities do not overlook the fact that the English have been and are active in attempting to interfere in American affairs.
>
> After Roosevelt suggested closing the *Tribune* by the Marines, who made the suggestion to get an indictment?
>
> Do you think Summerall would welcome some further gift like a bushel of apples or less, or would it look too much like subsidizing him?

Perhaps one of the most amazing assignments I ever got from the Colonel came out of Entebee, Africa, February 29, 1952, as I was preparing to leave for a Mexican vacation, "Must have accommodations for five rooms Tripoli March 1 or 2 at my convenience stop Absolute must." A similar cable went to W. D. Maxwell, then managing editor in Chicago.

This message reached me at 7 P.M., Entebee time, which was almost his March 1 deadline. I inquired at the State Department and learned that the American representative at Tripoli was John Stewart Service, about whose loyalty the *Tribune* had carried news and editorials. Nonetheless, any port in a storm, so I had the department cable Service. Then I went to the late General Hoyt Vandenberg, then head of the Air Force, and had him message Colonel F. O. Easley, commander of the air base at Tripoli. Naturally I cabled the hotel. We also contacted British Overseas Airways and the British Information Service. I would have phoned Tripoli, but there was no such line of communication. Meantime, Maxwell busied himself with Reuters, the Asociated Press, Pan American Airways, and other avenues I have forgotten. All our messages were signed, "Maxwell Trohan." I left for Mexico the next day wondering whether I would have a job when I returned.

Several days later I received a telegram in Oaxaca from Maxwell embodying a cable from the colonel which read, "Maxwell Trohan complete success stop express appreciation everybody." Later I learned that the Air Force commander had a military guard with band welcome the colonel on his arrival, cars were provided for transport through the efforts of Service, and the hotel manager had the staff standing by with thermometers in drawn baths. Still later, I found out why the colonel had upset the Washington bureau and the Chicago office. When I asked him why he sent such an urgent message, he said: "Veysey [Arthur Veysey, the *Tribune's* London correspondent] said we couldn't change our reservations, and I wanted to show him what *Tribune* people can do."

If I seemed to have stressed the curious and the casual, it is because these were the most frequent. None could be ignored, because the colonel was right too often when he seemed to be wrongest. As Robert E. Lee, former managing editor, remarked, "The colonel tosses apparent wild ones out of the twenty-fourth floor window, and they curve across the plate, beautiful strikes."

The day after Pearl Harbor, for example, he sent a message, "The Japanese attack couldn't have taken place if the Hawaiian commanders had been alerted. Why weren't they?" That was before America knew the extent of the blow. In May 1940 he wrote he had heard that FDR was planning to trade destroyers for bases in the Western Hemisphere. At this time the Navy didn't know anything about it, and, as far as I could ever find out, it was known chiefly to Lord Lothian and Roosevelt. The deal wasn't announced until about a year later.

In 1948 Colonel McCormick was the first to predict that Dewey would be licked if nominated for a second time. Often he sent his correspondents to news centers ahead of the story. The State Department has called the bureau to get the stories he ordered from Indo-China and Indonesia, when those areas exploded, confessing they had no information. His knowledge of history and military operations made him a great editor, if a difficult one. Certainly he had his idiosyncrasies, but they became our idiosyncrasies and we loved him for them, even when we smarted most under them. He was the greater editor for being human and having faults common to all. With all his faults he was a better editor and a better man than those who mocked and derided him.

INDEX